KEEPING THE
RED FLAG
FLYING

First published 2020 by Interventions Inc

Interventions is a not-for-profit, independent left wing book publisher.
For further information:
    www.interventions.org.au
    info@interventions.org.au
    Trades Hall Suite 68
    54 Victoria Street
    Carlton VIC 3053

Design and layout by Viktoria Ivanova
Cover photo: Sydney Mayday 1992, photographer unknown, from the
photo collection of John Percy. Used with the kind permission of Eva To.

Author: John Percy
Editor: Allen Myers

Title: Keeping the Red Flag Flying. The Democratic Socialist Party in
Australian Politics: Documents, 1992-2002
ISBN: 978-0-9945378-8-1: Paperback

Series: History of the Democratic Socialist Party and Resistance
Volume 3

NATIONAL LIBRARY OF AUSTRALIA

A catalogue record for this
book is available from the
National Library of Australia

Interventions is produced on the land of the Wurundjeri people of the Kulin Nation. We acknowledge the Traditional Owners of country throughout Australia, and recognise their continuing connection to land, waters and culture. We pay our respects to their Elders past, present and emerging. Their land was stolen, never ceded. It always was and always will be Aboriginal land.

This book is dedicated to the memory of John and Jim Percy, brothers and comrades. May their unwavering devotion to socialist revolution and the building of a party that could lead it inspire the present and future leaders of the working class.

KEEPING THE
RED FLAG
FLYING

THE DEMOCRATIC SOCIALIST
PARTY IN AUSTRALIAN POLITICS:
DOCUMENTS, 1992-2002

JOHN PERCY
SELECTED AND EDITED BY ALLEN MYERS

VOLUME 3 OF A HISTORY OF THE DSP AND RESISTANCE

INTERVENTIONS
MELBOURNE

CONTENTS

INTRODUCTION

The early 1990s, after the collapse of the Stalinist regimes in the Soviet Union and Eastern Europe, were a time of capitalist triumphalism. Capital's academic hirelings proclaimed 'the end of history', an absurdity nevertheless repeated in popular media. Really existing capitalism had been proven to be all that was possible, declared those who benefited from it. Socialism, along with the Soviet Union, was dead.

They were wrong – about both history and socialism.

In Australia, it was true that the left as a whole had been in more or less continuous decline since the early 1970s, with the waning of the 1960s radicalisation. Among the groups that realised that capitalism was not capable of solving its problems in anything but the short term – and only at the expense of working people – the largest was the Democratic Socialist Party, which had emerged as the most influential socialist organisation after the collapse and dissolution of the Communist Party of Australia.

With the new, widely read and respected newspaper *Green Left Weekly*, a sizeable nucleus of experienced cadres and Resistance, a vibrant youth organisation, the DSP was able to orient to the new political climate, including the growth of Green political formations, to seize on new opportunities and to grow modestly. Moreover, it was able to reach out to and help to influence some of the international efforts at rebuilding a revolutionary current.

Well before the turn of the millennium, 'the end of history' had become a sorry joke even for capitalist commentators. The DSP and other socialist organisations were a not insignificant part of ongoing history in Australia. Many of the campaigns and struggles they engaged in are now in danger of being forgotten – or, perhaps more commonly, misrepresented.

Today, as new generations take up the fight to stop capitalism from destroying civilisation, the history of these struggles can provide lessons and examples to help illuminate possible ways forward. The documents in this volume, consisting of DSP party-building reports by John Percy, are a very important part of a record that can aid the current generation of activists to learn from the successes and failures of those who have gone before.

The story so far

The first quarter-century of DSP history is described in two earlier volumes by John Percy. Volume 1 *Resistance* (Resistance Books 2005) covers the years 1965-72 and Volume 2 *Against the Stream* (Interventions 2017) the years 1972-92.

The story begins in the youth radicalisation of the 1960s, and particularly the movement against the Vietnam War. John Percy, a student at Sydney University, joined the campus Labour Club in 1965 and became involved in antiwar activities, in which he was soon joined by his younger brother Jim.

In the course of their activities, the Percy brothers were won to the political stance of Trotskyism, as advocated by Bob Gould and Ian Macdougall, members of a small and not very active group supporting the Fourth International (FI).[1]

In mid-1967, Gould, John, Jim and others they had persuaded of the need for an 'off-campus' and 'comprehensive socialist youth organisation', as John wrote at the time, established a group with the unfortunately flippant name of SCREW (Society for the Cultivation of Rebellion Every Where). The more serious name of Resistance was adopted in November 1968.

Resistance soon became internally divided between group-ings supporting the views of John and Jim and those supporting the views of Bob Gould. The former saw the youth organisation as only a step towards the eventual creation of a revolutionary political party, while Gould supported a strategy of 'entryism' – the idea that revolutionaries should organise only loosely and should conduct their political activities mainly through the Australian Labor Party, hoping eventually to win it, or a sizeable portion of it, to revolutionary positions.

The differences came to a public split shortly before Resistance held its first national conference in August 1970. To indicate the organisation's socialist political outlook, the conference changed the name of Resistance to Socialist Youth Alliance. A month later, SYA launched its 12-page monthly tabloid, *Direct Action*. The editorial in the first issue clearly set out the paper's intended role:

> To publish a paper without an organisation to build
> and be built by it is political irresponsibility ... Only
> when a paper has an organisation to build, and that
> organisation has a program to guide it, does a little
> left-wing venture such as ours take on any meaning.

The fledgling SYA benefited from the still continuing radi-calisation. The first five issues of *Direct Action* achieved average sales of nearly 8,000 per issue, and the organisation itself grew noticeably by the second conference in April 1971. By January 1972, the supporters of a party perspective were able to convene the founding conference of a new organisation, the Socialist Workers League. *Direct Action* moved to fortnightly publication and became the joint paper of the SWL and SYA.

The choice of the names SWL and SYA was a certain acknowledgement of the Australian groups' developing ties with the Socialist Workers Party (SWP) and Young Socialist Alliance (YSA) in the United States. The SWP was a supporter of the Fourth International, despite reactionary legislation in the US that prevented it formally joining. The goal of the SWL was eventually to become the Australian section of the FI. A fillip for this goal occurred at the end of the SWL founding conference, when members of the Labour Action Group (LAG), supporters of the FI based in Brisbane, decided to fuse with the SWL.

However, at that time the FI was riven by what became a prolonged factional dispute over the majority's support for a strategy of guerrilla warfare in Latin America and certain other questions. Most of the SWL, like the US SWP, supported the FI minority, while those who had come from the Labour Action Group supported the FI majority. The relatively inexperienced leaders and members of the fused Australian organisation proved unable to overcome the tensions caused by these differences, and only eight months after the fusion, the former LAG members split from the SWL, forming a new organisation called the Communist League (CL), which began publishing its own paper, *Militant*.

The divisions in the FI and the inexperience of the young comrades were not the only factors behind this split; objective circumstances were making it more difficult for socialists. The radicalisation of the 1960s began to ebb in the early 1970s, particularly as the Vietnam War wound down. While the 1972 election campaign and victory of the Whitlam Labor government was a time of mass rallies and heightened excitement at ending twenty-three years of Liberal-Country Party reaction, widespread illusions in Labor encouraged a shift from unions relying on their own strength to relying on promises of the ALP government.

During this time, members of SWL were frequently active in their local ALP branches as open socialists and supporters of

Direct Action; there was still real activity and political discussion in the Labor Party. But the main areas of activity were outside the ALP – in political movements such as support for Palestine, women's liberation and gay liberation, in student politics and in union struggles, which gradually revived after an initial downturn following Whitlam's election.

Large sections of the Australian ruling class had supported Whitlam's election, trusting in the ALP's ability gradually to defuse worker militancy. When international capitalism entered a major downturn in 1973-74, Australian capitalists took fright, fearing that Labor would be unable in time to rein in the working class sufficiently, and they therefore encouraged the Liberal parliamentary swindles that resulted in the sacking of the Whitlam government and the election of Malcolm Fraser's Liberals at the end of 1975.

The SWL had grown modestly and consolidated cadre in the preceding years, and in January 1975 a National Committee meeting decided that the organisation was ready to begin standing candidates in elections. The December 1975 election had of course not been foreseen, but the SWL reacted swiftly when Whitlam was sacked. The fortnightly *Direct Action* was immediately transformed into a weekly, and SWL candidates for the Senate were registered in the ACT and all states except Western Australia. At its conference in January 1976, the organisation decided to continue publishing *Direct Action* as a weekly and to change the name SWL to Socialist Workers Party (SWP).

In the following months, some members of the CL decided that maintaining a separate organisation from the SWP was no longer desirable or possible. Three leading members resigned from the CL and joined the SWP in November 1976, and others made a similar decision in early 1977. Later in that year, the majority of the CL decided to seek a formal fusion with the SWP. The process involved the preparation of several common political documents and the publication for several issues of a joint paper, combining *Direct Action* and *Militant*. The fusion was completed at a conference in January 1978.

In that year, the SWP decided on a major shift in its activity: the turn to industry. This was a party-wide campaign to get a large majority of the organisation working in basic industries. Such a campaign was seen as necessary because of the understanding that only the working class has the power to defeat the ruling class and begin the construction of a socialist society. The membership of the SWP was largely made up of students, former students and people in white collar jobs or jobs that were less central to the functioning of capitalism. So it was clear that the SWP would have to become a party of mainly industrial workers if it was ever to lead a successful struggle to overthrow capitalism.

But such an understanding does not by itself dictate a date by which a majority of a revolutionary party's members must become employed in basic industry. In this case, the impetus came from a mistaken analysis of the state of the class struggle, internationally and in Australia. The analysis, which was adopted at least in words by the FI, originated with the US SWP, which said that the working class was 'moving to centre stage' on a world scale: the crisis of capitalism had reached such a degree that ruling class attacks were certain to engender a widespread working class radicalisation, one that had already begun. Hence, revolutionary parties must be embedded in the industrial working class immediately in order to be able to channel and lead the coming struggles in a revolutionary direction.

In Australia, the SWP did carry out the turn and find industrial jobs for a majority of its members. Sometimes these workers were able to participate in and even lead valuable struggles. This was because the turn was carried out in a rational and careful fashion – unlike in the US SWP and some FI sections that followed the US lead and simply burned out cadre in vain attempts to relate to a radicalisation that was largely non-existent. When it became clear that the scenario of impending working class mass radicalisation was mistaken, the Australian SWP was able to reorient to developing social movements and layers such as students that were radicalising around particular issues. Part of this recognition of potential growth among students and youth was the decision in 1980 to change the name of SYA back to Resistance to make it easier to relate to radicalising young people.

The US SWP's rapidly developing sectarian degeneration, which soon spread across most of its politics, led to serious differences between it and the Australian SWP. The US group's leaders even tried to organise a faction loyal to them within the leadership of the Australian SWP, after which the Australians cut off all relations with the US party. Also in the mid-1980s, the SWP decided to end its affiliation with the FI, viewing that organisation as only one of many socialist groups around the world that it wanted to maintain relations with.

During the same period, the Australian SWP changed its analysis of the Australian Labor Party. From the beginning, the SWL/SWP had considered the ALP to have a dual character. On the one hand, it was considered to be a proletarian party in the sense that it was based on, and had been created by, the trade unions. On the other hand, its political program was support for capitalism. This analysis dictated electoral support for the ALP, at least until there was a major left-wing split from it or another party with a proletarian character but a better program came along. In 1984, the SWP changed its characterisation of the Labor Party, based on Lenin's argument that the fundamental determinant of a party's character is its program. On this basis, the SWP now described Labor as a bourgeois party that used union affiliation to conceal its real character from the working class. Therefore, no principle required automatic support for the ALP over other parties if these parties advanced demands that made them a lesser evil than Labor. The change in characterisation was timely, allowing the SWP to support enthusiastically the arrival on the political scene of the Nuclear Disarmament Party in 1984 and later various Green electoral formations.

Another change in political theory that broke with the FI and most of the world's Trotskyists involved a re-evaluation of Leon Trotsky's theory of permanent revolution.[2] The new look at this theory was initially spurred by the Nicaraguan revolution of 1979, seen as an extension of the Cuban Revolution. The SWP had previously followed the US SWP and most of the FI in try-ing to make the Cuban Revolution fit into Trotsky's theory; this required portraying the Cuban leaders as having been forced by circumstances (chiefly imperialist hostility) into a socialist revo-lution rather than following a definite Marxist strategy. The SWP rethinking of both the Cuban and Vietnamese revolutions led to the eventual conclusion that Lenin's two-stage theory, in which the democratic dictatorship of the proletariat and peasantry grew over uninterruptedly into socialist revolution, was a better guide than Trotsky's theory.

Increasing theoretical and political independence led to the establishment of a party full-time live-in cadre school in 1980. For a dozen years, the party school conducted one-month and four-month courses for eight to ten comrades at a time, with a strong focus on Lenin but also covering topics from current polit-ical issues to Marxist economics. In 1992, the school was closed, for financial reasons and because it seemed impossible at the time to spare such a large number of cadre from the demands of daily political activity. Reopening the party school remained a goal, but one that was never fulfilled.

The Hawke Labor government established its Prices and Incomes Accord with the ACTU in 1983. Many on the left, partic-ularly the Communist Party (whose leaders played a key role in creating the Accord), supported the deal or adopted an attitude of cautious criticism of the details. The SWP opposed the Accord as a class-collaborationist betrayal that would be paid for by working people and their unions. As the reality of declining real wages became more and more apparent, varying degrees of opposition to the Accord began to be expressed publicly on the left. This led to several conferences with titles like Fightback or Left Action, involving different left organisations, in an attempt to find some kind of coordinated action and/or combined organisation.

Among other things, this ferment led to the creation of a New Left Party Charter involving the SWP, the CPA and some non-party individuals influenced by the CPA, with the aim of creating a new party uniting the SWP and CPA. Charter group meetings were held throughout 1987, leading up to a national NLP conference in Melbourne in November. But at the last minute, the leaders of the CPA got cold feet about the whole process and cut off any real collaboration with the SWP. The CPA later established another NLP that gathered in no other significant forces and was only a thinly disguised way of disbanding the CPA.

The SWP also explored the possibility of unity with the Socialist Party of Australia. The SPA was formed in 1971 by ex-members of the CPA who disagreed with the party's criticism of the 1968 Soviet invasion of Czechoslovakia. The SPA was critical of the Accord, and supported *glasnost* and *perestroika* under the Gorbachev leadership of the Soviet Union, which the SWP supported enthusiastically in the hope that it represented the beginning of the political revolution advocated by Trotsky; this brought the two parties closer together. The SWP indicated its backing and hope for democratic change in the Soviet Union by changing its own name to Democratic Socialist Party in 1989. Since both the DSP and SPA supported Gorbachev in their own way, the SPA no longer needed to consider the SWP as anti-Soviet. Unity efforts included several joint election campaigns and a Socialist Unity conference of members of both parties in January

1989. However, there were two factions or groupings within the SPA – one favouring unity and one dragging its feet as much as possible. The unity effort collapsed after the Chinese government's brutal suppression of the Tiananmen demonstrators in June, which the SWP sharply condemned and which the SPA pretended hadn't happened.

Although the attempts at organisational unity had failed, the DSP continued to believe that greater collaboration on the left was both possible and desirable. This could occur particularly around issues such as protection of the environment, which most left groups could agree was a desirable goal. The DSP therefore decided to seek collaboration beyond its own members and supporters for a new publication, *Green Left Weekly*. Unlike *Direct Action,* GLW was not a party paper even though the DSP was the major organisation behind it. The paper consciously included articles by a wide variety of sources and had a much wider readership than did *Direct Action,* which ceased publication with the founding of *GLW.* At the end of 1992, when Volume 2 of John Percy's history concludes, the *GLW* website was the most popular political website in Australia.

The years since 2002

John believed that revolutionaries had to prepare for however long it might take to construct a mass Leninist party. But in the 1990s atmosphere of 'the end of socialism', many leaders and members of the DSP began looking for a way to avoid that long and difficult path.

The establishment of Socialist Alliance, intended to be a tactical experiment to create a more concentrated audience for revolutionary ideas, instead proved to be a heavy burden on DSP resources.

John and a minority of party leaders therefore advocated

pulling back from the Alliance tactic. But a majority in the organisation turned the tactic into a principled strategy, insisting that events would shortly bring an influx of members into the Socialist Alliance and propel it into an important position in Australian politics, including electoral politics. In the hope of such a development, they began downplaying the DSP's revolutionary program in favour of reforms that they thought might be electorally attractive.

The differences broke into open debate within the DSP in 2005. Despite the failure of all their hopes for Socialist Alliance advances, the majority refused to change course, and in 2008 they expelled the entire minority.

As one would have expected, John played a central role in the regroupment of expelled members as the Revolutionary Socialist Party. It was a difficult time, and two years later a substantial minority decided that it really was impossible to build towards a revolutionary party in the current climate, and they resigned from the RSP.

However, an important change was on the way. In 2012, Socialist Alternative approached the RSP with a proposal to explore the possibility of merging the two organisations. Since the major historical difference between the two tendencies – on the class character of the Soviet and Chinese states – had been removed by the changes in Eastern Europe and China, and since SA, like the RSP, was clearly committed to the construction of a revolutionary Leninist party, this was an eminently sensible proposal. RSP members voted unanimously to join Socialist Alternative, and this process was completed at SA's annual Marxism conference at Easter 2013.

John was one of the RSP members elected to the National Committee of Socialist Alternative. Despite declining health, he threw himself into building the united organisation, especially into distributing its new newspaper, *Red Flag*. He also continued his decades-long solidarity with the people of Vietnam as part of the Agent Orange Justice campaign.

About the author

John Percy was a central figure in the development of the Australian revolutionary socialist movement for half a century.

John and his brother Jim, his closest political collaborator until Jim's death from cancer in 1992, were key figures in the radical anti-imperialist wing of the movement against the Vietnam War in the 1960s. Their perspective was that it was necessary to start, now, toward building an eventual mass party that would be capable of leading an Australian socialist revolution, in the way that the Bolshevik Party of Lenin had been able to lead the Russian October Revolution. In this, they differed from most of the activists produced by the 1960s radicalisation, who tended to look for fundamental change to left capitalist politicians and/ or movements that would somehow know spontaneously what to do next.

It is difficult to write about John without writing a history of the DSP, because he was always centrally involved in initiating or implementing its major activities. John had an outstanding ability to combine firmness of political principle with great tactical flexibility – primarily because he had a very clear understanding of the difference between the two. He was good at party building because he was a team builder. He helped the DSP create a conscious culture of developing the skills of each member and combining them into a whole that was often more than the sum of its parts. This included particular attention to the training of women cadres and comrades from disadvantaged backgrounds. In both word and personal example, John emphasised that all the tasks of party building, including the most mundane, were to be valued equally and carried out by all members, as professionally as possible.

John was the editor of *Direct Action* during its early years, before spending eighteen months in New York City in 1974-75 as a journalist for *Intercontinental Press,* the weekly news magazine produced for the FI by the US SWP. On his return, he moved into party-building work in the Australian SWP National Office and Sydney branch. In 1982, he was asked to move to Melbourne to strengthen the DSP branch and help lead the turn to industry there; this included two years working on trams, one as a conductor and one as a driver. He returned to Sydney to replace Jim Percy as national secretary in 1991, when Jim became ill. He was widely known both inside and outside the DSP as the partisan of a regular, attractive and party-building revolutionary press. Over the years, thousands of people met John selling a revolutionary paper on the streets of Melbourne and Sydney, at demonstrations and picket lines - wherever he could come into contact with people who might be thinking about politics.

In 2008 John was diagnosed with throat cancer. This was eventually treated successfully, but involved months of radiotherapy and chemotherapy that drained his time and energy and left various long-term effects on his health.

In 2013, John passed out while selling *Red Flag* on the street in Glebe. He had suffered a small stroke, which in itself was not too serious. But the doctors' examination revealed another condition, an untreatable aneurysm in the brain. They described this as a time bomb that could kill him at any moment. Two subsequent strokes resulted in his death in August 2015.

About this volume

John understood the importance of revolutionaries studying and learning from their own history and experiences, and this moved him to write a history of the DSP and Resistance. John was always the unofficial DSP archivist, collecting shelf upon shelf and filing cabinet upon filing cabinet of documents, leaflets and posters from the Australian left, so he had extensive resources upon which to base this work.[3]

The first volume was published in 2005. Most of the second volume had been completed by the time of his death, and John had left indications of sources he planned to use, so it was possible to publish Volume 2 in 2017.

However, there was no partial manuscript or notes for Volume 3. But I did have available the organisational reports he gave to meetings of the National Committee and other bodies. Most of these reports are contained in the *Activist*, the DSP's internal discussion and information bulletin. I have therefore created Volume 3 as a documentary history of selections from those reports and talks.

In selecting what to include, I have sought to present the DSP's external and internal campaigns, their successes and weaknesses, while keeping the volume to a manageable size. Where a long-running activity or campaign might be mentioned prominently in several reports, I have tried to retain new information on its progress but cut material repetitive of an earlier report; therefore, readers should not assume that a campaign or activity given prominence in one year was dropped or downplayed in a subsequent year merely because it takes up less space in the reports included here.

The volume concludes in 2002 for two reasons. First, changing assignments in the National Office meant that organisational reports in the following years were usually given by a different comrade, and including those reports would have changed the character of this volume. Second, 2002 coincides with the beginning of the DSP strategic orientation to Socialist Alliance. While those events deserve their own history, they relate to a period clearly different from the one covered here.

A further explanation may be useful here regarding the language of this work. John was always aware and critical of jargon, and his writing generally avoids it. But in a report for DSP members, words that would have been jargon to non-members were quite clear to the intended audience. Rather than changing the language, I have tried to add explanations where necessary.

Acknowledgements

DSP *Activists* were digitised only from 1995. They are available online thanks to Corey Oakley, who arranged that at John's request. A few of the relevant 1992-94 hard copies were found in John's library. Sam King attempted to find more at Victoria University, but was ultimately unsuccessful. Ambrose Andrews found the remaining ones used in this volume, and also helped source photos for the cover. Nick Everett, Max Lane and Eva To assisted with research on references that had become obscure with the passage of time. Max and Eva read the manuscript, finding factual errors in my notes as well as numerous typos and stylistic inconsistencies. Eva, John's longtime partner and comrade, also provided much information and insight into John's library files, as well as unflagging encouragement and patience for the preparation of this volume. Thanks are also due to Janey Stone, who suggested a number of improvements, to the designer Viktoria Ivanova and the Interventions committee.

Allen Myers
February 2020

1. DEVELOPING A NEW GENERATION OF REVOLUTIONARY ACTIVISTS

Report to the National Committee 6-8 June 1992

Following the collapse of the Stalinist regimes in Eastern Europe and the related decline of pro-Stalinist parties in Australia, the DSP had emerged as the country's biggest socialist group, with the most popular left newspaper. The new situation brought new responsibilities and opportunities, but in a context in which the left generally was still small and weak. In this report, John Percy surveyed both the DSP's situation and that of the rest of the left. With no short-term prospects of regroupments, in contrast to the unity attempts in the 1980s, members needed to focus on activities that would directly build the party and Resistance, mainly by recruiting and training the new layers of youth beginning to radicalise despite the right-wing propaganda offensive.

At our party conference in January, we really began to get the suspicion that there'd been a significant turn in the political tide. The success of the conference surpassed most of our expectations. There was a tremendously high level of morale and enthusiasm among comrades.

Perhaps many of us had unconsciously swallowed more of the capitalist propaganda on the 'end of communism' theme than we'd been aware of over the last few years. Individually, we'd been beaten back a little by the media offensive, and it required the gathering of the clan, the coming together of all comrades, for us to realise that no, nothing had fundamentally changed, capitalism was still rotten, and we were still there fighting.

The youthfulness of the conference of course was also a tremendous boost for all of us more experienced comrades. The new generation of socialists isn't weighed down by past defeats or the strain of long campaigns, but brings a fresh energy and enthusiasm to the struggle

A good year so far

We've helped produce 19 issues of *Green Left Weekly,* at an average size of 28 pages. *Green Left* has included supplements for AKSI,[4] CISLAC,[5] Cuba, International Women's Day, EYA[6] as well as *Active Unionist,*[7] *Fantastic Sex Facts.*[8] We've used it to produce two DSEL[9] posters, the Indonesia tour poster, two Resistance conference posters, an EYA poster, *Student Underground,*[10] the Resistance O Week broadsheet.

Green Left sales have increased over the last year, by more than 600 a week. We had a wonderful special sales week, when we sold 7,250, or, by adding in Melbourne, which was out of kilter because of the Wills [Victoria] by-election, 8,500! We had more than 70 new sellers mobilised by the special sales week.

Resistance has had its best growth for years. Even before the start of the university year, we'd joined up about 80 new members, the majority at high schools. Then very successful O Weeks took this tally to more than 700 new members. But the most important feature was that this year a much bigger proportion of these new members got active, renewed their monthly membership, started selling *Green Left*, came to meetings on campus, came to meetings at the Resistance Centre.

The DSP membership is rising again also. We'd been shrinking a little over the last few years, but that has now turned around. Currently we have about 40 more provisional members around the country than we had in December, just six months ago. If we look at a graph of our membership fluctuations over the last 10 years, you can see that we hit a high point in 1984, dwindled down to a low in 1988, rose rapidly for the next two years after we abolished provisional membership to reach our highest point in early 1990, but fell back quickly from that. We bottomed out again at the end of last year, and have started growing again.

The tremendous campaign around the sex diary and our own *Fantastic Sex Facts* raised Resistance's profile and made local and national headlines. It was a model campaign of grabbing an opportunity, throwing the whole party and Resistance behind it and reaping the rewards: front-page coverage in many papers, features, interviews, debates and follow-up media requests on unrelated topics as well. The value of the publicity alone must have been worth tens of thousands of dollars, and we've made hundreds of great new contacts for Resistance, especially in high schools.

Our work to build EYA, which we projected as the major campaign for our tendency this year, has gone well. EYA had a very successful conference, committees are getting rebuilt in a number of cities, many EYA activists have joined Resistance, and the great new EYA paper now sets things up for a major expansion of EYA's influence.

Our Indonesian solidarity work, our second projected area of campaigning, has also gone well so far. We've been able to stimulate and open out AKSI committees in some cities, and the national speaking tour by Helmi Fauzi [a member of a new progressive youth group in Inconesia] has now succeeded in greatly expanding the possibilities for this work, with several hundred new contacts gained, good attendances at public meetings and campus meetings, and now real prospects for more active AKSI committees.

International Women's Day was a big success this year, in nearly all cities, and in nearly all of them our comrades played a crucial role, and sometimes it depended nearly entirely on us. There were bigger marches than in previous years in several cities. In many branches we organised well-attended Resistance or DSP forums associated with IWD. The broadsheet that we produced in *Green Left* was a great hit; some cities ran out very early.

We've participated in several election campaigns already this year – in the ACT, in Tasmania and the Wills by-election. Although our votes haven't been high, the campaigns were useful for the branches that participated in them, raising our profile and getting out our policies.

And across the country and throughout the year we've been getting consistently high turn-ups for DSP, Resistance and *Green Left* functions – fundraisers, forums, film nights, dinners, camps.

Our forum crowds have been generally larger compared to previous years. Our meetings on campus have been very encouraging. Some of the forums have been stunning, like Melbourne branch's forum on women's liberation, which packed 130 people into the building. In Perth we're running Politics in the Pub as well as our own forums, and they're getting good crowds. Hobart got 60 to a Politics in the Pub on the APPM dispute[11] last week.

Our dinner dances and social functions have gone well. Sydney's dinner two weeks ago was attended by 230 and had a fantastic atmosphere. Canberra had a dinner of 90. Cultural Dissent[12] functions are now occurring in Sydney, Brisbane, Adelaide and Wollongong. Adelaide crammed 60 into their headquarters for an African band night. Sydney had more than 100 here last Sunday for the women's cabaret night. Film nights have been big successes. Canberra got 70 people to one, Sydney's had 100 packed in here about three times.

We made a special effort on May Day marches and functions this year, and comrades felt good about them as well. Adelaide got 60 to the toast at their office; most of the active left was represented. Melbourne had a great toast.

We've played an important role in the Cuba tours and meetings. Some of the best meetings have been put on by us or depended on us. The Newcastle dinner was attended by 90 people, and everyone recognised the central role played by Resistance comrades.

During the last year or so we've stabilised CISLAC financially, and recently held a successful national consultation.

It's been a very hectic but fruitful five months. This experience confirms several things.

Firstly, it indicates the beginning of a change in the nature of the political period, as we move out of a focus on the collapse of Stalinism in the Soviet Union and Eastern Europe and the working class defeats and imperialist victories of the last few years. We seem to be moving into a period in which capitalism's crises move to the forefront of world attention again, when they're not so easily masked – the Gulf War, the international recession, the LA riots, the upsurge in Thailand, the strikes in Germany.

The subjective response we're getting to our functions, forums, events, and to *Green Left* must reflect partially that changed situation.

It also must reflect some things we're doing right ourselves. Our success reaffirms the correctness of our party-building orientation that we've stressed over the last few years.

It's worth quoting from the report Jim Percy gave to the party conference in January on 'The DSP and the crisis of the left'. Comrades should reread that, as well as his report to the October

1991 National Committee meeting on 'Party-building perspectives for the '90s'. Jim pointed out:

> In the last two years, and especially in the last year –
> 1991 – the party had passed through a rather difficult
> time. One might even use the word 'crisis'. There are
> a couple of elements to this. One of them was the
> further difficulty in trying to develop any broad political
> formation, and specifically, the failure of the Green party
> process. But a more significant factor has been the end
> of perestroika and the developments in Eastern Europe
> and the Soviet Union – the so-called end of communism
> and the capitalist propaganda barrage surrounding it.

This affected the left in general and us as well, leading to a crisis in the party and a certain demoralisation and decline in numbers:

> Over the last two years, and 1991 in particular, this
> meant the party had to go on a forced march to try
> to come to terms with what had happened in the
> world, to understand it, to review our own political
> thinking. Flowing from this, we began a discussion
> about the party itself, about our organisational project
> itself. This conference marks the end of that period.
> It's a crisis we've come through. In my opinion,
> we've passed the test with flying colours.

We overcame the crisis by our conscious hard work in 1991, and seem to have turned the corner in the first five months of 1992, recruiting well, building Resistance, increasing sales of *Green Left*, and starting to grow again.

But we should not underestimate the very real difficulties still in front of us, the difficulties in recruiting, training and developing a new generation of socialists. These difficulties arise from the absence of a healthy mass movement. We can't substitute for that, so we are not going to overcome these fundamental problems overnight.

The rest of the left

What about the rest of the left in this period?

Firstly, the New Left Party[13] – although I still prefer to call them the ex-CPA, since the NLP really hasn't properly got off the ground, and 'ex-CPA' encompasses the totality better.

They've finally made it out with *Broadside Weekly*.[14] All comrades would have seen it. In fact, the bulk of their sales so far have probably been through newsagents in the Chippendale area [in Sydney].

It's not a patch on *Green Left Weekly*. We were stunned. After all this time, we thought they'd labour and produce something that was slightly competitive.

Their 16 pages don't stand up to our 28. Their drab cover doesn't match our full colour. Their layout's boring. Their full-time journalists don't appear to be particularly scintillating, and there were few outside writers with names or authority. Their attempts at humour were embarrassing.

But their biggest handicap is their politics. Their link with the Labor left means they can't say much about federal or state politics. Labor was mentioned only twice, and only in passing. There was not a word of criticism of Labor governments. Their coverage of green issues is very scant also.

Their distribution will be mainly through their sub base. They do have links with some trade unions, which will be an added avenue for distribution, but will find it hard to match the links with the movements that we've built up, with the wide range of special supplements that we've been able to include. They have ceded street sales to us, with their in-principle position of not selling on the streets.

The political profile of the New Left Party itself around the country is minimal. In many cities, comrades report that it's literally non-existent. They don't hold public meetings or forums, participate in their own name at rallies or pickets, put out press releases.

The NLP invisibility isn't going to be improved with the appearance of *Broadside* either. They've made such a big point about not linking it to any party that it will be very awkward for them to promote the NLP and its activities. The alliance with some of the ALP fake left in the project is going to limit their options even further.

What about the NLP's attempt to link up with the Democrats, Rainbow Alliance,[15] some of the Greens and the Marxist Workers Organisation[16] in Melbourne? They've been having discussions for ages to develop a 'Work and Economic Justice Campaign' and statement. They're trying to work up a statement, and a broadsheet with articles contributed by each of the organisations. They also held a teleconference on 14 April, supposedly to finalise the broadsheet and make arrangements to launch it, but they weren't ready.

Perhaps they were caught up and diverted by the euphoria over Phil Cleary's election victory.[17] It seems they had high hopes of bringing him behind their projects, and also perhaps getting some jobs in his office. Those hopes certainly seem to have been dashed; Phil's own friends got the jobs.

Where is Cleary going politically? That's not clear yet. He's made some moves to the right, but there have been other good indications to the left, so we'll see.

In Hobart some former CPA members have participated in a group called SEECA – Social Ecological Economic Cultural

Alliance. This has been taken over by ALP left types and apparatchiks who hope to use it to bolster their green credentials.

In Adelaide there's also been an attempt at a local alliance, the South Australian Congress (modelled on the ANC!). It's mostly a collection of ALPers and NLP union bureaucrats generally.

The CPA's final fling, to 'broaden out' with the NLP, has further narrowed their base and killed off most of their remaining cadres. They haven't been able to renew them, and it's very unlikely they will be able to in future. There's still a little life in Left Alliance[18] – they had banners on May Day in Sydney, where the NLP did not – but it's still more a ladder for jobs in unions or government than a youth group that could develop cadres.

The decline of the CPA and its rebirth in smaller and weaker form as the New Left Party is really the biggest change on the left political landscape in Australia for decades. Twenty-five years ago, the CPA had around 5,000 members. *Tribune* was the dominant paper on the left. We, by contrast, were a tiny group located in one city. Today, in many cities our tendency is the left; there's no competition from the CP or anyone else. *Green Left Weekly* is the dominant, established left paper, and it's *Broadside Weekly* trying to catch up.

What of the other groups? The Rainbow Alliance might have seemed to have potential a few years ago, at least in Melbourne, but were unable to build on their large launching meetings. Their activist base today is extremely narrow. In Brisbane, they have little activity. On the whole, there are no great prospects for Rainbow Alliance.

We had some discussion of the Green Party situation and the varied green groups under the report on the state of the environmental movement. We know how tiny, weak and unprepossessing these groups are. They're divided among themselves (opposition to us united them, and now we've gone). They have a terrible oversupply of would-be tin-pot dictators. They're purely electoralist, opportunist.

What about the various Stalinist shells? The Socialist Party of Australia has shown signs of continuing decline, despite their efforts to shore up their members with the blind Gus Hall-style[19] 'Things were better with Uncle Joe' line. Some of their smaller branches are having trouble staying alive. The closure of the New Era bookshop in Sydney last December has been followed by the closure of their shops in Melbourne and Brisbane. (We've profited from this, managing to get a big chunk of basic Marx-Engels-Lenin stock from their Melbourne shop.)

In April the SPA approached us with a proposal to organise once again a discussion among the 'Marxist-Leninist parties' – us, them, the Association for Communist Unity (ACU),[20] the Communist Party of Australia (Marxist-Leninist)[21] and the Marxist Workers Organisation. We politely said, sure we're open to discussion with any serious forces, but we tried this a few years ago, and basically you missed your chance for unity then. Since then major events have occurred, and our parties have taken different positions, and we'd be on different sides on such issues as the split in the CPUSA.[22]

A small part of our attention can be devoted to finding a way to open up a political dialogue with those comrades from the SPA who are open to new thoughts, and deepening the differentiation between the diehard Stalinist types and any potential democratic socialist, Leninst lefts.

The CPA (ML) still survives, and [its paper] *Vanguard* is still coming out. But there's no sign of any new recruits, or any real political life around them.

The ACU is just a rump. They split over the NLP and *Broadside.* Their national secretary is Wally Pritchard over in Perth, but most of the rest of them are just in Sydney. They don't function as a party but as a trade union job trust. It's not even a junketing travel agency any more with the Moscow head office gone.

The Marxist Workers Organisation, confined to Melbourne, does function as a tiny Stalinist religious sect, but mainly persists through its hold on a few trade union positions, especially the ATEA.

It's clear that our main opponent on the left remains the International Socialist Organisation.[23] For quite a few years they've been our main rivals at selling papers, among youth and students. Their main branches are in Sydney, Melbourne, Brisbane and Canberra. They have a small group in Adelaide, and individuals in Perth and Hobart.

They have a radically different approach to politics to ours; i.e., they're an evangelical sect with a typical radical middle-class mixture of ultra-left and right-opportunist positions. So we will have to debate them, counter their views and tactics. We need to educate our own comrades, train our new members in counter-position to their perspectives.

They have been more subdued than we expected at the start of the year. They had a bit of wind in their sails last year, had some new recruits, and were extra happy with the working-class defeats in the Soviet Union and Eastern Europe. We thought they would begin the year with a lot of momentum, especially on campuses, but in many places their interventions were very low key and disorganised, even on campuses where we knew they had some strength. We joined up many more members than they did. Our campus forums, film showings and meetings were frequently better attended than theirs. As our Brisbane organiser reports, they're 'not together, not mobilising like they used to'.

They've been badly hurt by *Green Left*. The drubbing we've given them on sales with *Green Left* partly explains their offensive against *Green Left* over AIDEX[24] and the education demos. They ran around trying to get at *Green Left*'s sponsors on both issues, with little success. The results of one of their petition-type letters was in the last issue of *Green Left*. It turns out they added names without authorisation.

Their Sydney and Melbourne May Day contingents showed they are still a serious rival to us – they have some cadre, can mount interventions, are recruiting new members.

They're able to feed off the strength of their parent organisation in Britain, the Socialist Workers Party (SWP), which has some 5,000 members. But their turnover is high, and they have no infrastructure and apparatus like we have. They're limited by having only a monthly paper.

Nevertheless, we have to find further ways of combating them as our most serious left opponent, and there are lessons for us already from our experiences with them. Our comrades need more training and assistance in their interventions; we need to step up political education for new Resistance members; we need to give lots more attention to recruiting, to one-to-one talking to people.

As for the other left sects around the country, they're all tiny.

The Militant group,[25] still mainly in Sydney with a small group in Melbourne, has done some good work among working-class youth in Sydney's west. It will be interesting to see what are repercussions for them here from the split of their parent group in Britain, with the majority of them now out of the Labour Party.

The Communist League, the branch office of the US Socialist Workers Party, seems even weaker than before. They've retreated from distributing Pathfinder Press directly here, which was another windfall for us – we managed to grab most of their remaindered stock.

Communist Intervention in Melbourne is a grab bag of armchair Trotskyist sectarians, ex-Healyites[26] etc. Possibly they'll link up with [Phil] Sandford's little group of followers of Argentine Trotskyist cult leader Nahuel Moreno.

The supporters of the Fourth International here, Solidarity, are largely inactive as a group. Ken Davis in Sydney is a *Green*

Left sponsor and very friendly to us, and so is John Tully in Melbourne now.

The Freedom Socialist Party in Melbourne is only a handful of people, but they seem to have been able to relate to *Green Left* and use it in a non-sectarian way.

The Socialist Labour League, what used to be the Healyites and should probably now be called the Northites,[27] has dwindled. They had no contingents in Sydney or Melbourne May Day marches this year, in contrast to previous years, when May Day was a big focus for them. They've suffered a major decline over the last ten years – they possibly got as high as 150-200 members at one stage.

The Spartacists had more than 20 at Sydney May Day, but they're an ageing, increasingly irrelevant sect.

The anarchist milieu has probably grown a fair bit over the last few years, but my impression is the organised part of it is getting more rabidly right wing.

In Perth, there's very little on the left apart from us. The Troy group[28] in Fremantle has dissipated. The members of the Chilean Communist Party there are very friendly, and take their political lead from us, and help out with our functions, even our forum dinners. We probably should be checking out the Latin American left milieu, especially the CPs, in other cities a bit more, since they've been very much cast adrift by events in the Soviet Union.

Similarly with quite a few of the solidarity groups; many are in disarray following the downfall of Stalinism. The East Timor campaign in some cities is the largest movement; for example, in Adelaide they got 150 to a dinner. The party has good relations with Fretilin there.

This brief survey of the Australian left indicates there's not much out there and no great prospects for revival through some sort of regroupment of sections of it.

Reaffirming our youth orientation

Perhaps the most important general reason for our advance has been our orientation to recruiting and training young people as revolutionary activists through the work of Resistance. That's our trump suit, that's what's set us apart.

Our two best suits in the last year or two have been *Green Left Weekly* and Resistance, and we propose leading with these in the period ahead.

The main reason for our long-term success compared with the CPA has been the youth; that has been their failure from the second half of the '60s on. This has been the biggest contrast between us and other revolutionary groups, for example in the Fourth International, or the range of groups in the US. They haven't been recruiting young people in the last decade or more. This has always been our strength, and it's one of the principal reasons for our survival.

In this period, our orientation to youth and dependence on them for building our tendency will be even more important than in the past. We will also be recruiting people directly to the party, and also hope to save some of the remnants from the other left groups, but the core, the majority, will come through Resistance.

Understanding this, our party-building priorities are to assist Resistance to grow, to develop and recruit. More importantly, they are to recruit from Resistance, and to train, educate and integrate the new generation of revolutionary activists.

The party today is already made up of 70-80% youth. You could see it at our conference: the average age of the party has actually gone down. We know also the increasing role of Resistance in carrying out our movement work, and our decision at the conference to prioritise EYA and AKSI as our main areas of intervention. Resistance leaders will more and more be party leaders as well.

This central focus on Resistance will put an increasing strain on the Resistance National Office and Resistance branch executives. They will need all the help the party can give them in leading the work, in training and educating the new generation of activists, in backing them up.

As the proportion of older comrades gets smaller, and the younger comrades outnumber us in the party, it's clear this task has to be carried out by every one of the older generation. We can't succeed otherwise. All party comrades have to have as part of their assignment, perhaps their most important assignment, helping train the new generation.

We have to consciously break down some of the divisions that exist between the generations, between the party and Resistance. In our movement, there can be no generation gap.

We know that the organisational independence of Resistance is vital for recruiting and training the next generation. But it can be a hindrance, an obstacle, if we neglect the essential associated tasks, if we don't:

- Maintain the links between Resistance and the party.
- Provide the help, the education, the training, the discussion.
- Provide the glue of one-to-one contact, of talking to new Resistance comrades, making them feel at home in the revolutionary movement, passing on our experiences, knowledge and help.

We all have to be part of Resistance once again, in spirit and feeling if not formally. And that's not a bad place to be today. We have to attend Resistance's functions, raise the level of their informal political discussions, follow the Resistance pre-conference discussion.

This is the gain in consciousness that we have to register with this National Committee meeting – that all our party-building tasks have to be in the framework of helping build Resistance and training and educating a new generation of revolutionaries.

Education and training for the long haul

The task is to train comrades for the long haul, to educate them in Marxism, to develop their commitment and feeling of investment in the movement. We have to find ways to develop that long-term perspective but never to lose the enthusiasm and political excitement about politics, the idealism of youth that's essential for every revolutionary.

We're still in the process of adjusting our priorities, of reaffirming the party-building perspective versus the orientation to working in small committees that masquerade as social movements. We can get sucked in, diverted. Where our conference perspectives have been most consistently implemented, that's where we're making the most gains.

Our top party-building priority will continue to be *Green Left Weekly* of course. But let's do this in the new framework: educating, training and integrating the new Resistance members. We know a measure of the integration of new Resistance members is whether they've started selling the paper regularly. It's also a measure of how well we're training a comrade to be in it for the long haul of party building. So training new comrades how to sell, making them feel happy and fulfilled about selling, is fundamental.

Green Left is such a wonderful weapon for intervention, proselytising for socialist views in a general way, and intervening as though we're thrusting 30 or 40 separate leaflets into someone's hand. It's a wonderful aid in training new comrades in political situations, meetings, demos etc. We would feel defenceless without it.

Green Left is also the first step on the road to educating new comrades. If you read all of *Green Left* every week, you'd get a very thorough grounding in Australian and international politics, so we've got to constantly encourage this in new comrades

– ask them about particular articles, point things out, quote it in reports, at meetings, organise special reading circles if necessary.

The second facet of training and integration that we want to stress is the area where we've fallen down most over the years – personal integration and one-to-one training. All too often we merely set the formal structures for education in place and invite new comrades along, and leave the rest up to them. But the informal side of things is even more important.

We need to worry hard about the social integration of every single new comrade or contact. We all have to get to know new comrades quickly, spend the time talking to them (often doing political tasks at the same time, either around the office, out selling, at a demo etc.). Make sure they're included in social outings, organise special dinners. Include them in conversations, take the time to explain the background of an issue, or the jargon.

People join us for politics, so give it to them. Make sure at social functions that the discussions are political, not in-gossip or apolitical banter.

We have to take personal responsibility for new comrades. There's nothing more satisfying than having a new comrade come on board, seeing them develop politically.

The third aspect of integration of new comrades is that we learn best in action and flourish in a political atmosphere. Comrades join for activity – people who don't want activity stay at home and watch the box or end up down the pub. So always think about taking a new comrade with you when you're setting out on a political activity, whether it's a meeting, a demo or selling the paper.

The more activity we can involve them in, the quicker they'll learn and be integrated. But interventions have to be balanced and planned, and we have to select those activities that are most important politically and will also best raise political consciousness.

Sometimes the intervention might just consist of *Green Left* sales at an activity, or holding placards and chanting, but other times speaking at a meeting might be necessary. This can provide the best training for new comrades, if they're encouraged to speak, helped with their remarks or talk. In Sydney recently, Billy Bragg put on a little recruiting stunt for the Young Labor Association. Our comrades intervened and took him on, which was good. We could do more of this, especially going after the ALP whenever they raise their head with the line, 'Support us, or the Liberals will be worse'. Training new comrades how to intervene in that milieu would give them a very comprehensive education.

Training comrades in polemics and political infighting will be necessary as well, especially when the stakes are important. We're a very homogeneous party today, and I'm certainly not wishing for a faction fight to blow up in the party, but you certainly develop politically in those situations. So in the absence of any heavy internal debates, we can train comrades by launching them at the ALP right-wingers or fake left, or at the ISO if they warrant it.

A fourth aspect of training to be conscious of is that new comrades want to feel useful. They join the movement to be constructive. It's a great feeling to complete a task, and feel you've contributed to the cause in some way. It's another side of the active training process.

This also fits in with another vital need – to spread tasks and responsibilities around. It's the way to avoid overload on the longer term comrades. It's a real trap to think, just because we've been around longer, we have to do everything ourselves. It's one of the most basic responsibilities of branch organisers always to have a list of things that can be done by comrades coming into the headquarters – wrapping the subs; collating pamphlets; painting banners; doing phone-outs; HQ clean-up; sales; typing articles; filing; minding the bookshop.

If you're always conscious of asking and training other comrades to carry out tasks, then you create a better atmosphere in the branch. If all the tasks are on your shoulders, you can easily convey an atmosphere of panic, whereas with tasks spread around, you convey an aura of bustling efficiency, of activity around the place. That's the mood we want.

Can we get too 'professional', rely on the full-time volunteers too much? Perhaps there is a tendency for this in the large branches, where we have four or five full-timers. In smaller branches the tasks must be spread around, where there's only one or no full-time volunteer.

A fifth essential aspect of our training of new comrades is our internationalist perspective. This includes both the importance of our links and contact and discussion with like-minded revolutionaries around the world, and our activity in solidarity with other struggles.

Now that we're moving out of a period characterised by the defeat of Stalinism in the Soviet Union and Eastern Europe and into a period when imperialism is more unfettered, more naked, with a worldwide environmental crisis, with a widening gap between rich and poor, an international outlook will be even more essential for building the movement here.

We have to forge links with the healthy currents, those that have survived, those that are developing and growing, those that have split – to cook out a left internationally, but a democratic, revolutionary socialist left.

Some of the groups coming out of the break-up will move to the right in their disillusion with Stalinism. We have to do what we can to help and encourage those developing to the left. There are important debates happening on strategy, on the need and role of a party, on whether a Leninist-type party is necessary. We can participate, and through that, not only help others, but help ourselves and educate a new generation.

The role of *Green Left* in this will be very important, sending it further afield, developing an even larger network of correspondents. The proposal for a regional conference of revolutionary socialists, which we raised yesterday, could play a big part also.

As for solidarity work, our priority at the moment is Indonesia, through AKSI and our own activities. But we'll also be maintaining our Latin American solidarity activity through CISLAC, and our Cuba solidarity work, and secondary interventions in other areas depending on the local situation.

A sixth aspect of training is instilling in comrades a historical perspective. We have to situate today's struggles in the history of the movement, the history of the party and Resistance here, Australia's radical, working-class traditions and the international socialist movement's history also. Part of that history is also the culture, the literature, the working-class songs.

This not only provides an essential educational framework but also gives comrades the long view of history. It prepares them for the long struggle, prevents them developing false expectations of easy or early victories, and steels them against demoralisation when there are downturns and setbacks in the struggle.

A seventh aspect is the necessity of continuing to develop our working-class orientation. With the present low ebb of the labour struggles, it's especially important to stress the permanency of our working-class orientation, that we aim to build a proletarian party – a party that not only fights for the historic interests of the working class, but is predominantly composed of workers.

We're not proposing any sort of turn, but it is important to orient new comrades politically to industrial struggles, to help them get jobs where necessary, and to feature those comrades who are carrying out successful political work in industry and their union, for example, Andrew Watson at Mitsubishi.[29] And when there are upsurges around the world, such as the German strikes, or the US union elections, we should play them up.

The more structured side of our education and integration

work has not been as deficient as the more informal, unstructured aspects that I mentioned earlier.

Our class series are in place and functioning more or less well from branch to branch, reflecting the rate of new members coming round and the potential for growth. Hobart and Adelaide have had extremely well-attended class series this year, but most branches have had some good classes. The Introduction to Socialism and Introduction to Marxism[30] series seem to fill our basic needs, together with the classes on our program and our environment document. Both Sydney and Melbourne have found it necessary to hold special classes for a selection of the full-timers, since some relatively new comrades have taken on important responsibilities in recent years.

We want to suggest three possible special educational seminars or weekend conferences that we could hold around the country through the rest of the year. These could be roughly coordinated so we could get out some common publicity, but staggered so we share visual resources and speakers among the branches.

Firstly, we need an intensive weekend educational seminar in as many branches as we can organise on Indonesian politics and history. If we could use Max Lane and Helmi Fauzi for feature talks, assign some other comrades to prepare some classes, get some films and videos, it could be a great weekend, probably attracting many outside people.

Secondly, a weekend seminar on the life and ideas of Trotsky would be useful in giving a basic background of history and essential ideas to our new Resistance comrades, but could also be of wider use politically, directed at present or former members of the SPA or others from that milieu who need this slice of history, and secondly against the ISO, who associate themselves with Trotsky but reject some of his most important political positions. We could have a series of talks, as well as some videos, including the excellent documentary of Trotsky's life that was on SBS recently.

Thirdly, in early November we need our own way of celebrating the October Revolution, and another weekend educational series or conference might be the most useful for us. Again there are films and videos available as well, and the essential talks that need giving. On the Saturday night perhaps we could have a dinner with a rally, have a toast, raise some money, attract a wider attendance from our supporters and others on the left.

Individual branches might have proposals for other special educational events or conferences. Specifically DSP educational camps have also been very useful. A consideration to remember for classes, camps, seminars, talks etc. is our understanding that the person preparing and giving a talk always gets far more out of it than someone listening, so it's vital to involve the widest number of comrades in giving talks, as soon as possible after they join.

The second Resistance special training school will be held for three days after the Resistance conference. It will build on the success of the first, which was very much appreciated, and involve more intensive training in particular areas. It will be specifically aimed at raising the skills and capabilities of comrades leading the Resistance branches – the branch executive members, comrades heading up particular organising assignments etc.

We're not projecting holding a four-month full-time party school session this year, for personnel and financial reasons. We hope to have a three-week full-time school at the end of the year and another in January. We'd also like to investigate the possibility of organising shorter leadership courses at the school, but can't see the way to fit them in as yet.

In the period ahead we need to develop in the party a stronger culture of reading and theory. This can be done through all the informal considerations and through a more serious attitude to our formal educational activities. *Green Left* and our DSP publications can help further, and there is an important role here for our branch bookshops. Comrades are poor, and books are expensive, but we have to persist with this. A revolutionary without a library is a limited revolutionary. We've been fortunate this year in being able to get hold of a large stock of Pathfinder books, and Marx-Engels-Lenin from Progress Publishers. We'll also be stepping up production of our own pamphlets and reprints. So our bookshops have the possibility of stocking the basics and becoming added attractions to our centres.

Finally, I want to look at some of our party institutions from the viewpoint of training and integration.

Our fractions[31] have been the institution most neglected this year, and it's essential that we reverse this trend. Fractions are absolutely essential in training new comrades in how to intervene, in educating them politically, and teaching them how the party and Resistance function. Obviously, our student and EYA fractions were vital, but sometimes didn't happen. But in other areas they would help train and integrate new comrades also.

Sales committees are another party institution that has proved essential. The best, most improved, most regular sales have been achieved where successful sales committees are established. Brisbane's party-Resistance organising committee seems to be able to organise tasks like sales efficiently for a branch of Brisbane's size.

Forums, whether *Green Left*, DSP, Resistance or Politics in the Pub, should be conceived as both reach-out events and educational and training events for our whole membership. We should plan a more active role for comrades, not just passively sitting and listening. Work out possible interventions in the discussion beforehand, organise Resistance members to come along.

Branch meetings must be organised with a view to education of newer comrades, and the inspiration and continuing motivation of longer term comrades. We need the right balance, so that they're not just organisational events, but have a high political content. Comrades look forward to coming, because they know they'll learn something each time. They know there'll be interesting discussions, and decisions to take also; it won't just be a formality, listen to reports and go home.

We have to find ways of increasing the political content on executives, both party and Resistance. They shouldn't get swamped in organisational detail that (a) doesn't train the new members on the body and (b) doesn't efficiently get the work done. We can hive off many things to a temporary little subcommittee, or delegate it, or table a written report that comrades can check over if they want to.

But it's vitally important to make the leading party bodies intensely political. One step, which solves other needs as well, is to have *Green Left* copy discussed at every party branch executive meeting, to force us to be on top of political events in our city/state, and also to relate to national and international political events. The leaders of the branch must be on top of this; it can't be left to comrades who volunteer or non-members.

Finally, we have booked Hawkesbury[32] for a DSP educational conference 2-6 January. We know we'll need that gathering then; we felt the lack when we skipped a year. The conference will have an extensive selection of talks and classes that comrades can choose from, as well as feature talks, reports, fractions and workshops, and the usual features such as a rally, cabaret etc. Hopefully we'll also have some international guests.

Continuing to raise our party profile

Resistance is key, and training new comrades is central, but the complement to this is raising the profile of the DSP itself, as well as the consciousness about socialism.

We can use the DSP name to raise awareness about socialism,

to talk about the basic ideas. We have to let more and more people know that there is a party today defending and promoting those ideas, those ideals. We need to counter the right-wing offensive – they've already taken too much ground. We don't want a lapse into jargon, of course, or into schematic simplifications. We still need to pursue our efforts to express our essential ideas in accessible language, to find ways of reaching the mass of people.

But we can't be too cool, or so broad that we end up being defensive, embarrassed about the very word socialism, and some of our fundamental concepts and ideas that are straightforward, very clear, but very blunt. We have to find many ways and places to say it: yes, the DSP is for socialism; it's a goal we're proud to fight for. In the period ahead of us, clear ideas expressed firmly will find a hearing.

Green Left Weekly is still the essential expression of our growing influence. Its rhythm is ongoing compared to the one-off impact of a leaflet or pamphlet, or the broken rhythm of election campaigns. Its networking ability is thus far more important than election campaigns. So we need to explore ways to make better use of *Green Left Weekly* for this purpose. It's the essential building block for our party-building work.

The paper's so important because for the moment it reflects two essential aspects of the party's work: reaching out and bringing towards. It's been a tremendous success in reaching out. It has to succeed similarly in bringing towards.

Now, because of the particular stage of the mass movement and its weakness, which is reflected in the weakness of the subjective factor, i.e., parties, our present approach is to build *Green Left Weekly*, a non-party paper, which may be the situation for some time. But the purpose of the approach is not to leave people happy in their isolation from us in a party, not to set up an obstacle to us, not to leave people permanently distant from us. Even as we recognise that distance for the moment, our purpose is just as much to bring those closer who can come closer.

There are a number of things we can do to improve *Green Left* and address these questions.

Firstly, both *Green Left* and the DSP would benefit from the paper carrying more basic educational articles on socialist ideas. These will be harder to write than many other types of articles. They'll need more care, more going over by several comrades. But given the expanded readership of *Green Left,* these types of articles would be very appropriate and educational for our wide new readership, including the many young readers, new Resistance members etc.

For example, it would be great if we could get a regular column along the lines of What Socialists Stand For. If it was able to use a topical event to illustrate a classical fundamental point, all the better. Perhaps we could also submit more reviews of explicitly socialist books.

Especially when you consider that the paper has a large proportion of new readers, people who haven't had some basic socialist concepts explained to them, it's important to carry more of this material.

Secondly, we could have more varied ways of presenting our Marxist viewpoint. We have the *Green Left* editorials, and they've been important and effective. And our general positions do come across in most of the other articles written by our members. But we could also use the paper more effectively to present a wider range of DSP policy statements. There can be more *Green Left* statements, viewpoints, what we think type articles or short comments in boxes – in effect a second or third editorial, but presented differently. This can be used when it looks like we're not going to have an adequate coverage through normal articles of a major issue. Or there can be more comments or articles by comrades specifically identified as a DSP spokesperson, office-holder or candidate.

Another excellent part of the paper that we don't use enough, only in emergencies when prodded, is the letters column. Probably it's one of the most read pages. Short, punchy letters by DSP and Resistance activists would improve this feature immensely. It would shape the discussion in the paper more in the direction that we want it to head in, and allow us easily to increase the DSP profile without in any way diminishing the broad appeal of *Green Left*.

A third way to make even better use of *Green Left* is by using it more to set the political agenda that we want. We still haven't gotten used to having a paper which is the dominant paper on the left, and in the green milieu too. We often don't use it enough to promote our campaigns, to advertise our events, to build the movements we want to prioritise.

For example: EYA this year, its campaigns and successes. Given how well we've gone with this, and how we're continually recruiting to Resistance and the party through EYA, I think we should be featuring EYA even more. We need to approach EYA in the paper as though it's not our members who are leading it, but some other group of radical youth. If that were the case, I'm sure we'd be falling over ourselves to get interviews with them, publicise their activities and try to convince lots of other young people to join this very radical environmental group.

Indonesian solidarity was another area that we prioritised at the conference. We could play this up even further. People want as much information as they can get on this. *Green Left* must become the weekly source of news on Indonesia.

We can get a bit blasé about this – yes, Max Lane might be the translator of Pramoedya and probably the foremost Indonesian expert in the country, but he's our mate Max, we wouldn't want to big-note him in any way, would we? And Comrade Fauzi, we've all made friends with Helmi and regard him as one of us, so we wouldn't want to make a big song and dance about his trip to Europe, where he not only presented the case to the UN against the Indonesian government's attacks on human rights in Indonesia, but put the case for the people of East Timor as well, putting the case to the European Parliament, arguing against Indonesia's foreign affairs minister.

Another area that I think we could have featured more was the very successful International Women's Day rallies this year, which our comrades were very central to organising in nearly every city. Just compare our minimal coverage of IWD to the larger coverage we had of the Sydney Gay and Lesbian Mardi Gras, which we weren't involved in organising, and was less significant politically. We could have given more coverage to the IWD events themselves and focussed on some of our women comrades who led them.

Finally, I think we could promote and feature events and functions that we organise more: *Green Left* functions, DSP functions, Resistance functions. Sometimes we'll write a report of an outside event – a picket, or a meeting – that might be quite modest in size, but be bashful about reporting a larger event or meeting because it was a party or Resistance event.

We should also devote a little more space to promoting the distribution side of *Green Left*. Most people buy it in the street – let's strengthen that connection by talking it up in the pages of the paper itself. Let's praise our sellers who make a special effort, an excellent sales rate, some exciting new selling spots. Let's give credit to Resistance and DSP members where it's due. Let's also promote the other excellent efforts, Shell 63 in Darwin [a well-known political activist and *Green Left Weekly* distributor] for example. Or welcome aboard a new bookshop or movement centre that starts distributing. We could also get more chatty about some of our correspondents, especially our international ones.

The general point is that it's time we took ourselves more seriously. In the past, we reacted against the pompous self-promotion of all the left sects, the loud proclamations that they alone had the true word. But perhaps we went too far in self-efface-ment, as we tried to broaden out, or examined every possibility of unity. We need to redress that. Moreover, our weight on the left has changed, the importance of the paper has changed, and the period we're entering into demands a higher profile for us.

In the present climate, if there was a complaint, for exam-ple, that *Green Left* was playing up Resistance too much, we'd say, 'We'd be happy to play up any other youth organisation in Australia that was playing a similar role among radicalising young people. We'd be happy to play up an organisation that was responsible for selling half the copies of *Green Left* that get sold. Anyone who wants to constructively promote and distribute *Green Left* can join in.'

A specifically DSP theoretical magazine was one of the im-portant projections we made at the conference for raising our profile. We want to modify our original plan, and put on hold the idea of a separate magazine. We don't have the financial or personnel resources to launch it as initially planned.

Instead, we want to propose a quarterly magazine supple-ment to *Green Left Weekly,* sponsored by the DSP, just as other organisations have supplements. It could be called something like Socialism Today, consist of eight pages, carry longish theo-retical articles, discussion and reviews.[33]

The regular *Activist* will continue to fill an essential internal party need for information, reprints, discussion and coverage of our organisational campaigns. We've been able to halve the price, so no comrade should have any excuse not to purchase them. They are an invaluable source of information on our par-ty-building perspectives and experiences, and every comrade should be keeping them on file as references.

We aren't on schedule yet with all the publications we project-ed at the conference, but our new electronic duplicator has made a world of difference. As soon as we got it, it was straight into action night and day with the [sex] diary. It's made it so much easier and more economical for the *Activist* and Resistance Discussion Bulletin, as well as a host of leaflets, forms, circulars etc.

We've started using it for pamphlets, initially reprints of documents and historical material for new comrades since they required little extra writing, but we want to get out dozens more pamphlets this year, both reprints and talks by comrades. These are urgent; often it's just a matter of editing talks and we're ready to go. The new party or DSEL statements on different issues are a top priority for us after the NC.

We're just about ready to send the women's liberation book off to the printers, and hopefully that will be back in about two months.[34] We also want to prepare a new edition of *What Socialists Stand For*. There's not too much editing required for this.

We've already had quite a lot of discussion of our electoral perspectives. The registration of DSEL is our immediate task. We have to finish quickly getting 600-700 names. We have now relinquished the DSP registration, so registering DSEL is urgent. When we just put in the minimum effort, we get a great response; it's a lot easier than we expected. And many people want to do more than just sign: they'll pay the money and become part of our organised periphery.

DSEL is a way of raising the party profile, an immediate electoral vehicle for us. But we still have a sense of ghetto politics, and need ways to break out. But perhaps we shouldn't approach it primarily in an electoral framework. Perhaps we will just have to take our blows on the electoral front, after the end of the Greens option, for some time to come. The Greens aren't going to rise from the ashes easily. Cleary is a one-off phenomenon. If a broader electoral opportunity comes along, we can't be excluded. We won't miss it, especially if it has a working-class orientation. If it has any democratically functioning structures, we'll be in it.

We can't see it at the moment – there's less chance of it than in the '80s. But we'll keep our options open, just as we want to keep open our access to the Green name. We'll challenge them legally, try to get WA Green endorsement[35] and, if necessary, we'll round up the 500 names. Down the road we might need to stake more on a Green-type election campaign, perhaps a Green Left variant. We know of all our attempts to broaden out in the last 10 years, *Green Left* has been the most fruitful.

And we'll be flexible with our election campaigns, and won't want to push a branch too hard if they're not keen on a big campaign. Some branches will want to go flat out. We'll probably want to have a go with the next federal elections.

A campaign for democratic rights, perhaps in the form of a charter for DSEL, has been suggested as a possible way out of the electoral impasse. Perhaps we can launch it at our January conference.

We should be looking for new ways to raise the party profile in the media too. Quick responses to events with press releases and letters to the editor should be automatic for us. We can display a certain brashness as socialists to try to break into the media. Actions, stunts, demos and pickets in the party's own name sometimes, as well as Resistance's, might be useful also.

All in all, we want to take ourselves seriously as a party. In many cities already we are the dominant left party, sometimes the only organised left. Our aim over the next year or two is to take this position in all cities and nationally, to be seen as the natural party of the left.

But to achieve this, and to carry through the perspectives of this report, we must achieve our financial goals, and Reihana [Mohideen]'s report later will assess our progress and what needs to be done. The more we strengthen our financial base, the more we can build the party. It's all tightly balanced. We've had some success this year, but we still have very difficult tasks ahead of us.

'Socialism, now more than ever!' has been adopted as a public slogan by us. We should add: Party building, now more than ever!

The type of party we need for the long haul

We've always been a serious party and taken our party-building tasks seriously. We know we're in it for the long haul on the road to the socialist revolution. We always knew it wouldn't be easy, although sometimes we did have hopes and expectations that our goals might be a little closer than they actually are.

We have to consciously build the party to be able to undertake that long haul. The goal, our tasks, the period we're in now and the long road ahead determine how we have to shape it, the sort of party we are going to need. So what are the features of the party that we need for the long haul?

Firstly, we need planning and foresight about our actual tasks. We need the long view of the struggle, the big picture. We need to coordinate closely between the party and Resistance. We need realism about our tasks and our possibilities, and have to avoid over-projection, avoid overload.

Secondly, we need specific discussions about what to do, what to prioritise. We need flexibility, because there's no one model to follow. We have to think politically, not by rote, by habit.

Thirdly, we have to raise the level of political discussion in the party and Resistance, at branch meetings, at executives, in national bodies. We'll need a political membership and a political atmosphere to sustain the party in this period and find our way forward. It will be politics that recruits, trains and educates the new generation, but even more so it's politics that retains the old generation, and if we can't keep the cadre we've got, it's going to be hard to bring on the new.

Fourthly, we have to improve the level and tone of communication between comrades. We have to talk more, especially politics. And we have to be constructive in our discussions. This period will require enormous mutual support among all comrades. We can't afford any backbiting, sniping, cliquishness or gossip. We have to move away from general discussions that dump on individual comrades – there's been far too much of that in the past. The discussion has to be on how to go forward, how to solve political problems, how to help each other, how to build the party.

Fifthly, we know we can't build a model of the future socialist society within the party – the party's a tool to make the revolution. But let's not make this shitty capitalist society any worse than it is. The party won't be able to be a model of the future, but let's do our best. Wherever we can and our resources permit, let's encourage structures, relations that make life a little easier for comrades in this rotten system.

We can't level out all the inequalities we come into the party with, but some things can go in the right direction – our pledges and sustainer,[36] for example: we encourage what comrades can afford. Comrades who gain skills, professions, good jobs should be motivated to place their skills at the disposal of the party, to see their assets and advantages as something that can help the party, not something for their individual advancement. Comrades should be motivated to gain skills and qualifications, not to bolster their own ego, or for the pursuit of money or luxuries, but in order to advance the struggle.

We can help unemployed comrades find jobs. We can find support for comrades with special difficulties. Sometimes we'll need to support high school comrades who are forced out of home by hostile parents, find ways to support them, help them finish their studies if they want to. Comrades often live in party households out of economic necessity. Let's make virtues of that necessity, make them mutually supportive, special places to live. We can organise assistance for comrades with political study, with reading, with lending books. We can help comrades develop new skills. We are concerned about comrades' health, their happiness. We need to give them social support and help them fit in.

The party's a special type of organisation already, founded on human solidarity, made up of comrades linked by political conviction, of all ages, all backgrounds. We're linked through fighting a common struggle.

Sixthly, for this period ahead we need dedication and commitment. We are a party of 100 percenters, not dabblers, not summer soldiers. We throw ourselves wholeheartedly into the struggle. We give our all for the party, for socialism. And for this lifetime commitment and dedication we get a tremendous reward, the satisfaction of consciously taking hold of our lives, and not just being at the mercy of events, but doing something positive, doing our bit to fight this rotten system and taking a step down the path to a socialist future.

2. THE NEED FOR MEMBERS TO TAKE OURSELVES EVEN MORE SERIOUSLY

Report to the National Committee
30 December 1992

Continuing one of the main themes of the previous chapter, John Percy set out the implications of moving into a 'new era' marked by the fall of Stalinism and increasing working-class disillusionment with social democracy. The present period was a preparatory stage in which the DSP would need to strengthen a range of its institutions and activities in order to intervene effectively in whatever struggles were to arise from the continuing contradictions of capitalism, and the report outlined the strengths and weaknesses of many areas. The report was the given to the first meeting of the National Committee following the death of Jim Percy two months earlier. While this was a serious loss, John was also concerned to reassure members that it did not portend a crisis: over the years, the DSP had built a team leadership that did not rely on any one individual.

The unifying theme of this report is the need for members of the DSP and Resistance to take ourselves even more seriously, because of the increasingly crucial role our tendency is playing and will be playing, both internationally and in Australia. There's a bigger burden on our shoulders. What we do over the next few years matters.

On the international level, we're looking at the need to develop what in effect amounts to a new international, though such a new international organisation will be different and avoid many of the errors and rigidity of the earlier internationals.

The decline of Stalinism is the biggest change on the world scene. And although we've discussed this fairly thoroughly at recent conferences and National Committee meetings, we're still coming to terms with all the ramifications.

A less dramatic and somewhat different decline is the further removal of the social democratic parties from the left arena. Politically these parties could not be regarded as socialist since well before August 1914, but in the Western labour movements they retained their mass base, strong apparatuses and organisation, and played an important role for the bourgeoisie in disciplining the labour movement. In the last decade or so we've seen the further rightward evolution of this current in country after country.

So far it's only been in New Zealand that we've seen a real break, with the brittleness of the bureaucrats' hold on the workers and oppressed exposed by devastating implementation of their monetarist policies.

New international

The potential new international socialist network is emerging from parties with many different origins.

Firstly, there are the parties emerging from a Stalinist background. In the USA there's the promising development of the Committees of Correspondence; in Europe parties like the Party of Democratic Socialism in Germany.

There are parties grouping together former dissidents in the former Soviet bloc countries, and some former members of the CPs, like the Party of Labour in Russia, or Left Alternative in Hungary.

There still needs to be a further shedding of the Stalinist shackles on the world labour movement, and there will be a continuing differentiation in the old Communist parties; there must be if we're to go forward. Some forces are likely to move in a healthy direction, while others are likely to consolidate into a hardened international current of Stalinist sects, going through the old motions of Stalinist international diplomacy and resolutions. Another little international current that could be on the scene for a while also is the Maoist international – a loose gathering including the Peruvian CP (Shining Path), the Communist Party of the Philippines (CPP), the Pan Africanist Congress and a handful of tiny Maoist sects in Europe.

We heard yesterday about the struggle that's going on inside the CPP.[37] This Philippines party already plays an important role in the developing left network in the Asian region, and in some form, together with BISIG,[38] could be part of a new international network.

There are also debates taking place in the South African CP and the African National Congress. Parties like the CPI-M, and possibly other Indian left parties, are sure to be involved in the rethinking and regroupment process too. And then there are the ruling parties in Vietnam, Laos and Cambodia.

In Latin America and the Caribbean, the Cuban CP has been a beacon for over three decades, and will be central to any regroupment, rethinking and discussion. The Sao Paulo Forum, initiated by the Brazilian Workers Party (PT), has its fourth conference scheduled for Havana in July, and has already begun to provide a forum for discussion and regroupment following the events in Eastern Europe and the Soviet Union, bringing together the Castroist groups, the CPs some social democrats, Trotskyists, radical Christians.

Then there are the various Trotskyist parties around the world, primarily grouped in the Fourth International, which in spite of its faults is still a lot healthier and less sectarian than other Trotskyist currents. In addition to the groups in Europe, it includes a few quite large and active parties elsewhere – the Workers Revolutionary Party (PRT) in Mexico; a section of the leadership of the Brazilian Workers Party; a sizeable new group in Algeria; and the NSSP in Sri Lanka.

There are also some forces coming from left breaks with social democratic parties, such as the New Zealand New Labour Party, or with the potential to break, as with some currents in the British Labour Party.

And there are also newly emerging revolutionary forces in the Third World, ones we've encountered in our region, particularly Indonesia, and also in the Pacific, including in PNG.

Finally, there's ourselves. We're unique in our origins, a product of the '60s youth radicalisation, and formerly in the FI, and unique in our political development and perspectives. We already have some links with many of these forces that could make up the new international socialist current. Very few others have links with the variety of groups from different origins that we have. So in a very embryonic form you can see how we've developed as a bit of a hub a node, here in Australia.

We can assist the communication process, the discussion that's needed. We can help in the process of political clarification. So without going overboard about what a small party like ours can achieve, we can see that we have a role to play that could be very important.

Our increased role

In Australia also, we can see the increased relative weight of our tendency. This has resulted partly from our own stability and modest successes, but again, it is also the result of the default or retreat of others who might claim left leadership.

Unfortunately, we can't point to the healthy possibilities for regrouping the left here that we can see on the international scene. There's no group that's breaking, rethinking – thinking. There's no sign of a break from the Labor Party; most of the Green groups are small and highly sectarian, as is the Rainbow Alliance; and most of the small left groups are as narrow and sectarian as ever, although we might be able to work more closely in '93 with the FI supporters and Communist Intervention.

Green Left Weekly provides many examples of our bigger role and higher profile. Firstly, its increased circulation this year. Secondly, its increased use by different movements for supplements, or for advertising or mailing out their leaflets. Thirdly, its recognition by the bourgeois media as well.

We know how well *Green Left Weekly* has sold on the streets or at demos and meetings compared to other left papers, especially the ISO's *Socialist* – comrades report sales ratios of 5-1 or 10-1. The ISO has backed off from competing with us in a number of spots.

We're also very conscious of the genuine praise and admiration heaped on *Green Left* by anyone overseas who sees it – people in the FI, people in New Zealand and the US, people in Britain who put out the *Socialist*. In fact we're planning to get little 25-word testimonials for use in our promotional work from prominent international figures like Tony Benn, who's full of praise for *Green Left*.

Another measure of our success has been Resistance's media coverage in 1992, the enormous profile with the sex diary campaign, and the ease with which we followed this up on the unemployment issue. Resistance's leading role in EYA, the main youth environmental organisation in the country, is another indicator of the increased political importance of our tendency.

Many of the big forums and public meeting we've put on this year are also indications of our increased role and profile:

- In Melbourne, more than 200 people came to the *Green Left* forum on women and censorship.
- In Hobart, 100 people turned up to our Politics in the Pub with Ian Jamieson, Jim Bacon and the Liberal Party state president – the biggest meeting in Hobart for ages.
- Around the country many of our film showings have attracted very big crowds – obviously *Manufacturing Consent* in Brisbane, with 700 over five showings, but also other videos and films.

Another indication of our profile and how we've gone this year is the coming party conference. It's shaping up to be significantly bigger than last year's. People have been phoning up and sending in clip-offs to register. There's quite a range of non-members attending – people from Communist Intervention, the FI supporters, prominent individuals on the left, former members. People who have remained on the left have to acknowledge that since the Socialist Scholars Conferences in 1990 and '91, there's no one able to organise a discussion for the left apart from us. We could have built it bigger, recognising this and orienting to non-members more and getting out the agenda earlier.

We were able to respond quickly and flexibly to any opportunities that did appear in 1992 – our intervention in the Melbourne rallies; our response to Communist Intervention and the Janet Powell electoral alliance;[39] or efforts to get a broader trade union broadsheet off the ground.

And it has been a year in which our relative weight on the left has increased. Other left groups are still able to grow, of course, especially if they can find an area for themselves where we aren't active, but I think our way is clear in 1993 to further increase our leadership position on the left.

A good year for party building

On balance, 1992 was a good year for us. On the whole our comrades weren't affected by the prevailing pessimism. Not for us the doom and gloom of others on the left, especially independent lefts, academic Marxists – echoing the bourgeoisie's spin merchants.

Resistance and *GLW* were the two key areas of our work, the focus, the reason for our relative success, and our survival in difficult times. Our renewal in recent years has been through the youth.

Our attention to basic party-building tasks has enabled us to increase our membership a little this year, and most branches report quite a few active comrades around the party or in Resistance ready to join up, so there are further batches of recruits projected for the next few months. Some of the medium-sized branches, such as Adelaide, Perth and Brisbane, grew well.

We've succeeded in turning our membership drift around in the last few years. Perhaps the most interesting figure is the large proportion of provisional members now compared with one year ago. The average age of our membership is probably continuing to drop also. Comrades might recall the statistics from our conference a year ago, with the average age of those attending about 25, a drop from previous years. It will be interesting to see the statistics for this conference.

1992 was a good year for both press sales and fundraising. We didn't achieve all the goals we'd set ourselves, but we made a lot of gains. As an indicator of the increased circulation of *Green Left*, the *GL* business office received more than $50,000 extra in income from party branch bundles compared with 1991. That figure says a lot. Some branches almost doubled their circulation in '92.

The *GLW* subscription base is also considerably higher than a year ago. We've made the *GL* Fund Drive; branch sustainer payments to the party National Office have increased; our NO deficit has been reduced quite a bit, though it's still too large. Branch debts to the NO have been reduced slightly, but there's still a long way to go. We had to sell the party school, although that reduces our interest bill for '93 onwards, and makes it easier for us financially; it clears the decks a bit.

The higher public profile, the media success are nice, but we know the real measure of our success is the development of cadres, winning new young activists to the movement. A very noticeable feature of the development of our tendency in the past 12 months has been the large number of cadres developing through Resistance, ready to take on a bigger load, to carry larger responsibilities.

We need to continue the perspectives of the last three years, the bedrock of our party-building project – building Resistance, building *Green Left Weekly*, cadre training and education, raising the DSP profile.

A sad year also

But 1992 was a sad year also, and marks the end of an era. The party now faces the future without Jim [Percy].[40] We know the party leadership is weaker without Jim. The role he played in founding the party and guiding it for 20 years was irreplaceable – we'd be a very different party, if here at all, without his contribution. But his legacy, his contribution, was in building the party, getting us to this stage, and constructing a team that could work collectively and carry on in the absence of any individual member.

The DSP and Resistance, our tendency, is now a project with

its own dynamic, which won't be derailed by the loss of any one individual, even one who played such a central role as Jim. The team survives, and it's getting renewed, getting broadened further in the party executives, in the fractions, in Resistance, through our interventions. It's not dependent on the individual capabilities of comrades.

One of the biggest contributions Jim made to the party was in regard to our political confidence. He added an element of political confidence and courage that was able to direct the quick shifts that enabled our party to be quite nimble-footed, and to make those turns with most of our comrades still on board. That ability to act with the courage of our convictions flowed from the confidence Jim had, and the party had, in the ideas of Marxism, in our party project.

We can give reassurance to comrades by pointing to our collective leadership, which embodies many strengths, many levels of experience, and by pointing out that continued experiences and the tests of time and events will prove our party capable of the quick political responses needed in the future. It won't be a personal reassurance, in the sense of one individual playing Jim's role, but it will come from practice.

Of course no one can fill Jim's shoes, and some aspects of the style of leadership will be different, but the team will readjust, and different leaders will step forward. And we shouldn't underestimate the team approach of Jim, which was the essence of the party leadership in the past.

Although we'll sorely miss Jim's contribution, we'll have to compensate, and can compensate: We'll fill the gaps he left, many of us will try harder, some of us will learn new skills, more of us will be leaders. We'll learn from Jim's role. His skills grew from his dedication to building the party, his passionate approach to both the largest questions of political strategy and the smallest party-building details – working out camp menus, the wording of a leaflet, talking to the newest comrades etc. With that sort of approach, more of us will learn those skills.

Our proposal for the first project for the memorial fund is to produce a book of Jim's speeches and writings on party-building, especially the talks given since the beginning of the '80s. These were so rich in lessons and good ideas and will be of immediate use to all of us.

A new era

If it's the end of an era, then what political stage are we passing through today, and what can we anticipate in the new era? In order to set our party-building plans and make some projections, we have to fully grasp that it *is* the ending of one era and the beginning of another.

Firstly, it's the end of Stalinism. Stalinist parties linger on in power in some places, and Stalinist parties as declining sects will linger on in many countries for some time, but the 70 years of horrible distortions it engendered in the world workers movement are over. We still have to take into account that past, in order to prepare the future. Comrades have to be encouraged to study seriously Doug [Lorimer]'s pamphlet *The Collapse of 'Communism' in the USSR,* and follow the reports and discussions in *Green Left* and other magazines.

We should also take note that it's now 25 years after 1968, and comrades also need to understand the nature of that period and the processes since the youth radicalisation of the '60s. We need to give comrades the historical base, since most are very new. We need to know that historical background, so that our struggles of today and tomorrow are grounded in the lessons of past struggles, both victories and defeats.

We need to rescue our history from both the capitalist lies and mystifications and the distortions of former leftists and academic Marxists retreating in the face of the bourgeois offensive. We have to explain our unique history, our unique politics, to new comrades and potential members, without being sectarians or braggarts.

What's the potential for a new wave of youth radicalisation in this period, given the increasing exposure of the social democrats, the decline of Stalinism and imperialism's continuing economic crises and contradictions?

Firstly, we should note that the radicalisation that burst on the scene in the '60s has never been entirely snuffed out. Around the country, we observe an upsurge in environmental consciousness and the continuing radicalisation of new generations of high school students. And it's not confined to Australia – it's more the case that not many other left parties around the world have had the conscious youth orientation that we do, and an organisation to orient to young people with. Certainly, the campuses are quieter, but we saw how an event like the Gulf War could get young people back on the streets in large numbers quickly, and in Europe how young people are now mobilising against racism.

The social conditions that underlay the '60s youth radicalisation are still there. If anything, some of the factors are even stronger: alienation; the shadow of the nuclear bomb perhaps replaced by the shadow of environmental destruction; no meaningful job prospects for whole sections of youth. The hold of Stalinism and social democracy is qualitatively weaker today.

There's no immediate spark like the victorious revolution in Cuba or the heroic struggle in Vietnam, but in the next few years we might see a victorious outcome in South Africa, or big struggles in some other countries, that could inspire and encourage solidarity and politicisation in the West. But even without any revolutionary victories in the Third World, the social conditions for rebellion are still there, and the next phase of the radicalisation will build on the last one, with that higher consciousness on social issues, racism, women's liberation, ecology, gay liberation, sexual freedom etc. and an opposition to war and imperialism expressed in a lingering 'Vietnam syndrome'.

Campus students will again be central to the next big upsurge in the youth radicalisation, but it could be that the leadership will be given by students who have previously politicised at high school. Our experiences with high school students are that they have sometimes shown greater receptivity to radical ideas, been more ready to rebel, than campus students, who can be tied down by greater course loads, tighter job prospects, more conscious brainwashing.

Finally, what's the potential for mass working-class upsurges in the period ahead? We have to understand that the ongoing capitalist economic crisis will continue to influence the shape of political developments, in Australia and around the world. All the fundamental contradictions of the capitalist economy remain, and they're increasingly exacerbated by the urgency of the environmental crisis.

In this new era, we can be assured that the class struggle will break through. Workers will break through the restrictions on their independent action, the restrictions imposed by their treacherous leaderships, the restrictions imposed by the corruptions of imperialist super-profits, the restrictions imposed by the bourgeoisie's media brainwashing apparatuses. Big political breaks could occur in the '90s.

The new generation of socialist activists, who haven't seen such breaks, who haven't seen mass working-class struggles, have to be prepared for these developments. Many of the talks at the conference will explore this question. In the period ahead we need continuing education about past class struggle battles, training younger comrades for intervention in the working-class movement.

Our tasks are to prepare for future mass upsurges, and to

take advantage of any openings to move politics along in that direction. We have to convince new activists of the connection between socialism and the political issues they're campaigning on, and make them conscious of history and the lessons of past campaigns.

The future development of the party has to be based not only on our analysis of today's reality, and our program for the future, but on the past as well, on the historical experiences, the documents, the publications, the struggles. We have to acquaint the new generation with our proud record. It's a new period ahead, but we can and must draw strength from the past.

Our goals

What are our goals in the medium term, the '90s, looking towards the end of the century? We're a very ambitious party, but we also want to set ourselves achievable goals. We're always on the lookout for a major breakthrough and any new opening. We want to keep alive an atmosphere of seriousness about ideas, an atmosphere of discussion that can toss up new possibilities, create them even.

But there are also some definite goals that we'll be working away at solidly:

1. We want to grow. We need to recruit and develop more cadre, to really get us out of the small group league.
2. We need to establish a base in the working class, not measured necessarily by control of unions or official positions, but by a following among workers for our own union activists.
3. We need to develop an electoral impact, to force our way into that arena of politics, to get recognised as a regular player.
4. We need to further establish our hegemony on the left,

to be recognised by other groups, independent activists, the ALP left, as the decisively dominant socialist current, and to be recognised as the leadership of the different social movements and campaigns.

5. We want to have in place a more extensive publishing program – books, pamphlets, magazines – and outlets through our bookshops for distributing them.

6. We want to develop various business/political ventures, to lay a sounder financial basis for our political work.

7. We want to extend and consolidate our international links, doing more to develop an international network of socialist forces and help other groups to develop.

In addition, there are other possible ambitions for us in 1993:

1. A Darwin branch towards the end of the year.

2. An expansion of *Green Left* later in the year.

3. Assistance to the New Zealand comrades in producing a paper.

4. Making fuller use of our international news-gathering network, establishing it as a bureau that services others, and might make us money.

Tasks for 1993

As immediate tasks for the next year or so, we can start on the above, and lay the groundwork for some of them.

What can we see as the likely political developments and the type of political scene we'll be facing immediately in 1993?

- There'll be further attacks on our rights and living standards, either Kennett-like, Hewson-like or even in the manner of ALP governments.

- The ALP will get a little bit of a lease of life. Some on the left, for example some of the former NLP members, and some in the movements and community welfare areas, will join or rejoin. But the ALP has no serious future; the economic situation doesn't allow a major revival for it. We can't foresee a big influx of members, or a turnaround in workers' passive, cynical attitude to it.

- We'll see the further demise of the ex-CPA/NLP, the clearing of the decks on the left.
- In the unions, there's little likelihood of much of a fight back under the existing leadership. The unions aren't smashed, but weakened, and increasingly bureaucratised, unable to fight, unwilling to organise.
- We'll see the impact of the New Zealand elections later in the year. There'll be a higher profile for the Alliance[41] alternative across the Tasman. The media won't be able to ignore it as they have mostly up to now, although they'll try to undermine and distort it.

Again this year, the central tasks, and the most important weapons for our tendency, will be Resistance and *Green Left Weekly.* These have been the source of our success and survival in the last two years. We need to reaffirm their centrality to our party-building perspectives.

I'll also just summarise the key tasks already projected at this NC meeting in earlier reports, on our electoral work, our trade union work and our international work.

Electoral work

Pat [Brewer]'s report on our electoral work stressed the importance of our support for the DSEL campaign in the coming federal election, and how the specifically Democratic Socialist election campaigns will be our main focus in coming years. We'll be supporting some Green Alliance candidates as well. If any electoral alliances come along, we'll be in them, if we can, but there aren't any broad alliances shaping up. Getting ourselves on the board, and learning from New Zealand, will be the features of our work in the next few years. Immediately after the conference, branches will be running flat out on the federal election campaign.

We want to establish our electoral work as a more permanent aspect of our work, even working to build a base in a particular area. This will be especially important for our longer term comrades who might have permanently settled in an area, and also for our wide periphery of supporters, who are usually more settled than our comrades.

From this election on, we want to adopt electorates and do consistent work in them – build up lists of supporters, doorknock them; do consistent sales, get subscribers; letterbox with back issues of *Green Left* and leaflets; put posters up throughout the year; put effort into the local papers if possible, have the same candidates running each time. We should prepare for the possibility of running a big DSEL campaign in future elections.

As regards alliances with other forces, there seems little prospect at the moment. The SPA did approach us earlier in the year for their version of an electoral alliance, but there's very little to be gained by us in such an alliance, and their politics have even hardened up, defending their Stalinist shibboleths. In fact, *Green Left* has established itself as our main reach-out vehicle.

Industrial work

Dick [Nichols]' report on our tasks in the trade unions stressed the need for us to find ways of developing a base in industry. This is essential for the long-term perspectives of the party, and it's also essential for the training of the new generation, most of whom are from a student background.

One of the tasks for Resistance in 1993 will be to try to relate to, recruit and train more young worker activists, without detracting from Resistance's central focus on EYA work and students. We want to develop an atmosphere in Resistance that not only isn't alienating for the integration of young workers, but an atmosphere that encourages them, encourages the feeling 'I'm proud to be a worker, and my life will be satisfying fighting for our class and our socialist goals'.

We've projected a broader trade union broadsheet, and it's a real possibility, with important left trade union activists expressing interest. But we can't do bigger and broader things unless we have some cards to play ourselves. This means comrades getting jobs and doing party-building work in industry and starting some decent union work. We need to provide the education and direction for Resistance members here. We've also discussed how we can build more of a base in the working-class western suburbs of Sydney and Melbourne.

Internationalism

The reports and discussion of our developing international links were inspiring and exciting. Closest to us geographically, and closest in terms of similar political circumstances, is the development in New Zealand.

Firstly, we noted it's our duty to assist comrades there in whatever way we can – helping them get out a regular paper; campaigning here for the Alliance; touring New Labour Party and Alliance leaders; covering events in *GLW* on a weekly basis; organising exchanges of comrades so we can both benefit from the different experiences.

Secondly, we noted that we can benefit from any success there, and will gain from any identification with the New Zealand development. We hope it will give ideas to Australian workers that it can be done. We need to spread the NZ experience to other countries also, for example Britain.

We have to guarantee that it's we who benefit from the high profile of the alternative in NZ later on in the year. We can already see people trying to get in on the act – Janet Powell, Rainbow Alliance, we'll probably even see the fake lefts in the ALP hedging their bets. We need to revitalise ourselves politically, and we can use the exciting developments in New Zealand to help us do that.

A broad range of other international relations that we're developing, on a one-to-one basis with parties around the world and in the region, could lay the basis for a regional conference of socialists that we're tossing up, possibly sometime in 1994.

We also discussed the more open situation with the Fourth International, with the possibilities for collaboration on a broader magazine of theory and discussion, and using Paris as a base for future *Green Left* correspondents.

This year we hope to be able to make even better use of *Green Left*'s remarkable international news gathering network – our team of Frank [Noakes] and Catherine [Brown] in Western Europe, based in London; Renfrey [Clarke] in Moscow, with his increased access to news and articles; the contacts we developed in Eastern Europe; Sally [Low] and Peter [Annear] soon to be based in Cambodia, with access to Hanoi, Bangkok, Vientiane as well; Stephen [O'Brien] in Managua; comrades making extensive political trips, such as Lenore [Tardif]'s three-month tour of Cuba and Latin America; and all the other *Green Left* correspondents in New Zealand, the US, Russia, Europe, Mexico. Perhaps we'll be able to establish a regular alternative news service through Pegasus.[42]

International solidarity work

International questions and international links and solidarity are important for motivating both the longer term party comrades and the newer Resistance comrades. To some extent we've neglected that focus in recent years. Branches haven't mobilised for the major solidarity functions. Sometimes we've left it up to just one or two comrades to specialise in that area, and the newer comrades don't automatically get educated and inspired in the framework of the international struggles as they used to.

There are struggles and solidarity work in Asia, Africa and Latin America, and we want comrades to become familiar with all the most important struggles and movements around the world. But our priority at the moment is developing solidarity within the region, especially with the comrades in Indonesia, through our work in AKSI.

In 1993 there's great potential for really stepping up this work, through the setting up of the Indonesian Human Rights Centre, with Helmi [Fauzi] based here with real resources. There are possibilities of grants, and overseas funding, donations from some trade unions, and we can also use the resources and the base to raise further money.

In this area, as in others, we should be using our increased profile, prestige and the absence of the CPA block, to mobilise more prominent figures, academics, artists, etc. behind AKSI. We should be targeting individuals to sponsor and raise money. Perhaps in the earlier CARPA[43] days we did this better sometimes, so we have to resurrect those lessons – visiting people; sending individual letters to supporters; using the resources of computers to do targeted mail-outs; doing all this reach-out work much more systematically.

We also want to keep that aspect of CISLAC work up, since there's still a milieu that will support CISLAC and give money for its projects in Nicaragua and El Salvador.

There's also the possibility of a CISLAC tour of someone from the Brazilian PT next year, and we want to make sure that it's a success and gets the advance planning, organisation and support such a tour deserves.

It looks like we'll also have to mount an emergency solidarity campaign for Cambodia. Reports from Allen [Myers] and Helen [Jarvis], who are over there at the moment, stress that the situation is getting worse. The UN force is preventing the government functioning as a government, yet putting no barriers in the way of the Khmer Rouge's expanding terrorism. This is clearly in the interests of imperialism, Thailand, other neo-colonial regimes in the region and the Chinese bureaucracy. We need to do something here targeting the role of the Australian government, especially [foreign minister] Gareth Evans. We'll have good coverage in *Green Left* of course, but should also get out some party or DSEL press releases on the issue. We'll schedule Allen to give a special plenary report to the conference on the situation and what we should be doing.

Given the importance of the struggle, we'd also like to be able to do more solidarity work in support of the people of South Africa. In the past this work has been limited by the restrictions placed on it by the ANC and the sectarianism of the former ANC rep in Sydney. The new ANC representatives seem much more open and willing to work with other forces. In any case, the developments of the struggle itself in 1993 might force us to take more initiatives ourselves, especially if the Australian government takes actions that hinder the implementation of black majority rule.

Political campaigns

Our most important area of campaigning and mass work will be on the environment, but this will be overwhelmingly carried out by Resistance comrades active in the Environmental Youth Alliance. This will be a central theme of the Resistance National Council political report tomorrow, but party comrades have to fully back up this vital Resistance work, with political collaboration and help, and organisationally helping build the EYA national conference at Easter and the World Environment Day activities.

There will be a number of areas where we'll be able to intervene in the women's movement this year, in spite of the difficult situation in the movement itself and the retreat on many ideological fronts.

Firstly, there are abortion campaigns set up in quite a few cities in which we are able to be active, and the beginnings of a national campaign was set up in December. Claudine [Holt] was installed as the interim national coordinator, and it might be an opening we should be able to use to broaden out and democratise the campaign, and get some actions off the ground this year.

The IWD marches will again be an important intervention by some of our comrades. In some cities we'll probably be totally responsible for them again. This is OK as long as we don't get so snowed under that the leading women comrades can't do the party political tasks – putting our political views, selling *Green Left*, pushing Resistance and the DSP. If we do the work and win respect and recruits, that's fine. But here, as in other movements, we won't tolerate permanent independents or political opponents expecting us to service the movement, do all the shitwork, and then cop flak for airing our political views and raising the party profile.

It looks as though the IWD committees will again be supporting a supplement to appear in *Green Left*. Then in July there's the NOWSA[44] conference, in Brisbane this year, and as in the last few years, we'll be making a useful intervention.

In October/November there are the Reclaim the Night marches, which were quite large in many cities this year. We've intervened successfully by stressing the social conditions as factors in male violence in this society, against the right-wing feminists and social democrats.

Throughout the year we'll be carrying out a range of other propaganda activity on women's liberation issues – forums, leaflets, pamphlets, articles in *GLW*, promotional activities for our new women's liberation book. And we'll be presenting our views in the campaigns we're involved in – the abortion campaign, IWD, Reclaim the Night.

During the year different branches have also been able to be involved in a variety of other campaigns, such as on unemployment, or on peace issues, and in 1993 these again will vary from branch to branch.

Party profile

So while we can see many activities for comrades to get involved in – too many, in some ways, since so many of the small committees and campaigns seem to be clamouring for our time, our comrades, our resources and leadership in the absence of much else on the left – yet we can't see any major mass movements on the immediate horizon. In the absence of mass struggle, we can use the time to consolidate the party, to train and educate cadres.

The beginning of this new era, then, can be seen as a preparatory stage – training, educating and growing before the bigger struggles ahead. This is possible, since we are attracting a new generation of activists, although of course our training will be incomplete or distorted in the absence of the mass struggles to properly train and steel comrades.

The October 1991 NC meeting and 14th National Conference in January 1992 reaffirmed the party-building perspective that we'd been stressing for the previous year or two. They also gave it an extra push, recognising we needed to do more. The conference party-building report stressed the basics, the six Rs:
- Reaffirming the role of the party;
- Reasserting the party profile;
- Re-emphasising our working-class orientation;

- Recruiting to the DSP and Resistance;
- Retraining and educating the new generation of socialists;
- Re-establishing the socialist tradition.

In some of these areas we can report we've made some progress; in others, such as raising the party profile, there's a great deal more to do. Perhaps we feel the greatest weakness here partly because of the successes Resistance and *Green Left Weekly* both had in raising their profile and visibility. Resistance had some real media coups, and *GLW* is increasingly widely known and respected. We did have some successes. Nevertheless, this is an area where we need to step up the work and fulfil more of the projections we set.

The election campaigns, and our increased profile through DSEL, will be one way. The excellent Brisbane election result, with 9.2% of the vote,[45] is a pointer to the future. We'll be producing more DSEL posters in the centre of *Green Left,* and getting out a greater number of leaflets and brochures.

In 1993 we need to pay more attention to our media work, both from the National Office and in the branches. We have to do more to project ourselves as a serious political contender, be more professional in our press statements, leaflets and interviews. It's easier to break through in the small branches than in the larger cities, but we can work at it, make contacts, persist. And of course we're still not making nearly enough use of the alternative electronic media.

Publications

One of the main ways we projected raising our party profile was through stepping up our publications program. In 1992 we made some progress here, getting out a number of new pamphlets and quite a few reprints. Our electronic duplicator has proved a worthwhile investment, saved us money, and made possible the publication of many leaflets, pamphlets, posters that wouldn't otherwise have appeared. But we didn't fulfil all our plans, and have a lot more that we could do.

Our leadership problems, which we recognise and are trying to address and compensate for at this NC, are not just the gaps associated with the absence of Jim. There's a wider layer of long-time leadership comrades who have stepped back or are in the process of stepping back. Therefore, some of the things we'd like to do we won't be able to do, or not as well. One of these is a separate party magazine, or a DSP magazine supplement to *GLW*. In any case, we've heard already about the possibility of making use of a broader FI-sponsored magazine.

This will mean we'll turn even more consciously towards making use of pamphlets, and even small books. There are financial reasons too – they're more economical. They also last longer, date less and can be better for classes and study guides. Many of the talks from this coming conference, and a big backlog from previous conferences, will be published as pamphlets.

Our new women's liberation book, *Feminism and Socialism,* is at the printers and should be back here by [campus] Orientation Week. All branches need to prepare a big promotion campaign for it, and slot this into their schedule. We can hold forums in the party offices, and Resistance can organise campus forums to launch it. *Green Left* should do a major review, and we should prepare reviews for other publications, especially campus papers. We should try to get media coverage for the release of the book, do an advertising flyer for it, have branches do the rounds of the bookshops properly.

Then we'll also be getting out the book of Jim's party-building talks; a revised *What Socialists Stand For;* and we'll possibly need a reprint of our party program, since we seem to be going through the first thousand.

We have an enormous backlog of new pamphlets waiting to be

produced, in addition to many of the titles that are out of stock.

A listing of some of the new ones we'd like:

- A history of the left movement in Indonesia, by Max [Lane]
- A history of Wollongong Jobs for Women campaign, by Carla [Gorton]
- A history of our work in the student movement, by Tom [Flanagan]

In addition to these pamphlets, based on talks to our last national conference, there will be all the talks comrades have prepared for next week's education conference.

A topic that would be useful for a speaking tour, or perhaps for a feature talk at the Resistance conference, is 'The year 1968 – 25 years on'. It would also be useful getting it out as a pamphlet once the talk is prepared. Such a topic would be part of our campaign to combat the bourgeois mystification, reclaiming our history.

Another topic that could be a talk or tour and then a pamphlet would be to take head on the whole 'politics of difference' that has done a lot to derail the women's movement.

Yet again we could have a pamphlet on the nature of the tertiary education system today, perhaps prepared first as a talk for a forum or speaking tour. We could challenge the role of the universities as service centres for capitalist industry, counterposing them as centres of learning, free inquiry, research. Many of the themes raised during student struggles of the last 25 years need to be raised again.

We'll also be producing more specifically DSP leaflets. More resources will be available in the NO for these publication tasks. We'll also be able to give more assistance from the DSP National Office to *Green Left,* enabling us to carry out more of the projections from the last NC for sharpening the specifically socialist content of the paper.

We also want to produce more leaflets and pamphlets popularising our program. We need to learn to write in a more agitational style, pay more attention to the language we use and explore ways of getting out our full program in a way the masses can understand.

We also want to give a bit more attention to making our bookshops better outlets, open at regular hours through properly organised rosters, and with a good range of the most essential political books. Last year we obtained quite an extensive stock of Pathfinder titles, and in the new year a large consignment of Progress Publishers' Marx and Lenin titles will be coming from India.

Recruiting

In this period of consolidation and preparation, one of the main responsibilities of all of us will be recruiting. But we'll have to work for our recruits, work with them and talk to them individually, convince them politically, give them a long-term perspective, a historical perspective. Social integration of new people is vital. We have to make use of coffee chats, contacting dinners, talking politics in any situation.

And although all of us have to be recruiters, branches also have to make sure that they assign their best recruiters, the most experienced comrades, to recruiting. Efficient contacting systems have to be established, and today this means making proper use of our computers. If possible, contacting committees should be set up to organise and oversee the work.

One thing we have to be conscious of as we do more media work is that we can't let our party-building work, especially recruitment, get out of step with our profile work. Some branches had the experience this year of doing fantastic profile work, making the media easily, but not making a single recruit or lasting contact from the work. We have to make sure we integrate all our party-building tasks into our political work in the movements or with the media.

We've had a huge increase in the quantity of DSP and Resistance clip-offs to the National Office since we established *Green Left,* and 1992 was a big increase on 1991. Some branches also report a good response to clip-offs on their local leaflets. Melbourne got about 20 from the leaflet handed out on 10 November.[46] There's a bit of a change, too, in that people are joining from the clip-offs!

One vital lesson to hammer home is the absolute necessity of a speedy response to clip-offs and contacts. They should be responded to the day branches receive them, and at the outside within a week. There is an enormous drop-off in usefulness with each day or week's delay in answering an inquiry.

We've grown steadily this year, and many branches report a number of potential recruits for the new year, but we still haven't organised this area of our work systematically enough. Some of the branches that recruited best this year, for example Adelaide, set themselves a target for a membership drive, and this served to focus their energies. Perhaps for 1993 the National Office should help organise an ongoing recruitment drive over the whole year.

Training and education

Taking the decision to join the party or Resistance is only the first step in a long journey of training and education to become a committed socialist activist.

Training and education must be integrated into all our political activities, into the fractions, committees, branch meetings and so on. But we also need formal, separate, educational activities, sometimes related to immediate political questions, but at other times putting the effort into going into broader theoretical and historical questions. We have to inject into our educational activities the points I made earlier about reclaiming our history, about building on the past.

Another area where our new younger activists are lacking is in having a well-rounded Marxist world view, having an understanding of the materialist philosophy underpinning our Marxist political outlook, being able to counter the idealist notions that are prevalent, not just in conservative capitalist society, but also among activists in the new social movements. We need more classes on this, with experienced comrades helping the newer comrades with their reading and study on topics that can seem daunting at first. Too often comrades' educational activity stops at the current political campaigns; their reading is restricted to relatively shallow accounts of the latest movement issues. But without a grounding in the basics of Marxism, including philosophy, it's very hard to have a perspective of being in the struggle for the long haul.

We also have to take a number of steps to compensate for the absence of the party school from February.

First, we have a perspective for re-establishing the school as a live-in institution in Sydney, including getting our own building again. We'll find a way to do this, and arrange our finances in such a way that we won't have the crippling interest charges that we've had in recent years.

The Introduction to Socialism classes, the party program classes and the Introduction to Marxism class series will still be the core of our educational activities in the branches, essential for all new comrades to go through. We'll also be supplying a wider range of study guides from the National Office, for example on *Feminism and Socialism* and on Marxist economics.

The special training schools we instituted last year were very useful, and we'll continue them in 1993, both national ones after national events, and local ones.

Branches have to set aside enough time for serious study classes. We can also be more up front in advertising our educationals and classes on socialism – we can advertise our offices as training centres for Marxism and socialism. We also hope to be able to organise more tours by comrades from the National Office, with talks or classes prepared for delivery in most branches.

We also need to make better use of *Green Left* as an educational tool. Firstly, make sure comrades read it properly, give reports on articles, have reading circles if necessary. Secondly, we've very much neglected the role of *Green Left* in integrating comrades by getting them to write for the paper. Actively participating, having an article in every now and then, constantly thinking about whether your area of political activity needs to be covered by the paper that week, binds comrades in. It gets them more enthusiastic about selling the paper, and forces them to educate themselves. We need more worker and student correspondents for *GL*.

In the same way, more new comrades should be asked to give talks and reports. Active involvement and active learning are so much more effective.

We also need to consolidate the role of the *Activist*. It's vital for training and education. The *Activist* serves many purposes – it carries reports of our organisational campaigns, useful reprints not easily available, reports of our political work, our party discussions. In 1993 we want to use the *Activist* for monthly reports of our sales drive, our subscription campaigns, our finance campaigns. There's already a wealth of material in past issues that is indispensable for serious activists. Comrades need to get the back issues and keep a file of them.

Forums

Our public forums are an important part of our educational activity for comrades, as well as a way to reach out to new people. Most branches seem to have settled into the rhythm of building one big public forum a month, with more internal forums, educationals and branch meetings filling the other weekly slots.

The monthly forums should be built widely, casting our net in new areas, and recruiting from them. They can be under the auspices of Politics in the Pub, or a *Green Left* or DSP forum at the branch headquarters. We should have a very professional approach to them, charging for them, serving a decent meal and refreshments, really sprucing up the venue and having all the tasks on the night efficiently assigned to comrades. Specifically, there should be comrades assigned to chatting to new people, recruiting and contacting; we shouldn't just be relying on the anonymous boards getting passed around.

Other forums and educationals can be especially oriented towards members, and cater for their questions, develop their confidence and political understanding. These can be open forums or internal educationals.

In addition to the regular Resistance camps, we should continue to schedule weekend educational seminars at the branch headquarters. There were some successful ones held this year, and we need more, and we'll try to coordinate them from the National Office.

This year we want to plan our national educational tours and our international tours more efficiently, to organise them more in advance. There'll be a number of international guests – possibly Kendra Alexander and Peter Camejo from Committees of Correspondence, possibly even Angela Davis; probably someone from the New Zealand Alliance; probably CISLAC will be touring someone from the Brazilian PT; Catherine [Brown] will probably make a trip back here from Europe mid-year; probably we'll be touring some more Indonesian comrades. We need a qualitative increase in the planning and preparation of our tours.

Cultural Dissent has been a successful new institution this year. It's been a useful framework for our cultural events in several branches, raising money and bringing more people into the headquarters. We've also had a surprising number of Cultural Dissent clip-offs nationally. The big news for next year is the success of a major grant application that CD has received, to organise training for young people in cultural action theatre techniques, and make a video of it. So far three grants totalling about $27,000 are going towards this project.

Organisational methods

Over the years we've learnt a lot about how to organise a revolutionary party. But it's a constant process, developing our skills, refining our methods and institutions, and fighting a constant battle against bad methods creeping back in from the milieu we operate in – capitalist society.

Especially in this period, when the layer of experienced comrades is so thin, and there are so many keen new comrades, substitutionism is to be particularly avoided. This is the tendency for a comrade – particularly branch full-timers – to try to carry out all the tasks by themselves, to avoid delegating, not to entrust responsibilities to newer comrades.

This flawed method of organising creates problems for both the preservation of the older, experienced cadres, and the training and integration of the new. The traits of good organising are getting others to do things, delegating tasks (checking up to see that they're carried out also), training and developing others, making yourself redundant.

All of us here have to see ourselves not only as leaders, but as trainers of others. The educating and training role has to be even greater for the longer term comrades.

Structures

In the last period we've allowed a fair amount of flexibility in regard to branch structures and meeting frequencies, and that will continue in the year ahead. There will be variation from branch to branch, given the very different types of branches we have, in terms of size, composition, political milieu, competition etc. The important thing is that we're clear about the principles to follow, rather than making a fixed recommendation for all branches. There have to be enough opportunities for the developing cadre to have the training, education, discussion and political stimulation.

We need monthly branch meetings at the minimum. Some branches have found they needed more frequent meetings, and that's fine. What we need is a weekly event, a weekly gathering of the branch membership – it can be a large forum; a branch meeting; an educational; a small forum or combination meeting. Some branches have found the need for an organisation report at the educationals held between branch meetings.

Another general principle we should be conscious of in all our political work, but especially in relation to our branch meetings, is that we see ourselves as professional revolutionaries, and therefore we should have a professional attitude in our work. Our branch meetings are formal affairs. They can be called on to take very important decisions, and we should conduct them formally, with a proper lectern for speakers, the room set up for a meeting. It's somewhat different to Resistance meetings, and certainly to EYA meetings. We also have to strive for greater punctuality for our meetings and other events, and work at creating greater consciousness about keeping our offices clean, tidy, professional.

Fractions

The key role of fractions or working groups is to head up our interventions. They can also have an invaluable training and education role.

In 1993 we really need a major revamp of our fractions. Some branches might have had one or two of their fractions functioning reasonably well, but I don't think anyone can be really satisfied. So let's start with almost a clean slate, and begin the year with a confident note in the fractions, a campaigning tone, not a lackadaisical attitude. It's important that the fractions be regular; the actual frequency will vary from branch to branch and fraction to fraction.

In some branches, e.g., Sydney, the fractions will need to play more of the leadership role, given the large number of cadres who can take on leadership responsibilities. Comrades should recall some of the discussions of our past attempts to resolve the problems associated with organising a larger branch, where we attempted to divide the larger branches, or set up sub-branches based on the industrial fractions. The principle is that we should aim to get all the members of the branch involved at the level they can, and allow scope for the exercise of leadership abilities.

Small branches might find the more frequent meeting formula better, while the larger branches might move towards devolving responsibility and leadership more onto the fractions and organising committees. Without making any commitment to setting up a separate branch, Sydney is setting up a preparatory committee/task force to help expand the branch's influence in the western suburbs, with an initial agenda of sales, education, a public meeting and the election campaign. We have quite a few comrades working in the Fairfield-Bankstown area, and others living out west, and there are quite a few opportunities for political intervention and building the party.

Schedules

This year we should be able to do more planning ahead, both locally and nationally. We have the major conferences and national events mapped out, and we'll try to get the international tours organised as far in advance as we can. In January the NE will try to settle the schedule for DSP NC meetings for the year, leading to our 15th National Conference in January '94.

A calendar of events should be worked out at the start of the year by each branch, slotting in the national events, the main fund drive events, the main educational events, and starting to schedule the main forums. Regular DSP branch newsletters should be our goal – they help members, they help build and organise our growing periphery, and they force us to organise ourselves better.

Given our still extremely limited core of activists, we'll have to continue to be very careful in selecting our political priorities, and not get dragged into every new committee by accident without assessing the political gains we might make. In this period, there's enormous pressure on us to cover all the bases.

But at the same time, it's important not to put a blanket exclusion or limit on comrades' activities, especially in Resistance. We should be able to grab important openings if they occur, as we did with the sex diary campaign, or the anti-[Jeff] Kennett campaign [in Victoria].

Leadership

'Preparing for leadership' could be envisaged as the theme for much of our work in 1993 and coming years. This means an increased contribution expected from all experienced comrades – certainly the ones who are still playing central leadership roles and setting the pace and level of activism, but also those comrades who are currently taking more of a back seat. They need to be there for help, advice; they need to be ready for future upsurges, ready to step up activity again.

Even more importantly, we have to focus on the vital role of youth, their contribution in building our movement and the absolute necessity for the new generation of activists who have come on the scene in recent years to take increasing leadership responsibilities. This is particularly addressed to the leaders of Resistance on the party NC.

A key task where youth have led and must lead even more in 1993 is in *Green Left* sales. Resistance has to lead here, and lead the party too.

The Adelaide DSP and Resistance branches set the pace in '92 in this regard and showed what could be done, ending up averaging 700 sales a week towards the end of the year, and finishing with 1,200 'in order to pay the rent on their headquarters'!

Over the last five years we've been successful in bringing a layer of younger leaders onto the party's National Committee. This process will certainly continue at our conference in a year's time. But there's such a big layer of potential leaders developing that we have to provide many ways for these comrades to develop and test their leadership capacities – nationally and in the branches, in the party and in Resistance.

There are two seemingly contradictory processes involved in bringing on younger comrades to play more of a leadership role. Firstly, there is the party assistance, support and training. Secondly, there is the need for new younger leaders to develop initiative, to show independence, to grab the reins themselves. We can reconcile these two needs. The party will be open for Resistance comrades who want to lead, who want more responsibility, who demonstrate leadership capacity. We will stand back, recognising the 'obstacle' the older generation can be to new talent, with the experience and skills learnt over the years.

There are two paths on which young revolutionaries can develop in our tendency: by leading Resistance, from where more and more of our key interventions will be led, e.g., EYA, and by leading the party.

We must develop real competition to get on the Resistance branch executives and on the party branch executives – socialist competition of course; we want the best team leaders. We don't want the dog-eat-dog competitiveness of capitalism, but competition to help others, to contribute to our common goal. We need this sort of selection process in the branches, and need it for the Resistance NC, and at the end of the year for the party NC.

We need to make use of all the leadership talent in the party – leading in executives, fractions,

Resistance execs, party committees – but leading effectively, not just nominally. That is we don't want a multitude of meetings, but bodies that meet for a purpose, getting things done, intervening, discussing and deciding and acting. Leadership is leading in action, organising others, not just sitting in meetings.

In developing new leaders we won't be able to develop all of them in the framework of the formal bodies. For example, in Resistance there are many more potential organisers who would have already been asked to organise a Resistance branch in a previous period. There will be some new pioneering openings in the next year or so, but there won't be enough new cities for all the new comrades developing as leaders.

With the growing pool of talented comrades to draw on, we'll be calling on comrades to show leadership in the existing branches in many different ways. One way will be by drawing Resistance leaders in the branch into the discussions of the party's political priorities, playing a role in the administration committees that the larger branches have set up. Another way is by having Resistance comrades leading areas of the party's work, sales for example, and this is happening in many cases already.

There aren't limits on the possible leadership roles that the newer Resistance comrades can exercise within the party today.

So this is a special responsibility of the youth leadership. You have a double responsibility, leading the party as well, relating to people of different backgrounds. The Resistance leadership can't continue to think of themselves just as youth, that would be a cop-out. Party leaders on the NC and in the branch who are heading up assignments in Resistance have to see themselves as that – leaders of the party.

On tiredness

There are age differences in our party, and differing levels of political experience, but we don't want any generation gaps to become entrenched and limit our effectiveness.

The Resistance comrades, the younger party leaders, must develop more stability, and have the buck stop at them more often. They have to take on more party responsibility, more responsibility for educating themselves and others and leading theoretically; they have to develop the leadership qualities that will inspire others and show that they're serious about our long-term goals.

Resistance activists will be graduating as worker activists. We're only students for a short period of our lives. To become a serious Marxist party with a mass base, we must envisage ourselves as a party with a majority of workers. The majority of Resistance members must envisage themselves as becoming workers, struggling for their class, in it for the long haul.

One role of the younger comrades is motivating, inspiring, the older comrades, those who are still dedicated, but with a lower level of activism. The party, increasingly led by new activists, must still draw them in and find a meaningful role for them.

At the same time as continuing to address the problem of

tiredness among some of the older comrades, we can't allow it to infect the enthusiasm of the youth.

Confidence

In encouraging all comrades to take greater leadership responsibilities, we know a key element is the development of political confidence. We're conscious of the weaknesses of the party and Resistance in this area, and have to work on it. We're aware that political confidence can be based on at least three components.

First and most important is political understanding. The greater our level of knowledge of politics and history, and the better our grasp of political theory, the more confident we are.

Secondly, we also gain in confidence when we know we're part of a team and that it's our collective efforts that count, not just our contribution as an individual. As our DSP ad says, 'Working alone, you can change some things a little, for a while; working together with others, you can change the world'.

Thirdly, we can gain confidence from the atmosphere in the party and Resistance. If there is a crusading, confident atmosphere, it can be self-fulfilling. Revolutionary élan can encourage further confidence.

So in the year ahead we can all afford a bit more audacity and assertiveness. We won't behave in the haranguing, sectarian way that our opponents on the left have frequently done – we'll continue to develop our listening skills, our diplomatic skills, avoiding jargon in our explanations of our politics – but we can certainly afford to be more up front and confident about our political approach.

One result of our reach-out efforts during the '80s has meant we're a little reticent as a party about putting our views forward forcefully, and it rubs off on individual comrades. We entertain people at our forums and functions, rather than engage them and try to recruit and argue against their wrong ideas.

In Resistance, on campus, but also in the party as a whole, it's our lack of political confidence that's at the root of both our tendency to merely service the movements and also our failure sometimes to take the political initiative when we should. It's a further political argument for continuing to strengthen our party-building perspective.

In the absence of a mass movement, with ongoing campaigning activity, we can't substitute, but we can still introduce a campaigning atmosphere into all our political activity. We know a campaigning, enthusiastic approach to even the simplest tasks we carry out can be infectious, can enthuse new comrades, help integrate new recruits.

Party life

We can objectively assess that we have a high morale within the party and Resistance today. How can we build on it, and guarantee it stays that way?

A task for all of us is to work consciously at developing friendly, comradely relations among comrades, to encourage a happy, enthusiastic atmosphere in the party.

In addition to being a political machine, a unit for getting things done, the party is also a social unit, and we shouldn't forget that. We have to cater for comrades' social needs, to help them stick it out for the long haul, weathering the blows of capitalist society.

Resistance leaders, the younger generation of party leaders, have to address two needs. Firstly, they have to encourage and develop an active, attractive social scene for youth, an atmosphere where young people can learn, experiment, break out of a conservative background.

Secondly, they have to relate to all types of people, with different backgrounds. As the party becomes more successful in recruiting workers, sometimes older workers with more conservative lifestyles, families, we have to make sure they feel at home as well. We don't want to scare them off or make them feel out of place, with any sort of narrow reverse moralism, cliquishness, exhibitionism.

Conclusion

Even though we don't see any big openings for us at the moment, we'll be constantly looking. Our record and experiences in the '80s should hammer that home. We don't like the fact that we're a small party, we don't want to stay that way. But we don't want to make the mistake that former leftists and even former members of our party make, in attributing the fact that we haven't succeeded yet as somehow due to our Leninist orientation, our insistence on building a party of dedicated activists. Jettisoning the concept of a 'vanguard party' or even the idea of a party altogether is a guarantee of defeat.

There'll be different levels of breaks that will open up for us, from the full-scale opening such as in New Zealand, to a small regroupment, and we want to make sure we don't miss anything. Our practice in 1992 demonstrated that the party is still able to act quickly and respond to new developments. The crisis of capitalism worldwide means that the big breaks will come – we have to be astute enough to see them coming, and strong enough to be able to respond effectively.

3. A PERIOD OF PROFOUND CONTRADICTIONS AND OPENINGS

Report to the National Committee 2-4 October 1993

In March 1993, to the surprise of many observers, the Labor government led by Paul Keating was re-elected. In this report, John noted that this outcome meant another three years of the ALP-ACTU Prices and Incomes Accord, which would continue the process of destroying illusions in the ALP. This was one reason that revolutionaries should not talk down the current period too much. True, it was a difficult period, both internationally and in Australia, but it was also the case that there were many political opportunities; he pointed out that the DSP had more such opportunities than it had cadres to take advantage of them. John reviewed the party's experience since it had made a turn from efforts at regroupment to an emphasis on cadre building in 1990, pointing out a number of weaknesses, particularly in the organisation and functioning of party branch meetings, and emphasising the need to make interventions in social movements more consciously aimed at the party's political goals.

It's a new period, but we've emphasised that we're building on the lessons of the past, using the gains and tested methods of the past.

We've tried, and succeeded, with some very ambitious projects, such as the Socialist Scholars Conferences,[47] such as *Green Left Weekly*. In preparation we have the International Green Left Conference,[48] and the international magazine project.[49] And there is also quite an exciting range of contacts with new left forces that are developing, rethinking, regrouping internationally. We have an important role to play here. But we must have the base, the resources to fulfil that responsibility, as well as our responsibility of filling the gap on the left in Australia.

Party-building stress of last few years

I want to briefly review some of the goals and main themes of party-building reports to NC meetings and conferences over the last three to four years.

At our National Committee meeting in June 1990 we stressed the need to reaffirm our party-building tasks and continue to reach out:

> Comrades, the focus of this report is on the need for
> the party to reaffirm, re-educate in, and re-mobilise
> around our basic party-building norms and lessons,
> at the same time as continuing to do everything we
> can to reach out to, to regroup with, broader forces.
> These two aspects of our work are not in contradiction;
> in fact they're absolutely complementary. It's not an
> either-or choice for the party, but the two essential
> sides of our single party-building perspective.

At the April 1991 NC meeting we went a bit further: the

party-building report proposed 'a reorientation for the party, a change in direction that should be dramatised by seeing it as a turn. We want to propose that the party returns to a major focus on cadre-building, on recruiting, on party building.' We felt the need to dramatise this theme, arguing that reach-out and interventions could be done through party building, prioritising the party-building tasks – tightening up membership norms, raising the party profile, using *Green Left Weekly* to build Resistance and the party.

We developed this further at the October '91 NC meeting. Jim [Percy]'s report on 'The Crisis of the Left and the DSP' is vital reading for comrades, who should go back over it.

The party-building report I gave at that NC emphasised the need to raise the party profile in various ways, and using *Green Left Weekly* to tie together our party-building tasks: 'Party building now needs to "catch up" with our great weekly paper and our greater political maturity. We need a continuation of our push in 1990 and 1991 to reaffirm our basic party-building perspectives.'

Jim [Pery]'s report to our last [14th] party conference in January '92, 'The DSP and the Crisis of the Left', elaborated further the ideas in the NC report.

The party-building report to the 14th National Conference assessed our progress in the 'turn' to party building and stressed the basics that we were campaigning on.

Reihana [Mohideen]'s report to the 14th National Conference on 'Political Perspectives for the DSP' clarified further how we do our party tasks and movement work:

> So building the movements and building the party are
> totally interrelated tasks for us. But being interrelated
> tasks does not mean putting an equals sign between
> building the movements and building the party.
> Our purpose in building the movements is to build

> a revolutionary party. Our movement work has to
> be seen within this party-building framework.

At the June '92 National Committee meeting, we reaffirmed our youth orientation, stressing the training of comrades 'for the long haul, to educate them in Marxism, to develop their commitment and feeling of investment in the movement'.

At the January 1993 DSP/Resistance educational conference and at the NC plenum just before it, we outlined seven definite party-building goals and four ambitions for 1993.[50]

Comrades can assess what progress we've made in these areas, achieving some of the goals – for example, expanding *Green Left Weekly* to 32 pages, building major new international links – but the key ones are still ahead of us: recruiting and growth; establishing a working-class base; expanding our electoral impact.

And in June at our last NC meeting, Reihana's party-building report elaborated further, fine tuning our perspectives by recognising our need to put greater stress on education and training.

'The period'

So the last three to four years have been characterised by a push to reorient the party, to reaffirm our party-building norms, and adjusting the relationships between our party tasks and political interventions, fine tuning, learning more and succeeding on quite a few fronts, consolidating and growing.

And this success has occurred in a complex, difficult period, in the context of international defeats for the working-class movement, and the decline and disarray for much of the traditional left. So how do we stand today?

It's still a tough international situation, with imperialism on the rampage, carrying out new colonialist atrocities, fostering racism, and with workers' conditions under attack in country after country.

It's still a tough Australian political situation too, with Labor and Liberal governments doing all they can to boost profits at the expense of workers, pensioners and students, and attempting to restrict workers' ability to struggle.

But we should take care not to talk down the period too much. And we should consciously counteract the all too frequent talk in our ranks about it being a 'slow period', as many comrades pointed out yesterday.

It's good that we have another three years of ALP government and Accord – the better to expose them. It's good that, for the first time in Australia in the last 100 years or so, we have a breaking down of that very strong Laborist sentiment; the level of illusions in the ALP is much lower.

The youth radicalisation is still there. It's based on the gains of the past, many of which are now accepted wisdom, for example in the women's liberation movement, but new generations of young people are continuing to radicalise over a range of issues and in response to the general alienation of life in capitalist society today.

There is a range of activities, little campaigns, committees, fights back, breakouts. It's atomised, yes, but the potential for bigger, coordinated action is still there.

We should not succumb to the dominant ideology and lapse into 'talking down' the period. In fact, we should be actively combating it within the party. We've drifted a bit, got lazy, used it as an excuse for half-hearted measures, sloppiness – 'it's the period', 'it's dead out there'. It's not! Certainly we're not going to be like the ISO – off the planet, talking about a pre-revolutionary situation. But in reaction against their excesses, we shouldn't go too far in the other direction, which I think we have sometimes.

Certainly, we're still experiencing the dead hand of the ACTU-ALP Accord and the Labor government, but that's our chance. We want the Labor fakers in government, the better to expose them. We want them selling out so blatantly and disgustingly, all the better to attack them and win Australian workers away from their historic illusions in Laborism and ties to a bourgeois party.

Certainly, the left is smaller with the demise of the CPA and the collapse of Stalinism in the Soviet Union and Eastern Europe, but this should make it easier for us organisationally and politically, with Stalinist parties unable to block us. Of course, there's a much bigger responsibility on our shoulders, and we're still too small to take advantage of all the opportunities, but that's the task ahead of us.

We're not expecting major breakthroughs in the short term, but we can see action on a number of fronts, sporadic breakouts, breakthroughs even. In fact we've all recognised as one of our major problems not having enough cadres to take advantage of all the opportunities that are open to us in the face of the demise or default of most other groups on the left.

We can misrepresent the period by making invalid comparisons with the past: for example, nostalgia for the 1960s, and old-timers in the '60s would talk about the good old days in the '40s, and their predecessors probably raved about the '20s and so on. We should learn from the past, but not romanticise it. For example, in the '60s the level of illusions in the ALP was much higher than today.

Newer comrades don't see it as a slow period. They joined because they see things wrong and want action. We should also try to see politics through the eyes of a new generation. It's not a slow period for the working class; it's a period of sustained attacks.

This is actually a period of profound contradictions and openings. A key characteristic is the erosion of illusions in the ALP and in bourgeois political processes. Our response has to be to convince people of our perspectives. We need to use this period to recruit, to build, to consolidate, train and educate.

Another term that perhaps we should be wary of is 'the long haul'. Again, it's a shorthand term, which experienced comrades use and know what it means. But newer comrades can misinterpret it, get the wrong connotations, think it means that the struggle's a dreary uphill battle, never likely to be successful, so perhaps they waver in their commitment.

Certainly we want comrades to throw in their lot with the working class, to make a career of being a dedicated socialist activist, to be lifetime revolutionaries. We want to steel comrades so they're not discouraged by temporary setbacks, and don't expect shortcuts or easy solutions. But political life's exciting, now and in the future, as well as in the past, so let's steel and educate comrades without throwing cold water on their enthusiasm.

The state of the party

On the whole we'd give a very positive balance sheet of 1993 so far:

- *Green Left Weekly* is getting stronger, broader, better, more widely circulated. Claudine [Holt]'s report and the discussion yesterday went into this, and how we have to do better, go further, especially on sales, getting consistency in making 4,000 street sales, and on subscriptions, getting stability for a higher sub base.
- We launched *Solidarity*[51] as a great vehicle for our trade union work, and it's made quite an impact already.
- We've increased our links and contacts with socialists around the world, and are about to concretise this with some very exciting projects.
- Resistance has been going well, attracting new activists continually. But we know there are important areas where improvement is needed. Jorge [Jorquera]'s report today will go into that more thoroughly.

- We've made some gains with our finance campaigns, with the fund drive on target, the pledge income to branches and the number of comrades pledging up by 10% over the last three months, branch debts stabilised and the party's level of indebtedness way down.
- If we look at all the successful events this year, we can be extremely pleased. Our dinner dances, for example, were the biggest ever in many branches: in Sydney 240, Perth 200, Adelaide 170, Wollongong 110.
- Similarly with our forums, they were some of our biggest ever. Some branches have had great success recruiting. Perth has more than doubled.

On the negative side, we'd have to list:

- The loss of some of our more experienced cadres. We have to acknowledge that the sustained bourgeois ideological offensive has some impact on our party.
- The inexperience of our new members. We still suffer from a serious lack of education of our new young (and old) members, and often a resulting lack of confidence to intervene politically.
- We're still on the financial edge. We haven't resolved all our financial problems.

We'll be addressing all these weaknesses with a range of measures – international, educational, political activities and internal party tasks.

It's been an extremely hectic first half year, although we faltered a little in the last period. We didn't follow up on all the gains we should have. We didn't build on the excellent Resistance conference. We let recruits slip away, so that the membership has remained stable, with recruits balancing the lapsings.

Political answers

How are we going to begin solving some of these problems? Firstly, we have to remind ourselves that there's not going to be any mechanical panacea; a routinist organisational change won't do it. Two or three routinist organisational changes won't do it either. We have to resolve the problems politically, not merely through an adjustment of the settings. There are no simple, formalistic solutions. For any measure or change we propose, we have to answer the question: 'Are these measures expanding our political influence or not?'

It's not just a question of 'getting the priorities right', or 'getting the right balance'. That's important, we do it all the time; at each leadership gathering, we're constantly steering the good ship DSP. But we're a political party, of politically conscious comrades, approaching their tasks politically and applying political solutions to problems.

At all levels of our activity, we have to be conscious about understanding our enemy, understanding the dynamics of capitalism, its state, its institutions, its culture, its history, and also about understanding our own history, the history of our class, our traditions and resources and what we need to do to win. We have to understand the role of the party, as a dynamic formation essential for the victory of our class and its socialist goal. And we have to train all new comrades in this understanding.

The central theme in this report relates to our party-building tasks and our interventions, and how to mesh them together, and looks at the two 'sides' of our work:

- On the party-building side, focussing on the importance of branch meetings for training, integration, education and the democratic functioning of the party. The National Executive wants to recommend to branches that they think about holding more frequent branch meetings.

- On the interventions side, stressing the need for comrades to have the confidence to intervene politically anywhere, to debate, to defend our politics, to lead campaigns large and small. There's a lot of essential political work that has to be done, and it's essential also for training comrades. We learn in action, and we need action to sustain us. We can take initiatives and create our own, or we can intervene in activities initiated by others. We don't want to fall into the bad habit of either abstaining from a campaign or else feeling compelled to take it over and run it more effectively. In this period we do have to run some, but we can't be responsible for all.

And above all, we have to be careful not to see it in just black or white, internal tasks versus external. The two 'sides' of our work have to be seen as an integrated approach to building the party.

Branches and branch meetings

The NE feels that quite a few of our needs and problems can be partially explained and steps taken towards solutions by looking at our branch meetings. Nearly all aspects of branch functioning relate to our branch meetings – at least they should.

It's clear that we need to improve them. We need to make them more political, a more vital, democratic part of party life. To do this, we probably need more frequent meetings than the monthly schedule we've had for quite a few years.

This isn't, or shouldn't be seen as, a panacea. We're not proposing it as a prescription or an instruction, but suggesting that branches give it a go. Already some branches, for example Sydney, have discussed the idea, and are favourable to a change in this direction.

In any case, more frequent branch meetings are a conjunctural need for our pre-conference discussion over the next two and a half months. We need more frequent branch meetings at which to have as an agenda item or two, some aspect of pre-conference discussion. We shouldn't hive it off as a separate educational type meeting, at which only a part of the branch is expected to show up. It needs to be a normal branch meeting, with all the usual rights of members to move motions, set the agenda etc. There's been a tendency in recent years in many branches to treat pre-conference discussion as just an extra set of educationals, not a real opportunity for assessing our political interventions and strategies and really thinking about the best tactical approach for the future. The pre-conference discussion is an aspect of the democracy of our party that we shouldn't be slack about.

But beyond the conjunctural needs of the rest of the year, there are other problems in the functioning of the party that would be best addressed by going to more frequent branch meetings, even weekly.

Monthly branch meetings were first instituted from the July 1982 National Committee meeting, with Jim's report on 'Further Steps in Proletarianising the Party'. At that time we'd basically completed our turn to industry: 80% of the membership was either in industry and part of an industrial fraction or doing voluntary assignments for the party. Monthly branch meetings were seen as a further way to reach out, to make it easier for workers to join the party.

It was at a specific period, and in a specific context. We stressed the increased importance of the industrial fractions. We didn't want to take away from the important role of branch meetings, but many things were going through the fractions that previously went to branch meetings.

Jim's report looked at some of the concerns of the time, many of which are still with us: 'Is there a way of putting more real content into the democratic functioning of the party?', he asked. He noted that there was 'not enough active involvement in discussion at branch meetings. Sometimes the executive has over-prepared branch meetings, leached the life out of them.' The branch meetings were 'not necessarily providing a rounded political life'.

In 1982 we were starting to grow, after a period of attrition as we carried out the turn to industry. We saw the need to stimulate politically and train and educate new comrades, as we see the need today. But the difference then was that we had strong industrial fractions where that could take place, even subsequently experimenting with converting the fractions into sub-branches.

Well, we went through a lot of stimulating, invaluable experiences in the 1980s. We had high hopes for regroupment, made several attempts – the CPA, the SPA – made efforts to reach out – the Nuclear Disarmament Party, the Social Rights Campaign, the Greens – some small fusions. Many of these were gambles in a sense. We didn't hit any jackpots, although we got some side benefits, improving the political balance of forces, or preventing obstacles developing. And although we grew in the first half of the '80s, we were losing members in the second half. We spent our cadre wisely, as Jim pointed out. Without our ambitious attempts at reaching out, we would have been worse off politically, probably lost more of our comrades, and not renewed our ranks with youth so well.

One of our initial motivations for monthly branch meetings, making it easier for workers to join, hasn't worked out that way. And with our turn in the last three to four years to an emphasis on our party-building tasks, we've halted that attrition and are starting to grow again. We now need to round out that reaffirmation of our party-building tasks with a renewed emphasis on branch meetings.

Especially now, with a broader paper like *Green Left Weekly*, the needs of education, integration and consolidation of new comrades are not so easily served. A specifically party paper can serve that purpose; it's harder with *Green Left,* at least more subtle. The role of branch meetings becomes more important in educating and integrating new members.

One of the problems with monthly branch meetings is that they tend to get overloaded. When you have the opportunity only once a month to report on and discuss all the different areas of work comrades get involved in, the agenda can expand, the meeting can go on quite late, comrades leave before the end. Attendance can drop.

Similarly, if the organisers have only this monthly opportunity to get to comrades about organisational matters, there's a pressure to put an organisational report or a sales report and a finance report on the agenda each month. This skews the meeting. A heavy monthly exhortation can be substituted for the weekly one-to-one following up that needs to be done on the newest comrades or the comrades who have the lowest consciousness on these areas.

Thus the monthly branch meetings can take on the character of mini-task and perspectives meetings,[52] and the T&P meetings when they happen don't seem much different.

We certainly need the weekly rhythm of a regular event, whether it's the branch meeting or a forum or class. This is dictated to us by the weekly *Green Left,* the weekly collection of finances, but also the weekly pace of political activities nationally and locally.

The branch meetings need to be rounded events, but also different and stimulating each time, relevant to and helpful with each comrade's political activities.

We've always stressed that branch meetings should fulfil at least three functions:

1. Organisational. They should help plan and organise our work, such as *Green Left* sales, fundraising activities, our own meetings and events and activities, and our intervention in the political activities in the city.

2. Educational. There should be an aspect of disseminating new information and raising the educational level of comrades, either as a specific agenda item with a talk or report, or through injecting educational content into other reports.
3. Political. A key function of the meeting should be discussing tactics and strategies and taking decisions. This is the most important function. Of course, the organisational and educational aspects are also political, but this point stresses the role of our branch members as active, thinking, deciding cadre, and the branch meeting as the basic unit of the party in which we collectively hear reports on our political work, discuss it and take decisions about political positions and future actions. Unfortunately this hasn't been the case at many of our branch meetings.

It's important to stress all stages of the process: sharing information, discussion and decision.

Taking this into account, we think there's a need to redress a real imbalance between our branch executives and the branch meetings that has crept in during recent years. Although the role of the branch executive is to take the lead, set the agenda for discussion, provide political leadership for the rest of the branch, there has been a tendency for the executives to subsume much of the discussion that should take place in the branch, to discuss everything too thoroughly and end up leaching the political life out of the branch meeting. This trend has been exacerbated by the tendency to increasingly large execs. The execs are seen as the only place to train new people, because that's where the most extensive, interesting discussion takes place. The execs get seen as the place where all the real cadres are; the rest of the branch can become an increasingly passive membership. The attendance at branch meetings gets smaller, the executive gets larger!

The fractions can't substitute for an engaged, thinking membership at a branch meeting either. The fractions are part of the branch membership, accountable to the branch meeting, reporting to it and carrying out the decisions of the meeting in a specific area of work. We can't overload the fractions with the functions that the branch meeting should be performing, unless we were going in the direction of industrial branches based on particular industries or workplaces.

Fractions and executives have been distorted and will benefit also from restoring branch meetings to their proper function in the party. A real routinism has crept into the functioning of many of our party structures.

There's another more general problem. The administrative approach gets generalised. For example, branch administrative committees or secretariats have a useful role to play in organising the work of the branch between executive meetings, but if overused they can become part of this problem – they can start to take over the role of the executive committee. The democratic functioning of the branch gets undermined. Everything gets over-discussed. The same report is given two, even three times. This administrative approach is also getting duplicated in Resistance, and even by our comrades in EYA.

Comrades have less chance of learning how to intervene politically if everything is worked out already and the branch meetings are merely routine. They're less likely to develop a critically minded, self-active cadre. We have to lead, and plan, and organise, but not overdo it. We must allow initiative to have some play.

Branch meetings haven't been the decision-making bodies of the branches, except in the perfunctory sense of ratifying executive decisions. What we need are branch meetings where real discussions are held and real decisions are taken. It's necessary both for the longer term and the newer comrades. The longer term comrades need political stimulation, and the chance to help and intervene with their experience and ideas – they'll naturally be less interested in interminable organisational reports they've heard before and given themselves. The newer comrades need an atmosphere of debate and education, a forum where they can learn and start to test their own ideas and abilities. Potential recruits also need such a branch meeting, to see it as a place they want to be invited to regularly, where they learn, where it's exciting.

All of us need attractive, vibrant meetings that comrades leave feeling that they've learnt something, gained by attending, contributed to the decisions about the course of the party's work, got re-inspired, met all the comrades, got entertained even.

We also need to think about this in relation to Resistance branch meetings, and this will come up in Jorge's report. Resistance also needs that weekly frequency of activity, education and politics, and perhaps it can mostly best be done through a branch meeting.

I think these suggestions in regard to more frequent branch meetings are an important further step in the process of re-stressing our party-building perspective, of re-cadreising the party, that we have been concentrating on for the last three or four years.

Without this step, we feel it will be harder to succeed in or properly complete the party-building tasks, the measures we know are needed to strengthen the party, the themes we've stressed in party-building reports at NCs and conferences in the last four years.

Building a party of workers

One feature of our party-building perspective that we've stressed many times is our insistence that we're a working-class party, not only in program but also in composition and experience. We're building a party for and of workers, and that's the outlook we all need to have. We need the base of our party solidly rooted in the working class. We have to admit that we've made no progress on this front – in recruiting more workers, or getting more of our comrades jobs in industry, and in inculcating a working-class outlook among our younger student recruits. In fact, we'd probably have to admit there's been a serious drift in the party on this.

Even though our membership has increased in recent years, there's probably been a decrease in the number of working comrades who are able to do political work on the job or union work. Moreover, there's probably been an increase in the number of comrades with misconceptions about what sort of party we are and strive to be, not understanding we're a working-class party in which the normal life of members has to be in the workforce. We need to be that type of party politically (we know we shouldn't bother if we're just aiming at being a party of political dabblers, dilettantes on the fringes of the workers' movement).

We need to develop a bigger proportion of worker comrades in the party, worker cadres with a financial consciousness and commitment to the party. There are misconceptions among some younger party activists and leaders that you're only a real cadre if you're doing full-time voluntary work for the party, that working comrades somehow play a lesser role. We need to counteract this, by education, and by examples – aspiring leaders of the party need to lead on and get jobs. The real base of the party, in the future, will be the politically active working comrades.

There's a danger in the sort of social composition we have today. One manifestation is a problem of some comrades not bothering to look for jobs, or not being able to hold jobs, and the demoralisation of worker comrades in jobs. There are actual examples of comrades giving up well-paying jobs to go on the dole 'to do political work'!

That's not helping the party. Apart from the financial conse-quences for the party, these comrades are unilaterally and indi-vidualistically deciding that they should in effect be a full-time party staffer. That's the implication anyway. It's anti-democratic: the political activity of every comrade is directed by the party, and the party decides who its full-time staff are. The working comrades in jobs, with serious pledges and fund drive dona-tions, are subsidising the individualistic whims of these other comrades. That's a slippery slope. It erodes confidence in the party structures, our democratic decision-making bodies. Bad examples can spread. It can lead to the demoralisation of work-ing comrades, who might ask, Why subsidise such dilettantish behaviour? I'll wait for a real workers' party where members take seriously being a politically active worker.

This individualistic attitude is fostered by the capitalist education system, and comrades from privileged middle-class backgrounds are especially susceptible, expecting more from a job – they expect an intellectually satisfying 'career'.

We need to turn this around; we have to get rid of this attitude. For working-class comrades, it's normal simply to have a job, if you're lucky. That's just a normal part of life. That's the attitude that we must inculcate among all our members.

This does not mean a turn by the party to getting jobs in any specific areas of industry. Although there are things happening in the labour movement, some openings, there aren't the polit-ical conditions, we're not seeing a big upsurge where we want to motivate the great majority of our membership to get jobs in specific industries. We might want to do that sometime in the fu-ture – there were positive results of our turn to basic industry 15 years ago. But that's not posed for us today. However, we do need to begin changing our social composition, or else the political character of the party will be seriously undermined.

We need to have functioning jobs committees in every branch. Firstly, we need to help our unemployed comrades win jobs, but secondly, we need to help our student comrades get part-time work. We should always politically motivate the tasks of the jobs committee, link it up with our political work. We should also link it up with the financial needs of the party, as an important but secondary question.

We have to give special attention to educating our campus comrades, our new recruits, to understand what it means to be a professional revolutionary when they join the party, to understand that being on campus is part of their political assignment.

A party of full-time revolutionaries

We have to instil into the consciousness of comrades that there is only one class of membership in our party, that we're not a party of workers and intellectuals, but a party of worker intellectuals and intellectual workers.

We're not a party of full-time party staffers plus others, but a party of full-time revolutionaries, whether working for the capitalists or working voluntarily for the party.

We don't have two categories of members, thinkers and doers; we all participate in the discussions and process of reaching decisions, and we all participate in carrying them out.

Comrades in our party come from all different social backgrounds, with different skills, different levels of experience and confidence. We can't level out the inequalities of capitalist society, but we do try to help all comrades develop politically, become working-class political leaders. We ask all comrades for as much of their skills, their time, their resources, their money, as they can give to the cause. Some can contribute in these areas more than others, but that shouldn't be seen as a sacrifice, but as a privilege. Our best recruits at the moment – most of our recruits at the moment – are young comrades from a middle-class background. Often they're smart, well educated, they have many options in life. We have to convince them politically that they have to break with their past, they have to throw in their lot with the working class, with the class that has the power to abolish capitalism.

We do have to ask people to make sacrifices, looked at from the point of view of the capitalist world and bourgeois values. But our values don't encompass comrades setting their life goals on amassing a personal fortune, or getting themselves set so they can live a life of leisure, or becoming a star of some kind, or making a fantastic career for themselves. Our career is as socialist activists.

An attitude we have to combat, which you can detect among some of our newer comrades, even some not so new, is a holding back from that commitment to a life as a socialist activist. It can sometimes manifest itself in an attitude of being 'super-cool', which when you think about it is actually a direct imposition of the values and style of bourgeois culture. It's a stance of 'don't get too serious', we wouldn't want to get too fanatical about our beliefs, would we, confusing fanaticism with dedication and commitment. Any sort of supercilious attitude towards dedication and commitment is poison for a serious socialist party.

Being super-cool means you're going to fall short of being a 100% socialist activist, a dedicated full-time revolutionary. You'll always leave an out, keep your other options open, not close off your career path in the bourgeois world.

It's especially important to be conscious of this with a layer of Resistance activists who are in their mid-20s, have put in a good stint in Resistance and have to face the challenge of being party activists, socialist activists, for the rest of their lives. (It's sort of like a quarter-life crisis.)

There's a need for these Resistance comrades to take a further step in their commitment, not to drift or backslide once they're out of Resistance. They have to find ways of re-motivating themselves, and we have to give extra encouragement and help them develop as fully committed activists within the framework of the party.

We're training a new generation of party leaders, within the party and Resistance apparatus and outside it. There's a deep reserve of talent, and we have to make sure comrades understand that being a part of our voluntary full-time staff is not the only way to be a leader. Being totally committed is not equal to being part of the party's full-time voluntary staff. We want to give as many comrades as possible the experience of being part of our full-time staff. But we also want to ensure that all comrades gain the experience of a 'normal' working life. Sometimes comrades on staff will go off, get a job, make a little money, get a wider life experience, perhaps go back into the apparatus. But going off our full-time staff should in no way be seen as a stepping back from being a full-time revolutionary activist.

We also want our comrades who are party staff workers to be lifetime revolutionaries, that is, not to completely exhaust themselves while working for the party, not put in a Stakhanovite burst, then fall by the wayside afterwards. Our staff workers need a day off, need to be able to do their housework, to relax, to look after their health, to have decent meals. We're angry at society, and we know every bit of effort we put in counts tremendously, but we also need to enjoy ourselves, to enjoy life – we're not ascetics. Comrades should know they do have the options for the other aspects of life, such as overseas travel, having kids, enjoying cultural activities. We're not a sect, prescribing behaviour in all areas of people's lives, decreeing a certain lifestyle. Above all, we should enjoy politics. This applies to all comrades.

We have a duty to help all comrades develop their full political potential, to train and educate and pass on experience, and not to leave them to sink or swim on their own. This applies also to comrades who are assigned to our full-time staff. We have a duty to train the new staffers, the youth, not only in politics and organisational skills, but to be full-on party builders, to be 100 percenters for life – whether or not they are assigned to our full-time staff.

Recruiting

Recruitment is one of our main tasks in this period. We need to grow, urgently. We need a bigger membership to take advantage of the many openings, the many responsibilities. We know the possibilities for growth – Perth branch this year has shown how it can be done. Even groups with sectarian politics, the ISO, small groups such as the Spartacists, can grow at the moment.

Recruitment is something we can't leave to the branch organisers, or to the executive. All comrades have to be conscious of it; all comrades have to be recruiters. Certainly we should assign our best recruiters, our best educators, to giving classes, to recruiting, but it shouldn't be just them. All comrades have to develop the confidence to network with other activists, to talk about politics, to invite to meetings, to try to recruit while selling *Green Left* or selling subs.

We projected a membership drive at the last NC meeting, but we haven't had the resources to lead such a drive from the National Office. Hopefully, we'll be able to give more help for the rest of the year.

We'll produce a new double-sided recruiting leaflet shortly after this NC meeting. And we'll follow that up with a What Is the DSP? brochure, based on the old 16-page What Is the SWP? brochure. Early next year we hope to produce a 50-page pamphlet explaining in more detail what the DSP stands for.

While Resistance has produced some of the tools for its membership drive – a new recruiting leaflet and a new membership card, and will have a new edition of *What Socialists Stand For* – the party is lagging, in spite of our commitment to raising the party profile.

For the rest of the year, we do want to make a push on recruitment to the party, in conjunction with our pre-conference discussion and building our 15th National Conference and all the other tasks we want to carry out.

We should also note exactly what it means to become a provisional member and a party member. Becoming a provisional member should be easy, not requiring detailed understanding of our program, but agreement with our aims and general perspectives. Becoming a member is the big step, requiring a greater understanding of our politics and a tested commitment to political activity in the framework of the party.

We can't let slip in the branches the consciousness of the need to raise the party profile that we've stressed at recent national gatherings, not just have Resistance up front, but the DSP as well. We have to do more things in our own name – press releases, pickets, demos, forums, posters, stumps and stalls.

The finance report yesterday stressed the interrelation of our financial needs and our recruitment tasks. For the party's current needs and our future expansion, we need a stronger financial base, and recruitment of new members who are quickly trained in a serious financial consciousness will help provide this. We're still on the edge financially. We need to make full use of the party and Resistance offices, make them into real movement centres. In many cities they're already the best or only left centre, often the only left bookshop. They can become even more of a political focal point; we can make them more attractive, get other groups to make use of them – hold EYA meetings in the centres, for example.

Forums

As well as needing interesting, educational, more frequent branch meetings, we also need reach-out forums. Some Politics in the Pub functions are serving this need where we run them. In Adelaide, for example, we've held some very big ones. We need to avoid ritual forums that members don't come to, that Resistance comrades don't come to. For the rest of the year, we've got a very tight schedule with the pre-conference discussion, but next year let's organise them well. People want information and a place for a lively discussion. We should also develop our ability to schedule quick topical forums, and build them well.

Our forums serve several purposes. Firstly, they're useful for educating and informing our own members. Secondly, they're useful for networking, reaching out to other political activists. Thirdly, their aim is recruiting. But this doesn't happen automatically; we have to work at it. Comrades should be assigned to contacting at forums. Mailing lists should always be sent around, but we shouldn't rely on them, that's just a basic minimum, not a substitute for talking to every person who attends the forum and following up all likely contacts.

We should also be using forums as a training ground for comrades, training them to speak, to intervene, to get confidence, to learn actively. We shouldn't just leave it up to our speaker to prepare a talk; we should get other comrades assigned to study, read, and prepare interventions on the topic.

We've initiated the first Jim Percy Memorial meetings for this month. We haven't been too ambitious this year, but will be making them a regular annual event in the life of the party, and want to build them into important events on the political calendar.

We're producing a book containing four of Jim's last party-building reports,[53] which we'd like to be out by the party conference or soon after. These talks will be essential in educating new comrades. There's a wealth of experience in them. It's worth comrades re-reading them as part of the pre-conference discussion if they can get the copies of *Party Forum* and the *Activist* they originally appeared in.

Education

Reihana [Mohideen]'s party-building report to the last NC meeting put a big stress on education, on 'the need to put our organised educational tasks much more at the centre of our work in the next period', to campaign on it. We stressed how members need the theoretical and historical understanding, 'an intensive political education today, in order to orient themselves to the challenges and tasks we face today and for the long-term perspective'. We desperately need it to sustain us for the longer perspective.

We projected establishing regular activists' study classes, on top of our Introduction to Socialism, Introduction to Marxism and program classes. And we have seen some positive results of that push in the last few months. We also had Allen [Myers]' tour to various branches to give the Marxist economics seminars. And we've had some very successful camps and seminars as well.

But our overall education process is still haphazard. Often the comrades who need it most are the most lackadaisical about it. Often the educational events get squeezed out by other activities. Without the national full-time party school, we're still grappling with the need to systematise the education of comrades.

Even where branches are going exceptionally well, as in Perth, and recruiting rapidly to the party and Resistance, we face a crisis, because we have too small a layer of comrades able to educate others.

A further necessary step forward for our organised education program is for branch leaderships to pay more attention to each comrade's individual reading and study. We have to give them direction, indicate what they should read, show them how to get the books and articles. Comrades have to be encouraged to read newspapers and magazines regularly, reading them critically. The national education committee should draw up a reading guide of relatively accessible books that comrades should be buying and reading. We should be giving more direction to the branch bookshops about which essential books they should always have in stock.

The two-week schools that we projected for after this National Committee meeting in Sydney and Melbourne have been put off. We simply don't have the leadership resources at the moment to organise them. We now want to hold a four-week school after the party conference, from 10 January in Sydney, and a two to three week school in Perth in January also.

Political actions and interventions

The second main theme of this report is getting our interventions right in the framework of our overall party-building perspective, especially taking note of the importance of training comrades in how to intervene politically, and using interventions to train comrades and raise the level of political confidence.

And we need to tie all our work together more effectively. For example, using *Green Left Weekly* as a tool to intervene, selling at meetings, writing about actions, using *GL* to prepare speeches and talks. And of course our interventions have to be organised within the framework of the party, from the branch meetings, the fractions.

This is an area where many comrades have felt the need for a 'correction', an adjustment, where we've seen real weaknesses in our work, in our training of new comrades – getting political confidence, training to intervene and training through interventions. Comrades gain confidence through activities and action. Some comrades have not learnt how to intervene, some have unlearned.

This of course is always a danger when we're stressing party-building tasks, as we have in recent years. We can neglect developing the ability and confidence in newer comrades to intervene politically.

And we can tend to compartmentalise party tasks and interventions. We don't build the party as an end in itself, and not in a vacuum. We educate comrades in Marxism, not for abstract reasons, not for 'personal development', but in order to act, to intervene politically.

An important aspect of training comrades is training them to talk politics with others, with new people, with experienced activists, training them to network with other activists. Too often recently we've noted a certain timidity, even docility, on the part of many of our newer comrades.

How do we overcome this? Certainly it's a question of confidence, the confidence to intervene politically. How can we help comrades gain this confidence?

Education is part of the answer. Having a good grasp of the issues, and an understanding of the basics, the nature of capitalism and its contradictions, certainly raises the confidence of comrades. But it goes beyond this. Confidence can get eroded in longer term comrades, who might be well educated in Marxism.

There's a constant psychological barrage from the bourgeoisie against the idea of political activity, against people standing up and being confident. Part of the role of the party is to combat this influence. The varied aspects of life in the party help here: in addition to education, the support from collective thinking and action, the promotion of teamwork, the solidarity, the morale of other comrades.

Sometimes it's a question of will and persistence for new comrades. We just need to give it a go. Sometimes we need to push comrades into the deep end, or up on a stump, thrust a megaphone into their hands (and sometimes you'll find comrades then get a buzz out of it, get addicted to speaking in public!) Of course, there's more chance of comrades having good initial experiences if the preparation is done, the party backup is there, and the intervention's a team effort. Perhaps the interventions we made during the ACTU congress in Sydney[54] and the wonderful Perth Resistance action[55] – which I'm sure all comrades have heard about or read about by now – are the models for all branches.

Finally, it's a question of leadership as well. We can't lead if we don't inspire, and this is related to the question of 'the period' also: we can't inspire comrades if we're constantly talking down the period. We have to be very conscious as a leadership about how we express ourselves, how we conduct ourselves.

And part of our leadership responsibility is working out the balance between party building and political interventions. We're constantly adjusting, steering left and right, keeping the ship on course.

But we have to do both We can't let up on the party-building tasks. We have to carry out our party-building tasks while intervening, in the framework of the party. We need to integrate the party-building tasks and 'social movement' interventions – the *Green Left* sales especially, but also building our forums and dinners and other fundraising events, and all the education and training tasks of the party.

The most important part of this integration is the need to use the party framework for our interventions. We shouldn't encourage individualistic approaches, and we shouldn't leave comrades stranded without party backup.

Our interventions have to be backed up with education on the issues, fractions to carry out the work, branch meetings to decide on the action and hear reports on the results, executives to provide the political leadership and organisers to liaise with comrades individually. But at the same time, we don't always want everything so worked out that comrades feel unable to jump in in all situations, in emergencies.

At the moment the natural tendency of comrades is to hold back, not to seem too brash. We need to reverse this, get some brashness and aggression into our comrades and into the branches. This trait is partly a reaction against the bad example of the ISO – their arrogance and aggression, their sloganeering rhetoric. But comrades should not use this to justify a more passive approach.

There can be a danger from our current training of comrades in the mass movement. Often there's a tendency of all or nothing: we either abstain from a committee, or else we feel the need to run them. It's partly a misconception about our political line of mass action versus lobbying on the one hand and ultra-left stunts on the other. That's certainly our strategic approach, and we organise that where we can and push for it if it's appropriate, but it doesn't mean we abandon all other tactics and types of action. Small pickets, demos, petitions, delegations, leafleting, propaganda stunts can all be useful tactics, and sometimes necessary preludes to larger mass actions.

We need a variety of tactics, and a variety of frameworks for political activity:

1. Mass campaigns, united fronts. Of course this is what we'd like – large actions, mass actions, where we can really go flat out, intervene, learn, train, recruit. Most political activities today aren't exactly of this nature, but we learn from past campaigns and keep our eyes open for any possibility of big developments.

2. There are campaigns and committees in which we're playing a leading role – EYA, CISLAC, AKSI for exam-

ple. These are important, especially in this period, but they're easy. That is, they provide some training, but it's not much different from the training we get in the party framework itself. Mostly there are not big debates with political opponents, it's a friendly atmosphere, they're run efficiently.

3. Then there are a range of other committees, where we're not responsible for the course of the campaign. We should be involved in these other committees. We're missing out on some that are quite important, I think, for example on Bougainville, on East Timor. We should intervene in the party framework but not think that we have to run these committees.

   We should involve ourselves in them, to train comrades; to gather information and articles and sell *GL;* to be positive about the issue (even if the people involved aren't running the campaign as professionally as we might if we led it). The party has to show solidarity with all those taking progressive political action.

4. We also need our own initiated actions, called in the name of Resistance or the DSP. The excellent Perth Resistance action is an example of this. This sounds like it was extremely well planned.

   But we should also be able to call quick actions, emergency pickets, in our own name at short notice. For example, on Somalia, around the next US barbarity, we could consider quick actions. If we do this successfully often enough, our prestige will increase. And perhaps even more important at the moment, it will train our comrades, give them confidence, force them to speak in public. Placards can be prepared quickly; we don't have to wait on painting a big artistic banner. We should invite others, but not be beholden to them, let our own comrades' action be self-sufficient. Our comrades as the speakers, we get out the leaflets, paint the placards, lead the march.

5. Trade union and industrial interventions are also crucial. We should be quick in initiating or joining solidarity actions with strikers. Keep our eyes peeled for possible actions on issues mobilising workers. We need to be more conscious of this type of activity to orient comrades politically.

We had some good experiences at the ACTU congress in Sydney, with interventions on many fronts. It was a boost for morale, our best intervention at an ACTU congress for years.

Comrades do need public political activity, and also need to see gains, however tiny, victories, however marginal.

Comrades do need contact, action in the working class, not just the different movements, other sectors. Even if there's not much action, they need the contact. It's necessary for the long-term perspective, for sticking it out.

But beyond the immediate party-building needs, there are other important considerations regarding our political interventions. The collapse of the old left has been so rapid that we're already in the situation that we can't expect anyone else to initiate important actions; it's up to us. Who will take the first steps on major issues as contradictions deepen? Certainly not the ALP while it's in government. What happens when pressures mount? It's not automatic that things will break out. Probably in many cases if we don't make the move, take the initiative, it won't happen.

If we hadn't gambled on the openings in the 1980s, we would have lost more cadres, and as Jim Percy pointed out in his report to our last party conference, we spent our cadre wisely, and we gained many new cadre.

In the 1990s, should we also gamble? On Mabo/Aboriginal land rights, or unemployment? Certainly, we should be constantly on the alert for possibilities. We know the problems of campaigns on unemployment, or campaigns in the Aboriginal community, but we should be testing, probing, using *Green Left*, stepping up the party propaganda, using city stumps, using forums. We should be able to respond to new, unexpected developments.

The next step is to actually start a campaign, tap our allies, reach out to new forces – as in Adelaide with the anti-racist campaign formed from their Politics in the Pub forum.

People know something is wrong; there's anger out there, moral outrage, but we need a campaign to catalyse it. We need to counter the petty-bourgeois reformist projects, which demobilise people, miseducate them, demoralise them. So we need to have a go at something, to show comrades that we are impatient people.

Given the world political situation, what the US is doing around the world, the 'new direct colonialism', perhaps an increased sharpness and urgency are required in our polemics. Perhaps this is needed in order, firstly, to steel and educate our own comrades, secondly, to puncture the illusions of liberals in the left milieu and thirdly, to dramatise the situation, to save the best of the left milieu, the ex-CPAers etc., who'll otherwise tend to drift to the right.

Taking this sort of consideration into account, the type of movement, the type of campaigns and committees and actions could be important. For example, do we need a new antiwar movement that responds to specific acts, like Somalia? Not just a peace line. Even the anti-bases campaign focus is a bit general, pacifist.

Fractions

For carrying out our interventions, and stepping them up in the framework of our party-building tasks, we need to reinvigorate our fractions, restating their function and role.

Recently our fractions have sometimes been lopsided in both the party and Resistance. For example, in Resistance, with our monthly meetings, EYA fractions/working groups sometimes have been meeting even weekly. The branch meeting has not had the chance to lead, to monitor the work. Campus fractions sometimes have been having weekly meetings, but have not been integrated into or led by branch meetings, which have been meeting only monthly.

Yesterday we discussed our experiences and needs with our industrial fractions. We noted the cases of a number of longer term comrades who have sometimes been doing their own thing in the unions, and how we need to pull that discussion back into the fractions.

A big weakness recently has been the low level of consciousness among comrades about responding to political events, and therefore we haven't been properly training comrades.

International solidarity

Some brief points on our international solidarity. This is especially important for the training and education of new comrades. There have been some exciting developments in the Asian region, and also some special duties for us, with the role of Australian imperialism in the region.

We have to continue our Indonesian solidarity work, but we should also be considering how to organise our anti-imperialist work in the region as a whole, beyond AKSI, to include East Timor, Bougainville, PNG etc.

On the Philippines, of course, we've had a discussion of that, and have to step up our education on the struggle there, the history of the left, so that comrades are all much more familiar with it, and look for ways to do solidarity work.

Our CISLAC work has to continue, as well as our solidarity

work with Cuba. South Africa will also test our membership, as the ANC evolves, and opportunities for solidarity work open up. And also activities around the Middle East, solidarity with Palestine, could be possible.

We should also note some interesting possibilities for our women's liberation work: IWD meetings and marches; the NOWSA conferences; the Reclaim the Night marches; abortion work; and different women's groups being set up. We need to assess our work here and how we can improve it.

Darwin branch

We've been eyeing the possibility of setting up a branch in Darwin for some time, and are now in a position to decide to make a push on it. A core of leading party comrades has agreed to go, and now we're looking for about three or four Resistance comrades who'd like a pioneering challenge to make up the team.

I think Darwin has the potential for quick growth. We know how well *Green Left* has sold there for the last three years; we have a number of party supporters and at large members there; and Darwin's got a varied political life.

We'll make a feature of launching the Darwin branch at the party conference, give the comrades going there full backing so they're not isolated and use the launch to inspire comrades in the established branches to match the pioneering spirit.

International magazine

An ambitious project for the party, tying together many of the strands of our international work, is the idea for an international discussion magazine. We could see the first issue out by the International Green Left Conference, printing in late February. It's been given a big boost by the extremely favourable response from the Philippines – their commitment to take 1,000 or 2,000 copies. That sort of support and interest removes a lot of the uncertainty about its production.

This weekend we also got a fax from Jeremy Cronin confirming that the South African Communist Party would come behind it. 'I have discussed the matter informally with leading comrades in the SACP and there is considerable interest, in fact excitement', he wrote. He thought they'd be able to distribute 200, at a cover price of $5, agreed to serve on the editorial board, and would get someone else from there, probably from the Congress of South African Trade Unions. He also came up with a title that I think is the best so far: *Links. Journal for Socialist Renewal.*

The attraction of the project will be the broad input and support – the SACP, US Committees of Correspondence, NZ NewLabour Party, Sri Lanka Nava Sama Samaja Party, Philippines comrades, ourselves – but the coordination and the production of the magazine will be very much dependent on us. That's an indicator of our potential role, our impact on the left. It's also an indicator of what we've built and held together.

We should be modest, but it would also be a mistake to hang back. We should put our views. They are relevant, useful. We don't want to return to the style of the Trotskyist movement in more sectarian days, where you pontificate on everything, but perhaps we need to adjust a little in the direction of taking strong positions in the period ahead. For example, on the Philippines. We'll certainly carry their documents and articles in the magazine, but perhaps they won't even be the selling point in the Philippines; people will have access to them already. But they'll want to know our views on a range of questions. This is already indicated by their proposal for one of our leading comrades to go up there and give a series of educational talks to a few hundred of their cadres over the next two months, a proposal that we've readily agreed to.

The possible editorial board is shaping up along the following lines:

- USA: Carl Bloice, Peter Camejo, Malik Miah, one other;
- Australia: Peter Boyle, Max Lane, Reihana Mohideen, Doug Lorimer;
- Philippines: Francisco Nemenzo, Sonny Melencio, two other comrades;
- South Africa: Jeremy Cronin, plus one; New Zealand: Matt McCarten, plus one;
- Sri Lanka: A leading member of the NSSP.

We'd designate Jeremy Cronin from the SACP, Sonny Melencio from the Philippines and Carl Bloice from the CoC as regional editors. Then we'd have a much bigger range of contributing editors from all around the world. And we'd have one of our comrades as managing editor, coordinating the project.

Such an international discussion magazine would have a very positive impact on our party, on top of its positive contribution to facilitating discussion and improving collaboration between socialist forces around the world.

Firstly, it's going to be very important for the continuing education of our members.

Secondly, it would widen the party's horizons quite a lot.

Thirdly, it would provide a very useful boost to morale.

Fourthly, identification with a prestigious international magazine like this would help recruitment to the DSP and enhance any regroupment prospects.

Our membership and periphery and the *Green Left* readership will be the main initial market in Australia, but given the demise of *Australian Left Review,* and the ISO having decided to stop publication of their theoretical magazine, I think there are also good prospects for circulating it beyond our milieu. The International Green Left Conference will be a great place to launch it with a splash.

International Green Left Conference

The IGL Conference itself is the major task we have ahead of us for the next six months. It's going to take a lot of organising from the National Office, and a special effort from Sydney branch, but it should be high on the agenda of all branches from now on.

We now have the first brochure and poster out, and these have to be distributed quickly, to use them well before the end of the campus year. We'll have a follow-up poster and leaflets out later in the year. Branches should be planning comrades' attendance already, organising it in conjunction with the budgeting needed for the party conference.

An impressive list of international speakers has now confirmed, and the list will increase as the event approaches. Branches should start thinking about who they need to make special approaches to in their city, inviting left academics and political activists to attend and consider giving papers.

We have to build the conference properly, and make the most of it. We gained a lot from the Socialist Scholars Conferences, establishing enormous prestige for us in the left milieu. We'll gain even more from this, given the more activist orientation of it, and its link with *Green Left Weekly*. Branches should be seeing it as not only an exciting political and educational event, but as a huge recruitment opportunity.

We now have to start giving more attention to the agenda and purpose of the regional left consultation that we're holding in conjunction with the conference. The recent Philippines developments give it increased importance.

15th National Conference

The next three months are going to be busy for the party. We have important party-building goals to achieve – on *Green Left,* finances, recruiting, education, building the IGL Conference, different campaigns. But in addition, it's a special period in the life of the party, our pre-conference discussion leading up to our 15th National Conference, 3-8 January. We have to make sure this discussion is thoroughgoing, a real discussion, where comrades think and question and get involved. The likely agenda will be:

- International situation report;
- Australian politics report;
- Trade union and industrial work report;
- Campaigns and movements report;
- Party program report;
- International work report;
- Party-building report;
- Youth report;
- Finance report.

Even though the IGL Conference at Easter will be our main gathering of revolutionary contacts we have around the world, the party conference itself is shaping up as our most internationalist yet, with more international guests than ever before.

We're planning to have a similar format to our last party conference, with non-delegates having the option of attending an educational talk during the delegate discussion of a report. So we need to plan a series of educational talks that are comprehensive, that cater to both fairly new comrades who aren't delegates, and to more experienced comrades and contacts who aren't delegates. Some of the talks need to be breaking new ground, with comrades using the opportunity to do some research and serious thinking. We want to be able to publish some of the talks as pamphlets, and perhaps some of them as articles in the planned international magazine.

We'll also have the usual feature events – the conference fundraising rally, the cabaret, though not a slide show this time. We'll have the usual workshops and fractions too. Perhaps, given the extremely broad range of international guests, we can have a separate rally to launch the international magazine – most of the key supporters will be represented there.

Given it's a six-day conference this time, in the evenings I think we should have a range of social cultural events. We can make use of some of our newly acquired cultural action skills. We can make use of the bands and choirs that are getting formed in several branches. Perhaps we can have a presentation on alternative media – video, community TV and radio.

Branches have to get stuck into building the conference immediately after the NC meeting – the oral discussion, encouraging written contributions in the *Activist,* organising transport and comrades' finances for it, publicising it among our supporters and contacts. It's essential to get the maximum number of DSP and Resistance members there. It's going to be an intense, consolidating, educational decision-making process. We always get a great boost in morale from our conferences. Let's make the most of it, and not allow any comrade to miss out.

4. LENINISM IN AUSTRALIA TODAY

Report to the 15th National Conference January 1994

After the collapse of Stalinism, some on the left, seeking to understand 'what went wrong' in the Soviet Union, claimed to trace the problem all the way back to Lenin and the type of party he had built. Rejecting that false course was necessary, but not sufficient if it remained only on the basis of arguing about what really happened shortly before and after the Russian Revolution. DSP leaders believed it was equally important to explain what it means to build a Leninist party today, in an advanced capitalist country. This explanation of Leninism was also intended to reinforce the tightening of party norms that began in 1990, after the loosening of standards that had occurred as part of the party's regroupment efforts.

Comrades, why are we members of the Democratic Socialist Party? Why are we here, at this conference, and not still in our offices or workplaces, or at the beach, or watching the cricket? Why do we commit so much of our lives, our thinking, our energy, our money, our time, our passion to our political activity? It's because we are members of a party of a special type, with a very special goal.

Our aims are quite clear, set down in detail in our program, which we've updated at this conference, but expressed succinctly at the beginning of our party constitution. The updated formulation to be proposed in the session on our constitution tomorrow states:

> To abolish the capitalist social order in Australia
> and, in collaboration with the international
> working-class movement, to eliminate poverty,
> national inequality, sexist oppression, racist discrim-
> ination, war and ecological destruction, through
> the construction of a classless, socialist society.
> To achieve this by educating and organising the
> workers and other oppressed social groups, on the
> basis of the party's program, for a revolutionary
> struggle to replace the capitalist government
> with a working people's government.

We're building a specific type of party to carry out those aims. We're not merely an association of lefts, a network of progressive thinkers. And it's not sufficient to describe ourselves as socialists, since that has many meanings for different people. We are revolutionary socialists, our goal is the revolutionary overthrow of capitalist society. And we know from the history and experience of the workers' movement that a certain type of party is needed to reach this goal – a Leninist party.

With different goals, we'd be a different type of party.

If our aim was merely the reform of capitalism, the amelioration of some of its worst excesses, then a different organisational form would do. We could be just a loose grouping or network of people active in different areas of concern, meeting together every now and then to broaden each other's experience, meeting for solidarity, even for social reasons and to have a good time.

If our interest was solely intellectual, we could be content with a discussion club, with no real mechanism for activity, for implementing decisions. If we were really ambitious, perhaps an add-on might be a publication of some sort for seeing our brilliant ideas in print.

If our approach was purely parliamentary, to get into government and run capitalism better for the capitalists, we'd need a different type of organisation again, not one where political ideas and program were important, and involvement and activity and education of the membership were key, but one where the numbers and personal power were the dominant concern.

But our goals are different (although we fight for reforms, and we need discussion, and we make use of parliament). Our goal is the overthrow of the existing order, and for that we need a Leninist party, a cadre party of dedicated activists, able to discuss and take decisions democratically, and organise to act in a united way.

The notion of a cadre party rests on a military analogy, We're the highly trained force that provides the framework, that can lead a mass of new recruits at times of mobilisation. At times of upsurges, we'll be able to lead struggles, and because of that, recruit massively. It won't be necessary (or possible) at that time to educate each one of these new recruits in all aspects of our program, our history, as it is in a period like now when we're recruiting to a broad set of ideas, recruiting in ones and twos. With a mass influx we'd educate and train on the run, and during lulls in the battles.

So when we talk about a cadre party, a Leninist party, it doesn't mean we make a virtue of being small. We do want to become a mass party, but a mass cadre party. It's exciting to be in contact with and learn from a party such as the Communist Party of the Philippines that is further down the track than us on this.

When planning the agenda for this conference, we deliberately put it in the title of this report and discussion, to make a point – that we are a certain type of party, that we are staking out the name, the tradition of Lenin's party.

The word by itself is not enough of course. We need to explain Leninism, what it means, why we need this type of party, and relate it to today's conditions, and express it to potential recruits in a way they can understand.

It's actually no big problem explaining to newly radicalising young people, who are the main source of recruitment to the party today, why this type of party is necessary. It all makes sense. They thirst for knowledge, for the experience and understanding that can be passed on from longer term comrades. Our experience is not that the young people involved in the range of struggles are cynical, or scared of the 'hard' concepts of revolution, class struggle, cadre party.

No, it's not the youth, but some of the older generation who are baulking at these words, and they're actually rejecting the concepts.

Why is this so? Some are rejecting the words for political reasons, equating Stalinism with Leninism. Others are giving up completely on the task of building a revolutionary cadre party. We'll debate this out in Australia, and internationally. And we'll educate our new recruits in our tradition, which is the tradition of Lenin, of Trotsky, of Cannon, and our own experiences over 25 years.

In the face of the anti-socialist offensive following the collapse of Stalinism in the Soviet Union and Eastern Europe, a range of people – ex-CPAers, ex-lefts, some of our former members, some movement activists, even some of our own comrades – get tired, get demoralised, waver. But in the end, the best way to re-motivate these comrades, many of them with a wealth of experience to offer, is to build a strong, aggressively confident, campaigning party – a Leninist party.

These crucial times for the left cry out for such an organisation. It's when Leninist organisational norms come into their own. Wishy-washy organisation in the end means wishy-washy politics.

Our membership needs to be well versed in the basic concepts of Marxism, and then learn how skilfully to convey our basic concepts to a larger audience in a language they understand.

Unfortunately, words such as socialism, revolution, Marxism, Leninism have not only been corrupted by the bourgeoisie, they've also been debased by the Stalinist experience. There is some hangover, some vestiges of Stalinist parties, clinging to 'Marxism-Leninism' as a religious icon. But we need to retain these concepts and words for our own understanding and for the education of the vanguard, while expressing the concepts in a transitional way to broader forces. We need the terms, because they are precise and scientific and enable us to read the classics, and thus to assimilate and understand the great thinkers and practitioners of scientific socialism. We'd suffer if we don't tell potential recruits until they've been in the party for a while that we are a Marxist party, that we're a Leninist party.

Because of imperialism's counter-revolutionary successes in recent years, and the constant media barrage, there are many hesitations before socialism among working people – doubts about its possibility. And there are many hesitations about joining a party. But that's just what's needed to counter the capitalist offensive, to coordinate and lead the counterattack. So the party question, and our role, are crucial, as our draft political resolution points out.

It also helps clarify our dual attitude to other organisations like the CPA (when it existed) and the Greens. The draft political resolution gives an assessment, and the right balance, pointing out they're both potential allies and obstacles to building the revolutionary socialist movement.

Nature of the period

At our October National Committee meeting, we made some corrections to how we had talked about the nature of the period. We pointed out that while it was still a difficult political situation internationally and nationally, we should take care not to talk down the period too much.

We're not expecting major breakthroughs in the short term, but we can see action on a number of fronts, sporadic breakouts, breakthroughs even. And we've stated many times that we don't have enough cadre to take advantage of all the opportunities. So it's not a slow period, even though it's not necessarily a period where we can expect massive growth.

But even in the last few months we've noted a number of further encouraging signs on both the international and Australian level: internationally the range of election victories for left parties, or defeats for the main capitalist party, and the range of workers' struggles; nationally, some very large meetings and demonstrations around Mabo, Aboriginal land rights, the largest Reclaim the Night demonstrations yet, some exciting high school and university actions on education cuts, the PSU Challenge ACT election victory.[56]

In the party-building report we adopted at our June 1992 National Committee meeting, we began by noting that we were starting to see the beginning of a change in the nature of the political period. In 1993 we can be firmer on this, it has gathered pace, and we can expect 1994 to be quite exciting. The underlying anger, resentment and political consciousness of people are there; what's lacking is a clear political alternative to organise and focus their disillusionment with capitalist politics.

Some fascinating insights into the nature of the political consciousness of young people appeared in the Sydney press in recent months.

Firstly, the *Good Weekend* reported the results of a survey of student attitudes by the Sydney Uni paper *Honi Soit,* which asked the same questions that a survey carried out by *Honi Soit* in 1968 asked. Students are supposed to be more conservative today, right? Just the opposite! Here are some of the most interesting comparisons:

- In 1968, 51% of students surveyed voted Liberal /Country Party, compared with 17.6% in 1993;
- Back then, 71% of students supported a quota on Asian immigration, in 1993 only 35% did;
- In 1968 36% supported military conscription, now only 9% do;
- Back then 70% said they believed in God, today 52% do;
- New questions indicated overwhelming support for free education and Aboriginal land rights.

Another survey on youth attitudes appeared in the *Sydney Morning Herald* and the Melbourne *Age* towards the end of November, perhaps in other papers as well. They had headlines like: 'Study paints a picture of lost, dispirited youth' and 'Life at 20: no views, no hope'. This survey, conducted by an advertising agency, was also fascinating. The papers tried to focus on the apathy, portraying young people as apolitical, but if you read to the end of the articles, you got a much clearer picture – overwhelming alienation and disillusionment with the system. Some examples: 'Politicians were held in contempt: "For them politics is only concerned with the material issues that may eventually affect their lifestyles and wellbeing. They simply don't think about quality of life or community issues".' The report continued, 'They tended to vote green or independent, simply because they were not mainstream parties'.

'The women were not concerned with feminist issues', but 'the gains made for them by feminists in the 1970s were taken for granted'.

It confirms all we've said: the ideological gains of the youth radicalisation of the 1960s are still there, on a range of issues: antiwar, anti-racist, anti-sexist. There's apathy, yes, but that's very much because of their healthy disillusionment with the two-party system, the corruption, the cynicism at the top, and because we haven't yet reached them with our campaigns, with Resistance.

But that widespread disillusionment with the major parties has not led to a major break. The campaigns and little breaks are over specific issues.

In recent years we've compared this with developments in New Zealand, and looked wistfully across the Tasman at the growth of the NewLabour Party and the Alliance. That it hasn't happened here is due to many factors, but is testimony to the success of the ALP's Accord project, as our draft political resolution points out.

It's also testimony to the role of the fake left, especially the Communist Party of Australia, because this was their project. But a good by-product has been their self-destruction; it was so successful, it wiped them out. There's hardly a whimper of the CPA left.

In contrast, we can be quite pleased with our successes in the two years since our 14th National Conference. And an evaluation of 1993 from a party-building perspective is encouraging:

- *Green Left Weekly* is getting stronger, broader, better, more widely circulated and respected.
- We launched *Solidarity* as a great vehicle for our trade union work and building alliances with others in the labour movement.
- We increased our links and contacts with socialists around the world, and are concretising this with some exciting projects.
- Resistance has gone well, continuing to provide a stream of recruits to the movement. It's had a range of experiences, even in the final stages of the year.
- We're going closer to balancing our budget, and completed

the fund drive successfully, although we're still on the financial edge and haven't resolved all our financial problems.

- We've had many extremely successful functions, the biggest dinners ever for many branches, and some of our biggest forums.
- We have a stronger, more even branch leadership.
- Education has been better prepared and organised, although we still suffer from a serious lack of education of our new young members.
- We've made progress in the organisation of branch meetings and fractions.

Our party-building perspective

When talking about our party-building perspective, we can think of it on two levels: firstly as a permanent aspect of our work, and secondly as a turn back to it in the '90s, stressing it as an area we'd neglected as we made the necessary responses to potential opportunities for broadening out.

We've slipped a little with our terminology, talking about 'party-building tasks' and by referring to them like that, often counterposing them to our campaign work, our united-front work around particular issues, our public political interventions. But of course there's no counter-position; in fact all our interventions and campaign work should be seen as party-building tasks. Perhaps it's better to get back into the habit of talking about our basic party-building tasks.

The fundamental party-building perspectives of the DSP are summarised in the last section of our draft political resolution, Part VII, titled 'The Role of the Democratic Socialist Party':

> The DSP is still a small cadre party, despite the considerable body of political understanding and

experience it has built up. Through its history of trying to build alliances and regroupments with any force breaking from reformist politics and through its persistent struggle against Laborism, the party has evolved to a position of being the main force on the – admittedly weak – Australian left. Today the party faces larger challenges and responsibilities than ever. Nonetheless, the development of the party is still at an early stage: it does not yet lead masses in action and must continue to grow through propaganda for socialism and recruiting new members 'one-to-one'.

There are no gimmicks, we can't jump over objective reality. We're certainly always on the lookout for opportunities, and we'll respond to any opening, as we did in the '80s. This perspective has been repeated in most of the party-building reports from the last three or four years.

The central theme of the party-building report adopted by the October [1993] National Committee meeting related to our basic party-building tasks and our interventions, and how to mesh them together.

And Reihana [Mohideen]'s party-building report to the June 1993 National Committee meeting adjusted another important dimension, 'the need to put our organised educational tasks much more at the centre of our work in the next period'. We stressed how comrades needed the theoretical and historical understanding, an intensive political education, 'in order to orient themselves to the challenges and tasks we face today and for the long-term perspective'.

Throughout this conference, we've stressed the party-building approach to all our areas of work, and this has been reflected in all the reports and discussions on campaigns, on trade union work, on international work.

Recruiting

What's the most basic party-building task? It's recruitment of course.

We didn't grow as much as we'd hoped in 1993, despite having some of the biggest events ever and the largest number of contacts on our mailing lists.

Part of the reason of course is the general political situation, something we have little direct control over. The capitalist class, as is its nature, conducts a permanent anti-socialist ideological offensive, which has intensified following the collapse of the Soviet bloc. And even though there's anger on issues, the Accord and Laborist politics have had a deep impact on social consciousness. The collapse of the old left, the CPA in particular, has had the partial effect of weakening the general left milieu, adding to the pervasive anti-party feeling and movementism.

On the other hand, we are stronger relatively on the left. The problem is this can be seen as being a 'bigger fish in a smaller pond'. In short, we have the combined task of both convincing people of the general socialist viewpoint, as well as of the necessity of joining a revolutionary socialist party – our party.

We have to recognise that there's no shortcut on this. Changing our name, or toning down our politics, won't magically make us grow. We can keep our eyes peeled for special opportunities, openings for regroupment, as we did in the '80s, and will continue to do so. But there's no substitute for the basic task of recruitment (a science, as Comrade Jim McIlroy puts it) – the propaganda, the party events and activities, the interventions, the education, the one-to-one talking.

But we've never done it properly. We have put it down the list of tasks. So really we need a major national recruiting campaign, centrally planned and led from the National Office, and with the branches allocating the necessary resources to carry it out.

It should be a campaign to join people to the DSP, but it should be a joint campaign with Resistance, because most of our recruits will, as always, come through Resistance.

In the past we've talked about recruiting campaigns, but in practice they have always played third fiddle to the key campaigns on *Green Left Weekly* sales and finances. We have major sales and finances campaigns on an ongoing basis, but the third pillar of our party-building project, recruiting, has always tended to be pushed aside in practice. Sales bundles and sustainer and fund drive targets have always had a looming immediacy in the eyes of overworked branch organisers, executives and committees.

We need a campaign to make contacting and recruiting a central task in the eyes of, especially, the leading and most active comrades, but also all party members. We need to involve the whole party in the recruiting campaign, not just the full-time organisers.

We have to organise this campaign, we have to lead it, from the National Office. We now have a stronger NO and should be able to do more. We're planning a recruitment committee in the NO, and similar committees should be organised in the branches where possible.

Why now? We can always say we need to grow as fast as possible, and we need to give as much attention to that intervention, or this area of work, as possible. (We're impatient, and we want to do everything right now.)

But there is a question of tempo involved in how we allocate our resources, our time, our comrades and our priorities. We can plan ahead, and think, OK, we'll invest in a particular tactic, or an area of work, for future gains, three or four years in the future, say. Or else we could just look at the most immediate gains, today, this week, this month, and plan our work with this in mind.

But from our present standpoint, in January 1994, we know we need some results this year and our plans, our basic party-building tasks will be targeted so that we grow appreciably this year.

There are some pressing reasons to grow:

- There's our need to intervene more effectively on the national political stage – elections, propaganda, raising our profile, trying to influence the political direction.
- There are the opportunities, and needs in different cities – new branches like Darwin (and in future, other towns also: Geelong, Launceston, along the northern coast of Queensland) but also larger or more branches in the bigger cities where we already have a party branch.
- There are the needs of the movements, which need our comrades – the trade unions, the women's liberation movement, the environment movement, the student movement, the different solidarity campaigns.
- There are the needs of the international movement. We're at a very important turning point. Links are being developed, rethinking is going on, the movement is getting rebuilt.

So if we don't succeed in growing this year, some of these opportunities, these moments, will pass.

One-to-one recruiting

Central to this national recruiting campaign is the idea of one-to-one recruiting. We have to put this idea up front, and convince comrades of their ability to do it. This is still the main way to recruit, and will be for some time to come. We're a small cadre party, still very much at the propaganda stage. Even for the CP in the Philippines, a cadre party with a mass base, recruitment is one by one, training, testing, integrating, educating. There are no shortcuts, there or here.

The problem of recruiting is our ability to talk socialism one to one. Even though we'll be getting out a better range of propaganda material, that hasn't been the real problem.

We need to revive the practice of visiting; more contacting dinners; more teaming up with new contacts, for sales, for political interventions; more talking to new people at all our functions.

At the IGL Conference, perhaps we should be assigning 50 cadre just to recruiting. We need to get comrades feeling confident and aggressive and competitive about recruiting to the party at such events. That is, it's not an assignment for comrades to sit behind a recruiting table, although we will have that, but for these comrades to fan out through the conference and start up conversations with participants they don't know – with or without introductory props like *Green Left* or a leaflet.

Recruiting can be a question of confidence, sometimes a question of will! We have to be determined we can do it. And all comrades should be recruiters.

There are many misconceptions about recruiting, such as the idea that only experienced comrades can recruit, or the idea that young people have to understand all about Resistance before they join.

Integrating all our work

We already have many of the tools and structures in place for this campaign, and we'll be relating our other basic party-building tasks to this central, but hitherto neglected, task:

- Selling *Green Left Weekly,* to recruit;
- Building Resistance, to recruit;
- Holding forums, not as an abstract intellectual exercise, but to recruit;
- Organising our political campaigns and interventions, to recruit;
- Holding classes, to recruit (and integrate and develop the recruits);
- Building the party's profile, to recruit, and to assist in later

recruitment;

- Building the IGL Conference, to help us recruit.

In short, recruiting can be treated as a way to integrate all our work.

We need to make full use of our interventions, our campaign work, so that we're properly oriented to recruiting.

We do need more and better recruiting material: books, pamphlets, leaflets, in addition to the range we already have. We already have the wonderful propaganda vehicle of *Green Left Weekly,* of course, and we can use that more directly for recruiting. But neither *Green Left* nor any other piece of literature, no matter how brilliant, is a substitute for each individual comrade's ability and passion to explain our politics. We need more campaigning and recruiting stalls, stocked with *Green Left,* leaflets, books and pamphlets (particularly those the party itself produces), petitions.

We should be actively and openly campaigning for socialism. We need to continue to implement our intention to build a higher party profile. We need DSP press releases; more national tours; better use of *Green Left Weekly;* promoting our party leaders as spokespeople; more public use of our more experienced comrades.

We must take the campaign into Resistance, so that Resistance leaders think about recruiting to the party, so that they're conscious this is a central part of their assignment to Resistance.

The role of Resistance in recruiting is crucial, the main source of our cadre. But recruits at the moment are not all coming from campus; we are getting people with broader life experience.

The Perth branch experience needs to be generalised. Branches do go through cycles of growth; it was Perth's turn last year. But it shows what is possible in this period. All branches can grow.

Our recruitment targets

Branches should be thinking, planning, organising to meet ambitious targets for the number of new provisional members joined up in 1994.

We have to make full use of provisional membership, be more outgoing. We have to be seen as an open party, easy to join, without actually lowering our standards and level of activity for full members.

In 1993 the total numbers of full members and provisional members grew by only 6%, but our full membership, our real membership, grew by 17%. This has been a significant consolidation, even though it's not a large growth. We've made some progress but know there's an enormous amount of untapped potential.

In 1994 we should aim for both a large number of new provisional members and consolidation into party members and cadres as well.

Our needs, and the objective possibilities, mean we should be looking for about a 30% increase in our national membership over the course of 1994.

It's possible. We know Perth branch has grown by about 100% in membership in a year. Many branches already have lots of contacts, potential recruits around them. Witness our dinners, our large contact lists, the periphery through *Green Left Weekly*. Resistance has good prospects for growth, with strong bases on many campuses to begin the year with. And the stepped up political tempo we've observed points to the possibility for recruiting large numbers to the party and Resistance.

Consolidation

But the real question of course is how many of them become cadre, so we have to be conscious of all the different stages of recruiting:

- Bringing people around us, through our political activity, our meetings and functions, through *Green Left* sales, our leaflets, etc.
- Convincing contacts to join the party as provisional members.
- Educating and integrating provisional members into the party and our political activity.
- Joining provisional members as members of the party.
- Continuing the education and training of members into cadres, into professional revolutionary activists.

The question of the size of our basic party units and the development of cadre through the taking of leadership responsibility needs investigation. It's easy and simple to grow and develop in small, new branches. Comrades are forced to take on major responsibilities, to lead politically. They can't wait for someone else to do it or even show them how – they're on their own. In larger branches it's often harder. There are a larger number of comrades to carry out the tasks, the individual responsibilities are smaller, newer comrades can be neglected, not given major assignments, and drift, so they might not develop as fast as they would in smaller branches, despite the advantages of all the experienced comrades to help them.

It's a problem of size that we still haven't resolved properly. In Melbourne and Sydney and later in Brisbane, we made several attempts to divide the branches, set up smaller units in the suburbs both to intervene in the political life there and to try to recruit in those areas. But an important consideration was always to try to spread leadership responsibility, and thus train and develop cadres quicker. This problem is still ahead of us. As we grow we don't want the size of our basic party units becoming a limiting factor on further growth and integration of comrades.

In the future, as we grow, we'll need to set up several branches in the major cities and create district structures. But we should be very conscious of this factor even now: how to develop comrades through giving them important responsibilities, challenging assignments.

We should work out how to make better use of teams, to take leadership responsibility and lead and show initiative in a particular area. It can be a fraction, a campus team of comrades or other teams to carry out specific projects.

An activist party

After recruiting, and then consolidating, there's the question of retaining comrades, keeping them in the struggle for the long haul. We know how important education is here, but there are other important factors we must consider too.

In the written pre-conference discussion, a number of comrades raised the question of the continuing drift of 'older members' or, a better term, 'longer-term comrades'.

We understand a number of the reasons for this. There can be tiredness, after a long stint of dedicated activity. There's always the pressure of bourgeois ideology that bears down on us. It can be hard when we see no immediate victory in sight here in Australia, and a number of setbacks, the Accord, the collapse of the Soviet Union. So some comrades retreat to personal concerns, or academia, or demoralisation.

But some questions shouldn't worry us. We will be a party of young people, if we're a revolutionary party. That's the nature of revolutionary organisations – the comrades who've been to the Philippines report the same type of age spread in the Manila-Rizal organisation of the CPP as in our party. We're not likely to grow from the old, tired left. We will grow from the newly radicalising youth.

There's also the question of the level of activism. We are an activist party, and we want as much from comrades as they are able to give. Obviously comrades in some circumstances won't be able to be as active as others – child care or other family responsibilities or certain types of jobs will limit some comrades' time available for political activity. But we don't want to encourage a low level of activism; we want, we need, an activist party. Also, we shouldn't assume that older people will automatically be less active. That's not the case. Comrade Betty Downie in Sydney, for example, would give many younger comrades a run for their money.

The question of the level of activism is really a question of politics. Those stepping back are just a small number, and not necessarily the older comrades. The pace in the party has to be set by the activists, because we are a party of professional revolutionists.

But of course we have to make use of all the different generations in the party, all the backgrounds etc. Certainly we should not make older comrades feel out of place, discriminate against comrades because of their age. And we are joining people from different age groups, and drawing them into activity. We are also reactivating people: a number of delegates here have had a break, and are now back in the thick of things.

The point is, how does the party make the most of the different contributions each member can make, from whatever background? And how can we mesh all the different activities, and different experiences, and different origins, into a homogeneous party?

It's been raised, what about introducing a party supporters category again? We think that would be a mistake at this time. A formal supporters category now would both send the wrong message to comrades and create an organisational burden for us that's not necessary.

Raising the party profile to recruit

One way to increase our possibilities for recruitment is by raising the party's public profile.

We should issue press releases in the name of the DSP much more frequently. Press releases would force our thinking on political questions, as would more DSP statements and interviews with party spokespersons in *Green Left*. We need to promote our national leaders more, giving more talks and forums, and speaking tours.

May Day this year falls on a Sunday, so branches could plan meetings and forums and dinners to promote the DSP and having a high profile at official marches, where they stagger on.

We can use our victories more openly, let our members and periphery know about them. We should be using *Green Left Weekly* more openly, and not downplaying the role of the DSP as much as we have in the past. We should have our writers identified as DSP members, quote DSP members, quote DSP press releases.

Every month, we should have at least one DSP leaflet in subs, e.g., 'What is the DSP?' We should have a listing of our addresses on page 2, letting readers know how to 'Get *Green Left Weekly* in your city'.

We can have more specifically DSP supplements. The first one this year will be a DSP supplement on women's liberation for IWD. Some DSP inserts don't necessarily need to be on a single issue, but might be rounded recruiting broadsheets, on different aspects of party interventions, party life, party analysis of issues, interviews with DSP members, an article on the politics behind some of our projects, for example, the role of the IGL Conference in building the Australian left. We can have analytical articles in supplements by *Green Left* staff who are DSP members, so identify them as that. We think we can do all this without taking anything away from the broad, open nature of *Green Left*.

We now have a new DSP logo, so let's institutionalise it around the country. Artwork and files will be available for comrades to incorporate it into their branch leaflets. We should also reinstitute our membership cards.

We should be more conscious in Resistance of talking about the DSP, and seeing recruiting to the party as a central task. We shouldn't hold back from reminding new Resistance members of one of Resistance's main aims, giving support to the DSP.

Certainly we shouldn't get beyond the stage we're at in building the party; we shouldn't be posturing, shouldn't be giving ourselves airs. But we should act seriously; we have to take the party seriously, given the serious goals and tasks we have set ourselves.

Public campaigning

I think it's necessary briefly to reaffirm some of the points made in the conference campaigns report and by the October NC meeting about the importance of relating our public interventions to our party-building perspectives.

We can be very flexible about the form and nature of public campaigns, committees, activities, and this should include the possibility of carrying out actions in our own name. We missed the boat on a number of actions that could have been called by us in the absence of initiatives from anyone else – Somalia; broken ALP promises in March; community TV; Mabo; Bougainville; the Yeltsin coup.

There have been some cases where we did grab the opportunity; the Canberra high school action is one very good example.[57] We acted quickly, we were open about our leadership of the action, and we were very conscious about recruitment and party building throughout.

Of course, we don't have only this approach. We need the broader committees, we need the united front campaigns if we hope to draw in broader forces. But we can also be conscious about bridging between the two. For example, in leaflets published by campaigns, we can list the sponsoring organisations, including the DSP and Resistance.

We have stressed the need to professionalise our basic party-building tasks in recent years. Having already improved or being in the process of improving on many of these fronts, we can now be feeling a little impatient to test out a range of opportunities, which is exciting, taking our integrated approach into campaigns.

We need to be seen as activists, to inspire and recruit others. The party needs to be visibly identified with the oppressed, to be bold and brazen. Our interventions in campaigns have to be multifaceted – sometimes some comrades leading the action, others networking, talking to people, recruiting, selling *Green Left,* promoting our events, getting articles for the paper.

A discussion contribution by Comrade Jonathan Strauss made an interesting analysis of our history from the '60s on, but I'd make one adjustment. He wrote that in the 1960s and '70s 'our tendency was built primarily as a faction of the ALP'. Not really, because although we had a mistaken analysis of the ALP, our practice was different. What built us was our independent work, our Resistance work, our party paper *Direct Action,* our independent interventions in political campaigns, including running our own election campaigns. We had that ALP orientation as an albatross around our necks. Certainly, there was a different situation in the ALP then and today, and we would have had to relate to it more, e.g., after the Whitlam election campaign in 1972.

Jonathan also outlined the direction we'll be moving to, but we're not there yet: 'Now, as the main force on the left, we are increasingly ceasing to be primarily a propaganda grouping, becoming instead mainly a party of practical struggle'.

Not quite yet. We're still primarily a propaganda grouping.

It's a process, yes, and we've made some steps in that direction, yes, and we certainly feel the pressure on us to play the role of leading the struggles. It's useful to be conscious of the direction, the needs, the possibilities, but we have to be very conscious of succeeding in growing, recruiting, as a propaganda group, in order to play that necessary role of leading practical struggles.

Green Left

We're all well aware how *Green Left Weekly* has been our main weapon, our biggest success, for three years now. It's helped us reach out, broaden out, and been a partial solution to our regroupment needs where other efforts have failed. It's helped establish us as the strongest party on the left.

We have three major tasks in relation to the paper:
- We need to continue to broaden out *Green Left.*
- We need to ensure its success through making our goals on sales and subscriptions.
- We need to use it more to build the party and recruit.

We want to project a sales drive from 1 May to Resistance's 23rd National Conference [1994], which begins on 2 July. We'll work out the focus of the drive, what targets etc., in the coming months. But this sales drive doesn't mean any relaxation on sales for the first three or four months of the year. We know how important *Green Left* is for all areas of our work – recruiting, building our events, finance etc. It will be a very busy first three months this year, so sales and other basic party-building tasks mustn't suffer.

But after the IGL Conference, we will have the chance for a major sales drive, in conjunction with building the Resistance conference. We're proposing a nine-week sales drive. It can be launched with major *Green Left* or DSP functions around May Day.

For *Green Left* subscriptions, we're not proposing a drive as such from this conference. Instead we want to build on the experience of our subscription campaigns last year and treat the whole of the coming year as a time when we'll be making a continuous push on subs This involves raising consciousness on sub selling so we do it automatically, in all our political work and while selling *Green Left*. Sub cards should be a part of every bookstall, every meeting, and clip-offs should be on every mail-out.

Secondly, we have to regularise the chasing up of renewals. We fritter away subscriptions, and thus sales, every time we delay for a week on following up renewals. We know the universal experience, that a large percentage of subscribers will renew if we follow them up, but will let their sub lapse if they don't hear from us directly.

We're going to make a special offer at the IGL Conference, offering people who register for the conference a discounted sub if they subscribe at the time they register.

Other promotions from the National Office include arranging exchange inserts with other publications, encouraging more movements and organisations to pay for special supplements in *Green Left,* and some special promotional mail-outs. We have several lists – libraries, women's organisations, green groups, high schools – that we'd like to mail to if we had the money, or could get free postage.

Campaign 4,000 will be broadened out to include other aspects of using *Green Left Weekly* – reading *Green Left,* writing for it, using it, promoting it. Perhaps we'll change the name of it so it's seen as both a newsletter to promote the campaigns on sales and hours and subscriptions, but also a general newsletter used to build the party and Resistance, to educate and recruit and network.

From the first issue of *Green Left* this year, we'll raise the consciousness about recruiting and talking to people while selling *Green Left*. There should always be a party or Resistance leaflet with us, with a short recruiting blurb and clip-off. We can have a number of standard formats. We need to organise more tables, more stumps, so we have a collective approach to recruiting, and teach newer comrades how it's done. There should be Resistance membership cards as well as sub forms with every table.

We need to raise the DSP profile in *Green Left Weekly,* at the same time continuing to broaden it out. For example, we haven't really pushed much to get new shareholders and sponsors recently. Each branch should go through the sponsors list, contact everyone, see if they're still interested and update the list to include most current supporters of the paper. At the very least we should be contacting every sponsor to make sure they have a current subscription.

Branch executives should have a regular item on their agenda each week – *Green Left* copy. The paper has been fantastic. We know there's nothing like it around the world. But we know one area we can improve is local copy.

There are some interesting results from a statistical analysis made of the sales figures of the last two years of *Green Left*. Over the two years, the national sales have remained pretty constant. The rate has decreased, but this has been compensated for by an increase in the number of hours sold. The main factor contributing to the decline in the sales rate has been the decline in the street sales rate. There were a number of factors that didn't influence the rate, according to the survey. For example, green covers, women's covers, the price change and winter didn't affect the rate.

Another interesting revelation was that our sales campaigns haven't led to a lasting increase in hours. There has been a general increase, perhaps influenced by long-term raised consciousness from sales campaigns.

Education

A key task for all of us in the period ahead is the education and training of the next generation of revolutionary socialists, so that they in turn can give political leadership, educate a further generation, and build the party.

We'll be putting real resources into this immediately after the conference. We've got a four-week school in Sydney, with ten comrades attending on a full-time basis, that begins a few days after the conference. We also have a three-week school in Perth, and there's a four-day school in Melbourne.

The infrastructure of our basic class series is all there – though the study outlines for the Introduction to Socialism and Introduction to Marxism series need updating.

We should also resolve to continue with the branch activist classes this year, or to institute them in branches that haven't yet started them. We've already seen some very positive results from these classes where they were carried through. And weekend seminars and lecture tours, such as those carried out last year by Comrade Allen Myers on Marxist economics, should become a regular component of our education program too.

We need to encourage a more rigorous attitude towards theory and our political line. Comrades can get lazy, too ecumenical, adapt to the accepted wisdom of the milieu, whether it's the women's liberation movement, where a theory of patriarchy is dominant, or the aid and NGO milieu, where self-help solutions rather than political action and change are promoted.

How do we counter this, especially in the absence of our full-time party school? And unless we act more consciously to counter it, the fact of having a broad paper like *Green Left* instead of a specifically party paper can also exacerbate this problem.

Apart from the general needs of education, perhaps we need to encourage a more polemical attitude among comrades. That is, to debate more among ourselves in search of clarity, and polemicise with others on the left to advance our views.

We also have to ask ourselves why there's been a decline in reading in the party, especially of the Marxist classics. Certainly there has been a change in left culture, a collapse of some left culture. In Australia today it's our role to create, to prop up, to stimulate a left culture, at many levels, to promote a working-class culture again, inject a working-class political perspective into the cultural scene. For example, we need to take up the debate with idealism, debunk any 'new age' mysticism. It's not just the directly bourgeois views we have to refute, but all the diversions and dead ends.

Comrades need to be encouraged in their reading, and it's the case that you're more inclined to read if you're reading with a reason, for a debate or polemic.

Branch meetings

Following the last NC plenum recommending more frequent branch meetings, we've had a positive response from most branches. So in 1994, we should implement that perspective, and fully absorb the motivations contained in the NC report.

We're not saying every branch should go immediately to weekly meetings. Some might. Some might be fortnightly. We recommended more frequent meetings. And we always have to keep in mind the two sides of democracy. We want to avoid situations where we only have time to talk and go to meetings, but no time for activity. So branches have to balance out these two things. The principles are political effectiveness, what educates and trains and develops cadres best, what best enables us to take the right decisions and implement them. The principles aren't abstract democracy or a certain frequency of meetings.

So we've got to balance out this rounded role, with the need for smaller working bodies where every comrade gets responsibility and develops their leadership abilities and organisational skills – sales committees, recruiting committees, fundraising committees etc.

Fractions can play part of that training role. The campaigns report clarified some of the fractions we'll need in 1994. Fractions should be very conscious of recruiting as a responsibility in their area.

And forums should be regarded as very much recruiting events, in addition to raising the party profile and educating our comrades.

Our international work

Reihana [Mohideen]'s report on our international work and the discussion that followed really reaffirmed the extremely important role of our international work in building the party. Of course, it can't be a substitute for building a base among working people here. But it can be a tremendous complement, and a source of inspiration and education. It can also be a valuable insurance against narrowness and chauvinism.

Internationalism raises the political level of comrades here, where the class struggle at the moment is generally more subdued than in some other countries, especially in the Third World. Comrades need the international perspective to help them make the political connections, that socialism is realisable, that revolution is necessary. The world political situation today makes international work even more important at the moment.

Part of our perspective is to build an international movement for socialism. We cannot build a national revolutionary party without building an international revolutionary movement. Leaving the Fourth International didn't mean we rejected that view. The key point was our recognition of the limitations and narrowness of the FI for building an international revolutionary movement with mass influence.

As we noted in the discussion on our international work, the exciting Philippines development reorients our party in the coming year. It's not merely our internationalist duty to orient to it and respond, but it will benefit the Australian revolution in the short, medium and long term. It's a tremendous boost to morale; we all feel less alone in our political perspectives.

We'll have closer links, exchanges, joint activities with the Filipino comrades. I really recommend comrades try to visit, perhaps for the May Day rally.

The Philippines development helps change the balance of forces on the international left, and it emphasises the importance of solidarity work this year.

We can learn a lot from the Philippines comrades, and through our discussions and interactions with them: how to do mass work; how to build a base in the working class; how to organise a large party.

It's a historic opportunity. It's the most significant development in renewing the socialist project since the collapse of Stalinism in the Soviet Union and Eastern Europe. In this respect it's probably the most important and thorough break with Stalinism for many, many decades.

Finances

There'll be a separate finance report to the closed session tomorrow, and some of our financial needs will be explained in the party-building rally tonight, but I want to briefly outline our main financial campaigns and goals for the coming year.

Firstly, we have an ongoing campaign of increasing the national pledge base as a means of increasing the sustainer paid to the NO each week.

Secondly, there's our fund drive. We did very well in 1993 with our fund drive. Many branches went over their quota, and some have been able to use the extra to purchase equipment for the branch.

This year we're projecting a target of $125,000.

It's a party-building fund drive, for the DSP, not simply a *Green Left* fund drive that the party runs. A big part of it, around $100,000, will be needed to keep *Green Left* going. And we'll run *Green Left* fundraising functions to help raise that money. But there are other party-building projects that we need money for:

- Darwin branch, to help them set up.
- Our international work, which has become much more important and exciting – *Links;* setting up a *Green Left* bureau in Johannesburg; more trips to the Philippines and exchanges.
- A range of books and other publications.
- We need to update some of the computer equipment in the National Office.
- Maintenance work on our National Office building – it's sorely in need of a paint job. We've been talking about it for years; let's get the money to do it this year.

Last year's fund drive success benefited from many extremely successful dinners. Nearly every city was more successful than in the past. We'll continue such events, and plan well ahead in 1994.

A number of Cultural Dissent events were very good fundraisers too, while Brisbane's Green It Up ended the year on a very high note, attracting 200 people to the final one and making $1,000.

To reach our fund drive targets, we need to be conscious of the lessons we've learnt:

- The importance of an early start. Let's not let the IGL Conference and other activities stop us planning a fundraising schedule that gets under way as soon after the conference as possible.

- We need to get fund drive pledges in early. We hope to get a big proportion of our target pledged at the rally tonight, and we need to get most of those pledges in to the National Office in the first part of the year.
- Central planning will help us achieve our goals. Those branches that planned fund drive events far in advance and devoted the most political resources its success, were the most successful last year.

Publications

We say it's a propaganda period; therefore we certainly should be serious about producing more and better propaganda. The list of books we need to produce is growing:

1. The new edition of the party's program that we adopted yesterday. We should produce it in book form quickly.
2. A new edition of *Socialism and Human Survival;* we need to update it with a new introduction and new cover, and aim to get it out before the IGL Conference.
3. A book on Maoism. There's a big demand for it in the Philippines.
4. A book containing Jim Percy's four most recent party-building reports. It needs an introduction and some editing, and also should be out before the IGL Conference.
5. Later in the year, a pamphlet with our new resolution on lesbian and gay liberation.
6. A number of Marxist classics need reprinting, and to be made available to comrades in the Philippines, Indonesia and other countries where new socialist movements are developing or evolving.

We need to keep expanding the materials available for our own education. Perhaps what's needed also is an organisational handbook for the DSP and Resistance, which could bring together material from old documents and recent party-building reports. All the different sections might be best treated on two levels, firstly expounding the general principles, and secondly outlining our norms and procedures and lessons for our specific situation and the particular period.

Alliances and elections

There are no immediate prospects for alliance building and regroupment with any existing forces on the left, although we'll always be on the lookout, as our draft political resolution makes clear:

> Besides intervening vigorously in the struggles of
> working and oppressed people, the party must be alert
> to all breaks, no matter how hesitant, with capitalist
> politics and continue to probe all opportunities to
> construct a broader 'red-green' political alternative.
> The party reaffirms the need to continue these
> attempts at alliance building and regroupment.

The WA Green senators took a good stand on the Mabo legislation, but received no real support from their own party, or from the national Greens. We should be looking for openings for united work with them, inviting them to speak at the IGL Conference, continuing to cover their activities in *Green Left*. We should try to support any future progressive stands they take with backup actions, demos, pickets, whatever, since their own party is incapable of this.

In future elections we'll be searching for alliances and non-aggression pacts as usual. But we'll mainly be running Democratic Socialist campaigns, or sometimes in the framework of Green

Alliance. Perhaps we'll be faced with a NSW state election this year, depending on the outcome of the North Sydney by-election. The Brisbane City Council elections are coming up, which we should participate in. And there are elections in the ACT in early 1995. We should plan well ahead for this; the elections will take place on the basis of two five-member seats, and one seven-member seat.

But the main frameworks around which healthy independent activists can regroup at the moment are the structures we have already set up – *Green Left Weekly, Solidarity,* and our broad public conferences, first the Socialist Scholars Conferences, and now the International Green Left Conference.

There are many demoralised former leftists, former CPAers floating around. One task we have is to try to rescue some of them, any that retain some vision of the future, that have escaped the demoralisation and cynicism most have succumbed to. Some are active on a particular issue. Although of course the overwhelming source of growth and new strength for the party will come from fresh forces, especially the youth, we hope we can win some former activists back to a socialist perspective.

Most, however, are lost. Some are even part of the problem still. Under the guise of rejecting sectarianism or the authoritarianism of their past political allegiances, they can often adopt the most sectarian attitude to those who are still fighting for socialism, those still with a vision and hope for the future – us. Some have got niches in the trade union bureaucracy, in aid bodies, in government departments, in academia. It's clear that sectarianism is in no way a monopoly of the far left, but can be worse among the non-party left. And our continued existence and growth are a constant affront to their past, an embarrassment to their current capitulation.

Boldness and passion for socialism

We have to train and educate our comrades to be eager to engage in polemics – taking on board all we've learnt about tactics and language and diplomacy. Comrades need to develop their confidence, even aggression, and hone their debating skills.

A polemical approach is needed against the milieu that defends, and is dependent on, the continued existence of capitalism, while being involved in progressive causes and speaking the language of 'social justice'.

It's needed against sectarian currents that remain on the left, and talk the language of socialism while abstaining from or blocking real movements and campaigns that can assist the struggle for socialism.

We have overdone the humility bit in recent years. We don't face a problem of ultra-left posturing in the party. We need to be seen as the revolutionary cutting edge. We have to be out there winning people to socialism! We're not just promoters of progressive causes. We shouldn't just be identified as the best activists on particular issues, but as members of a party, a revolutionary socialist party.

We have a special responsibility for helping young comrades who join Resistance. They've rejected capitalism, but often are not clear about what being a revolutionist actually means. It's the responsibility of all party comrades to lead, to show, to patiently explain.

We must help them develop their understanding and skills, as well as their passion and seriousness. We must help them understand that they don't just belong to the party, the party belongs to them. Ownership is vested in the comrades here, the membership, expressed through the delegates at our conference. And with ownership comes responsibility. So all comrades here, and everyone who joins, has a responsibility to learn, develop politically, and lead as an individual, because the more you step forward the more the party benefits, but also, and more importantly, the responsibility to build the party collectively, to do your utmost to help others and the party as a whole, to get satisfaction from political advances and the growth of the party.

Our party is a wonderful instrument that is so much more than the simple addition of its individual components. An essential component is our team leadership concept – at branch level, at national level. Seeing the party cadre here at our national conference, hearing the full range of our experiences and involvements and skills and strengths, you realise what a powerhouse for socialism our team, our party, is. We should be extremely confident about what we've got, and where we're going. Our friends, as well as our enemies, recognise that strength.

A good year ahead

1994 is shaping as an exciting year. There's confusion and crisis in many of the traditional bourgeois political instruments, and we saw a range of little victories, the beginnings of struggles in 1993.

And as we emerge from all the coming rich struggles and stimulating activities, there will be many more of us, because throughout this coming year, we're all going to have up front the goal of recruiting, and all our areas of work will be linked to this and will benefit from our success and our growth.

5. COMBINING REACH-OUT AND CADRE BUILDING

Report to the National Committee 11 July 1994

With a certain layer of older comrades becoming less active or even dropping out, while Resistance and the DSP were still recruiting youth, finding ways to educate and train the new layers became a more pressing task. This report was intended to speed up the process of integrating new members, through a range of measures, including a decision-making conference held a year earlier than the usual biennial schedule. A factor not directly addressed in the report was signs from the Perth branch that some newer members grouped around Steve Robson, a long-time member of the National Committee and the Perth branch secretary, were seeking to weaken party norms in the hope that this would lead to swifter recruitment of new members.

What's the year been like for us since our 15th National Conference in January [1994]? On balance, I think we'd all have to agree that it's been very successful. Just look at some of the highlights:

- Resistance organised an extremely successful O Week intervention, joining up 1,200 new members.

- We organised a very successful International Green Left Conference, with more than 800 people attending, and a big range of international speakers.
- We've launched *Links*, with two issues out now, and expanded significantly our international relations with other left parties.
- We've expanded our trade union work through our PSU activity, getting good experience with the national election campaign, and from our comrades, who are PSU organisers.
- We ran a very good campaign in the Brisbane city council elections.
- We've made some steps forward in our Asia-Pacific solidarity work, publishing *Suara Aksi*,[58] the continuing hounding of [Gareth] Evans, the Manila East Timor conference.[59]
- We've broadened out our women's liberation work, and initiated or got involved in a number of abortion campaigns.
- Resistance has had some good campaigns against cuts, the youth wage, on youth rights, for World Environment Day.

And besides all of these, there's also our biggest ongoing success, which we tend to take for granted – *Green Left Weekly*. It's been going for three and a half years now, and too often we're blasé about it, but a 32-page left weekly newspaper of such quality and such circulation and such broadness and such respect doesn't exist anywhere else in the world. Even parties a hundred, a thousand times bigger than us don't have such a paper! And its influence continues to grow.

So it's been a very good six months. If you posed the question, not just to our comrades but to other left observers, 'Has the DSP's political weight in Australian politics gone forward or back in this period?', the answer would definitely be forward. Our role has become distinguishably more important.

And there's a lot more potential: all the campaigns discussed over the last three days at the Resistance National Conference; the international work we discussed this morning; our PSU work; women's campaigns; stepped up solidarity activity; and all our basic party-building activities – recruitment, consolidation, *Green Left* sales and promotion and raising the DSP's profile in various ways. And even though there's been no broad upsurge, there are dozens of little campaigns that we've been involved in or could get involved in.

As for the weaknesses so far this year, I think we're all very well aware of them: sales; finances; recruitment, consolidation and education, i.e., the central, basic, party-building tasks, where we haven't fulfilled our potential or met our needs.

Comrades should recall the party-building report to the party conference in January, and the projections we set on our party-building tasks, especially the points about 'integrating all our work'. I won't repeat a lot of that, but it's worthwhile for comrades to reread it, and take this report in the context of all the party-building reports of the last few years.

Our continuing main concern

So our continuing main concern is to succeed in this push on our basic party-building tasks. We're very conscious of the particular difficulties facing revolutionary socialists in this period, the weakening of the workers' movement, the strength of the bourgeois ideological offensive and its control of the media, the demoralisation of many on the left around the world.

We're feeling the continuing impact of the collapse of the Soviet Union and the demoralisation even among some comrades and people in our periphery about the prospects for socialism in the near future. There has been a drifting of some comrades. Sometimes it's been a function of graduating from Resistance, or of reaching 30, or of reaching 40. There's also been the impact of the difficult economic situation and capitalist austerity, and the feelings of insecurity about jobs, their future. Being a revolutionary today is 'tougher', it seems. But of course this is very subjective, and very relative. You only have to consider the conditions of life for revolutionaries in the Third World, for example.

The first half of this year has been a contradictory period also in the sense that we didn't allow for the impact of some of our successes on our basic party-building tasks.

For example, the very successful IGL Conference made us a lot of gains, but it was also a lot of effort. It took place very close to the party's national conference, which made it harder. There was that double financial burden on comrades, and the effort of the IGL Conference disrupted sales and fundraising.

There's also the example of the big success Resistance had with its O Week recruits. Resistance cadre had to focus on integrating as many new members as possible, educating them and providing political leadership. In some branches *Green Left* sales probably suffered as a result, although the longer term impact should be different.

Thus it's been a very busy six months for us, with more opportunities than we can properly take advantage of. So do we cut back on some things? This would be hard. For example, if we lower our sales goals, it means more pressure on fundraising; if we schedule fewer fund drive functions, it means more sales are needed; if we do less recruiting work, it means long term problems for sales and finances; if we cut back on our outreach and interventions, it's harder to build the party and train new cadres.

There will be some areas we can trim. We won't be able to finance as many international trips as we'd like, even though now, with *Links,* it's an ideal time. Perhaps we won't be able to print as many copies of *Solidarity* for free handouts as we'd like. Perhaps we won't be able to run in all the election campaigns we'd like to run in. And we're going to have to prioritise political functions that make us money, rather than costing us. But throughout our political work in the next few months, we have to reaffirm and weave in our push on the basic party-building tasks. The main task is developing cadres, recruiting, educating and consolidating new forces for the party. We know it's possible to recruit people at the moment, in fact we know it's easy. Doing it is another thing, however: giving the necessary attention to recruiting.

But the next stage – consolidation and training – is even more important. A big weakness we've been conscious of for some time, and it's getting more acute as our political responsibilities increase, is the lack of skills, the lack of confidence to lead by our new and middle layer members.

In that sense, the next six months are a period of consolidation. But that doesn't mean we intend to be inward looking; we won't retreat into our shell, sect-like.

We also want to continue to reach out, to maintain our areas of political interventions, to look for any new allies in the struggle, and for all comrades to have a well-rounded political life.

Doing both

Can we do both? Can we do the reach-out work and the cadre building at the same time? Yes! It's what we're trying to do on many levels, the international political level, the level of Australian politics, the level of day-to-day work.

On the international level, it's clear. Firstly, the task of regroupment, uniting, reaching out and sweeping aside the remnants of sectarianism from the workers' movement. And secondly, presenting and defending principled socialist politics, engaging in discussions and presenting the fundamental positions of socialism.

Both tasks are desperately needed today, and the conditions are ripe for a renewal that includes both a regroupment and a reaffirmation. Just an ecumenical sentiment for unity is not enough. And just having the right line is not enough.

The collapse of Stalinism, the final outcome of the disaster in the Soviet Union, has had a positive outcome, the breaking of a political logjam, opening up the possibilities for discussion, for regroupment, for lowering sectarian barriers.

We're doing this very well, with the possibility of having an impact. *Links* is a most impressive instrument for doing exactly this.

On the level of Australian politics, this dual perspective is what we've been doing very consciously since the early '80s. In the '90s we've put the emphasis on reaffirming our Leninist perspectives for Australia, and concentrating on party building. But we're still very conscious of trying to reach out and draw around us broader forces and also maintain the gains of the broad, non-sectarian politics, although the prospects for alliances or regroupments are a lot smaller in this period.

In our basic party-building tasks, we can see many instances of this dual approach in practice. For example, we need to educate our new comrades in our revolutionary politics and in our high standards of activity and commitment, but at the same time we have to do our best to retain the older generation of comrades who might have lowered their activity, not drive them out because they're not matching the activity of the youth.

On all levels, this dual need is accentuated by the nature of the period, a period of difficulties and defeats, but also a period of renewal and regroupment. In a more revolutionary period the line of march is much straighter.

Compare the practice of the sects, who often seem to be stuck in a time warp. For them, it's always only the first aspect that they look at: 'Lenin laid down such and such conditions for admission to the Third International ...'. 'You can never ally or unite with people you don't agree with, or even be polite to them.' It's always very simple, and of course not successful in actually developing revolutionary Marxist cadres. Growth's not a worry. In difficult periods, it's just 'Circle the wagons', 'Our day will come'.

But we know we have to do both the reach-out and the cadre building. This is at the heart of the central party-building problem for us in this period: educating and training the new generation of socialist activists.

We've noted frequently the cadre 'scissors' problem – the fact that we have a thin layer of experienced comrades, and a majority of new, mostly younger, comrades. The thin layer has been educated, and to an extent steeled, by valuable experiences over the years, and the experience of the party is vested in them. Our task is to close the gap, have the new generation and future new members of the party link up with that tradition. It's a process of reaffirming our strategic perspective of building a Leninist party. If we departed from that perspective, we'd lose all the gains we've made.

Party conference

Up to now we had not projected a decision-making conference for January next year, only an educational conference, but we now want to change that and call the 16th National Conference of the DSP. There are quite a few reasons why we think this would be useful and necessary.

The main motivation relates to the need to consolidate and integrate the new generation of party members. It's important that the new generation is reinforced in their commitment to building the party, that they grasp the responsibility for actively leading the party. A decision-making conference that involves the whole membership in discussing out the political situation and our tasks would meet this need much better than a relatively passive educational conference, with just the National Executive and the National Committee discussing the perspectives and presenting them as talks.

Some new party members recruited from Resistance still don't think of themselves as party activists, even when playing leading roles in the branch, on party branch executives or heading up areas of party work. The party to them is still just the party members not assigned to Resistance. There's frequently a feeling that it's just the responsibility of the non-Resistance party comrades to do the recruiting to the party, rather than this being the central responsibility of party members working in Resistance, who are in day-to-day contact with the new potential party members in Resistance. This thinking can get reinforced by the artificial division we have in tabulating *Green Left Weekly* sales – 'party sales/Resistance sales' – when most of those Resistance sales are by party members assigned to Resistance. We have to continue encouraging, forcing, these younger party leaders to take full responsibility for the work of the party. That's the only way to learn thoroughly, to go the whole way.

A party conference will be the best way to speed up the integration of the newer party members who are active in Resistance, to get them to think of themselves first and foremost as party activists, having to discuss and decide what the party's tasks and perspectives will be.

Secondly, we feel there's a real need for a discussion on a range of questions in the party, especially many of the international issues, such as the new situation in South Africa, debates in the FSLN and FMLN, the Palestinian struggle, the whole perspectives for the socialist movement in the post-USSR world. In fact, this discussion is already taking place in the party, at branch meetings, forums, informally at dinner tables and down at the pub. We're being driven to a discussion by real developments. It's best for us to formalise and democratise it, and generalise it across the country so the whole membership participates on an equal footing. Also, there's possibly a lack of clarity on our party-building perspectives, for example relating to our failure to grow much in this recruiting campaign, or the central role of *Green Left Weekly.*

Leaving it for another year would run the risk of greater levels of confusion. It's best to have a democratic discussion, with the whole party involved, and thus to politically homogenise the party, rather than a long, permanent discussion without the clear focus of a decision-making conference.

Thirdly, a party conference this January is more likely to fit in with the schedule for our reach-out needs. It's hard to get large numbers of non-members to a live-in conference at Hawkesbury. The Hawkesbury conferences are really best for our membership and close contacts. And we want to leave open the option of a large, broad conference sometime in 1995 or perhaps 1996, that serves our educational needs, our reach-out needs, perhaps even our alliance-building needs. An educational conference in January would cut across that a bit.

A decision-making conference would be a 'tighter' conference; that is, it would focus on decision making and consolidating our newer members, and not try to get a lot of non-members to it. We'll still have a range of educational talks and classes at the conference, as we did at the last two party conferences. And we'll still aim to get a range of international guests, many of whom would be more likely to come and benefit from a full conference than just an educational conference. For example, it would be good to have a central leader of the Manila-Rizal CPP attend.

We'll prepare the conference fully from the October National Committee plenum, opening the oral discussion then. We propose to open the written pre-conference discussion on 1 August.

We don't think we need a major new resolution on the political situation – our resolution from the 15th National Conference [January 1994] will not be fundamentally outdated. But we will need to make more precise our Australian political perspectives, especially our election tactics. The conference could help launch a range of election campaigns that we could be involved in next year.

In the pre-conference discussion bulletin, we could print the Democratic Socialist Electoral League policy statements and invite DSP members to make suggestions as to how these statements could be improved, updated etc.

In the report on the party program adopted by the party conference in January, we projected drafting a new resolution on the struggle for gay and lesbian rights, opening a special written discussion on the draft leading up to the October NC plenum. The National Executive simply hasn't had time to do this. Instead, we propose to prepare a draft resolution on the gay and lesbian rights struggle for discussion by the October NC plenum and for presentation for a vote at the party conference in January.

We also propose that the NE prepare a revised draft of our resolution on 'Socialism and Human Survival' for a vote at the party conference. The existing document, which was adopted by the party's 13th National Conference in January 1990, is out of print, and could do with some additions and updating – for example, the changed nature of the nuclear threat with the collapse of the Soviet Union, the UNCED conference,[60] more on the environment movement itself and its political reflection in the various Green parties, the potential they had, and the reality they exhibit.

Discussion of the international questions would be a major aspect of the conference. Another agenda item could be the expansion of our international solidarity work, especially Asia-Pacific solidarity. It could also be used to give a further push to our union work and improve our industrial implantation.

The youth work report could be less a conjunctural report and more a general report on the present situation with the youth radicalisation, the role of a youth organisation, party-youth relations etc. This could be the basis of a future *Links* article. Other parties could benefit from our experience on this.

There are also some changes to our constitution that we'll probably want to make. One amendment foreshadowed in the constitution report adopted by the last party conference was the proposal for limiting submissions to the nominations commission[61] to elected branch delegates and consultative delegates. Another that the NE wants to foreshadow is removal of paragraph 3 in Article 6 requiring members to attend at least two branch meetings within a three-month period and at least three branch meetings within a six-month period. With most branches having a fortnightly instead of the previous monthly meeting schedule, this provision no longer provides an adequate standard of the minimum requirements for party activity. To tighten it up, for example by setting something like at least four branch meetings within a three-month period, would begin to push us in the direction of an administrative approach to developing comrades' party activity. Our tradition has always been to set minimum constitutional requirements for activity, and to rely on political education and motivation to get comrades to be as active as they are able. Although we obviously still want to encourage attendance at every branch meeting, we do not think that making this a rule will help us attain that norm.

Finally, we'll benefit from the election of a new National Committee. The transition in leadership in the recent period, with more younger comrades taking responsibility for leading the party, needs to be reflected in the composition of the National Committee.

Recruiting

Our main goal this year was to grow and consolidate and educate new members, so we set a recruiting campaign. We had very ambitious goals. How have we fared? Not as well as we would have hoped, I'm afraid, although we certainly have made some gains. Comrades can see the results from the charts being circulated.

An important point to note, however, is that the bulk of the lapsings were provisional members, so it is not as though we suffered a serious decline in the level of experienced comrades in the party as a whole. Certainly it's inevitable that we will have a high turnover of provisional members; that's what the category is designed for, a testing period. But we certainly need to find ways to improve our integration, consolidation and education of provisional members. We should also remember that, compared with the rest of the left, here and overseas, we're not doing too badly, to actually grow and continually renew our party, keeping its average age in the mid-20s.

The figures on where the recruits this year came from are very interesting. The largest group was campus students. We would have expected that, but 40% is a large proportion. The next largest came from reading *Green Left Weekly* in one way or another, 21%. Then came solidarity work, 15%, half from Asia-Pacific solidarity and half from Latin American solidarity. These figures confirm the relevance of the priorities we've set. The reports from branches also confirm the absolute necessity of immediate follow up of clip-offs that come in – invite them for a coffee and chat the same day.

To get that number of provisional members in the first half of the year is not bad, and I think we should be able to recruit a larger number in the second half. A number of branches have already indicated there are people about to join. Many other branches also have quite a few potential members around them. So it should be realistic to expect that we'll make about two-thirds of our initial target.

Consolidation

However, the really important task for the next six months is the consolidation of our current provisional members into full members of the party, and of our newer members into active cadres who are taking responsibility in the party.

But there's another important task for us – retaining the longer term comrades. How do we reconcile setting ambitious norms of activity to develop cadres, and retaining comrades who are stepping back for a while?

It's a fact of life that some comrades are stepping back. We haven't done anything wrong in relation to these comrades and certainly we need this layer, their education, their experience. They will revive in an upturn; some are even getting more active now. It's better for them to be in the party than out, so branches should check that they're not too harsh with comrades still in political agreement with us.

Will it lower our norms, keeping the less active comrades as members, and make it harder to train new comrades, and instil in them real revolutionary commitment? Avoiding that is our big task. I think it can be reconciled, I think we can do both. It will require skill on our part, tact, tolerance. But let's do our best to retain the experienced comrades, find ways to give them new inspiration and challenges.

We won't be a completely homogeneous party in terms of levels of activity. We never have been. But we'll be stronger. And at this stage the democratic framework of the party is not really threatened, that is, the democracy we guarantee by being a party of activists. Let's praise the enthusiastic activist, but also find ways to appreciate the longer term comrades who are less active and the contributions they have made in the past and can still make now. We need to find satisfying political tasks for them – there's lots to do.

Nevertheless, our main task is still to retain and educate and integrate the youth. This is the main source of our recruits, and will be the bulk of new members in the immediate future. So what are the main points to consider as we tackle this task of consolidation?

1. *Politics.* It's hard politics, especially if you're involved in a mass struggle, or a political fight, that really educates. Comrades need that political involvement and engagement.

2. *A working class orientation.* Getting jobs, doing union work is essential to the consolidation of party cadres. Comrades have to understand the concept that their career is as a working-class revolutionary.

3. *An internationalist outlook.* Comrades need to develop a world view that sees it as one struggle. Our party as a whole and individual members benefit from contact with, and by giving help to, other struggles.

4. *A historical perspective.* Comrades need not only an understanding of past struggles, but a feeling for the dynamics of revolutionary change, and an ability to see human history as very limited and brief up to now, and thus have an inkling of the possibilities of the future.

5. *Education in Marxist theory.* Without a grasp of the basic theoretical ideas of our movement, and ongoing attention to deepening their understanding of Marxist theory, comrades will eventually lose their revolutionary perspective. But such study can't be undertaken in a vacuum, in the abstract. It has to relate to today's concerns and struggles.

6. *Activity.* We need to give new members both satisfying political tasks and concrete tasks where they can see the results of their activity.

7. *Loyalty and identification.* Comrades need to fully

understand the essential role of the revolutionary party, and of our specific party-building project. Identification can be helped by a high party profile.

8. *A supportive social milieu.* The party's a framework within which comrades will be struggling side by side. It's primarily political, but a friendly, supportive milieu, a lively party cultural and social life, tied and subordinated to our political work, helps integration and cohesion, helps comrades stay in it for the long haul.

And we should remember also that there are extra considerations, extra difficulties, for those members joining the party directly, not coming through Resistance.

Education

Thorough education in Marxist theory and politics, in the history of the working-class movement, is essential if we're to properly integrate new comrades and give them the outlook to keep going. It's actually an ongoing need for all of us.

Our education needs to be both formal – classes, talks, organised reading – and informal – talking politics at all opportunities, one-to-one discussions, and political education in a social or cultural framework too.

One consequence of the political period we're in at the moment, with its limited mass campaigns and no major upsurges, is that the practical link is not so easy to make with comrades. So in this period, how do we get engagement, encourage commitment? One partial answer is to encourage polemics, counter-positions, debates. The international discussions that are taking place will be useful in this regard.

Comrades need to become totally familiar with the day-to-day details of Australian politics. They need to read the papers.

Green Left Weekly, yes, that's first and essential, but comrades have to read the capitalist press too; they have to know what the enemy is saying. They have to learn how to read them, how to interpret them, ignoring the bullshit and sycophantic drivel. Even marking, clipping the papers. This is a task for each branch, for the *Green Left* copy committee, but all comrades should be conscious of this. We should make sure comrades know the positions of other parties on issues and are able to counterpose our policies and respond confidently to questions from contacts, *Green Left* buyers, radio or TV interviewers.

We have to develop our own political culture, a 'counter-culture' that actively engages the ruling class culture, knows how to answer it, combat it, not just ignore it because we know it's rubbish.

We now have a very comprehensive series of classes available, and branches should at the very least be using the Introduction to Socialism and Introduction to Marxism series. We need feedback from National Committee members on how the ITS and ITM series have been going. Let the National Office know of any suggestions for improvement.

From now until the October National Committee, when oral pre-conference discussion will be opened, branches should consider reinstituting the activist classes if they're not already doing them. There's also the possibility for camps and weekend seminars in this period.

Once again we want to reaffirm the usefulness of our full-time party school. We'll try to have more of the three-week schools without the building, but it's our goal to re-establish a permanent school with our own building.

But to really ensure its return, we need to be successful with the next stage of cadre building and consolidation. And we need success on our finance campaigns.

Reach-out

Green Left Weekly is our main weapon, the scaffolding for our political work, and we need to make full use of it, as the Resistance conference emphasised time and again. Thus *Green Left* circulation and promotion should be a central part of any party-building discussion.

We reach more people with *Green Left* each week than with anything else we do. We reach our own members and periphery of course, but also other committed left activists, people who are starting to radicalise, and hundreds and thousands of people who are totally new to left ideas.

So comrades shouldn't just regard *Green Left* as 'sales'. It's much more than that. It's our main political weapon, and our main way to reach out.

Although we didn't succeed in making our target of 4,000 street sales during our sales campaign, we did make significant gains. Our national sales average during the campaign was 700 papers more than before the campaign. Hours were significantly up in Brisbane, Hobart, Newcastle and Sydney.

There are a couple of interesting statistics that indicate the areas where we can hope to make a big difference in future.

Firstly, the sales rate is clearly lowered by inexperienced sellers. The non-party Resistance rate is two papers an hour less than the rate of party comrades. We should be able to remedy this by training in sales techniques, by help from the more experienced, skilful sellers, by political education that increases the confidence of newer comrades.

Secondly, in 1993 Resistance members sold 63% of the total on average, while in 1994 so far they've only been selling 45% of the total. Yet Resistance is stronger, with many excellent new members, and a big periphery. There's no reason this shouldn't be turned around as well, with more Resistance sellers, putting in longer stints each week.

The Resistance conference addressed this problem, and the Thursday sales stump, the sales rally, and the emphasis on *Green Left* during the conference should be a good start to a campaign to change this. Resistance really has to adopt *Green Left* as its own paper, to campaign with it, have more Resistance articles in it, bigger ads for Resistance, have more Resistance comrades on staff in future too.

We started to improve our suburban sales with the successful special day in the suburbs. We should be targeting Sunday as well as Saturday for sales in the suburbs, so that a meeting or demo on Saturday won't disrupt sales. There are many selling opportunities – markets, shopping centres, cinemas. We'll possibly schedule other special days this year.

Comrades should also pay attention during campus breaks to sales outside city cinemas, to make up for the loss of campus sales. With high schools usually on holiday at the same time, these spots have all-day potential, and good rates are possible.

And let's remember the possibilities from country trips. Hobart's recent experience reminds us what can be done – in Launceston two comrades from Hobart sold 60 papers in a day; in Burnie, one comrade sold 25 papers during a three-day trip.

And also the importance of stalls, stumps, collective selling and training, and the need for comrades to integrate other party tasks into selling *Green Left* – selling *Links,* selling *Green Left* subs, distributing leaflets for our functions, making contacts, getting addresses.

For the next stages of our sales drive, we want to step up the promotion of *Green Left,* with a new poster, stickers and more exchange ads. At some stage we'll possibly organise a big national dramatisation, a sort of relaunch of the paper.

But to succeed in our sales goals, our sales needs, the party and Resistance leaderships will have to set the example. That means comrades on this National Committee, our organisers, our full-time voluntary staff.

From this National Committee we will be organising a special push on subscriptions. Again, we know what needs to be done. Where branches do the basics, they get excellent results, whether it's selling new subs or organising renewals. Some branches and some comrades might feel that they can't do everything at once, so something has to slip, and often that's sub selling.

But the important thing is to make sure that selling of subscriptions is totally integrated into *Green Left* sales. That way it won't require extra hours – you're going to be selling *Green Left* anyway, why not ask every buyer about a sub, and about *Links* also? Similarly on phone renewals, tell them about the next forum or *Green Left* fundraiser at the same time – it will save money on phone calls too. We should be using our subscription lists and expiry lists as a way to network.

Links

Now that the second issue of *Links* is out, we should be using it properly. It's an important tool for educating our comrades, drawing them in to be part of the international debate on perspectives for socialist renewal.

It's a very prestigious magazine, and can help us win people to the socialist movement, so let's not waste it. We need to spread it far and wide to help us get our money back anyway. It should be part of every *Green Left* sales kit, every stall, given a high profile in our bookshops, reviewed in local or campus papers. All vaguely progressive or liberal bookshops should be asked to stock it, and for shops that haven't taken the first issue, we can take along both issues, now that it's established.

Party profile

We intend to continue and expand the projections we made at the January party conference to raise the party profile. Raising our profile in *Green Left* (with the Democratic Socialist insert, for example), is one of the most important ways. Being more upfront and confident in our political interventions is obviously vital too. But we also need to be more conscious about the party's image, facilitating identification with the party through party symbols, a party image, our logo.

In the coming months we'll also maintain our ambitious publications program of pamphlets, recruiting leaflets and books.

Jim Percy's book of party-building speeches is just about ready to go to the printers. It will certainly be available by the October National Committee and the second Jim Percy memorial lectures.

Then in the last quarter of the year we should have Doug Lorimer's book on China and Maoism[62] out, ready for the party conference.

We should be making better use of our bookshops. It's an important way to raise our profile, it reaches out into the community to bring in contacts, and with better stock it can even be a modest source of income. Once the National Office finances are stabilised, we hope to be able to provide more stock centrally. But it is important to keep them open regularly, advertise the hours and stick to them. People do get pissed off if they come in and find our bookshops shut. We can make better use of our less active, or retired, or student comrades to staff the bookshops.

Geographical expansion

One reason we desperately need to train and consolidate more cadres quickly is the opportunities for expansion of the party. In Darwin we will have a functioning Resistance branch soon, but to get a party branch up and running we will really have to send them a couple more cadres, so put the word around: see if any comrades would be interested.

And some Sydney comrades are itching to get a western suburbs branch established. That's an encouraging sign, showing the enthusiasm amongst comrades, and where the party is at. But I'd just repeat what we said at the party conference: we'll be able to make expansions like that when we achieve some of the party-building goals we set, especially on recruiting and consolidating and training more cadres.

Financial resources

A number of the contributions at the Resistance conference demonstrated clear understanding of the importance of finances for the revolutionary movement. It's a question of what needs to be done, and what we need in order to do it, financing the party, financing our interventions, a question of the necessary resources. It works on several levels – raising the resources themselves, and cadre building through raising financial consciousness.

We began the year with a very large deficit, and by June it had grown by 50%. If this is left unchecked and left to grow at this rate, it would be unmanageable and would cause real financial difficulty.

Our financial performance in the first half of the year was not good. Our fund drive at the end of June was around $16,000 behind target, despite real improvements over May and June. The pledge component had more than $30,000 of the more than $50,000 pledged still outstanding. And the events component is way down also, since branches have heavily weighted fund drive events towards the second half of the year, with few events before the IGL Conference. Comrades can see from the graph that we're behind where we were this time last year, with a much lower target last year. The curve started to rise a bit in May and June, but it needs to be sharper. We need to step up the payment of pledges and devote sufficient branch resources to fundraising events.

The sales debt from branches to the National Office has increased in 1994. The total income received from *Green Left* sales has been exactly the same as for this period last year, but remember that last year the price was still $1 until April, so sales are down this year. Like the fund drive, sales income improved in May-June during the sales campaign, but we can't afford to drop back again. A key element in our finance campaign for the second half of the year will be stabilising sales income – bundles of at least 4,000 are the bottom line financially.

Likewise our sustainer payments to the National Office have been down this year, which reflects the ongoing fragility of the pledge base and branch budgets. We have succeeded in raising our national pledge base, with almost all branches making a little progress and Sydney quite a jump. But many branches are still failing to balance their budgets. The result is unpaid sustainer to the National Office.

The key to turning around this situation is further increasing our national pledge base. This can be achieved by, firstly, the integration of newer members into the party's financial norms, and, secondly, the success of the jobs campaign. For example, if 30 unemployed comrades found work, increasing our pledge base by an average $40 per week, we'd get a $1,200 per week increase in our national pledge base and have a chance of meeting our national needs.

It's important that branch executives assign someone to talk thoroughly to new provisional members about our financial system and structure, why the party needs the money, why high financial consciousness is important. This campaign could benefit from visible charts in branches of comrades' pledges, just as we do, or should be doing, with sales, and a chart on the progress of the pledge campaign.

As a result of these shortfalls – bundle debts from lower sales, sustainer debts from insufficient branch pledge base and other debts – there's been a large increase in branch debt to the National Office.

The first quarter was very difficult financially, with the run up to IGL and the dislocation that followed. In May and June there was considerable improvement, and further consolidation is needed in the next six months. Continuing the consciousness of the sales campaign, a continuing push on pledges and the jobs campaign have the potential to get us there.

We need to reach our higher fund drive target of $125,000 if we're to cover our deficit and enable us to carry out the urgently needed (really emergency) maintenance work on the National Office building. And in both the National Office and branches, we need new technology to make our work more productive.

Workplace implantation

One of the party's biggest failings at the moment is the weakness of our base in the unions, and the limited understanding and experience in this area of our new generation of cadres.

This weakness has even been shown up by the opening with PSU work. This was our strongest implantation, and even here we were very weak. This is a big drift from our overwhelming concentration following our turn to industry 15 years ago. We spent that accumulated capital, in exploring possible regroupments, in surviving, and now we need to replenish it.

We need a 'mini-turn' to increase our implantation in the labour movement. The main reason for it is for the education and training of our cadres, and the future political health of the party. It's not for particular conjunctural needs, although having a stronger PSU fraction and other fractions would be very useful. We're not expecting an upsurge in the working class and the unions just around the corner, which was one of the false motivations of the turn to industry in the late '70s.

But without turning this situation around, we will miseducate the new generation. They won't understand our project, they won't last. This is a long-term basic orientation of the party.

Certainly we still expect to get most of our new recruits from campus, and we'll continue with this orientation, even be more scientific with it. We know what can be done, and are learning to do it better. So we shouldn't expect a lot in the way of recruits from a stepped-up implantation, although Canberra is having some results with their PSU work. It should be seen as the next step after being integrated in the party, a logical place for a Marxist to be, with the working class.

So that's a proposal for this National Committee, that we carry out a concerted and systematic drive to increase the number of comrades with jobs in areas that can enable us to step up our union work. The immediate goal is to get our unemployed comrades into jobs. A by-product of this project is that it will be good for them financially, and good for the party financially. We know how to do it, through a well-organised jobs committee; the experience from the turn to industry is still there, and we can make use of the experience of the longer term comrades who undertook the turn to industry.

To start with, we'll just be looking for any jobs, wherever possible. Of course, comrades should be seeking employment in areas that can help us strengthen our existing trade union work. But this shouldn't be used as an excuse to ignore any other employment opportunities. The priority for unemployed comrades is simply to get a job. That's a good goal for the end of the year: full employment.

After getting any job for our unemployed comrades, the next

goal is for branches to help comrades change from politically barren workplaces to better, more politically interesting, jobs. This will be an ongoing task.

We also need to stabilise the functioning of our trade union fractions. Until we get more comrades into jobs, this will be very difficult in a whole number of branches. And we need to step up our education in our revolutionary strategy and tactics in the unions and also the history of the Australian labour movement. The projections we made about education and training in the report on our trade union work adopted by the last party conference are conditional upon improving our implantation in the workforce.

The party conference next January will be able to give a push to our mini-turn. We hope to have made good progress before the end of the year, especially in getting our currently unemployed comrades jobs, but this will still be an important orientation next year.

Political perspectives

The analysis of Australian society and our political perspectives that we adopted at our 15th National Conference [January 1994] are still fundamentally valid. Pat Brewer's recent National Executive report that was circulated brings that analysis up to date.

The main development exciting the bourgeois media, the [Alexander] Downer-[Peter] Costello change in the Liberal leadership, doesn't mean any real change in the situation. On real policies, there's little difference between the lot of them still.

We can contrast this analysis with that of other left tendencies – the Labor 'left', the ex-CPA, SPA, ISO, other sects. All of them have some remnant of illusions in Labor, and hope for a 'new right' Liberal Party to find some difference with Labor.

We need to accentuate our differences with their approach. It's not the case that because it's tough times for the workers' movement, therefore we need to unite with the ALP against the Libs. No, the ALP and the trade union bureaucrats are the cause of the problem – the capitalist class is the enemy, but Labor has been their agents very openly and successfully for the last 10 years.

We now have the chance to explore this connection better than ever before, and expose it. We can use our analysis to educate and consolidate our new comrades, our periphery, *Green Left* readers. This also ties in directly with much of the international debate on strategy for South Africa, the question of class-collaborationist accords between capitalist governments and the trade unions.

In exposing and countering the Labor Party and its hangers-on, we have to do all we can to establish and boost a counter-milieu and ideology and culture to the Laborist outlook. This outlook is prevalent among the traditional left milieu and the union movement, and obviously still dominant at the electoral level, but is not there among young people, and increasingly not there among activists.

So our independent socialist electoral campaigns are vital in this period for building an alternative, and important for educating and training our comrades. In practice we can get respectable results.

There's still some support for alternative/independent/ Green candidates, as the 24% in Tasmania and the 20% for the Green candidate in Coburg [Melbourne] indicated, although here we should also take into account the fact there was no Liberal candidate (indeed, I got more than 20% in a local council election in Glebe [Sydney] about 15 years ago when there was no Liberal candidate!).

The interesting statistic from the polls is the youth support for 'other parties' (not merely independents). And even the Sydney Greens got up to 35 people at their meeting for the Parramatta by-election.

The possibility of regroupment-type alliances is not on the horizon; that was the '80s, when we did our best, but the possible allies proved wanting. We're in a different period now, and there are no potential groups with which we could merge our forces.

So building alliances today is very much a party-building question, tactics for building the DSP as it is: how we get a mass platform. We retain our identity as a party. But we also retain our approach, our non-sectarian, outward-looking stance, ready for any opportunity that might arise, whether it's possible alliances on issues or local alliances.

We have some trump cards which we can always play, if we're thinking about a national campaign or conference that might try to put together an alliance:

1. Our national spread;
2. Our international links;
3. Our organisational ability, and experience with conferences.

A number of state elections will take place next year: in the ACT, in February probably; in NSW, in March; in Tasmania, and possibly elsewhere. We'll want to stand in at least some of these, and though the main responsibility will be on the branches, we'll want to coordinate our electoral work and literature from the National Office. It's clear that our main goal is raising the Democratic Socialist profile, and so we'll support DSEL candidates where we can. DSEL should try again for registration federally. DSEL could also be useful for involving our periphery and some ex-members.

Where we've been able to establish a good base in the community, such as in Brisbane, we get consistently good results – Susan Price's 8% and 9%. The comrades in Brisbane have a contact list of 200 for that electorate, and have built successful party events from the campaign. People there are beginning to see us as the alternative. Where we put the work into a particular electorate, we can often win as much support as the Greens.

Interventions

A feature of this period is that, with our bigger weight on the left, we're finding not only more openings for political work, but more expectations of us. We find we've got increasing responsibilities: campaigns and committees and actions needing our assistance.

We can make our life a bit easier and maximise the campaigns we can be involved in if we link them properly with our reach-out work – selling *Green Left,* advertising our activities, networking, getting contacts, recruiting. And also if we combine them with our whole party-building approach, intervene with a view to education, training and integration of new members.

Our fractions are essential in this regard, for training in a collective way. Fractions should be efficient, streamlined, not overloaded with tasks that should be done by branch meetings or other committees or classes, but organising our interventions and training to intervene.

There's a lot of variation from branch to branch as to which campaigns we can take up, and there should be flexibility. But there are certain priorities, such as our international solidarity work, at the moment concentrating on Asia-Pacific solidarity, and our women's liberation work. There should be an element of persistence and continuity in campaigns such as these in this period. That is, new campaigns won't necessarily be on new issues, but surges forward on issues that are already established.

International solidarity

Our Asia-Pacific solidarity work has gone well this year, and there's the need to do more. AKSI branches are functioning well in Sydney and Brisbane, with varied activity in other cities, and *Suara Aksi* is well received and paying its way.

We had been planning to get out a Philippines solidarity bulletin of some kind, but now think it would be more useful to publish a broader Asia-Pacific solidarity bulletin, with the early issues obviously having large amounts of material on the Philippines, but also covering Indonesia, East Timor, Bougainville and other news from Asia. It could be produced as a four-page insert in *Green Left* and called something like Asia-Pacific Networker or Asia-Pacific Campaigner. We won't project an organisation behind it, but will have it sponsored by ourselves and a few other supportive names in Australia, and significant figures in the region.

There are better possibilities for useful work in the quite healthy East Timor committees around the country, especially after the Manila conference, and with Max Lane one of the Australian coordinators of the Asia-Pacific Coalition on East Timor.

Our Central America solidarity work is picking up now, after the decline following the Nicaraguan election defeat. There are also a lot of opportunities for recruiting amongst Latin American exiles who have settled here, as the groups they set up here lose their cohesion or dissolve.

The Dulce Maria Pereira tour[63] was very successful in raising the party's prestige and raising CISLAC's profile. Nationally and in a number of branches, it has succeeded in effectively re-establishing CISLAC. The national CISLAC consultation will be in Melbourne, 10-11 September.

Women's liberation

Our assessment at our last party conference that there was the possibility of a bit of an upsurge in the women's movement has proved correct. Confirmation was provided during O Week, when more than 70% of our 1,200 new members joined to Resistance were women, and on some campuses this went up to 80-90%. All the major national events we've been involved in have been successful – Reclaim the Night last year, International Women's Day this year. We've gained many benefits from these events. They've been good training and political inspiration for our new young women members. They've been useful for networking with other activists in different movements. And they've been very useful in building our own events and enabling us to reach out with *Green Left* and other literature.

There appears to be real interest in some form of national abortion law repeal campaign. In nearly every state, there's some form of interest or an already existing broader coalition wanting to campaign on this.

The time we've spent exploring the women's student collectives has been instructive. Sometimes these have been dead ends, but sometimes we've been able to recruit. This NOWSA conference could be bigger than last year's. We'd want NOWSA to continue to be built, and in the coming year relate to the escalating attacks on student unionism. For that reason, we'll push that next year's conference be held in Melbourne.

We've been tossing around the possibility of a national conference on women's struggles. Such conferences have been very successful in the past. The South Australian women's liberation group has jumped in and called such a conference. It's a small group at the moment, but we have one comrade involved, and they're open to us, so we'll throw our weight behind it. They're planning to open it with Christabel Chamarette,[64] and finish with a demo. At the moment they're talking about 21-23 July, but it might be better pushed back just a bit.

The rest of the left

During the first half of this year, the rest of the left in Australia has probably declined even further.

The former CPAers are less and less likely to be able to reconstitute themselves into a group as time goes on, even with all the Search Foundation[65] cash. We should be conscious of trying to relate to and recruit any who still want to be active. Comrades know the story of the Brisbane group that organised the folk music fundraiser for *Green Left,* without knowing the DSP was behind it; they're friendly. In Adelaide, some ex-CPAers turned up to our May Day toast.

The SPA continues its slow decay. In Brisbane, to try to resolve their bitter factional situation, they've now disbanded their state committee, so that the branches just relate to their National Office, not to each other.

The old Stalinist left has moved into the Australia Cuba Friendship Societies, at least in Sydney and Melbourne.

The ISO, our only real rivals and the main competitor for the allegiance of radicalising young people, hasn't been doing so well this year, although they've still got a lot of students in Sydney, Melbourne and Canberra, and about forty members in the Public Sector Union. They've backed away from their madness of a 'pre-revolutionary situation' and if anything are more characterised now by an orientation to the ALP.

Leadership

We have built up a strong team in the national apparatus; it's probably larger than at any time in the past, and we have a large National Executive resident in Sydney. We know this strong national apparatus is needed, however, both for the particular tasks that have to be carried out, and because of the stage we're at in developing the party.

But we also need a strengthening of branch leaderships. We hope to be able to do that through training new comrades to take responsibility, to take on leadership positions and full-time assignments. We will need a range of transfers, with some of our more experienced comrades going from Sydney to strengthen Melbourne, for example.

This year we have a larger NE Standing Committee, and replaced the Secretariat with a number of working groups. The working groups have not worked well, however (although a lot of the work has got done). We're certainly in a transition stage, and in 1995 there's the possibility of some changes in our leadership structure, perhaps a smaller NE.

In the last year many comrades with assignments leading Resistance have stepped forward to take on responsibilities leading the party. This process will continue in the coming year, and that's an added reason for deciding to hold a party conference in January.

Conclusion

We're fortunate that the Resistance conference has already discussed many of the details of our party-building and Resistance-building work so far this year. So I'd urge comrades in the discussion to address the central problems we face, especially how to succeed in consolidating the new generation of cadres.

That's our key task, cadre building, without cutting back on our political activities and projections. We are going to do both. We have been an ambitious party in the past, and the responsibilities we face are greater than ever before. We're in a position to be able to take important steps forward in building a Leninist party in Australia; and also in a unique position to give some help in the development of Leninist parties in a number of other countries.

So our main party-building projections are:

- Recruit, consolidate, train and educate the next generation of cadres.
- Make our sales targets, and make the finance-campaign goals.
- Continue our political campaigns, integrated with our party-building and outreach tasks.
- Make a push to get all comrades jobs, a mini-turn to labour movement work.
- And bring it all together in a consolidating, educating, clarifying and unifying party conference in January.

6. THEORY, PRACTICE AND WHAT UNITES THEM

Report to the 16th National Conference 6 January 1995

The beginning differences in the Perth branch, referred to in the intro-duction to Chapter 5, came out into the open at the October meeting of the National Committee. There followed a wide-ranging written and oral discussion. At the National Conference in January 1995, the dele-gates overwhelmingly voted against the positions put forward by Steve Robson, and in favour of the line of this report, delivered by John Percy. While the minority position won very little support and had little im-pact after the conference, this report is important in showing the party's traditional attitude to internal debate: encouraging thorough discus-sion to attain maximum clarity on the differences, and not holding the minority's positions against them. Thus, the conference re-elected Robson to the National Committee, believing that it could benefit from the presentation of another view as new events arose. However, Robson resigned from the DSP shortly after the conclusion of the conference.

Comrades, we've just come through a challenge to the party, a discussion and a conference that make me even more confident about the party we have, the party we're building towards and the fundamental party-building perspectives we defend.

In my opinion it's been one of the best discussions in our history. We've printed 16 *Activists* containing: two draft resolutions; 15 NC reports or other party information; 70 pre-conference discussion items from more than 50 comrades; and 25 informational reprints.

But even at the same time as we've been having this very extensive and intensive discussion, our level of activity hasn't dropped off, and we've had a series of successes that are encouraging signs of the healthy state of the party.

So we've come to the end of a good year for us, and come to the end of the discussion – three months of oral discussion and nearly five months of written discussion, a discussion that was quite fundamental, and at times very heated in Perth branch.

Fundamental issues involved

Fundamental issues were involved, involving two different perspectives for our party. However, getting the underlying political differences out into the open proved hard. Often the challenge to the party's position was indirect, or on the organisational questions, or endless questions, or smokescreens. But by the end of the discussion it was quite clear.

It's not as though the issues were new. They're mostly the same issues raised by comrades who lost faith in our project and the need for commitment in the '80s and '90s; they also mirror the self-doubts and pessimism about their party that engulfed the CPA during its last few decades; and they're similar to issues raised in the socialist movement around the world in recent years also.

We've come out of the discussion stronger. We've lost some comrades, and will lose some others who are demoralised, but that's not a result of the discussion, but a result of the miseducation and mis-training that had already taken place.

In the end the alternative perspective amounted to only a very tiny minority, two votes in Perth branch, although there would have been other supporters of this view who didn't turn up to vote.

The overwhelming majority of the party has reaffirmed its confidence in our perspectives. But the importance of the alternative current goes beyond its numerical size. This debate is important, and clarity on the issues is vital for us, because:

1. This alternative perspective *does* reflect trends outside the party, the viewpoints of individual activists, some not-so-activist, permanent non-party types, 'independents' (independent of left parties, but not independent of ruling class influences).

2. The issues raised repeat some of the refrains of opposition viewpoints in discussions in the party in the '90s (and the '80s). Even some of the specific proposals have been resurrected from earlier discussions.

3. The complaints and charges against the party, or against the party leadership or 'regime', are common to a number of comrades who've drifted out of the party in recent years. Most often these differences were raised only after they'd dropped out of activity or left the party. There are even social networks of some of our former members, mostly who are not very political or not very active, but who raise some of these complaints, and Comrade [Steve] Robson even referred to this in the discussion.

4. And finally, there's quite a lot of confusion on many of these same questions internationally. Many misconceptions and wrong conclusions have been drawn from the experience of Stalinism by the socialist movement around the world, and following the col-

lapse of the Soviet Union, there's been further pressure to equate Leninism with Stalinism, and to reject the whole Bolshevik experience.

Different perspectives

So, in spite of the limitations of the discussion, and although the alternative current ended up being quite small, more than enough was stated and written for us to be clear about the alternative perspectives involved. And Comrade Robson has conceded that two very different perspectives have developed, two different political lines are involved.

The analysis made in the report I presented on behalf of the National Executive to the National Committee plenum last October, and adopted by the NC, made a number of characterisations of the position he put forward, and where they headed. Three months ago we summarised Comrade Robson's alternative perspective in the following seven points:

- He was against our concept of team leadership, downgrading the role of executive bodies.
- He was for a party with lower membership norms and levels of activity.
- He was for reduced emphasis on *Green Left Weekly*.
- He was against our concept of norms as 'moralism'.
- He was against the idea that we have organisational principles, and rejected our traditions on this.
- He had a different reading of our experiences in the '80s and a different analysis of the period.
- In the end it amounted to a different concept of cadre and a cadre party.

In the course of the written and oral discussion, these positions have been repeated and reaffirmed, but some new differences have been added. Specifically:

- Comrade Robson has indicated different perspectives on Australian politics.
- He advocates opening up the party to 'campaign activists'.
- He advocates making it possible for people with different political perspectives to join.
- He thinks we have 'an apparatus too large for the size of the party today'.
- He argues that the 'party is in a crisis', that it's 'stagnating'.
- A number of further claims have been made about the tone of the discussion and the democratic functioning of the party.

We should also put into the picture the positions of Comrade [Michael] Boswell, who proposed the alternative platform, made a contribution to the pre-conference discussion, but didn't turn up at the Perth branch meeting for the election of delegates and hasn't come to the conference. Some of his views in motivating this alternative platform were:

- 'Allusions to history like that of the Russian Social Democratic [Labour] Party ... serve no useful function.'
- 'We have no party tradition', and anyway it should be ignored because it 'alienates novices from full participation in the party'.
- 'It seems that the only purpose of membership is to support a party bureaucracy overstretching its human and financial resources.'
- The financial contributions that the majority of comrades make are more onerous than the church taxes of the Middle Ages.
- He argues against the 100 percenters; he even argues against people being 1 percenters.
- We 'need to develop a need for a loyal opposition in the party'.
- There's 'a subconscious fear of open debate in the party about the party'. There's only 'a small window of time' for debate 'held at best every two years'.

- He approvingly quotes the ex-Stalinist Katharine Susannah Prichard, 'Don't sacrifice your life to work and ideals'.

This report rejects the line of Comrade Steve Robson's October NC counter-report, his pre-conference discussion contributions, his actions and proposals. It also rejects the line and the specific charges of Comrade Michael Boswell's contribution.

But besides rejecting that alternative line, the report clearly reaffirms our Leninist strategy of party building, the fundamental political perspective we've had throughout our history.

The 'turn' in the '90s

We've learnt from our experiences over the years, and understood the nuances better each year. But there is a basic perspective we've adhered to since the founding of our party twenty-three years ago. So when we talk about 'our turn to basic party-building tasks' in the 1990s, we always have to bear this in mind. It wasn't a turn to party building in the '90s, but a 're-cadreisation', or in Comrade Jim Percy's words, 'getting back to the sort of cadre party we were in the '70s'. And we also need to clear up some myths about the '80s.

We made a turn in 1982 to open up the party, putting a lot of hopes in the possibilities of a working-class upsurge, and experimented with some of our organisational forms. A few years later we ended that period of experimentation, reassessed things, realised we'd overestimated the possibility of an upsurge of labour radicalism, underestimated the hold of the trade union bureaucracy and the ALP parliamentary careerists over the labour movement. We reinstituted weekly branch meetings, a fixed dues system and a bigger emphasis on building Resistance.

In 1986, however, we turned our attention away from directly building our own party towards regrouping with other organised left forces.

The tactics we were contemplating in 1986-87 – preparing for an entry into the CPA, really, like the US Trotskyists' entry into the Socialist Party in the '30s – have been blurred, extended, mythologised, and some comrades today try to draw totally false lessons from that experience.

We weren't giving up our perspective of building a revolutionary party, but contemplating a possible detour that would get us there quicker. This was made abundantly clear in Jim [Percy]'s report on 'Building the Revolutionary Party' adopted by the October 1987 NC meeting.

Jim pointed out that this particular party-building tactic was not a break with our past strategy, but a way of doing it, and indicated we were still in the framework of a propaganda group. The problem was that the words 'new party' seemed to imply something drastically new, and this infected our comrades as well as the petty-bourgeois leftist milieu. The biggest political error we could make, he said, was not understanding that without the *old* party there won't be a new party. We weren't dissolving our tendency, and could be in a minority in the new party.

For example, in his report to the October 1989 NC meeting, Jim stressed that we'd had a successful year because we asserted the fundamentals, we 'continued to build a vanguard party'. He pointed out we'd experimented with loosening up, and rapidly ran into a crisis. If we hadn't had the party, we wouldn't have been able to take advantage of the different openings, he said. How to do party building today is through, firstly, continuing the organisational form, concentrating on the basic party-building tasks, and. secondly, the regroupment process.

But at our June 1990 NC plenum (where we adopted the perspective for *Green Left Weekly*), and even more so at our April 1991 NC meeting, we stated that what was required was a reorientation, what amounted to a 'turn'. The fact that we'd started *Green Left Weekly* in February 1991 meant that we actually had the means to *implement* such a perspective, at the same time as continuing to reach out, build a bigger periphery, do any regroupment that was possible, through the paper.

It was hard enough defending our revolutionary perspective in the '80s, without any breakthroughs, with the dead hand of Laborism doing its work for the ruling class. We, as well as the rest of the left, suffered attrition, comrades dropping away, finding the going too tough. And the effects *have* been felt in our party, on the morale of the party, and more comrades dropping away. But just think what we have been able to achieve in that period – difficult as it was – and look at where the rest of the left is, internationally and in Australia.

We've been able to continue to win new youth to our revolutionary perspective, replenish our ranks, even grow a little. We've built *Green Left Weekly, Links, Solidarity;* organised the Socialist Scholars and International Green Left Conferences; developed new programmatic documents for the party; led and intervened in campaigns on a broad range of issues; and continued to reach out, continued our openness, and not withdrawn, sect-like, in difficult times.

But it's all been dependent on our fundamental strategy: building a revolutionary party, and beginning to build it now, along Leninist lines.

We made an adjustment for our false expectation of a big working-class upsurge in 1983-84, and we made an adjustment for our manoeuvre with the CPA during the New Left Party process.

And there was a slippage on our norms and functioning partly due to those adjustments, but also from the pressure as we continued to swim against the stream throughout the '80s and into the '90s.

So there's a fundamental continuity between the '80s and '90s too. We're sticking to our political positions, our party-building perspectives; it's Comrade Robson who wants to change.

The first signs of a different line from Comrade Robson were the questioning of the concept of norms, which he raised at the NC meeting last July. Then in Perth branch his different conceptions were concretised in the form of some actions he took as branch secretary. There was a further elaboration and clarification of his positions before the October NC plenum, in his counter-report at the NC meeting itself, and in the written and oral pre-conference discussion since.

'Opening up the party'

Comrade Robson's oral and written discussion contributions involved many questionings, niggles, attacks on our organisational principles, traditions, tone, 'hardness', language etc. But the major change proposed, the *real* issue in the debate, is what sort of party we are building. He made his perspective more explicit toward the end of the discussion. He wants to:

- open the party to the mass movement activists, and
- open the party to people with differing political perspectives.

We also want to 'open up the party to movement activists', but on *our* program, *our* politics, *our* norms. We don't want to *adapt* the party to the *politics* of independent activists, who are most susceptible to the pressures of ruling-class ideology or to the politics of other left tendencies. That would only change our party for the worse.

Any who agree with us and want to be active are welcomed into our ranks. That's the actual experience. We take the question of membership very seriously, and would welcome them as members. Nevertheless, our main area of recruitment in the future will be among youth, as it is at the present and has been in the past.

There *is* a milieu of people who are hostile to the party –

the minority of ex-members who have a grudge, the hardened anti-party independents – but there is little chance this layer could coalesce into an actual party or organisation. They are united by both their non-partyism and their cynicism towards activism and commitment.

And this milieu is increasingly outnumbered today by the real periphery of the party. This periphery's the largest we've ever had:

- Look at *Green Left Weekly* readership and influence. Every week the party branches sell it or send out subscriptions to 4,000-5,000 people at least. If you take into account the casual buyers, it's probably 10,000 people. If you take into account people who read other people's copies, you're probably looking at 20,000.
- Look at the attendance at our dinners and similar functions in a twelve-month period. The total who come to our dinners in the course of a year would be more than 2,000 around the country. If you add in other functions, forums, Green It Up-type events, it would be several thousand more.
- Look at the number of young people who joined Resistance campus clubs and branches last year, more than 1,500.
- Look at the people who came along to the Socialist Scholars Conferences or the International Green Left Conference, about 1,000 each time.

Our periphery is bigger than it's ever been. Compare us with the International Socialist Organisation: Comrades were at a meeting of one of their Melbourne branches in December, and they were bewailing the fact that they had practically no periphery.

We *are* relating to the former members of the CPA, to the genuine Greens, through *Green Left Weekly* and our other events and activities. But we're in a position to politically influence them, not have them influence us with their essentially left-liberal politics.

And we're not *that* isolated. Certainly we have only a small influence in the unions and in the working class as a whole. We've discussed the political problems there. But we're not isolated from mass struggles. Compare our situation with those who have left our party – there's no other way to keep in touch with left politics today than through the party and *Green Left Weekly*.

But we should not blur the distinction between members and periphery. We reach out to them, try to draw them into activities, try to influence them, try to make them active. We should relate to them openly and honestly. We should state clearly our goals and objectives, and not manoeuvre with them. Comrade Robson's approach would lead to fewer members and a smaller periphery.

Party and class

But, it's been said, the sort of Leninist party we're trying to build now is not really appropriate at this stage of the struggle, when the working class is not revolutionary and we don't have a mass base; a democratic-centralist vanguard party was appropriate for the Bolsheviks because they had a mass base in the working class.

At what stage of the struggle, or at what size of organisation, does such a party become justified? There's the quote from Lenin's *'Left Wing' Communism* that we're very familiar with, where he explains that 'one of the fundamental conditions for the Bolsheviks' success' was the maintenance of the strictest, truly iron discipline.

The thrust of this pamphlet by Lenin is directed against ultra-leftism, but he begins with an attack on Kautsky and other renegades who deny the possibility of revolution, the revolutionary lessons of the Bolshevik victory.

We've pointed out that a program is part of living struggles, and the Leninist party is a party that is itself a product of the living class struggle, not of cadres who ideologically defend the 'true' program and 'proclaim' themselves the vanguard. Of course, there's no 'Leninist concept of party-building' separate from program, orientation and tactics. Our party program very clearly sets out our understanding of the role of the revolutionary Marxist party and its relationship to the masses.

Note, all the conditions Lenin points to: the class-consciousness and tenacity of the vanguard; the party's links with the masses of workers; the correctness of the party's leadership, program, strategy and tactics, which assume final shape only when it is able to establish links with a 'truly mass and truly revolutionary movement'.

Lenin stresses that these conditions cannot emerge all at once, they are created by prolonged effort. It's not the case that the party has no role to play until then, and shouldn't try to win political leadership of the masses and organise its ranks, select its membership etc.

Any attempt to start with a politically heterogeneous, loosely organised group, to try to win a mass base, and then try to turn it into a tight Bolshevik-type party, would end in disaster. It wouldn't have revolutionary politics.

Such an approach would take us back to the pre-1914 Social-Democratic type party, refusing to look at the lessons of the history of all socialist organisations since then. It ignores our criticism of the all-inclusive socialist party of the [Eugene V.] Debs model. Theoretically it's a step back to Engels' false idea that '… the simple feeling of solidarity based on the understanding of the identity of class position suffices to create and to hold together one and the same great party of the proletariat among the workers of all countries and tongues'.

We're Leninists because of the test of *practice*. Lenin's party was successful in making a proletarian revolution and starting the process of constructing a socialist society. Where has the alternative strategy, of building an all-inclusive party, ever been successfully applied? No socialist revolution has ever succeeded without the leadership of a combat party. Some weren't Leninist – the Chinese CP for example – and thus there was no proletarian democracy. But there's never been a case of a loose organisation without trained cadres being able to lead a socialist revolution.

How to get there

Understanding the danger of sectarianism, the clowning of self-proclaimed vanguards, is just the beginning of wisdom. The real task, in today's political landscape, is *how* to build a Leninist party, to get a party of the Bolshevik type with a mass base, with deep roots in the working class.

A serious combination of building a Marxist party or group to link up with and win a base in the working class has been our approach – open to regroupments, merging with real forces if they emerge, but still building our organisation. In this scenario, what sorts of organisational norms are best for the Marxist group? Is the Leninist organisation principle of democratic centralism irrelevant until that link with the masses is forged? Can the very existence of a Marxist-Leninist cadre group be an obstacle to the eventual emergence of a mass formation that could develop later into a Leninist party with a mass base?

We do not think so. A party like ours is needed at all stages of the process. There's no evidence of the spontaneous emergence of a Leninist vanguard party. Certainly the particular form can vary according to the political circumstances. Certainly a smart, flexible approach – characteristic of Lenin – is needed. But a Leninist-type party is still required.

It's needed especially at this time, following the collapse of Stalinism. The ideological leadership role of revolutionary Marxists can be crucial in the regroupment of healthy forces, in explaining political developments, the nature of Stalinism etc., in providing education, educational material, in providing infrastructure. On a small scale, look at what we've been able to do with *Links*.

And when did the Bolsheviks themselves actually become the vanguard party of the Russian working class? Not really until the middle of 1917, in the full sense of the word. They had a mass base among advanced workers before the revolutionary upsurge of 1917 to an extent, but in periods of reaction and retreat for the working class, they were sometimes isolated, sometimes quite small, and the Mensheviks might be said to have had a bigger base in the working class for much of that time.

It's vital we recognise where we're at. We can't act as if we already have a mass base, to the neglect of patient development of Marxist cadres. Although we always act from the point of view of the interests of the working class, we act to try to *win* the masses, to have a mass approach. A false understanding of where we're at can lead to a fake populism, a rejecting of our Leninist position, and a neglect of cadre building and our basic party-building tasks.

Jim Percy put it very clearly in his party-building report to our 11th National Conference in January 1986:

> We should understand we're still a propaganda group.
> We've said that plenty of times, but today it's modified by
> our understanding of how we build a vanguard party.
> You don't build a propaganda group by doing
> propaganda. You build a propaganda group
> by massive intervention into every struggle
> that is going on. That's what we've learnt.
> Maybe it's wrong to use this phrase, but I use it
> to emphasise one of the key struggles we still
> face: to build a vanguard party in this country.
> That's the ideological, political struggle …
> But we emphasise that we have not yet won that
> political struggle, the centrepiece of which is

> *Direct Action.* That's where we engage in most of
> that discussion and struggle, and that's why we
> have to say that we're still a propaganda group.

Nine years on, that's still a good description of the stage we're at in building the party. The difference of course is that we have *Green Left Weekly* rather than *Direct Action*, a much better propaganda tool.

How to develop cadres

The development of cadres is a conscious, active process, and there are two sides to it: theory – education, reading, under-standing capitalism and the history of the workers' movement; and practice – involvement in struggle, activity, learning from struggles of workers and other oppressed.

There's a 'third component' that binds these two together: the party. The framework of the party enables the theory to be put into practice; it unites that activity and political experience; our program progressively encapsulates that experience. The party framework allows revolutionaries to discuss collectively, decide collectively, act collectively. Unity of theory and practice can be just a mantra without the structure of the party. The party is the instrument for struggle, the collation of the experiences of the working class movement internationally and locally.

Can revolutionary cadres be developed if you begin with a rejection of democratic centralism and a vanguard party? At the very least, you'd have to agree it would be a lot harder.

Apart from the overall political weakness of any strategy for revolution that begins with such a flawed perspective, it makes it almost impossible to train and develop revolutionary cadres. You might develop activists on an issue, or smart academics, but not cadres. Even when you look around at non-Leninist left organisations, often you find that many of the leading activists got their skills and training in a cadre formation.

This approach, of making a principle of no democratic centralism, no vanguardism, no unity in action, is like spitting in the well from which the socialist movement in the future will have to draw. What might be seen as a necessary tactical position in constructing the party today, or a retreat forced on socialists by the weakness of their forces, gets converted into a permanent block on the road to any further advance towards a stronger party. It would lead to the wholesale miseducation of a new generation, preventing the creation of revolutionary cadres.

Are we sectarian?

Are we sectarian, as all our political opponents on the right think of course, and as some of our ex-members maintain? Are we a caricature of a Leninist party? Are we 'sect-like', 'church-like', as Comrade Robson states in his final pre-conference contribution?

Well, yes and no. There's partly an element of truth in this characterisation. We are certainly still in a semi-sectarian existence, in difficult conditions for winning the masses of workers in Australia to a revolutionary perspective. Of course the reformists, the careerists, see us as a sect; their perspectives are totally within the institutions of capitalist society, ours are outside them.

Lenin at one stage in the development of the Bolshevik party also characterised their organisation as a 'sect'. But whether they were leading the advanced sections of the working class in revolutionary struggle, or just struggling to keep alive the skeleton of their organisation in difficult times, the Bolshevik leaders always maintained the necessity of their revolutionary cadre party.

In the difficult year 1909, Lenin polemicised against those who wanted to abandon the Bolsheviks' course, liquidating the party outright, or more subtle suggestions for doing the same thing.

'Whoever finds this work tedious, whoever does not understand the need for preserving and developing the revolutionary principles of Social-Democratic tactics *in this phase too, on this bend of the road*, is taking the name of Marxist in vain.' The Bolsheviks' party tasks now, he said, 'consist in patiently training up partyist elements and knitting them together, in building up a really united and strong proletarian party'.

It's been raised in the discussion, though not committed to paper yet, that the degeneration of the US SWP under Jack Barnes flows directly from the Cannon[66] tradition, that the Cannonist method of building a party is fatally flawed and sectarian. But we pointed out in the January 1984 NC report, presented by Comrade Doug Lorimer and printed as *The Making of a Sect,* that the organisational abuses of Barnes flow from the politics – the continuation of incorrect expectations of the turn to industry. We corrected our line; they didn't, and thus had to have a bureaucratic regime and organisational abuses to maintain it. We still defend the Cannon tradition. In fact, it was our assimilation of its lessons that helped us to avoid following the Barnes leadership's degeneration into a sterile, abstentionist sect.

National tactics and international tactics

Is there a contradiction between building a politically homogeneous party here in Australia – a Leninist party – and our open, ecumenical, regroupment approach internationally, with *Links,* for example? We say there's no contradiction.

Firstly, our international approach reflects the reality internationally, attempting to rebuild, regroup all those still genuine about socialism, about revolutionary struggle, following the collapse of the Soviet Union and the decline of Stalinism.

Secondly, let's remind ourselves of the understanding we reached of the difference between the functions and structures of national and international organisations. It's worth re-reading some of our documents from the early '80s, when we broke with the US SWP, and left the Fourth International, analysing the problems of Cominternism.

Thirdly, comrades should know that we're not excluding the possibilities of regroupment, of an open approach here in Australia. Let's remember our efforts in the '80s, the quick response we'd have if there was any real possibility again today, and our actual efforts with *Green Left Weekly*, the most effective regroupment vehicle there's been.

Our Australian approach reflects the realities and the possibilities here in Australia. Our international approach reflects the realities and the possibilities internationally.

It's the *same* approach, taking account of the different roles of local and international organisations. A national revolutionary party has the task of leading the working class in the struggle for power against its own bourgeois state and ruling class. Even with the development of imperialism, the internationalisation of capital, the need for the international workers' struggles to be coordinated, and the impossibility of creating socialism in one country, this fundamental task is still the same.

Individual socialist activists join a political party at the national level. Parties relate to each other at the international level.

Political activity at the national level requires unity in action, requires democratic centralism. But any concept of democratic centralism at the international level is totally inappropriate. It's the hallmark of sects today – the ISO/SWP, the Spartacists, the US SWP and its little groups of acolytes. The way the Bolsheviks operated in the early years of the Communist International is very instructive on this. In spite of their immense authority as the leaders of the first successful workers' revolution, their practice was not to insist on international democratic centralism, even as they strove to remould the socialist parties attracted to the revolution into communist parties. It was only under the Stalinist degeneration that the system of issuing orders and changing and controlling the leaderships of national parties set in.

In the last few years there's been a significant expansion of our international work. The collapse of the Soviet Union has opened up a number of avenues for collaboration that were closed before.

Our open, non-sectarian approach has enabled us to develop better contacts with other revolutionaries around the world than we've ever had before – comradely party-to-party exchanges and collaboration. This has culminated in the launching of *Links,* a very impressive initiative for a party our size that has won tremendous respect already and is winning more support with each issue.

So the success of this international work, and the way we carry it out in our relations with a range of parties and individuals from diverse political backgrounds, have perhaps led some comrades to extrapolate from our international relations back to our Australian situation.

The pluralism, the diversity within certain parameters, is a useful trend in the international discussion, where it's a process of recomposing, renewing the left, and building links between the genuine socialists who might come from different traditions – former Maoists, those from the CP tradition, those from the Trotskyist tradition, those breaking with social democracy.

But pluralism is not a principle as such, and certainly not a principle in building a party here, where we're striving for clarity and for unity in action.

'Culture of debate'

Comrades Steve Robson and Michael Boswell charge that there's not 'a culture of debate' in the party. Comrade Boswell bemoans that the constitution allows only three months discussion every two years.

Let's put aside the facts of our actual practice in recent years, for example a written discussion for ten of the last eighteen months! More importantly, our *normal* practice of democratic discussion doesn't exist in any other party here, and not in the CPA when it existed either.

Look at the real culture of debate that we've fostered: with our periphery, the left milieu, through *Green Left Weekly*, nationally and internationally too, and with *Links* as well.

Although our strategy is to build a politically homogeneous party on Leninist lines, we've shown time and again that we're flexible, open to regroupments, and willing to build an inclusive team leadership. That's the actual experience over the years.

The question of hardness

Another charge that's been made in this debate is that the NC majority has been 'too hard' and that our tone and style have been too sharp.

It's the historical experience of Marxist parties that those who raise the question of 'tone' or 'regime' are the ones trying to obscure the discussion, or sit on the fence. Our tone has been exemplary. We have to be sharp to try to get clarity.

The National Executive intervention in Perth branch, limited as it was, was to uphold and implement the decisions of the *majority* of the party, taken at our last national conference, and at NC meetings. Some Perth comrades were undemocratic in flouting this, and the majority of the branch executive was correct in pushing for the implementation of the party's position.

The intervention was absolutely correct. Such action is part of the responsibility and accountability of leadership. This was questioned by Comrades Robson and Boswell and other comrades in Perth, as somehow bureaucratic, or Stalinist. But *not* to have intervened would have been an abrogation of our responsibility.

I'm not saying that we made no mistakes in past struggles in the party. But at each major struggle, at each step, we did the right thing. We learn, we avoid some stupid errors and idiocies, we learn how to do things better, and some of this gets codified in our constitution or in our organisational principles and norms.

Norms and rules

One of our most important organisational norms, and one that's been challenged in this discussion, is that of team leadership and collective decision making by executive bodies. One aspect of this norm is that discussions on proposals for action should be taken collectively and given as a report on behalf of the executive. Another is that deliberations should be kept to members of that body, making it possible for members of the executive committee to feel free to express their views without feeling that they would have to defend or be responsible for whatever they said before the entire membership. That's a norm, not a rule or regulation. It's a norm that executive discussions are not open to every branch member to participate in or observe, not a rule that members are forbidden to report to others.

Similarly, with reports to branch meetings on NC decisions. It's the norm for such reports to be given to all the members of the branch, not a select few. But in a situation of serious political differences, it's obvious that such norms would not be maintained.

As the US SWP degenerated in the early '80s, the central leadership around Jack Barnes converted these norms of the Cannon-type party into rules and regulations that brought disciplinary action for every infraction.

Why do comrades leave the party?

Comrade Robson has pointed to the problem of attrition in the party, members leaving, even experienced comrades, NC members. Obviously the party as a whole, and the national leadership too, was not unaware of this, and not happy about it.

It's not just a phenomenon of recent years. Throughout our history we've had the problem of a turnover of members and leaders of the party. It's a feature of revolutionary movements in all countries, and at all times – revolutions, and attempts at them, are devourers of people in this sense. The dropouts in recent years can also in many cases be seen as responses to the particular political conjurcture worldwide, a difficult time for the socialist movement.

But the real question is how should we react? It's *not* a solution to jump overboard after them. Throw them a life raft where possible, perhaps, but we've still got a ship to steer, a party to build. We shouldn't just bemoan the fact, without a solution, or a false solution, or add to the problem.

What are the reasons comrades have left? There are two categories.

Firstly, the younger, newer comrades who leave. In general, that *is* our failure, our failure to politically integrate and educate these comrades. It's something we've addressed in recent party-building reports, and will be taken up in the party-building tasks report tomorrow.

Our real fault has been in the inadequate use of provisional membership, in not educating provisional members in our politics and organisational principles, in not giving them help and guidance in their political interventions. There's always likely to be a layer of comrades like that, not very well integrated into the party and its politics. It becomes a real problem if it's the dominant trend in the party. That's possibly what happened in

Perth branch.

Secondly, there are the longer term, experienced, comrades, including leaders of the party. Here the reasons for comrades dropping out can be a bit more complex.

There would be many different individual components to the reasons, but you can't leave it just at the level of individual psychology, and certainly at this time you can't ignore the question of the period, the difficulties socialists face today, the tremendous ruling class ideological pressure that bears down on anyone who dissents, let alone those who make a fundamental challenge to the capitalist system.

That's the relevance of the graphic metaphor of the 'ideological bullets of the bourgeoisie' – it might be less physically dangerous than being a revolutionary in other situations, but it can still be destructive of the revolutionary. That's why we need a party of a certain type, to help ward off those ideological bullets, to counteract the ideological batterings from ruling-class institutions and propaganda, to help explain and collectively resist the carrots and sticks.

The bourgeois ideological offensive against the workers' movement, against socialism, is very consciously directed. They don't feel secure, in spite of their public bragging. They're much more class conscious than the overwhelming majority of workers at the moment. They're using racism, sexism, nationalism, their labour lieutenants, religious bigotry, the perversion of language, the promotion of individualism, the denial of social solutions, sops and bribes to consciously weaken the workers' movement.

To make advances in building a revolutionary workers' party in this context requires clarity, organisation, dedication, commitment and perseverance. Some comrades will get worn out by the effort, become unclear about the goals. And over time, the class struggle pushes comrades back, the current gets too strong.

Comrade Robson never relates his concerns about the resignation of longer term comrades to the class struggle. For him it's just a question of individual psychology, which the party is held responsible for failing to deal with.

Comrades can get demoralised when we don't have victories or get pushed back, and become more susceptible to the bourgeois pressures. But it doesn't automatically mean the party was on the wrong course; the objective situation, the odds against us, might just have been too great at the moment.

And it's false to argue that people leave because we demand too much of them. Let's get it in perspective. What are our goals? An extremely ambitious project, to lead the working class and its allies, millions of people, in overthrowing the rule of the capitalist class and replacing it with the rule of the working class. It's not going to be achieved by half-hearted efforts. If we don't ask for dedication and commitment, if we don't expect sacrifices, and yes, heroism too when required, we should give the game away right now. Without that commitment, we won't have cadres; without cadres, we won't have a revolutionary party; and without a revolutionary party, we won't be able to lead a socialist revolution.

It's no solution at all to comrades' demoralisation and dropping out to propose that we lower our norms of activity and commitment. The way to counter demoralisation is through activity and successes, through education and politics. Revolutionary politics *is* satisfying, and can continue to be satisfying. What's the alternative? Make peace with the system?

Having said all that, it's worth saying again, that we shouldn't write off former members. It's only a small minority who go really off, move rapidly to the right, become hostile to the party. We'll always be open to comrades who want to resume their political activity after a break – we're very welcoming of prodigal sons and daughters. And if comrades who leave still want to support the party in some way, or work with us in some area of common struggle, that's fine, as long as they respect party members' right to continue to build the party as we see fit, and don't engage in hostile acts against the party.

Some who leave are just stepping back temporarily, and will be reactivated by new events, by an upsurge of mass struggles. Some will put time into bringing up a family, paying off a house, but after a while will realise the problems of capitalism are still there. Comrades will be motivated to have a second go. New anger, new events, can lead to them casting aside their demoralisation and jumping into the stream again.

Are we doing too much?

Even though we have ambitious goals, and we're trying to build an activist party and train cadres through education and engagement in activities, are we perhaps trying to do too much? Perhaps the stress on comrades is too much, we're overloaded.

We all recognise that even in this period, at what are supposed to be difficult or impossible times for socialists, we are confronted with many opportunities for building the party, for intervening in the class struggle, for reaching out to new people with our socialist ideas. There are many openings for us, yet far too few resources, far too few comrades, to take advantage of all of them.

And it's also true that party life is quite hectic, with meetings or activities on most nights at branch offices, packed calendars, comrades running around, sometimes frazzled, trying to get the tasks done.

But even though we're overloaded in a sense, we don't think there are any major cutbacks in our activity that we should make. *Some* tasks we won't complete. *Some* things we won't do as well as we'd like. *Some* tasks will have to be relegated further down the list. Let's try to complete as much as we can, as best we can, and not allow a feeling of panic.

Sometimes we've said that we have an apparatus suitable for a party many times our size, and that now we need to put more flesh on our bones. Well, that's true in a sense, but with more flesh, more cadres, I think we'd quickly want to have even more comrades on full-time assignments, to try to take advantage of further opportunities. Comrades Robson and Boswell have accused the party of having an apparatus that's *too* big.

The charge of too big an apparatus has sometimes been raised in previous discussions, and by former members. But with a smaller staff, we'd get *less* done. We'd have to be content with a smaller, less attractive, perhaps less frequent, *Green Left Weekly*. We'd publish fewer books and pamphlets. Perhaps we mightn't manage to produce *Links*. The pace of party life would certainly be slower, there would be less activity expected of comrades, and less political impact.

We know how much more we could do, with a larger party, with more resources, with more full-time staff, more activists, more 100 percenters.

But for now we're short, and can sometimes feel overloaded. The national and branch leaderships will have to be very conscious of this in planning our work.

The first thing is to make sure we get our priorities right, and get our basic party-building tasks covered. Our mass work has to be planned within our party-building framework, and our interventions prioritised accordingly.

Secondly, we can all work at being much more efficient than we presently are. We can be a lot better organised, we can spread the load of work among comrades more efficiently. And we can carry through further the integration of all the different aspects of our party-building work.

The balance sheet of 1994

The balance sheet of our work in 1994 has been positive, if you look at the actual strength and achievements of the party, the education and development of cadre and the response to the challenge in Perth branch.

The *real* failure of the party this year has been our failure to integrate, train and educate enough of our new youth recruits.

In the year ahead we have to succeed on this. Our perspectives for the coming years depend on it. Unless we train a larger number of cadres, we won't be able to recruit, we won't be able to grow, and we won't be able to lead the coming struggles to successful outcomes.

We need to present ourselves as a politically 'viable' alternative. We're the only organisation really presenting a different political perspective, a working-class political perspective. We're small, yes, but we know we can grow.

We need to act more as a party – seriously, responsibly, confidently. We don't want to engage in bragging, false projections, the ridiculous hype of the left sects. But we do need to raise the party profile. Comrades need confidence, even aggression in some circumstances, when they talk to new people, intervene in campaigns, on campus, on the job. We need to inject a tone of anger, outrage, in our agitational leaflets, our talks, our election literature.

The opportunities for the DSP *are* greater today than ever before. But unless we try to act as a serious socialist organisation, our members and supporters can lose confidence in the party project, can drift off to their private concerns, can seep back into the ALP, back to 'the marsh', become part of the problem. The defeatism of those who adapt can thus make the tasks for socialists that much harder.

7. PERSPECTIVES UNDER THE NEW GOVERNMENT: BUILDING BASES

Report to the National Committee
9 June 1996

The federal election held on 2 March 1996 was a landslide for the Liberal-National Coalition on a swing of more than 5 percent. Labor lost 31 of its 80 seats in the previous House of Representatives. With the change of government, a reorientation was necessary to relate to a new political context, in which sharper neoliberal attacks were to be expected. With the ALP now in opposition, the possibility arose of united fronts against particular government actions. Therefore this report went into some detail about how to utilise the united-front tactic.

We are now in a new period, blessed with a conservative government led by Neanderthals like [John] Howard, [Peter] Costello, [Amanda] Vanstone, [Peter] Reith and their gang, after 13 years of ALP government and Accord politics.

We're entering a period of increased and intensified class conflict. The stepped-up attacks on workers' rights and conditions and social services and jobs by the Coalition are guaranteeing that. The large rallies and demonstrations by students and staff defending education were very encouraging. We have already seen some union actions, some more fights back are being organised.

But the current bureaucratic leaderships in the trade unions have neither the will nor the ability to stop Howard. There will be sell-outs – it's happened already in the CPSU – and we can expect defeats. It's likely we'll have post-budget defeats, leading to demoralisation and an initial downturn in the level of struggle.

Nevertheless, there are still more opportunities for action, for struggle, for radicalisation And any fight is better than defeats without a fight at all, which is what we got with the attrition, the retreats, the weakening of our unions through the Accord years.

The capitalist class's neoliberal offensive will be implemented by whichever government is in office in Canberra. The ongoing discontents on economic and social issues will be a permanent and deepening feature of social and political life. But the anger will not automatically be channelled through the ALP, as it would have been prior to 1983. The Labor politicians have been slow and clumsy in getting back into opposition mode, have not been able to put on much of a left face and absorb or sidetrack the anger and opposition.

So even though this will be a hard period – workers and students and the poor in general are going to suffer, the capitalist class will create even better conditions for enriching itself – we can also make gains. This period will radicalise workers and others; it will make it easier for us to recruit, to build the party and other organisations of resistance. We can and must extract the maximum payment politically for the Howard offensive.

It might be only a brief period of relative upsurge before the demoralisation of defeats sets in, but of course we hope it's a more extended period of struggle; we hope that significant setbacks can be dealt to the Howard offensive. But we're very painfully aware of the extent of the destruction of working class organisation – trade unions – and working class consciousness. There's a lot of ground to be made up.

Our assets and gains

What's the balance sheet of our party-building efforts during the 13 years of ALP government? What are our gains?

First, we're still here, which mightn't sound much, but compared to the decline or disappearance of other left parties here and around the world, it's an achievement. We've had relative growth compared to what the left was 13 years ago.

We've recruited, kept and trained a valuable cadre force. The party is educated and experienced, with an invaluable acquisition of our party program and other political documents that express that experience.

Look at the political tools we've developed – *Green Left Weekly*, *Links* and the *Activist*, books and pamphlets and other publications; our geographical spread; our assets and resources that can make our political activities possible (since 1983, we've acquired the Sydney, Melbourne, and Brisbane buildings).

Most importantly, we've continued to recruit and train young people. Resistance has been a yearly source of strength and renewal for the party. The average age of our tendency is still in the mid-20s.

We've not only survived through this difficult period, but are now undoubtedly the strongest organised tendency on the Australian radical left.

What are the negatives from those 13 years? We've suffered like the rest of the left, from attrition, dropouts; even experienced comrades from our leadership who have fallen by the wayside. We have a very limited base in the trade unions. We have a large potential periphery out there, but it's only partially organised through *Green Left Weekly*, DSEL etc. We didn't succeed in an electoral project that would elevate us, make a breakthrough.

It has been a continuing uphill battle to expand our forces here. The working-class movement is weak, after 13 years of ALP government and Accord. The upsurges of struggle that develop are all too transient, falling away quickly, with few apparent lasting gains. The class-collaborationist Laborist bureaucrats still dominate, and we're even still battling the dead hand of the CPA.

Nevertheless, there's been a modest but real increase in our own weight, and the responsibility we take for campaigns and struggles:

- In 1995, the DSP and Resistance played leading roles in building the large mobilisations against woodchipping and the French nuclear tests. Without our leadership, the anti-tests mobilisations would not have continued after Hiroshima Day.
- Our comrades led and organised the IWD marches in most cities in 1996; they often wouldn't have occurred without us.
- We were instrumental in getting the anti-uranium mining protests going this year.
- We've been the major current in the East Timor solidarity campaign, through Resistance, ASIET and broader initiatives.
- We've maintained an ongoing Latin American solidarity campaign, through CISLAC.
- We've been able to have an increasing leadership role on campus, in campaigns to defend education.
- And we've played a crucial leadership role in the fight to force the CPSU national leadership to initiate a bans campaign against public sector job cuts.

What changes with a Coalition government? It *is* different with the Liberals in. The change will have consequences for our functioning and requires a change of attitude on our part and a change in our tactical orientation.

The mobilisations are still likely to be short-lived and the radicalisation shallow. Radicalising workers and students will still seek the line of least resistance to the Coalition's attacks. They'll still look for electoral salvation rather than more radical solutions. How do we counter this, how do we make the best of it, how do we take the party to the next stage of growth and influence?

How to break through?

In particular, how can we significantly break through what seems like the barrier that's roughly been our size for about the last 13 years? We've had modest growth in the last six months. There was a slight drop in the full members, but a good increase in the number of provisional members. There's still a process of attrition, some of the longer term comrades letting their membership lapse.

We need a *political* plan for growth. In recent years, as well as throughout our history, we have run hard. Our comrades have been active, self-sacrificing. But our growth has never matched our ambition.

In response, often we've tried to campaign for growth, to *will* it. In difficult periods we've sometimes set recruitment targets, set targets for the number of recruits. But of course it's better to have the political perspectives and the targets of *political projects* that will lead to growth.

We're still a propaganda group, not a mass party, and our fundamental task is to recruit radicalising workers and students and educate and train them as Marxist cadres. But we must also always put forward proposals for the workers' movement that are in the best immediate interests of the working class and the longer-term socialist struggle. And we must act as though we are leaders of our class, although we know we can't call the masses into action in our own name as yet.

But there's also a third component of our strategy that connects these two components: we have to organise to get intermediate bases, partial gains, organisational targets, so we can both build the party and recruit, and better aid the defensive struggles of the working class and its allies, putting forward the correct line of march. We need other goals, other targets, to focus comrades, to organise their political work, to inspire them.

How will we grow now?

Remember of course that it's not just recruiting, but educating and training our members: keeping them, convincing, steeling them for the long haul.

Now that there's a new period (all proportions guarded), we need an advance in party building, in recruiting, to break through the ceiling we seem to have become stuck at throughout the late 1980s and '90s. We need to do better in all aspects of recruiting – propaganda, leading campaigns and united front work.

But how do we improve the process of, and consciousness about, recruiting in the party? And how do we concretise, register and secure the gains?

How can we better stabilise, and confirm, the positions we gain in relation to others on the left, and develop permanent bases of influence and leadership? This is going beyond publicising ourselves better, raising our profile, having better propaganda.

How to do it in the context of a Coalition government, with the ALP-ACTU Accord at an end, the possibility of some in the ALP putting on a bit of a left mask, with old ghosts rising and simplistic ultra-left sects able to pick up members by raising their flag?

Let's look at it specifically in our main areas of work – trade unions, students and international solidarity.

Trade union work

Firstly, in the trade unions and our industrial work, which is the most important area, and where we're weakest, relatively, especially compared to the ALP but also compared with the ex-CPA, even the SPA and ex-ACU – in terms of official positions anyway.

Our first and most important task is to get more comrades into the right jobs, where they're able to do political work in the trade unions, and recruit more workers to the party where possible. And in this framework they'll be doing the basics, getting delegate positions, talking socialism on the job.

Secondly, winning positions from which we can aid the struggle, broaden the consciousness of wider layers of militants, radicalise workers, lead struggles, raise our profile and keep the gains and results of our work. In particular:

- The public sector fight, our CPSU work. We need to set targets for increasing our implantation and building a stronger base here.
- The Telstra defence.[67] This is another important campaign which won't just be trade union work, but can involve other sectors of the community.

Also, we want to develop better union implantation in other sectors.

We also want to give support for militant, class-struggle unionism, for example, full backing to the Shearers and Rural Workers Union[68] and any other class-struggle breaks – through *Green Left Weekly*, picket lines, liaison.

And there are all the basics: recruiting fellow workers, talking socialism on the job, distributing *Dare to Struggle*[69] – for all this, fraction organisation is essential.

We need to set targets to focus comrades' work, to aim at some goals that are achievable that will take trade union work one step further.

Having milestones to pass, hurdles to overcome, positions to win to register progress, helps focus and organise and motivate the work.

Building campus bases

Our second main area of work, among students and youth, has been and still is the main arena for recruitment and growth, and competition on the left, and it's very promising and exciting.

So it's still vital that we do all the basics right on campus to build Resistance clubs – sell *Green Left Weekly*, have stalls, forums, leaflets, do all the propaganda work, raise our profile, and link up with the Resistance and DSP branches and our other political activities.

But it's also vital in this period that we engage and confront our political opponents on all fronts – in the SRCs, in NUS, in the various committees defending education, that we become an integral part of political life on campus.

The timely change in our tactics on NUS[70] enables our student comrades to better relate to openings, run for positions, raise our profile and gain confidence and learn in struggle. We'll be setting targets in hegemonising certain campuses. We'll be looking at where we can establish some more lasting 'bases' – SRC positions, NUS footholds, campaign committees.

International solidarity work

The East Timor and Indonesia Solidarity report outlined how we have already established some bases in this area, and how we want to consolidate and extend them;

- Consolidating ASIET as the main solidarity organisation in this area;

- Building the 25 August actions,[71] the East Timor conference, other East Timor events.
- Strengthening the Indonesian solidarity side of things.

We should also note the continuing importance of our Latin American solidarity work, the wonderful effort comrades assigned to this work have put in over the years and how that's still registered in the continuing existence of CISLAC. Gains that we make get registered in organisations like this that we keep going.

Compare the fight of ASIET versus the remnants in the East Timor campaign today, and the CISLAC-RACLA[72] fights in previous years. RACLA is no more; but even with the relatively low priority we've given to CISLAC in recent years, we're still able to preserve the gains, the benefits of the work.

The factional hostility of the lobbyist cliques in the East Timor solidarity movement is a symptom of that organisational struggle and transition, the struggle for recognition of the work. In effect, they're trying to prevent registration of our gains, recognition of our bases.

International solidarity work remains essential for recruiting and training new young comrades in a revolutionary internationalist outlook, in a period when the class struggle will still be at a modest level in Australia. International solidarity work through ASIET and CISLAC and our previous experience with CARPA allow the intersection of our revolutionary perspectives and liberal concerns.

It's important for youth and students, and important also for raising and broadening the consciousness of workers we come in contact with. But it's also an important arena for organising and fighting for the allegiance of the petty bourgeois liberal milieu. We should be on the lookout for other campaigns to mobilise them and orient them towards us, for example the World Bank appeal.[73]

Green Left has been excellent for reaching out to this milieu.

Our large conferences and speaking tours like [John] Pilger's have also been invaluable for this. We can also make better use of Cultural Dissent activities to reach academics, artists, musicians etc. We can build a financial base here, and it gives points of support for other campaigns, through petitions, appeals, dinners, public meetings.

Other areas

Some of our other areas of work, such as the women's liberation movement and the environment movement, won't have quite the same priority for us in this period, partly because we can't see the organisational structures through which we could do work and have gains registered. Of course we'll continue to propagandise on the issues, especially in *Green Left*.

A whole new layer of young women comrades were assigned to the IWD committees and learnt heaps; it was great training. But mostly we weren't able to consolidate the many contacts we made. Probably this would have changed in some branches if we were better known as socialists, if we had a higher DSP profile. Branches can try to revive the contacts, catch the threads again, through running women's liberation and socialism conferences in the second half of the year. But IWD itself is not enough of a structure for us, and in the future, hopefully, there'll develop a fighting women's organisation that we can build and keep going.

In the environment movement we had to let EYA slip; we weren't able to maintain it, which was a pity. There's no other healthy ongoing campaigning structure at the moment that activists can join. The peak bodies are still lobby-oriented, even with a Coalition government.

The anti-uranium campaign is not galvanising huge numbers. And given the narrow base of the committees, we can't continue to take major responsibility for it. It's better to have a focus on issues that mobilise more people, or have a sharper political focus, for example, East Timor, which exposes the contradictions of Australian imperialism. But this varies from city to city. It's an issue where branches can best decide.

Targets and bases

Fundamental, of course, is building the party: the politics, the program and the organisation itself. But there are also other ways to register gains, to concretise the past work, that assist the building of the party.

On the other hand, there are dangers of campaigns without gains. There's the problem of sect parasites parachuting in. We do the work, and they smother it with placards on the day. We can counter this with our own high profile, and our own propaganda in quantity. Or we can organise actions in our own name, if there's no real possibility of genuine joint work.

There's also the danger of burnout of comrades from covering everything, and not doing the recruiting well in any of them. We can economise through doubling up: do *Green Left* sales *in* interventions; recruiting, talking to contacts, *at* demonstrations. We can revive old comrades and thrust responsibility on new ones. If comrades can see the permanent gains, they're less likely to feel tired.

Green Left Weekly in this period

One of the problems posed for us in this period of heightened class confrontation is that *Green Left Weekly* is not a party paper. Of course it's only a partial problem; the gains we get still far outweigh any negative aspects.

Nevertheless, how do we adjust, compensate for the drawbacks? We don't go back to a party paper, but raise the socialist content. We make the paper more directed, controlled, with a conscious reflection of the party's activities and views. Perhaps we give more weight to the first half of the paper. We should be covering the DSP, DSF members, Resistance more openly. Let nobody who buys a copy be mistaken about the main tendency behind the paper. Let's keep the virtues, but improve it for the period.

Green Left needs to have comprehensive coverage of all the actions, all the fights back. At the same time, it should give direction to the campaigns, and draw out the political lessons. There's no problem in carrying all the type of articles *Direct Action* might have carried in the past. We need this anyway to give political guidance to our members and our wide periphery.

But also in this period *Green Left Weekly* can really come into its own as the paper that unites all the campaigns, is the resource, the arena for discussion, for all those fighting back. Use the paper to build and reach out into the movements. It can regroup the activists.

We want *Green Left* to house the debates. Branch leaderships have to go after the left liberal milieu for *Green Left* copy. Target the *Frontline*[74] writers, for example. Get the more interesting names from the former CPA milieu to comment or write in *Green Left* – [Jack] Mundey, [Frank] Stilwell.

We should put more effort into involving others in writing, for example on the campaigns, on women's, environmental and gay and lesbian issues. This would have the advantage of allowing our comrades, on *Green Left* staff or not, to concentrate on the socialist perspective articles.

And we need a full range of other propaganda, socialist literature, pamphlets, leaflets, books. A propaganda group without propaganda is pretty pointless. We want to project a DSP pamphlet series that's frequent and topical. They can be sold regularly with *Green Left*. Some of the pamphlets might be reprints, or collections of articles, or a transcription of a talk.

We need a higher profile for the party and for socialist ideas, as we've emphasised at recent national gatherings. Let's not be conned by the capitalists or our political opponents, even our ex-members, who say socialism's dead, out of date, that it's uncool to talk about changing the system.

Wins to break the electoralist consensus

But how can we challenge the predominant parliamentary/electoralist consensus? How do we go beyond propagandism? The radicalisation and the mobilisations in this period will still be weak. People could still fall back into electoralism, drift back into the framework of Laborism, or else we could see the Greens or the Democrats with their own slightly more left version of parliamentarism, of liberalism, reap the gains.

The socialists, the class-struggle current, need to have a win, or to show that you might have a win, that it's possible.

We need a sustained platform for projecting our politics. Winning bases or leadership within institutions is an extra goal of our work, but a goal that extends the resources and tools we have to build the party, extend its influence and recruit. It also provides a series of projects that can focus energies and provide a medium-term goal which the party and its members can strive for that is within our capability to reach even in current objective conditions.

It would be a major advance for the party to win permanent dominance of student politics in a number of campuses over the next few years, or emerge as the permanent left opposition inside the CPSU, or emerge as the recognised militant section of the East Timor solidarity movement. But it would not be a substitute for intervention in any big break that develops in the electoral arena. Rather, the development of bases increases our capacity to reach people, to recruit and build the party, and position ourselves better to orient to any such break.

Without these additional resources, we'll be substantially hindered in responding. Developments in Europe and New Zealand have shown, for example, that it is highly advantageous to be able to respond to upsurges in mass anger from platforms that already have some authority and visibility in 'mainstream politics'.

We have to both counter parliamentarism and compete with it. Our vehicle for the moment will remain DSEL, so we have to succeed with it, get the registration so we're ready for a July 1997 election if there's a double dissolution. We can also use it for increasing the identification of our periphery, bringing them closer to the party. We should note here the good performance by our 12 candidates in the March federal election, and our two candidates in the Victorian state election.

Is there potential for something more innovative on the electoral front? Even within the DSEL framework? Will we run in the Senate? Is the best tactic a specific socialist pole? Or should it be broader, should we try to regroup with others in a general anti-capitalist framework? We should have a more thorough discussion on election tactics at the next NC meeting.

The ALP and types of united fronts

Right now the key political question we need to be clear on is the united-front tactic. After 13 years of ALP government, we're not used to having to work *with* ALP members in joint actions against government cuts and attacks on rights and conditions.

For 13 years, the ALP has been the target of our protests. And ALP members kept their heads low. We have to make them pay, still, for the sell-outs, the betrayals. They're still our main opponent in the workers' movement. But now we have to make better use of the united-front tactic. Let's be careful we don't just have a knee-jerk reaction to the ALP; we need more subtlety now.

The united-front tactic is used in a situation where we don't command the overwhelming support of the mass of workers and oppressed – the case now and for some time to come. It's for circumstances where they still have illusions in other parties (which is still the case with the ALP, even though workers are a lot more cynical after 13 years). The dual purpose of this tactic is: to provide unity in action, on principled issues, for reforms, or to oppose particular attacks of the ruling class; to get a hearing among the masses, to win over the ranks, to expose the reformist misleaders through struggle.

Our party program provides a clear and succinct guide:

> To be effective, united fronts should be formed around clearly defined issues, should be founded on a dem-ocratic attitude towards discussion of the best means of pursuing the joint objective, and should involve respect for the right of all participants to continue expressing their views and to act on other questions. Inherently, the united-front tactic involves seeking agreements with non-revolutionary political forces. Concessions in the interests of establishing and main-taining the united front should not undercut its central purpose – the mobilisation of the broadest possible forces against the policies of the capitalist class.
> The united front is not an end in itself, but a means to unify and mobilise the masses, to draw them away from the influence of pro-capitalist leaders and to win them to the party's policies and revolutionary perspectives.

The ALP leaders are fairly wily; they'll try their best to smash, to marginalise their left opponents. Some even read their history;

they know about the united-front tactic from the other side. They want to bury the lessons of the Accord's thirteen years.

So how to guarantee they pay? How to make sure we can raise our program, and our profile, most effectively in contexts of united-front actions against the Coalition? So that we expose the Labor traitors' past errors, as well as their inaction today and in the future?

We certainly won't make our critiques preconditions for united-front actions. But we certainly will raise our critiques in *Green Left Weekly*, in other pamphlets, forums etc. And at the same time as not imposing unacceptable conditions to the ALP for their participation in actions, neither will we go quietly when they try to impose unacceptable conditions on us.

We'll also look to other political and organisational forms to register the real lessons of these 13 years. In the trade unions, perhaps a militant minority, a broad left type formation.

The Comintern's Fourth Congress theses on the united front stressed:

> It is particularly important when using the united front tactic to achieve not just agitational but also *organisational results.* Every opportunity must be used to establish organisational footholds among the working masses themselves (factory committees, supervisory commissions made up of workers from all the different parties and unaligned workers, action committees, etc.).

So we want both the basic organisations of the united front – trade unions, shop committees, campaigns against the Coalition's attacks. And also united-front organisations that are based on recognition of the ALP's betrayals, anti-Accord, for class struggle, not class collaboration.

United fronts, alliances and regroupments

What about alliances on a more general level, on the electoral level? Unfortunately the word 'alliance' has become a coverall, embracing very different political projects, and we need to differentiate:

- Joint actions, a united front that engages in *action*;
- Alliances that help promote and organise a *break* from class-collaborationist politics;
- Alliances and projects that tie the struggle in behind the ALP, keep it within the framework of the capitalist system, within the electoralist consensus.

Our program is again an invaluable guide:

> Because the underlying assumption of all ALP politics is the preservation of capitalism, there can be no permanent and generalised alliance between socialists and the ALP. Socialists enter into alliances with the ALP, or with sections of it, to defend the interests of working people, to improve the strategic position of the progressive and socialist forces, and to foster motion towards deeper mass political consciousness, particularly among those sections of the masses that look to the ALP for political leadership.

The experience of past generalised alliances – popular fronts – overseas and in Australia has been disastrous, saving the skin of the bourgeoisie and demobilising workers.

The CPA in its last decades was involved in a whole series of efforts aimed at tailing the ALP – the People's Economic Program, alternative budgets, culminating in the Accord. Last month the Search Foundation organised a series of meetings and seminars in the main cities, on 'Which Way Forward?' with

Beatrix Campbell![75]

The ALP for decades was the stumbling block for the CPA, and now that they've finally capitulated to it, can they rebuild something outside? Certainly they can use their union positions, their welfare positions, their ALP positions, to get a propaganda campaign 'alliance' going, aimed at the Libs, not challenging the ALP or 13 years of the Accord.

But could they provide enough backing to make a Bob Leach[76] type alliance effort more realistic? Could they get in the game with the Greens and Democrats? It would be more troublesome if they reconstituted another 'party' type effort; we would have to go through a lot of the old shit again.

The Greens, at least Drew Hutton writing in the latest *Arena*, want a (tame, genuinely reformist) social democratic partner for the Greens and Democrats.

Can the Search Foundation ghost provide such a social democratic partner, cobble something together?

The possibility of something falling short of a genuine political alternative was canvassed by Peter Murphy[77] at a Sydney seminar, attended by fewer than 100. He sketched a possible political program for an organisation, which sounded more like a political think tank. It all seemed oriented to education and propaganda, rather than a program for fighting, for action.

Their agenda is limited, perhaps one of helping to revive the Labor left. Their political line on the ALP still defines them. It allows them to canvas a limited 'alliance' against Howard, but prevents them rebuilding a real alternative to the ALP, or a new party.

So what are our tactics? On one level, we know they're not for real; therefore let's not waste time and energy on them. But we know they still have (a) money, and (b) connections and positions in unions and other bodies. Therefore we have to continue to keep an eye on them.

So we counterpose unity in action on specific campaigns, an *action program*, against their likely revival of 'unity behind the ALP' manoeuvre.

Other currents

We also need to look for opportunities to make approaches to the Greens and Democrats even though they're moving to the right, putting up proposals to them for united action on such things as defending Telstra, approach [John] Woodley[78] for example to support the East Timor campaign, to sponsor the August 25 action. There'll be competition among them for the space to the left of Labor. We can propose joint work, have a united-front approach, but fight against their politics. They're vulnerable, since they've got so few activists on the ground.

There's a danger of the more astute and active ALP lefts, such as [Anthony] Albanese, now trying to muscle in to regain some credibility, offer themselves as patrons of organisations, trying to absorb the anger, channel it back through the ALP and parliament. We counterpose action. Get them in organisations supporting action, but not hide away or lessen our criticism of their past crimes, and their future inevitable sell-outs.

The SPA is on a big 'unity' tack. Their call for a united front of action sounds partly OK, a common front between all left and progressive organisations – unions, parties and community groups – for actions, and a common front in parliament to reject the Coalition attacks. But their orientation to the Greens in the elections was tailist, and they refused to support our socialist campaign, attacking it in their paper's letters column.

How important is the question of Stalinism now? How to handle it, internationally and here? It's not just a historical question 'over there', not just a question of workers' democracy in a socialist state. Stalinism was above all a class-collaborationist political current within the international workers' movement that peddled its political poison under the banner of 'Marxism-Leninism'. It's not totally superseded, but now there's a changed balance of forces. We can be firmer, even aggressive on the politics, and while they shout 'unity' (for them it often means 'shut up'), we can throw the call for unity back at them, on a principled basis. There *is* a real yearning for unity in action.

And we shouldn't ignore the ultra-lefts. Comrades should be warned not to act too superior to them. If we ignore them, they could steal a march in some areas, win people that we should win (they already have some of those). In this period the united-front tactic can be usefully pushed up to them as well.

But a key point is that comrades have to relate to, argue and debate with *all* the left groups. It's essential to engage all individuals in left groups, even the most sectarian, in debate, for training, getting confidence, swatting them down and even trying to win some of their members. They do have some that we should have recruited.

Comrades should be encouraged to have a go, even if they're not totally confident; this is the way to learn, to get confidence, to test the arguments.

A final note on left sects and sectarians. You have to have more respect for them than for those giving up the struggle, rejecting Marxism on the grounds of rejecting sectarianism.

Priorities and campaigns

How do we keep well ahead of the left sects, and remove their chances for growth in a period like this? We know that anyone running up the socialist flag in an energetic way can recruit today. There's a Chinese saying, I'm told: 'In times like these, even the salted fish come alive and start swimming!'

There will be some salted fish reviving, both from the right and from the left. So don't relax now; now's the period for activity, seizing the initiative, running hard, leading, taking responsibility, building the party. Yet at the same time we have to provide the responsible alternative where we can, in the unions, for youth, in solidarity work, in the different campaigns.

So setting priorities can be a constant worry for branches, for branch executives. We're still very small, there are not enough cadres, too many openings. The '90s exacerbated this problem, with the abdication of many of those won to radical politics in the 1960s and '70s. We're filling the gap without having caught up in terms of actual strength.

Thus we have to set all our political interventions in the right framework – a party-building framework.

We intervene to build the party, through (1) recruiting, (2) expanding our influence and credibility and (3) training Marxist cadres through theoretical education and action, intervention, even confrontation.

This National Committee meeting will set our national priorities in the trade union area, the campus area and East Timor solidarity work. But there'll be a range of other activities and campaigns where we must intervene.

We need the flexibility to jump into important new campaigns. We should be able to react quickly. It will be a period of intensified class conflict, and intensified competition on the left. In a slow period our stability helps us keep going, but we must adapt to the new tempo.

The exact priorities will also have to be determined to some extent branch to branch in this period, taking into account our resources nationally and in the branch, and also taking into account who else is involved – healthy new activists or just a few tired former lefts.

We can expect many more activities. We'll try to cover them, to hit all actions, demos, pickets, rallies, meetings – with *Green*

Left sales, that's the absolute minimum of course; sell subscriptions, try to recruit, get contacts, get names on petitions, set up stalls, have our placards, our banners, our contingents, write articles for *Green Left*, take photographs, involve the activists in *Green Left.*

And as we've stressed so much at recent NC meetings, we have to raise the party profile, raise the specifically socialist banner.

We have to be conscious too of *how* we project ourselves, what image we project for the party and Resistance. It's important we're seen both as socialists and as genuine builders of campaigns, of the fight back activities, and that we're not seen as 'parachutists' by the independent activists.

Often it will be our role to provide leadership not just to our comrades and independent activists in campaigns, but also to the members of other, opponent, tendencies in these areas.

There's also the importance of having targets and building bases outlined earlier, to consolidate our activity, to reap the gains.

This also helps refute any charge of parachuting against *us.* We build permanent bases, make organisational gains. Then the other charge gets tossed up, of takeover, or competing with the existing ossified committee: CISLAC/RACLA, ASIET/Friends of East Timor. But that's inevitable if we're to take the movement forward, revive it. There'll be much louder squeals as we get in a position to assault the more important reformist bases, the trade unions.

Leadership

A central point we emphasised at the December NC plenum was the need for Marxist political clarity, for sharpness, rather than tolerating 'broader' wishy-washy politics, obscuring the fundamental class questions and playing down differences. We said this would be 'a guide to the debates we need in *Links* and with the broader left milieu internationally, now and in the future'.

The party-building report continued: 'We're not proposing that we relinquish our open, flexible approach, able to take up any opening, any possibility of regroupment, but that we should emphasise the fundamental political questions more, drawing the lessons from the past, educating in those lessons', but:

- 'We need to talk and write about our socialist ideas and politics more.
- 'We need to raise the DSP profile higher.
- 'And we need to step up the education and theoretical development of our comrades.'

Secondly, the report stressed the importance of increasing the participation of comrades, giving comrades more responsibility, through devolving responsibility onto smaller teams for the elections, encouraging more active involvement in the areas of recruitment, in Resistance, in education work: in essence, training and encouraging all comrades to be leaders.

Of course, there's their leadership and ours. 'Leadership' was the ALP's March election slogan, highlighting Keating's arrogance in implementing capitalism's dictates as though it was a guaranteed vote winner.

Charisma and confidence are helpful, yes, but most important is political leadership in action. Leadership is taking responsibility. We don't equate leadership with formal authority. Authority has to be constantly earned, re-won. You earn respect by taking responsibility. But leadership's not an obsession, a separate subject divorced from action and politics.

The socialist struggle constantly requires new leaders. We've suffered from the demoralisation of some of the old gang, comrades who were recruited and who put in good service in the '70s and '80s, even some of the more recent recruits, some of the middle layer of leaders who've stepped back.

We've also suffered from what is in effect a bleeding split of the last seven to eight years. You can see the trends among some of our ex-members. It's an unfortunate product of the move to the right of a section of the left following the collapse of the Soviet Union, and demoralisation over the prospects for socialism. Why does the collapse of the Soviet Union have the wide effect it does, for example, even on the Greens? It's not so much the collapse, but the triumphalism of the ruling class. But that can be more easily undermined than creating a new Soviet Union. A few victories for the working class, or a few disasters for capitalism, can turn things around.

An upturn in mass struggles will be an opportunity to revive some of the older comrades, and some of the tired youth with less excuse to be tired.

We can also network with our supporters better, contacting them more regularly, and organising them through DSEL and *Green Left Weekly*. We need to provide a social link – dinners, Cultural Dissent, forums, informal contact – to prevent too solid a coming together of our ex-members as a hostile bloc.

But most importantly, this new period must provide the opportunity for us to recruit new forces and grow significantly.

Where will inspiration come for the long haul? Most importantly, from having a firm grasp of Marxist theory, understanding history, the big picture, the long march of humanity away from barbarism towards the socialist future.

It will also come from an internationalist perspective, and activity in international solidarity, as with Vietnam, Central America, Asia-Pacific.

It can also come from looking at the history and experiences from our movement, here and internationally, the problems and principles in party building and developing a leadership. Jim Percy's book with the party-building reports from the '80s, for example, the 1982 *Socialist Worker* with three of his reports in it, the booklet, *Organisational Principles and Methods of the Democratic Socialist Party*. All of us could benefit from rereading them.

A leadership transition in the party is happening at branch level. Comrades in their 20s are stepping in. We have to prepare a more active leadership transition at other levels. There are plenty of openings for leading in new, small branches; for leading in trade union work, campus work, organising our East Timor solidarity work.

How do we ensure that comrades grab these opportunities? Are there structural obstacles we can remove? Are there pushes we need to give, or incentives we need to offer? Are there mental attitudes that we need to change?

Taking responsibility

It's vital that all comrades take responsibility. At the December NC plenum, the party-building report covered four areas where responsibility could be broadened: through election teams, in recruiting, in Resistance and in education.

What's been the balance sheet of the teams experience during the March elections? The feedback from branches indicated there was good potential for this approach: we did get newer comrades taking responsibility, there was wider participation.

A by-product of this focus has also been to remind us of the basic institutions of the branches where responsibility has to be taken, through our committees and fractions.

We have to allow, encourage, comrades to take more initiative. We need to convey a sense of ownership of the party to the newer, younger comrades who are faced with a choice about what to do with their lives. Sometimes they can tend to phrase their hesitations as 'Why didn't you do better?' rather than 'Why didn't *we* do better?'

Resistance

In Resistance the role of responsibility, involvement, engagement, is vital. We constantly have to assess the balance between training, guiding, on the one hand, and independence, standing on one's own feet, on the other. The need in this period, with this composition of comrades, is to lean towards independence.

What will help the separation, the independence, of Resistance and the DSP?

Firstly, we should let Resistance take more initiatives, more responsibility, think things out for themselves. They should be encouraged to take up and lead the fight in various arenas, especially the student arena. Where possible, the campus fractions should be Resistance fractions, with DSP-only comrades invited along.

This proposal doesn't mean we shouldn't convene a DSP-only fraction when necessary. And it shouldn't stop us taking the discussions of Resistance and campus work into the party branch – it's going to be needed for the integration and education of youth recruits, and also important for the *inspiration* and mobilisation of party comrades.

We'll encourage Resistance to shoulder more of their own financial responsibilities, and tend toward Resistance taking responsibility for their own *Green Left Weekly* bundles.

The key point is for Resistance comrades, for all comrades, to dive in, to learn, to gain confidence, in action, in polemic and debate, and through taking responsibility.

Fremantle branch

Last week Perth comrades took a bold step forward for the party – on Perth branch's recommendation, the NE chartered a new DSP branch in Fremantle and established the Fremantle-

Perth district.

There were good reasons for the step, reasons specific to Fremantle and to Perth branch, and those that are general in this period:

- We can see a general political opening to increase the scope of our propaganda.
- We've noted the current weakness and inactivity of the WA Greens.
- There's been real membership growth of Perth branch – from 18 to 24 since the Easter conference, with at least three other potential members in the short term. These are activists wanting to do things, not former activists in retreat.
- There are the local factors of Fremantle, a real second centre. The left has a long history there. We had harboured the thought for quite a few years that it would be easier to divide Perth branch than the larger branches of Sydney and Melbourne. It's a genuine second political centre.
- We wanted to give a chance for more of the Perth comrades to take responsibility for leading a branch.

The immediate tasks for Fremantle branch are to sell their initial *Green Left* bundle of 100; to help take responsibility for Murdoch University Resistance work (initially there won't be a separate Resistance branch in Fremantle); to concentrate on East Timor solidarity work in the community there. There's also CISLAC work in the Latin American community, and we should be looking at running a DSEL candidate in Fremantle in the state election.

Naturally enough, this exciting step makes us think about future projections, both dividing branches within cities, and looking at branches in smaller cities and towns. Lismore, for example, could possibly be our next target. There are some very interesting developments there, with a radicalisation on Southern Cross campus, and significant *Green Left* sales and subs there over the years. But there are other small centres where we know we could grow – Townsville, Toowoomba, Launceston, Geelong, Armidale, Cairns, Bathurst, Frankston. Party growth and setting up new smaller branches could provide the springboard for qualitative advances in the organisation and structure of the party in the larger cities.

Inspiration

Our perspectives are clearer and our prospects are more optimistic than they've been for a long time. More of our specific projections will be presented in the party tasks and organisation report, especially *Green Left Weekly* sales and subs, education, propaganda and raising our profile, our schedule for the year ahead.

We need a sober assessment of our possibilities, what's objectively possible in this period, but we also need to be able to inspire and motivate our membership. It's time for a little bit of 'voluntarism', an extra push, even getting hyped up, as I think we all started to feel during the discussion on student work. Be confident and aggressive.

We know the dangers of mad over-estimations that have plagued the Trotskyist movement over the years. But we also have to look for the openings, make use of the possibilities to the maximum.

In this period, we have to be able to act quickly, so our national priorities for campaigns certainly won't be set in stone for a year, for six months even. The party, the branches, have to be able to respond immediately to any new issues. But the main areas of our work, the trade unions, the campuses and our international solidarity work, especially on East Timor and Indonesia, are clear. This is where we want to build bases or strengthen our existing ones. We'll set targets to aim for, intermediate goals that are necessary for building the party, and for the political education and inspiration of our comrades.

Jim Percy outlined what we saw as four special features of our party, at our September 1980 NC meeting. We were inclusive, independent, Leninist. We are all those, we reaffirm it now, and have reaffirmed it over the years. We also need constantly to reaffirm that fourth feature, we're an *ambitious* party.

Today's the time for energy and activity, not complacency. It's a time for vision, not routinism; a time for boldness and daring in expanding our base and building the party.

8. NATIONAL AND INTERNATIONAL PERSPECTIVES

Report to the National Committee
5-7 October 1996

*In reaction to many of the attacks of the new Coalition government,
there were demonstrations and campaigns, but these were often
short-lived. The report wanted to call attention to the opportunities
to intervene and recruit from these events, despite their weaknesses,
especially now that the CPA was no longer a major competitor and
the ALP had trouble putting on a left face after its thirteen years
of neoliberal government. The report reaffirmed the emphasis
of earlier reports on orienting to radicalising youth, including
by plans to expand into areas outside the capital cities.*

This report has to set forth our immediate party-building
perspectives for the rest of this year, and also prefigure the perspectives we are likely to be presenting to the national conference
in January to guide us internationally and in Australia for the
following two years.

Links magazine

Links has proved an invaluable vehicle for our international work. It was established on the basis of our broad range of international contacts, but there's been an expansion of our contacts as a result of it in the last two years.

This is likely to be reflected in a larger international attendance at our conference than ever before. Thus we plan to hold a *Links* public meeting in Sydney on the Friday night after the conference, as well as an organising and planning meeting for those involved with the *Links* project.

Two processes are going on simultaneously with this project. Firstly, there's the process of broad reach-out and regroupment, the networking, breaking down old barriers. This has been an undoubted success, in some ways unique on the international left, drawing together parties from different origins and traditions.

Secondly, there's a process of political clarification – initially often just exchange of experiences, but also drawing the lessons, steering the discussion, the movement in the right directions. The second process is now starting to become a bit more important. The reach-out is still happening also, but a change in the relative weight of the two processes is developing.

This dual process did not begin with *Links,* of course, but was a feature of our international work since we broke out of a semi-sectarian mould in the early '80s.

Evolution of our international work

In the early to mid-1980s, breaking with Trotskyist sectarianism under the impact of the Nicaraguan revolution and the FSLN, we made a closer examination of the Cuban revolutionaries, and studied Lenin more closely. We set up our own school, our Lenin School. Our rethinking led us to look for new ways, to new thinking on old shibboleths, to opportunities for regroupments in Australia, to new collaborators internationally. We broke with the US SWP in the early '80s; we left the Fourth International in 1985.

In the second half of the '80s, we had hopes for a residual positive component of the Stalinist parties, internationally and in Australia. We grabbed at the possibility that glasnost and perestroika might herald a real change for the better, and attempted regroupments with the CPA, and later the SPA. They were tested and found wanting yet again.

In the late '80s and early '90s, we had hopes in the Greens, in green-left formations internationally and here. Unfortunately, their general evolution has also been to the right.

Green Left Weekly has been primarily an Australian project – our paper but also a *de facto* regroupment when no organisation was up to it – but it also served as an international tool, for our correspondents to travel and report, to gather other international correspondents, to have an impact on other currents.

It prepared the ground for our specific international initiative, *Links* magazine. *Links* is a very important initiative, even though it's not fully used by us here, or even internationally. It was an effort to reach out internationally, to draw together the healthy elements from different traditions we'd made contact with. Following the collapse of the Soviet Union, the process of political clarification, rethinking, and regroupment made this initiative very relevant.

That political clarification, even division, in some mass formations is continuing – in the FSLN, in the FMLN, in the PRC in Italy, in the Brazilian PT, in the SACP, with an ongoing and interesting debate.

During the last two years our contacts have expanded further. We developed a much bigger range of contacts in Latin America. We built up contact with Militant Labour in Britain. We made contact with an interesting range of parties on the Indian sub-continent, in India, Nepal, Bangladesh.

This year we got to know the German PDS better, and they got to learn about us, especially through the attendance of Andre Brie at our educational conference in January. We made contact with the ODP, the new fused party in Turkey, and a regroupment in the Dominican Republic. We made direct contact with a small group in Japan that supports *Links*, as well as the Canadian distributors, the former CPers there. We also expanded our contacts through the East Timor conference, other overseas trips, and participating in the Zapatista conference.[79]

Anti-Stalinism

We'll continue to reach out to broader forces internationally, and make new contacts, bring more groups into the *Links* project. There's still an unravelling of ex-CPs going on.

A clarification on Stalinism is still taking place. Some currents are hardening up in their old dogmas. Others are carrying out revolutionary policies in practice, drawing their lessons from Lenin's time.

At our educational conference in January we emphasised those important political 'dividing lines', Stalinism and social democracy. It's not a question of origins, of course. Some revolutionary parties of the future will come from a Stalinist background. Some that we are working closely with today have those origins, and it's a tribute to our ability to think politically, and not scholastically, that we've been able to make those links, unlike dogmatic sects who can't see change, who think in terms of labels and timeless categories, mistaking form and content.

But parties that can renew the socialist project need to be clear on both the problems of Stalinist politics and practices implemented today, and also on historical questions, especially the

'30s. That's important, because a future revolutionary party can succeed only in *opposition* to that disastrous tradition – firstly, to be able to win over, convince, the mass of the working class, and secondly, not to repeat the mistakes, the crimes, of Stalinism.

But we've also seen the dangers of an emotional rejection of Stalinism, without a proper Marxist understanding of the phenomenon, how it can lead to a rejection of Leninism, the rejection of a revolutionary perspective, of the possibility of socialism. The Committees of Correspondence in the USA look like they're going down this road (unfortunately they've also retained most of the CP's political line, supporting the Democrats, for example). The unfortunate demise of Line of March/*Crossroads* seems partly due to this too; at least Irwin Silber's book[80] was a bad case of it.

The retreat to the right of former Marxists, in the name of rejecting sectarianism or Stalinism, or reviving the line that Leninism leads to Stalinism, even gives a little breathing space for Stalinist throwbacks.

Anti-sectarianism

A rejection of sectarianism can also easily slide into a rejection of a revolutionary socialist perspective, as people get cast off from sectarian Trotskyist groups, or these groups harden up in their sectarianism.

This seems to be partly the case with a number of the ISO/ [British]SWP splits around the world – Socialist Alternative here, the New Socialist Group in Canada, and splits in South Africa and Britain etc. The new groups seem to have both left and right characteristics, but in reaction to the bureaucratic regime of the ISO/SWP, an anti-Leninism is getting entrenched.

Also, some comrades involved in regroupment processes around the world have had the misconception that renewal and regroupment must mean a shift to the right, an accommodation to reformism. In the USA, for example, discussions have taken place between Solidarity, CoC, Democratic Socialists of America, Freedom Road Organising Committee and the Socialist Party. There are good comrades and good intentions involved in all of these groups, no doubt, but sometimes I've seen their self-characterisation as 'the anti-Leninist left'.

Positive developments

On the other hand, there have been many positive developments in the socialist renewal process around the world as well. The most exciting and important developments have been taking place in Asia:

- In Indonesia, the emergence of the PRD as a class-conscious workers' vanguard in the largest country in our region is an extremely exciting and encouraging development. The comrades are young, but have displayed a very mature political sense, grabbed openings and managed to insert themselves much more centrally in Indonesian politics in the lead-up to and aftermath of the 27 July events.[81]
- In the Philippines, the comrades in MR are reorganising and maintaining, even expanding, their mass base in the Manila region. As Sonny [Melencio] reported on Saturday, they've still not succeeded in uniting with splits from the CPP in other regions, and are still working on the organisational and political questions involved in making the transition. We should help build and publicise their counter-APEC conference in Manila 21-25 November, and attend it if possible. The close collaboration between the Philippines and Indonesian comrades and ourselves has the potential to help further the development of revolutionary socialist parties in the Asian region.

- In India, we hope to develop closer links with the CPI (ML) Liberation. They have Maoist origins, and still have those trappings, but don't have a Stalinist, class-collaborationist program. They're a healthy party, with a big and expanding mass base, and open to debate on revolutionary strategy, on the Trotsky-Stalin fight in the Soviet Union. There are interesting developments also in Nepal and Bangladesh, and of course there's the NSSP in Sri Lanka.

We hope to be able to develop further our contact with Militant Labour in Britain. They now have someone on the *Links* board, and hopefully they'll distribute it seriously too. They've not only been able to lead important struggles in recent years, but also able to make a healthy reassessment of many past positions, although they're still stuck on Ireland. Their international work still has two sides to it: opening up to parties outside their current – the FI, ourselves, large parties such as the PDS, the PRC – but then putting their main emphasis on the fostering of little clone groups as part of their Committee for a Workers' International in as many countries as they can, often groups with only a few dozen members, while cutting themselves off from much larger revolutionary parties. We'll see what the repercussions of their current discussion there are, and what fallout there is from Militant here breaking off discussions with us.

The Sao Paulo Forum set a good example in the wake of the collapse of the Soviet Union, and provided a meeting place for the Latin American left, but seems increasingly oriented to parties relying on the parliamentary arena.

The EZLN conference provided another dimension of 'broadness', but little political clarity.

What direction do we hope our international collaboration will go in? Which are the links we value and respect the most?

We value the left, the militants. We'll develop and maintain fraternal relations with those moving to the right, and still hope to influence them, and work with them where possible. But we're also realistic about the directions in which some parties are heading, and what politics are needed for a successful socialist renewal. Broad milieus, such as the Sao Paulo Forum and other broad international gatherings are needed, but we also need greater political clarification now. So the political role of *Links* is even more important.

International collaboration on campaigns needs to occur. The PRD defence campaign could be one such useful rallying point, so that's another reason for us to go flat out on it.

Building the DSP, developing a Marxist cadre

There are obviously different tempos for the international renewal and for our party-building work in Australia, building the DSP and Resistance, but there are some similarities. For example, you can look at the balance between:

- The recruitment, consolidation and education of a Marxist cadre. This aspect of building the party is always the basic goal, the bedrock.
- The less direct ways of building the party, such as our unity attempts of the 1980s

You can also compare the relationship, the balance, between those basic party-building tasks and our interventions in campaigns, our united front work. *Green Left Weekly* itself embodies this duality, being both a de facto unity effort, reaching out, when the possible candidates for unity had collapsed, and a basic party-building tool.

We always do both, but there's a different balance at different times, in different circumstances.

Our basic party-building perspective is outlined in the draft perspectives resolution for the conference:

> 22. While our goal is to build a mass revolutionary
> workers' party capable of leading masses in struggle,
> we recognise that we are not such a mass party or
> anything approaching it. We are the propaganda
> nucleus of such a party. This means that all our activities
> are propagandistic in their goals, that is, aimed at
> reaching out to radicalising militants with our ideas
> and winning them to our ranks. It means that we put
> priority in our activity, including in the mass move-
> ment, on explaining and popularising our ideas ...

But this does not mean we have to circle the wagons, batten
down the hatches. It certainly doesn't mean we just engage in
propaganda activities (along the lines of the quintessential sects
such as the Spartacists). The resolution continues:

> 23. While we are too small to directly alter the ob-
> jective political situation by calling into being mass
> struggles, this does not mean that our role is limited
> to commenting on events from the sidelines. We can
> initiate modest-sized actions that can set an example
> to broader forces on how to struggle. Where these
> actions raise issues and demands that connect with
> the concerns and sentiments of the broad masses they
> can have an impact on the class struggle by forcing
> the labour bureaucracy, the capitalist media, and the
> bourgeois parties to address these issues and concerns.
> Moreover, the majority of radicalising workers and
> students will only be won to a class-struggle perspective
> as a result of their exposure to Marxist propaganda
> drawing out the lessons of their own experiences in

struggle. Our propaganda work is therefore most effective
if we are actively involved in the mass movement.

In this period we can even take modest initiatives ourselves,
and intervene in other campaigns that crop up. We'll be seizing
every opportunity to lead in practice, even though we're too
small to change the balance of class forces. But we'll be increasingly leading what struggles do take place, increasingly critical to
whether it happens, how it goes.

This link between our propaganda work, our basic party-building tasks and our intervention in the class struggle is the
key concept to get clear in this period.

Building bases

The party-building report to our June NC meeting tried to
clarify this relationship further, and introduced the concept of
us striving to develop permanent bases as a way to better understand our party-building tasks.

Our progress in the past four months on these targets has
been good. I'll recap those positive interventions:

- Trade union, especially CPSU, work. We've developed a
  relatively large network of militant delegates through the
  DEETYA campaign.[82] Tim [Gooden] was elected as secretary
  of the ACT government section, and will now be on the CPSU
  National Council. We've trained a good layer of comrades in
  trade union work.
- Campus, high school and TAFE work. We've had some
  successes in SRC and NUS elections. We can see some
  campuses where we can build a strong base. NUS
  conference will be very different for us this year, with an
  organised intervention. We can see the potential of national
  high school work next year, the strongest high school base for

many years, which we can plan next year to more than double it.

- International solidarity with Indonesia and East Timor. 25 August, despite the sabotage attempts, was a big success for us. We also had the successful East Timor conference. We've begun to build ASIET into a broader, stronger national solidarity organisation. There's the PRD defence work – the publicity, information, initiation and coordination of actions so far.

The balance sheet of the last few months must also include the results of our specific party tasks. That's the next report, but comrades are well aware of the pluses and minuses:

- The *Green Left Weekly* sales and subs campaign, where we've failed so far. A major focus for the rest of the year must be to remedy this.
- But we've had a major success with our financial campaigns, our fund drive, the budget, in spite of the big shortfall from *Green Left Weekly* sales. That's something to make us very confident, proud.

Party building in 1996

1996 has been a good year for us so far, politically and organisationally, and the last four months since the June NC plenum have been hectic, successful and productive. You get the feeling we're a much more *engaged* party, more in touch with more of the real struggles, and in a position to make gains.

The party this year has grown only modestly – there's too much turnover of newer members, and attrition of some longer term members still continues. But recruitment is balancing attrition. Our overall membership has stayed steady since the June plenum and there's been a slight growth since the end of last year. We'd like to have grown more, but compared with the rest of the left, we're doing well.

Resistance has grown in the past year, with a larger number of dues-paying members. And many branches have a good list of potential members, so we will grow between now and the conference. As comrades heard yesterday, branches have 33 Resistance members on their lists to be asked about joining the party.

The party has responded well to the new period. We've intervened in what struggles have occurred. We passed the test on 19 August, mobilised 130 comrades for our propaganda intervention, and politically responded to the events.[83]

This will continue to be a period of retreat for the leaderships of the mass organisations – the trade unions and other peak bodies. Thus there will be defeats. But it's not a period of retreat for us. This situation gives us the opportunity to actually lead some modest-size campaigns.

This reflects the good side of the end of the Accord, the good side of the collapse of the Soviet Union, the good side of the dissolution of the CPA. There'll be a difference with the last period, and previous periods, of radicalisation: there's less chance for cooption. The leaders of mass organisations, peak bodies, will be less in evidence in united fronts and any actions. We'll be on a more equal footing. Where they try to exclude us or the left organisations, they can come a cropper.

There are more openings, more possibilities, than we can actually handle. We're confident in the party's ability to grow. We can look forward to the prospect for modest but sustained growth in 1997.

Movementism

But to succeed, we must get the relationship between our party-building perspective and our interventions in the campaigns correct. Let's be on the lookout for the danger we've identified as 'movementism'. Trade union work gets counterposed to party-building work; building the education campaigns gets counterposed to building Resistance or the party. We can lose track of the interconnection, forget which is our most important task, building the party, and forget how it's done while engaged in all other political activities.

It's a bourgeois idea, a bourgeois pressure. It's a pressure that's strong outside the party, and gets reflected inside too.

Many wish the party would just go away; it embarrasses them for us to raise our profile. For example, we've come sharply up against the fear and loathing of the old East Timor cliques this year. We've stirred up the fear of the trade union bureaucrats, with their accusations of 'other agendas' and 'factional interests'. And we've seen the fear of our political opponents in the student movement: the outright red-baiting by the ALP right, and the more subtle pressure by the ALP left or the 'non-aligned left' not to raise our flag. Even red-baiting about parties from Militant.

This issue comes up in some of the debates around the world too. For example, how many times have you seen misused the line from the *Communist Manifesto*, 'The Communists ... have no interests separate and apart from those of the proletariat as a whole' as an argument against building a party, which was the very project of the *Communist Manifesto* itself.

Our political priorities

We set three main political priorities at the last NC plenum, and these will continue:
- Solidarity with the PRD.
- Our trade union work.
- Our student work, and building Resistance.

We also want to maintain our CISLAC work at its current level. There are also a number of areas of women's liberation work we'll be carrying out. We want to continue our involvement in the IWD committees, and build IWD in 1997, especially in the face of an assault by ALP women to take over the committees in some cities.

Reclaim the Night marches might emerge as possible foci for anti-Howard actions on cuts to women's services, and we should make sure we cover the actions well with our propaganda and have our own profile. We should be prepared to participate in campaigns defending the right to abortion, especially if decent committees or actions are initiated.

For other interventions our priority will be propaganda, raising the party profile, networking. We aim to cover all political events with *Green Left Weekly* and our leaflets, stalls etc. and recruit. Getting out our propaganda, building our profile and recruiting, must be an essential part of all our interventions.

Recruiting

The key to recruiting is to have the branches and their institutions functioning well. We need to build a political milieu, with also enough welcoming social events. Everybody must be a recruiter to the party, conscious of it all the time – while selling *Green Left Weekly*, around the HQ, in our political campaigns, on the job.

Recruiting is also a question of confidence; you need the right confident stance, aggression as well as clear Marxist politics. We've heard already of the successful experience of Melbourne comrades' intervention at Militant's high school camp. It was partly a result of Militant's inability to present their ideas, or a basic case for socialism, but also a confident stance and clear politics on our part attracted the independents there. Another example I think is Wollongong comrades successfully taking on NAL [Non-Aligned Left] on campus, not tailing or hiding our politics, which is one of the reasons for their success this year.

We need to get all comrades used to political debate, to train them in polemics with our opponents, all the while being open to real possibilities for united action by the left. We also need to organise the recruiting and contacting properly, make proper use of our scaffolding, *Green Left Weekly*, integrate the tasks.

But the key task is consolidation. We're meeting many potential recruits, especially youth, from all our political work, from *Green Left Weekly*, from clip-offs in *Resist!*[84] The task is to educate, train and consolidate them.

Looking at the experiences of the months since the election of the Coalition government, the new period, we can reaffirm one of our main pillars – our orientation to radicalising youth. That's where we continue to recruit from. Compare our recruitment in the student milieu and actions – universities, high schools and TAFEs – and the slower, harder process in the trade union movement.

Yesterday we discussed whether the radicalisation expressed in the actions last year and this could accurately be described as 'shallow', given the short-lived nature of the campaigns, and the fact that while many got involved in the actions, those involved in the organising or follow-up were few. The political understanding of activists is certainly mixed, with consensus acceptance of many of the progressive issues being challenged continually by the bourgeoisie's neoliberal ideological offensive. But at least on the issue of illusions about the ALP, and the ease with which the ALP can coopt or derail campaigns, we're much better off today than in the past, after the experience of 13 years of ALP government and craven Accord politics. Rejecting the ALP has to be part of any real rebellion today.

Another big difference of course is the absence of the CPA, which in the past would have been the major benefactor of the campaigns and the major component of organising committees.

So although the radicalisation and campaigns today have contradictions and weaknesses, the possibilities for us to intervene, lead, recruit and build the party are greater.

How to keep the youth

A vital question is how to keep the youth: how to ensure they take the next steps.

Firstly, after the first flush of excitement at breaking out, at getting an activist, progressive view of the world, but then realising that it's an enormous, long and difficult task to change it. Then, after being assigned out of Resistance, adjusting to a longer term, serious struggle.

It's a continuing battle against the ruling class culture. One angle is the question of 'careers', what to do with your life. Our initial revolutionary commitment signifies a break with that road, but it's a constant battle.

Most jobs in capitalist society are unrewarding, unsatisfying – of course. Smart working class youth can escape partially, and sometimes even a step in the direction of socialist politics can be a first step to consciousness and an alternative life or career. We've seen some like that pass through our ranks.

Sometimes middle class youth can take that first step towards revolutionary politics, and a 'career' as a socialist revolutionary, and last longer through not having the same desperation to escape through an individual solution. Sometimes a temporary escape can be provided by niche jobs – academia, social work etc., that mightn't be quite so alienating as most.

It's OK if it's just a temporary expedient, or if we have the political consciousness to still put politics first. But such careers have a pressure of their own, to impart a petty bourgeois outlook. The pressure's on to make your career the priority, or to guarantee financial security for the rest of your life, or give yourself regular overseas trips or other luxuries. Then revolutionary socialist politics becomes an embarrassment, or a drag, holds you back from what you've set as your goals, makes financial commitment to the party ever more onerous, selling the press irksome. Individualism, personal solutions, are put before social, political ones.

What do we have to throw into the battle against such ruling class values and inducements?

- International solidarity. Which heroes can we look to? In the '60s, it was Che, Cuba, Vietnam. Today, can it be the PRD? Yes. Budiman [Sudjatmiko], Dita Sari and other comrades will be on our posters.
- Marxist education. Getting a historical perspective and a theoretical understanding.
- A working-class perspective. This of course is linked to Marxist education and our political activity. Some wins, making some bases, will also help.

Marxist education

A serious approach to Marxist education is always essential for us. The socialist movement needs an understanding of the dynamics of capitalism, class society, the history of the workers' movement, all its experiences, in order to chart a strategy, to make the right tactical decisions.

Individual revolutionaries also always need both the collective framework of a party and Marxist theory to withstand the bourgeoisie's ideological assault.

Furthermore, the youth, the inexperience, of the majority of our membership dictates that we give Marxist education a high priority. A culture of politics needs to be developed in the DSP and Resistance, where comrades debate politics rather than petty gossip, where there's a thirst for political knowledge.

And given the variety of experiences, the variety of exposures, and the variety of manoeuvres and tactical measures we've had to take in the last 15 years, education and steeling of our cadres are vital. Overall these different experiences and experiments have been positive, but we're also aware of the negative, unsettling effect this can have on comrades too.

There's always the danger when going through manoeuvres that some comrades will convert our tactical necessities into political principles. Entrism becomes a permanent principle. Alliances become the required form, even without real content. Broadness becomes a permanent orientation rather than a conjunctural response. Anti-sectarianism can even become anti-socialism, anti-Leninism.

Then there are all the charges and accusations flung at us by our political opponents, from right and left. The slanders step up of course as our relative weight increases and our profile grows. Without education our members can either bend, or shut up, or simplify and defend our tactics and strategies with dodgy arguments.

So Marxist education is vital. We need to raise the profile and importance of education across the party, and implement a clear national plan. Each branch needs a clear plan for classes, educationals, reading, seminars, conferences, camps and educational literature for members. And it needs to carry out the plan, make sure the classes happen, follow them up.

The formal, basic education is vital, but we also recognise the need for *active* education, not just passive book learning. Comrades need to be steeled in action, standing on our own feet, learning through struggles, political fights, polemics.

Our goal is to build a politically homogeneous Marxist party, to be in a position to make sharp turns and take the whole party with us, ultimately to be in the position to respond rapidly in a revolutionary situation. We're certainly not in that state at the moment; we're rather creaky, rusty on the theoretical, political level. To reach that goal of a homogeneous party, we need a free and democratic atmosphere of discussion, a membership trained in debate, in polemic and practice.

Responsibility and participation

We've hammered away at recent NC meetings on the importance of more comrades being encouraged, forced, to take responsibility. We want a bigger proportion of the organisation to take responsibility; we want more activists, fewer 'back-seaters'. This will allow us to achieve more; it will help us recruit too.

Setting up more small branches is one way to involve more comrades, to have them take responsibility, participate in all party activities. We've been inching in this direction in recent years. Having more branches in more cities and suburbs is also a way to maximise our propaganda reach.

We've had some very positive experiences with our smallest branches this year:

- In Wollongong, we've rebuilt Resistance from practically nothing. Now we have a strong Resistance branch, and an excellent base on campus, that's engaged with the political struggles and doing the main tasks well, e.g., *Green Left Weekly*, with up to 50 sales a week in the Mall. Now Wollongong is a young branch, whereas for so many years it was seen as a holding-on operation by the longer term comrades.
- Newcastle branch was also pretty much down to the bones at the start of the year, but has joined two new recruits in recent months.
- Darwin branch has been going for nearly three years now, and it's been a good experience. The geographical isolation will always make it hard, and we're still small, but the branch has

recruited, and comrades have won a high profile for the DSP and Resistance.

At the June NC plenum we reported the establishment of the Fremantle branch. The branch has now obtained an office in a house near the centre of Fremantle, holds meetings and classes there, and has some potential recruits. A key task will be to establish responsibility for Murdoch Uni, and build a Resistance base there.

At this plenum the NE proposes the chartering of another new branch, in the Penrith-Blue Mountains area. There are two already existing components of the branch – longer term comrades and contacts living in the Penrith-Blue Mountains area, and high school comrades recruited to the party and Resistance in the lower Blue Mountains. These comrades often find it hard to get to Sydney branch meetings anyway, so this is a very logical step. At the first meeting, two more comrades will definitely join the branch as provisional members: another high school comrade, and a close supporter who was formerly in the SPA. So, with an initial group of transfers from Sydney branch, the branch would begin with 10 members.

The branch would be centred on Penrith, with responsibility for the area from Parramatta westward to the Blue Mountains. Saturday sales stumps would be held at Parramatta, Penrith and Katoomba to begin with, looking to expand to other spots in Springwood, Blacktown etc. The advantage of this location is that it's distant enough from Sydney to have to stand on its own feet, and would have clear specific areas of responsibility.

The branch would hope to get some presence on the University of Western Sydney campuses at Penrith, Richmond and Westmead. There are some local political, environmental and union campaigns that comrades have already been involved in, and in the Blue Mountains last year we brought together a meeting of left and progressive people that decided they wanted to do East Timor solidarity activities.

District structures are needed where there's more than one branch in a city, so we will be proposing the NC constitute the Sydney and Penrith-Blue Mountains branches into a district, and appoint an interim district committee consisting of Dave [Wright], Chris [Spindler] and Wendy [Robertson]. District fractions will also be necessary, e.g., CPSU, other trade union, other main interventions.

In Melbourne, the branch has set up an organising committee in the Frankston-Dandenong area, to orient to and hopefully recruit from a large milieu of sympathisers at the Frankston TAFE college. Classes are being held in the area, with some Melbourne comrades assigned to attend. We hope to recruit as many as possible, and then would like to assign a few experienced comrades to look for work or study in the area, and eventually charter a branch there. So far three have agreed to become provisional members, and more are likely.

Also next year we'll be looking to establish a branch in the Lismore area. Two comrades will move there next year, possibly followed by two or three others. We know the Lismore-Byron Bay area has always been very lucrative ground for *Green Left Weekly* sales, there's a fair base of subscribers and former subscribers; the Southern Cross campus has mobilised large numbers of students on education cuts campaigns in the past year; there's a high consciousness on environmental issues; and there's an East Timor committee run by some *Green Left Weekly* supporters.

We're not proposing some sort of ISO turn with these new branches; we don't have illusions about the period, or illusions about building a 'small mass party' that they have to import from Britain. We note the ISO here has had to retreat from most of the extra branches they set up. Their projections were unreal. But each of our new small branches or steps towards a new branch has been a response to some specific political openings, or not wanting to lose the possibility of some new recruits.

Our thinking about new branches has been prodded by the openness to our ideas and *Green Left Weekly* in country centres particularly. We should be considering special trips for *Green Left Weekly* sales and subscriptions combined with political meetings in many of the larger country towns.

In the future, especially with a bit of growth under our belt, we can look at places such as Townsville, Toowoomba, Cairns, Launceston, Geelong, Ballarat, Armidale, Bathurst etc., for new branches.

Of course there are dangers and disadvantages in small branches. They can't be as rounded as larger ones. The formal education and range of experiences available to comrades might not be as comprehensive. Therefore the national educational institutions and national propaganda from the party become even more important. And cheap quick communication via the internet can bridge the isolation.

But the other side is that standing on one's own feet, with the backing of the party NO etc., can also speed up education and integration.

In other branches, we should be aiming to get back to full-time secretaries for Perth and Adelaide, with part-time secretaries for the smaller or new branches. We also need to make more efficient use of rosters, even volunteers from among our supporters, to get the basic work done around the office.

Green Left Weekly

Green Left Weekly has now been going for nearly six years. The tasks and organisation report today will go into the serious drop in sales, even subs, we've undergone recently, and present proposals to address this crisis. But it's not just campaigns and harder work that will be needed. We need to understand the political importance of the paper.

We still underestimate what we've achieved. We're not boastful to say that it's the best left paper in Australia, possibly in the world. That's not just us talking, we hear it from others. But it's very much underutilised!

We know it's the scaffolding that integrates all our work – our interventions are led through the paper, we build the party around the paper, we use the paper to advertise our events, forums, literature. We need to use it more for educating party members, Resistance members, sympathisers, and as the vehicle for more debates, polemics.

There are pros and cons of a broad non-party paper such as *Green Left Weekly*. It can become and is becoming the paper of record for the left, as well as its calendar; it's becoming the place for debate – we've had wonderful letters pages this year. It's become an international news magazine. *Green Left Weekly* is a bit like *Intercontinental Press*[85] in its healthy days. There are so many countries, where our exclusive coverage is unsurpassed, unavailable elsewhere – Indonesia, Philippines, East Timor, Bougainville, Russia still, Latin America. We'll develop all these aspects, and continue to still reach out, but definitely not let the form restrict our party-building needs.

Other propaganda material

We also must do the theoretical work to back up our dominance on the ground, consolidate the hard work we've invested in a huge range of campaigns, our persistent activity, through *Green Left Weekly* etc.

We must encourage the whole party to take theoretical work more seriously – study, research, thinking, reading, debates, polemics. It's not academic, but for a purpose, directed to a political end. Although it can seem disguised at the moment, since we're not engaged in any overt faction fight, in reality it's a huge political battle, firstly, against the bourgeoisie's neoliberal offensive, and secondly against the many confused and confusionist currents in the working class and progressive movement.

We want to publish more books, pamphlets and propaganda. In many cases it's just a matter of editing and publishing material that's already there; the work's done. In other cases we have to write it. Our bookshops are vital for the education of our members, and for building a political culture that encourages comrades' reading, buying books, subs to magazines.

Let's use *Links* more in this way, to educate our members. Have discussions around articles. The hectic pace of the last period delayed the latest issue, but it will be back from the printers immediately after the NC. After that, let's keep to the regular schedule, and promote it and distribute it better.

We want to retain the *Activist* as a combination internal magazine, for discussion, education, reprints and organisation of our members. We need a more conscious approach to reports for the *Activist* from branches, from important interventions and areas of work.

Also let's make full use of *Party Campaigner* to organise our party-building campaigns with more feedback from branches, and possibly back to a four-page *PC*.

The consensus seems to be that *Resist!* was very useful, so we'll plan more of them, finance permitting. Sometimes perhaps they won't have a run on, but just be an insert in *Green Left Weekly*.

We need to significantly expand and upgrade the DSP and Resistance web pages, together with those for *Green Left Weekly*, *Links*, DSEL, ASIET, CISLAC, Resistance Bookshops, CPSU Challenge. We can't be left behind on this; it's an important new medium that reaches out around the world.

DSP profile and recruiting

We want to schedule branch Easter or post-Easter educational conferences in 1997, with a clear socialist or Marxist theme
(80 years since the Russian Revolution might be a possibility).
We want to make an early start on planning them and building
them, certainly so they're ready to go completely by O Weeks.

The NE proposes that branches start advertising their classes
publicly, in *Green Left Weekly* and elsewhere. We don't have to
give the exact time, and can have a filter, via a phone number,
and require confirmation to keep out nuts and opponents. But
it will attract some extra contacts. Perhaps more importantly, it
will let our supporters, potential recruits and *Green Left Weekly*
readers know that we do have a serious attitude to Marxist
theory, that we run classes on an Introduction to Socialism,
Introduction to Marxism, the DSP's Program, Feminism and
Socialism, Introduction to the Marxist Classics. We can run the
ads regularly in the *GLW* calendar, put them on branch leaflets,
an extra little box. Perhaps we can have even larger *Green Left
Weekly* box ads now and then listing all branch classes.

For the Jim Percy memorial meetings this year, unfortunately
Renfrey [Clarke] won't be back [from Russia] in time. So we'll
have him do a tour next year, a topic like '1917-1997', perhaps
cover some of the Easter conferences. For the lectures this year,
we were proposing that leading comrades in each branch present
a public talk on party perspectives, an argument for socialism,
perhaps linked to the Russian Revolution anniversary, but the
suggestion of Indonesia and the PRD sounds good.

Party schools

We definitely want to hold one or more party schools in
January, two or three weeks long, and perhaps a one-week

December school in Melbourne. The party needs them, comrades want them.

The difficulty of holding longer or more frequent schools at the moment is a problem of freeing up enough comrades from their branch assignments or work. But we all feel the need in this period to restart this institution as a permanent feature. With a bit more growth, and greater financial stability, we'll want to regain our full-time party school.

Also, branches need to schedule enough weekend conferences, camps and seminars throughout the year.

Next year, we need enough forums and branch meetings to have regular good political discussions, to provide political stimulation for old and new comrades, and to have something to bring new comrades to, and recruit.

Some branches have cut back to fortnightly executives, because of too lengthy discussions. But it's better to make the exec smaller, more efficient, task-oriented, and meet weekly, more briefly. We're likely to build a more unified, functioning team this way too. Executives need to be efficient bodies, to get the work done, to provide leadership and direction and coordination for the branch, and provide communication both ways with the National Office. Executives aren't the place for long, repetitive discussions. They shouldn't take away the life from branch meetings and forums.

Pre-conference discussion

What should we hope for, expect, from our pre-conference discussion? The written discussion's been open since June, but from now to the conference the written and oral discussion has to be a bigger part of comrades' political life.

Firstly, it's a time for conveying information and generalising experiences. This is something we try to do year round, but we step it up in the pre-conference period.

Secondly, it's a time for longer term reflection, for trying to work out our perspectives, trying to get clarity on problems that have been held over. Do we have all the answers? No, so get working.

And finally, it's specifically a time for hammering out differences over our tactics, strategy and theory, if they exist. We should not schedule educationals and think that they're pre-conference discussion. They're *not* the same at all. However, the discussion *will* be very educational in essence, even more so if genuine, serious debates occur.

The task for the party leadership, for NC members, in this PCD, is to take the lead, give political direction, but also open up the discussion in areas where we need greater clarity, encourage debate.

Firstly, on all the reports and the draft perspectives resolution coming from this plenum. But there's a whole list of particular questions that *I'd* like to see comrades take up. For example:

- The stage we're at in building the party here, and in the recomposition of the Marxist movement internationally.
- Our regroupment experiences in the '80s and '90s: what lessons can be learnt from them.
- The united front, what is it, how it applies.
- The ALP; the Accord experience; union affiliation. Would Australian workers be better off or worse off if there was no ALP? no union affiliation, like the US Democrats?
- Leninism, the party question again, the vanguard party, its relation to movements; Marx, or Lenin too, i.e., the Russian Revolution question, again; what is sectarianism?
- The Cannon tradition. What is it? What are the aspects we defend? What's being attacked by the IS-[Max] Shachtman tradition, with their attacks on 'the Cannon regime'?
- The politics of Militant and Militant Labour.

- Debates in the SACP, key debates in other parties.
- Small branch experiences.
- New experiences in the student movement, the unions.
- The evolution of environmental groups, peak bodies, the Greens.
- Indonesian perspectives. Popular front/united front.

Comrades here have to get writing, gear up for debates and intensify your study and reading to back up your contributions. Some topics will be debated anyway; comrades will want to write, want to discuss. On other issues it will be worthwhile to stimulate the process, to provoke, to get comrades thinking, even toss up challenges.

Something to consider for next year is whether to keep the *Activist* open for discussion. We think it would be useful to have it open for discussion on theoretical and historical questions, and discussion of ways to implement our perspectives, even open for bright ideas, or worries. The party would benefit from a more open approach that encourages more debate and discussion.

Today an organisation with a free and open democratic discussion will be attractive to radicalising young militants. Such a discussion is possible and needed today, without preventing the possibilities of centralised action when it's needed.

Change in relationship of forces on the left

The draft perspectives resolution points out:

> 24. There has been a striking change in the relationship of forces within the radical movement since the last federal Coalition government. Under the [Malcolm] Fraser government of the late 1970s the radical movement was dominated by the social-democratic left in the ALP and its allies in the Communist Party. Today

there is a partial vacuum on the left, resulting from:

    a. The incapacity of the labour bureaucracy and the various liberal-reformist leaderships of the other social movements to break with bourgeois electoralism.

    b. The collapse of the social-democratic left as an identifiably separate force on the Australian political scene owing to its uncritical support for the Labor government's neoliberal austerity program and its withdrawal over the last decade from involvement in extra-parliamentary struggles to immerse itself in the bureaucratic machine politics of the ALP.

    c. The destruction of the Communist Party due to its support for the class-collaborationist alliance between the labour bureaucracy and the ALP government.

25. Owing to these circumstances, and the still small size and influence of the revolutionary left, the initial struggles against the Howard government will be disconnected and fragmented instead of being programmatically and organisationally coordinated through the influence of any single leadership. However, unlike the situation under the Fraser government, these struggles will arise in a context in which we do not have to confront the hegemonic domination of a relatively large pro-ALP left-reformist party. The relative strength of the DSP within the organised left puts us in a better position today to win the political leadership of the radicalising workers and students that will emerge out of struggles against the Howard government.

26. In the wake of the dissolution of the old Communist Party, the organised left consists of ourselves and a range

of smaller petty bourgeois leftist sects, all competing
for the allegiance of unaffiliated young radicals. In this
context, mobilising broad forces in independent mass
political action requires bringing together a diversity
of elements in united-front type coalitions aimed at
building a broad base for mass action on specific issues
directed against the Howard government. Because of
our relative strength within the organised left and our
understanding of how to apply united-front tactics,
our party can play a crucial role in initiating and
holding together such united-front type coalitions.
Joint action, however, does not entail the suspension
of political differentiation and polemical struggle
against our petty bourgeois leftist opponents. To
the contrary, we must be continually on the alert
for concrete situations in which to effectively counterpose to their false ideas, positions and methods
the proven program and methods of Marxism.

So we'll toss up challenges, adopt a united-front approach to
the rest of left, to build the campaigns we initiate or are involved
in. We can expose their limitations, their sectarianism, their
inadequate politics.

The discussion on Saturday addressed the question of what
chance or likelihood there is of the ALP rising again to try to (mis)
lead the movements, make a fake left turn and divert or coopt
radicalising young militants. The consensus seemed to be that
there was no sign of revival, no hint of a left turn. So we're not
seeing much of them, and the united front is rarely posed in this
period. But we'll still pose a united front to them on actions over
issues (not the tailist caricature of a united front that the CPA
followed and the SPA follows) but recognising:

- On many of the issues they're not going to be able to support even the basic demands of most campaigns, their policies are so rotten. On so many of the issues and campaigns, Labor was so complicit in preparing the ground for the latest attacks – privatisation, weakening the unions etc. – that a decent campaign and slogans can't avoid making the connection.

- They're so sectarian, (and wary) they'll refuse, demand that it's just them on a platform, certainly not us or other lefts (that doesn't stop us tossing it up to them, of course, to expose them yet again).

Is there any chance of winning over individuals? That should be the aim, the purpose of the united front tactic, 'to steal their supporters'. We won't do it by accommodating to them, so scathing criticism, sharpness, is needed. The most likely recruits are from those already disillusioned, the many who've already turned their backs on the ALP. Many are angrier than us. So trenchant ongoing criticisms of the ALP and the Accord record are absolutely essential.

We'll win people in struggle, yes, but also in debates. Raising a socialist flag, putting a clear Marxist analysis, in this period is essential.

Failure of Militant

The one group on the left that we had some hopes for in the first half of this year, Militant, has taken a step back, deciding to break off discussions on exploring the possibility of unity with us.

They've decided instead to take in most of the membership of Solidarity and Communist Intervention. This means they've taken in a few rather hardened sectarians, with their own factional agendas. It will make interesting watching the digestion process.

The regroupment could give them an initial boost. They'll certainly be aggressive, with extra confidence. They boast of tripling their membership in Melbourne, claiming 25 now, but with six in Sydney, and a few in Perth, that still doesn't put them much over 30. They'll be looking for quick fixes.

They're unencumbered with a range of interventions, a range of responsibilities, so they, and ISO, and Socialist Alternative, and other small groups, can concentrate on a campaign or two, plus the weekly forum/meeting recruitment focus. We have to cover them in the campaigns, not allow any of them to get a jump, and match them with our aggressive recruiting and political discussion. We need to schedule enough party events, forums, functions, to build in *Green Left Weekly*.

What it means to be a revolutionary today

What does it mean to be a revolutionary socialist today? What are the new features, or the challenged concepts that we should reassert? What are the questions important for recruitment and consolidation of new members? What are the issues that motivate us, and will inspire others and ensure the party develops?

Firstly, we need seriousness, professionalism, commitment. Commitment and dedication are essential, a point we've always stressed. But you notice, around the world and here, that rejection of 'sectarianism' too often gets misinterpreted to mean rejection of revolutionary commitment, dedication and activism. You get the 'paper sellers' charge – from people in US Solidarity, to the anarchists of the Newtown Political Collective, to Militant here. There's cynicism about commitment and activity. You see scorn about handing over money to the party. There's contempt for any idea of party loyalty. Cynicism on these questions is fatal for a revolutionary party. You'll never build anything.

Secondly, we need a collectivist approach. A proletarian approach to politics is fundamentally collectivist. The party's an instrument for a specific task – leading and organising the transition from capitalism to socialism. We can't reproduce the future socialist society in relations between comrades today. But we should do what we can to avoid reproducing all the worst of capitalist society inside the party – competitiveness, individualism, a dog-eat-dog attitude to others.

We're engaged in a joint project. We should all be multiskilled. We don't want a special caste of thinkers, and a lower caste of doers. All comrades should be thinkers, theoreticians, all should have a chance to study, be encouraged to speak out, write, lead. And all should do shitwork (cleaning the HQ, 'menial' tasks). We've had indications of some new young Resistance comrades seeing the relations between comrades in hierarchical, individualistic terms. We'll pay a political price for such attitudes. It will miseducate others; it sets the wrong example; it's likely to demoralise other comrades. It runs against our party-building needs. A collectivist approach is non-hierarchical. We want genuine equality in the party. It's the efficient way too.

In the struggle, we know we need leadership. That's the project of the party itself. So all of us are leaders. But we build an inclusive party and a team leadership. Teamwork is the proletarian norm. We aim to build a team of comrades engaged in the most important task there is.

But also vital is initiative, thinking for yourself, standing on your own feet, taking responsibility. That's the third point – engagement, participation, taking responsibility. That is, you get the conviction that you're connected to the struggle, in important ways that *you* can make a difference. And we all have the feeling of 'ownership' of the party.

We've been pushing on this over the last year or two, trying to encourage comrades to take more responsibility, learning through having a go, participating. We should also understand that *now* is important, i.e., don't put your political activity and commitment on hold, until you think the class struggle might heat up, and concentrate instead on your personal enjoyment and betterment.

Fourthly, developing theoretical confidence, through education.

Fifthly, political boldness, ambition. We need to break out of routines, try new challenges, try new tactics. Our fundamental strategy for building the party has been unchanged, but we do try all tactics. Comrades should be bold, innovative too. We're still a centralised party, and need to set our priorities; because we're small, that's absolutely necessary. But we should be open to initiatives.

We should be aggressive, confident in our debates and polemics, during our interventions, in what we write.

And we won't allow small sects to falsely claim that they have the left ground. They're usually only pseudo-left on demo tactics, smashing a window or door, and overblown macho posturing, but tailing the ALP on the main political questions.

We need to claim the left ground for ourselves, raise the party, the socialist, the Marxist profile. We're activists, leading and intervening in the main struggles with no illusions that we're able to lead masses in struggle yet. But there's no need to make a permanent habit of modesty, being diplomatic about our politics, when there are no broad forces there to unite with, to work with, when the main recruits will be coming from the radicalising youth.

Solidarity with the PRD

Sixth, and finally, we have an internationalist perspective. Here I want to stress again the special importance of solidarity with the PRD. It's important, firstly, for basic reasons of internationalism; it's our fundamental *duty*. Those brave young worker and student activists need our help against the vicious repression of the brutal Suharto dictatorship. They're in the vanguard of the struggle for democracy there, and leading a clever and heroic fight.

Secondly, *Australian* imperialism has fostered a special relationship with the Indonesian military dictatorship, for sordid economic reasons. As our draft resolution states: 'Victories won by the movement for democracy in Indonesia not only help alter the relationship of class forces in Indonesia to the workers' advantage, they also help to weaken Australian capital. Every advance made by the workers in Indonesia in their struggle for democracy directly helps to strengthen the working-class movement in Australia.'

Thirdly, they're *our* comrades. We've developed a close relationship with them, we see eye to eye with them, we've helped them in various ways.

There's a fourth reason too. We should prioritise the defence of the PRD for the education, training, inspiration and steeling of our own cadres. *We* benefit. It directly contributes to building our party here. Since we don't lead the mass of the working class here, there are likely defeats ahead and potential demoralisation for our comrades here. The events in Indonesia provide a bigger horizon, an international perspective, a more immediate revolutionary example. The struggle of our comrades in Indonesia can inspire and spur on our comrades here.

This solidarity campaign is a perfect illustration of the interconnection of our international socialist renewal work and our party-building work in Australia. It's a vindication of our course over the last decade.

Perhaps also the reactions of sectarians to events in Indonesia provide a second vindication – 'there but for the grace of god go we'. If we hadn't broken with a sectarian, pure 'Trotskyist' framework, would we also have regurgitated our slab of text on Permanent Revolution and wagged our fingers at the PRD?

At our national conference, 3-8 January, a major focus will be on the PRD, on solidarity with the struggle in Indonesia. The venue will be decorated with banners, slogans, displays on the struggle in Indonesia, with portraits of the jailed comrades. There'll be a report, videos, feature talks, panel discussions.

With this, and all the international guests, and all the interesting discussions, and all the new young comrades there, and experience of a very successful year, and good prospects for 1997, we'll have a great conference.

9. RECENT INTERNATIONAL WORK

Report to the 17th National Conference 3-8 January 1997

This is an excerpt from the international work report to the National Conference. It gives a concise description of the range of the DSP's efforts to increase international ties in this period.]

During the last two years, our international contacts have expanded further. Comrades' trips to the Philippines and Indonesia have been invaluable. Graham Matthews and Karen Fletcher attended the PRD founding conference last year. Dick Nichols attended the Philippines Slam APEC conference in November organised by the BMP, the socialist workers' centre. Reihana Mohideen was based in Manila for most of last year, and was also able to visit Japan and make direct contact with the small group in Japan that supports *Links*, as well as other left groups.

We made contact with important parties on the Indian subcontinent, in India, Nepal and Bangladesh through visits by Sujatha Fernandes and Michael Tardif. Especially important has been our contact with the CPI (ML) Liberation. Sujatha worked with them for all of last year.

We developed a much bigger range of contacts in Latin America, through Steve O'Brien, and Dick Nichols' trip, attending the Sao Paulo Forum. Steve attended the conference in the Dominican Republic that formed FR (Revolutionary Force), a fusion of four parties. It's an interesting regroupment for us to follow, and they've sent greetings to our conference.

Chris Spindler, Trish Corcoran, Neville Spencer and Sandra Wallace attended the Zapatista conference in Mexico. Comrades have attended the Fourth International world congress and IEC [International Executive Committee] as observers, and developed closer contact with some of the better parties in the FI.

We developed contact with Militant Labour in England and Scotland, which we hope to be able to develop further. Lynn Walsh, one of their leaders, is now on the *Links* editorial board, and hopefully they'll distribute the magazine seriously too.

Last year we got to know the German PDS better, and they got to learn about us, especially through the attendance of Andre Brie at our January educational conference, and collaboration on Indonesian solidarity work.

We also expanded our contacts through the East Timor conference we organised in Sydney in June, meeting other activists from different countries in Asia.

We've renewed our contacts with the Trotskyist groups in Hong Kong, and one of their comrades had initially planned to make it to this conference. We made contact with the recently regrouped ODP in Turkey; one of their leaders visited Australia.

Maurice Sibelle was able to attend the Committees of Correspondence convention in July. He also made contact with the Canadian distributors of *Links* in Toronto, the former CPers there, who operate through the Cecil Ross Society. Chris Spindler and Trish Corcoran attended the Solidarity convention and summer school this year.

We've maintained our contacts with the New Zealand

NewLabour Party and Alliance. I attended their conferences last Easter.

Sam Wainwright was able to attend the French LCR congress last November. We also received an invitation to the French CP congress held last December, and Sam was able to attend that also.

Comrades have made follow up visits to South Africa, Latin America, Europe.

That's a wide range of contacts, and I haven't exhausted the list. We're working with both large parties, with much more mass influence and strength than us, as well as smaller organisations and individuals. There were invitations to congresses we were unable to attend, such as the PRC in Italy, and the Portuguese CP. And there's a big range of greetings to this conference.

The 1990s have been the period of our most intense, and fruitful, international work.

10. WINNING AND KEEPING YOUTH

Report to the National Committee 5 October 1997

A major task of this report was to focus attention on the problem of fatigue in some layers, which affected not only older members but also some younger comrades. This was seen as mainly a product of the difficult political environment: in addition to the Coalition government's attacks and the lack of serious resistance from the union movement, the lack of a political project comparable to the 1980s regroupment attempts. John also addressed the question of whether a misunderstanding of the united-front tactic was making party interventions in campaigns less effective than they could be.

What achievements can we look back on so far this year? We've carried out an extensive and successful range of interventions.

We can be proud of the work we've done in the anti-racism campaign this year. We initiated the anti-[Pauline]Hanson demonstrations in many places. We were key organisers in others. We provided the necessary political leadership and firmness too.

On campus, we participated in practically all actions, and led quite a few of the struggles recently.

We organised a successful range of Indonesia solidarity activities, including the ASIET conference, tours, demonstrations, meetings.

There's a range of other campaigns that we've been active in, often playing the leading role, for example, in IWD, high school actions, CPSU Challenge and CISLAC.

We've made some modest progress with our basic party-building tasks. We've made some progress on *Green Left* sales and subscriptions. We've made steps forward on literature production and distribution, with new titles, improved distribution. The finance report will show we're continuing the progress of recent years towards balancing our budget. Of special note is the building refurbishment, a major achievement, costing more than $65,000.

Membership overall has been static during the last few years. Recruitment has been steady, in some cases strong, even easy. We're attracting more people than we can integrate, but it's been counterbalanced by the loss of some comrades.

There are two sides to this: (1) There's a necessary selection process: we keep the serious comrades, the activists (some branches report they've got a more *effective* membership, even though it might be less experienced). But (2) we hate losing cadres, all that investment of training and education. There's tremendous lost potential, and so many good comrades we wish were still with us.

Morale is generally high; comrades feel we've done well. Even in difficult situations like Melbourne, with a raft of left opponents, comrades feel they're getting on top of it. The political weight and authority of the party are high in anything it intervenes in.

All the radical left groups reflect the dilemma of this political period. The period is hard in some ways – Australian politics is not the most exciting. Conservative forces are confident, and outright racists are able to raise their heads. And we're still suffering the ideological fallout of the collapse of the USSR.

Nevertheless, there are still tremendous opportunities in Australian politics for growth, especially among youth. And other tendencies, even moribund ones like the CPA, can grow where we don't have a presence. So it's very much a competition, a race, on the left for youth recruits.

We still have to run hard to win that race. We might be the largest, in addition to being the most sensible, and with the best politics, but it's only a small margin. If we stop running, we'll be overtaken.

We are and will be going at a hectic pace. There's lots to do, we *are* overworked. But we shouldn't lapse into any tone of panic. There's going to be stress and stressful situations. But comrades have to find their own individual ways to handle that, and resolve it in a political way.

Revolutionaries *should* be busy. If we didn't have more than enough things to do, a huge range of tasks and openings, there'd be something wrong. There'd *really* be something to moan about.

At this NC plenum, as well as at recent NC meetings, we have recognised more openings than we can effectively handle. Thus setting clear priorities is absolutely important. We need to give priority to the things that build the party. That's the criterion – the recruitment, consolidation and education, the creation of cadres.

Integration and development of youth

But most important is the recruitment, integration and development of youth. This is our key task. Recruitment of youth has kept the DSP going, and Resistance has been an integral part of our development. We need to keep that youth recruitment flowing, and step it up. But also, we need to close the back door, prevent younger comrades dropping out after a few years in the party, reduce the attrition rate at least. We'll always have a high turnover in Resistance, that's partly the function of the youth organisation. And we'll also have a turnover of provisional members, it has that testing role. But the worrying trend is the too high a turnover of young comrades who've been in the party for a few years.

We think we understand the reasons for the attrition rate. It's fundamentally a political problem. Comrades who've dropped out or stepped back have succumbed to the direct or more subtle arguments of the ruling class, and are making their peace with the system.

But to succumb, in most cases, is the result of a limited political outlook in the first place. Clearly the comrades on the verge of dropping out have assimilated only a superficial understanding of Marxism.

How does the process work? There are lots of halfway houses on the road to making peace with the system. Thus it's worth getting comrades to examine more thoroughly the differences between, for example, anarchism, movementism, liberalism and a revolutionary Marxist perspective. All those have a flawed understanding of the nature of state power, the process of revolutionary change, and the key question of the revolutionary party.

Without a clear understanding of the party perspective, how it unites all other political problems, how it's necessary for the long term, but also for the immediate struggle, a comrade is not going to last too long.

We are all aware of the pressures to retreat from that consciousness. 'Grow out of it', 'Go beyond your youthful enthusiasms' are the refrains. We know the many pushes, the pulls, the inducements, the bribes, which are possible in a rich imperialist country like Australia. You *can* have an easy life, if you're smart, or inherited a bit, or escape the chains of consumerism, or compromise your ideals.

But having gained that Marxist consciousness, can you shut the pressure out? As an individual, can you resist all the ideological pressures, the media barrages, all the other avenues? It's not very easy, really not possible unless you have a party framework.

Key to retention of comrades is Marxist education, education in our line, but it's also important for comrades to be steeped in the culture of the socialist movement, its history and traditions. To know of, and identify with, the past struggles, the past sacrifices, the expectation of the sort of life to lead.

James P. Cannon, in a 1953 speech, put it this way:

> The revolutionary movement, under the best conditions, is a hard fight, and it wears out a lot of human material. Not for nothing has it been said a thousand times in the past: 'The revolution is a devourer of men' ...
> It is not easy to persist in the struggle, to hold on, to stay tough and fight it out year after year without victory; and even, in times such as the present, without tangible progress. That requires theoretical conviction and historical perspective as well as character. And in addition to that, it requires association with others in a common party.

A new generation to take the reins

Retaining *all* our comrades, especially the younger recruits, is a general problem. But there's also the specific problem of comrades reaching a certain level of political understanding and assuming a certain level of responsibility, and then pulling back.

At our last NC meeting in June, I intervened in the discussion on the tasks report trying to address this issue – the attrition – and more specifically the stepping back of some younger party and Resistance leaders once they'd reached a certain point, and should have been on the verge of taking on even more responsibility.

I made a specific appeal to NC comrades, to step forward, to volunteer for particular assignments, such as branch organiser: to take the reins of the party, in a small, medium or large branch, to volunteer for a transfer, to volunteer for a full time assignment, now or in the future.

I got a few takers (although unfortunately probably just as many comrades have been giving an indication that they wouldn't mind stepping back a bit). So I'd make that appeal again. Volunteer for a particular assignment, say that you'd like a challenge, that you want something that will stretch you. Volunteer for the harder assignment. Motivate yourself; don't wait for a call from the NO. Be bold and confident in yourself. And be bold and confident about the role of this party and the role you have to play in it.

High school work

Youth are the guarantee of the future of the party, and high school students can be the guarantee of our youth work. Our tendency has had a long, successful history with radicalising high school students. In recent years, during the '90s, there have been consistent mobilisations – on uranium, the sex diary, French [nuclear] tests, environment, anti-racism, education issues. We need to continue to be the leading force among high school students, and step up our recruitment.

High school students can be the guarantee of our successful campus work. Recruiting more high school students, integrating them, and then having them strengthen our campus fractions when they come to university can be the way to making the qualitative jump on campuses.

The campus club versus the downtown branch dilemma for

university students was tackled with the formation of Resistance in 1967. The downtown centre was a much needed escape for high school students, from home, from school restrictions. For university students, campus facilities and relative freedom provided their own lure, a counter-attraction. We should maximise use of our centres for high school students, welding together young workers and unemployed, campus students and high school students, through our political activities, a social milieu and tasks and activities to cater to their idealism and energy.

Resistance high school students can organise through many structures: *Student Underground* or other news sheets; secondary student unions; no work for the dole committees. We've learnt further lessons this year, but the key thing is, given the special difficulties of high school organising, how can we recruit and train more high school students as Marxist cadres?

Resistance leaderships have to give this constant attention. We have a big responsibility here. We have to look for ways that raise the political consciousness of our high school students: organisational steps that consolidate them to a party perspective, beyond an issue-based view. There are more restrictions on high school students, so grab any opportunity. For example, the NE wants to raise the possibility of a special January school for high school comrades going on to campus in 1998. It would prepare year 12s for political life at university, so they would have a head start as campus activists. How many high school comrades do we have in this situation who would be able to attend? Let's check this out over the next few weeks.

Another special task for high school comrades would be to help out with the ACT election campaign during January-February. A few extra full-time activists could be extremely important for this major intervention.

Also there's the use of *Green Left* internships, for our comrades. It's useful help where it's always needed, and a week or more on

Green Left can contribute an enormous amount to the training and integration of high school comrades.

Project, focus, target

One problem of the stage we're at, the political period we're in, is that as a small propaganda group, with the class struggle in Australia at a fairly low ebb, we lack a clear project, a focus for our activity, a clear target for comrades to direct their fire at.

It's not just a question of tasks, or campaigns in general. We've got a full swag of those, many openings, many tasks. It's the on-going campaign or battle, the major significant *project* that we lack.

In a general sense there's capitalism, bourgeois society, the ruling class, the whole caboodle, there's plenty to get angry at. But we're still at the propaganda stage, so there are no battles on anything approaching equal terms (not even any guerrilla skirmishes really).

On a second level, aiming our fire at the secondary lieutenants of capital, there's the ALP. But it's so rotten today, making such a meagre effort to distinguish itself from the other main bourgeois party, it's harder for us to get to grips with.

On the local scene, we sometimes worry that perhaps we're missing out on a few too many of the local campaigns, especially the urban environment ones: freeways, airports etc. But generally these local struggles haven't involved working class communities under siege and in revolt. Mostly the natural leaders have been the petty bourgeoisie.

Australia-wide campaigns that have occurred in the recent period have often been the responsibility of Resistance, not so much the province of the party. For example, the student fees/free education campaign gives a national campaigning focus for Resistance. The anti-racist campaign has given some focus, but also mainly to Resistance. The party still lacks a dominant campaign focus.

Of course, there's *Green Left Weekly*, which is a project in its own right, not just a paper.

And we have a hunch that the 'big project' will come internationally, from the region. The region's undergoing tremendous change, and with the huge, growing working class populations in India, China, Indonesia, there'll be big struggles there.

Options, other paths

The 'new mass workers' party' can be a useful slogan and perspective, as in our *What is the DSP?* brochure, which devotes quite a bit of space to the concept, but it's not currently a realisable project. Compare our experiences in the '80s and '90s. There were some possibilities of uniting with actual forces in motion – the NDP, the Greens – or regroupment with larger forces in decline – the CPA, SPA. Today, the pathetic response to the NLP shows the lack of reality of it.

Also, compare the British Socialist Party. Their propaganda for a new mass workers' party is really a call to 'join us'.

But are there things we can adapt from the populist approach, the experiences of the European left parties, the left social-democratic parties of Stalinist origins, the PT in Brazil, the New Zealand Alliance? For example, the ex-Maoist Dutch Socialist Party has recruited rapidly (up to 20,000 members) and developed a high electoral profile by adopting a left populist approach, with a clear slogan, 'Against', catering to the anti-austerity sentiment, with attention to image (tomatoes) and a PR-oriented platform, with limited analysis or education for their members. But their parliamentary success is also partly related to the specific circumstances they're in, with a conservative-Labor coalition government, and the Green Left party shifting to the right as well.

We can learn some things, but not apply them mechanically.

Would it be possible to build both a revolutionary party of cadres and a broader left-populist party? Facing a more repressive state and the need to work underground, such multilevel organisational forms are necessary. But how would it work in a liberal democratic imperialist country?

We've had direct experience of some of the contradictions and tendencies a dual structure would impose, or a watering down of the Leninist type party, for example, as in Perth in 1994. As we've reaffirmed at party conferences since then, we need the cadre party.

But we should assess the question regularly, incorporate any new information and think again, if only to be clearer and reaffirm our perspective. And we should measure any alternative options against the other specific problems we face too, for example the attrition of youth. Would a new project help retain them, or just ease the slide out to an easier political perspective?

There's tremendous pressure to adapt, not just from the ruling class and its direct mouthpieces, but also from the liberal milieu. The continued retreats and betrayals of the traditional trade union leaderships and the NGO liberals, who never considered an alternative, means there's a pervasive milieu thoroughly committed to the status quo.

So is there another project, another step to be transitional, yet still maintain our revolutionary socialist perspective? Are there lessons on elections for example, we should be drawing from some of those European experiences, where left reformist parties' or left populist parties' electoral votes are growing?

From the same milieu and experience there's another 'lesson' for us to ponder, a *third* question for us to work on: the nature and value of united-front work, versus doing things in our own name. For example, the 'Tomatoes' are involved in few united actions and generally do things in their own name. Their leaders asked Max Lane when he met with them and was describing our views and activities, 'And what gains do you get from all these campaigns you run?' It's a pertinent question. We'd better be sure we have the clear answers to it.

This of course is something we've always noted about the social democrats and liberals. They put up front building their own profile, they abhor united action with others, they prefer to do things in their own name. Should we be following suit?

Do we sometimes misunderstand or misapply the united-front tactic? Do we sometimes tend to make it a universal tactical approach, a style, even a principle? Do we sometimes fail to raise our own profile and do things in the name of a committee, when we could still make it broad, with more direct gains, in our own name?

Misinterpretations of the united-front tactic

The united-front tactic was developed in response to a very particular situation. Following the October Revolution, the split of mass social democratic parties into their revolutionary and reformist wings and formation of the Communist International, the task for the sizeable Communist parties, especially in Western Europe, was to win the rest of the workers away from the social democrats. The initial formulation, and still possibly the most succinct, is in Trotsky's 2 March 1922 theses for the Executive Committee of the Communist International.

The united-front tactic was a proposal for action, joint action, since 'the working masses sense the need of unity in action, of unity in resisting the onslaught of capitalism or unity in taking the offensive against it'.

After breaking with the reformists, according to Trotsky, the Communists had to 'learn how to guide all the collective activities of the proletariat in all spheres of its living struggle'.

The theses had to polemicise with those who argued just for the 'united front from below', that is, just approach the masses, not the reformist leaders. The task was to 'drag the reformists from their asylums and place them alongside ourselves before the eyes of the struggling masses'.

But in united actions the revolutionary party retains its independence, and its freedom to present its political perspectives. The theses continue:

> We broke with the reformists and centrists in order to obtain complete freedom in criticising perfidy, betrayal and indecision and the half-way spirit in the labour movement. For this reason any sort of organisational agreement which restricts our freedom of criticism and agitation is absolutely unacceptable to us. We participate in a united front but do not for a single moment become dissolved in it. We function in the united front as an independent detachment. It is precisely in the course of struggle that broad masses must learn from experience that we fight better than the others, that we see more clearly than the others, that we are more audacious and resolute. In this way, we shall bring closer the hour of the united revolutionary front under the undisputed Communist leadership.

It was certainly the correct tactic for the early '20s, correct for those circumstances, but how should it be applied in other times and other circumstances? An extremely successful more recent application was in the movement against the Vietnam War, here, in the USA, around the world. It still is applicable today, in the right circumstances, but it's not a universal panacea, and we shouldn't lose sight of the central political purpose of the tactic.

The key criterion is: what will build the revolutionary Marxist party? Sometimes it will be a united-front approach to other parties. Sometimes it will be independent action by ourselves. Furthermore, the size of the revolutionary forces themselves is not irrelevant: whether there's any real possibility of forcing the leaders of the reformist or liberal parties into a united-front action, or at least making them pay, exposed before their supporters, if they refuse.

The closest thing to an application of the united-front tactic today would be us calling on the leadership of the ALP and the leaders of the trade unions to unite in a real fight in defence of workers' rights and conditions. But after the Accord years, it rings a bit hollow. Nevertheless, at the June 1996 NC plenum, we thought we had better prepare for the possibilities of some action, and opportunities to propose action to the ALP, or at least expose any revived bursts of left rhetoric.

The united-front tactic involves a *serious manoeuvre* with opponents. It's not enough to simply set up a committee and declare it, and expect the ALP to join in. Today, the ALP doesn't even want to sit in the same room with us. Thus CAR [Campaign Against Racism] is narrow – us and the ISO often, while the ALP sets up closed committees to organise reconciliation or cultural diversity concerts.

So, in the absence of the ALP in the Accord years and since, we've tended to substitute campaign committees, with the small left groups and some independents, and confuse them with a united front. Too often, the 'united front' is a pitiful grouping of the small left groups. It's certainly not what Lenin and Trotsky had in mind.

The united-front tactic is not primarily aimed at exposing the *inaction* of the liberal reformists, the ALP. If they don't act, everyone knows this. The point of a united front is to demonstrate to a broader audience that we are better leaders and fighters than the liberal reformists. We can't do this without getting some common action going.

Therefore we have to make *serious* approaches to the reformist leaderships, serious efforts to entice, cajole, force them into joint action. But if that fails, we have to do our utmost under our own banner.

So have we, by not appreciating the differences, drifted into a distortion of thinking on the united front? It will be valuable for us, but it's not a universal panacea. Otherwise, we will drift into errors, for example, not raising the party banner; or not doing our propaganda work properly and thus limiting our recruiting possibilities; or misunderstanding the class basis of the political positions of others in the 'campaigns' milieu.

Some certainly do have a distorted view of the united front. For example, Solidarity in the US seems to think that raising your own banner in campaigns is sectarian. Solidarity seems to think socialists should never organise campaigns in their own name, or in the name of a committee you dominate. It always has to be at arm's length. For example, their members castigate the Workers World Party, a pro-Maoist split from the US SWP in the 1950s, as sectarian for the campaigns it organises, which are sometimes extremely large and broad, but nevertheless dominated by Workers World.

We keep urging the integration of our work, but sometimes our party-building tasks seem to be in conflict with the tasks, the perspectives, the actions of the fronts and coalitions we establish or prop up. We should examine each case on its merits. The Resistance high school rallies, for example, have been great.

Compare our use of CPSU *Challenge* with the ISO's *Red Tape*. A lot of our work in the CPSU is now done through other fronts, so should we use *Resist!* more for our statements?

I'm not proposing we shut down any current committees. But we have to know when to act in the name of the party and when in the name of a committee.

The general principle should be, pursue our primary objective: build the revolutionary party. Generally we should do things in our own name, raise our own profile, unless there's a good party-building reason not to. Good reasons might be:

- A classic united-front situation, which we're far from at the moment;
- A united action campaign or coalition that would lead to significantly larger mobilisations than we could organise on our own, or which would allow us to engage in necessary debates with political opponents;
- To reach out to potential recruits, either new or supporters of other parties;
- To expand the reach of the party, with extra organisations that are seen as associated with the party;
- To enable us to tap sources of funds for party projects or causes that we wouldn't otherwise be able to reach.

Sectarianism

A misinterpretation of the united front can also be linked to a misuse of the term 'sectarian'. We know the social democrats denounce everyone to their *left* as 'sectarian', yet maintain the most sectarian attitudes, in the real sense of the word.

It's *not* sectarian to raise our own profile, or to put forward our political positions, or to do things in our own name. It would be sectarian to refuse united action on issues of importance to the class, or to set ourselves apart from the real struggles, content we had the right program, but not attempting to reach the masses.

One of the most frequently misused and misinterpreted quotes from Marx is that from the *Communist Manifesto*: 'The Communists do not form a separate party opposed to other working class parties. They have no interests separate and apart from those of the proletariat as a whole. They do not set up any sectarian principles of their own, by which to shape and mould the proletarian movement.'

But taken with the rest of the *Manifesto,* and Marx's other writing and practice, it's clear it's essential for communists to form their own party, put forward their program. It's not sectarian. How we relate to other currents, forces, groups, individuals is determined by the longer term interests of the class, and that's directly related to building the party.

If it's a campaign that involves just small left groups and independents who are liberal obstacles, perhaps we're better off campaigning on the issue in our own name.

We've stressed repeatedly the importance of the integration of our political interventions and basic party-building tasks. Perhaps, sometimes we can achieve an even closer integration, where we can do things in our own name without narrowing the possibilities of the action at all.

We need to refine our perspective of establishing bases. The feasible base we can establish soon is on campuses. The 'base' in the Indonesian solidarity campaign is more a question of hegemonising that area politically, and we're heading in that direction. A base in the CPSU is still a long way off, and requires significant growth in the party to achieve it.

Raising the DSP profile

Again we need to stress the theme of recent NC plenums – raising the DSP profile. In campaigns and interventions and leaflets and press releases, we'll use the DSP as the sponsor unless there's a clear reason to do otherwise. For example, if we'll reach a significantly broader audience, or if we can tap into funding that we wouldn't normally reach, as with API[86] sponsoring the Easter conference. There's an order of priority: DSP, DSEL, Resistance,

Green Left, ASIET, CISLAC, API, Cultural Dissent, others, and sometimes we'll connect the lot.

We've continually stressed the central role of the press, of *Green Left Weekly.* We've never had any doubt about the importance of the paper. But a further question is, how much can we increase the identification of *Green Left Weekly* with the DSP and Resistance? There are the obvious gains for us in building the DSP immediately. The question is, how much would we lose, in the way of independent supporters, from any increased identification? This is something we should be monitoring and assessing constantly.

We've taken some important steps recently towards a higher party profile in the paper: the 'Arguments for Socialism' column; the Resistance page; better use of DSP ads; the use of party spokespeople; pushing for a more active role by branches in preparing copy and using the paper.

We can think about further features in the paper, on fundamental issues, important historical lessons from the workers' movement. Perhaps further down the track we can contemplate a major move, some structural changes in the relationship with the party.

Initially at least, we need a major effort to reach out to the supporters who subscribe, and the former subscribers.

One coming opportunity for connecting the DSP with *Green Left* will be the ACT election campaign. We can test *Green Left* again in the ACT in newsagencies during the campaign, with *Green Left* ads on election literature – 'follow the news about the Democratic Socialist campaign'.

We should be beating our own drum, about *Green Left,* and ASIET, CISLAC and the other things we do. That is, an election leaflet that explains what we do and are, not just our policies. We connect it all up on our web sites; we can do it with other leaflets, for example, 'Join the DSP, read *Green Left*'.

We should make full use of the internet to promote the party, not just with our web sites, but also using any local or national mailing lists or discussion groups. We won't spam, but send useful content – our events, our views. We can use the net for press releases, it's cheap, and promote our web page addresses and email addresses on all our literature.

My experience in preparing the DSP web site reinforced the realisation of what an impressive array of publications and literature we have. Our assets are our accumulated politics, but expressed in words, pamphlets, books, magazines, newspapers, class series. The web site starts to take advantage of that. It plays to our strengths, making use of that political archive.

We should be more aggressive with press releases, in the branches as well as the NO. Swamp the media. We can reuse the text for leaflets and *Green Left* articles, and put them on our web sites. There's a difference between small and large cities in receptivity, but we can break through. Especially let's use our scoops, for example Jim Green's exposés on Lucas Heights.[87]

Regular public forums are important for keeping a high party profile. But let's make sure we do them properly, all the necessary tasks to build them well, all the right things on the night, so that they're proud DSP events. Our main targets are firstly, new contacts, recruits, youth, and secondly, our periphery, our supporters.

For our stalls, we should be developing a Resistance *and* DSP profile. Especially in suburbs where we want to stand in elections, we should highlight the party. It's best if we can have a task, a focus for the stall, in addition to selling *Green Left* and other literature and dishing out leaflets. For example, an election campaign focus, or gathering DSEL memberships to get registered.

Growing the party

Even though we haven't been able to grow in absolute terms in recent years, recruitment has been happening in all branches, and actually from Resistance, a lot. The key task is keeping, educating, training and integrating comrades. We've had some very positive experiences with recruitment and stabilisation in small branches.

Darwin comrades have made a big impact on the city, and have new recruits around. Newcastle and Wollongong, although we've squeezed those branches for cadres, are still recruiting youth. Hobart has been an exporter of cadres for some time. The Resistance branch in Lismore is doing well, with new recruits, a large periphery and some impressive successes, although there's no party branch there yet. Penrith-Blue Mountains branch has a periphery around it, and has recruited two new members, but the main problem is the lack of a youth component, though we know there's potential at the University of Western Sydney and among high school students out there.

Unfortunately, we had to retreat from a separate Fremantle branch. It was partly circumstantial; in the end we didn't have enough leadership to run both branches in the Perth district. And perhaps we also learnt a little more about the political demographics of Fremantle, that it's now an old political community and increasingly a petty bourgeois milieu. But also it's a further illustration of the difficulties of dividing a branch in one city, something we still have to solve.

But in other cities and regional towns, we can see the potential; there's plenty of room for expansion. People want us, are calling for us to come. The anti-Hanson demos in regional towns were another indication of the possibilities. We just need a little more solid growth, and we could expand to a few more places.

Perhaps we should be ambitious on the side of geographical

expansion. These are challenges for comrades, the chance for a couple of enthusiastic comrades to really take on responsibility and see tangible results. The fact that we're not hitting Launceston, Rockhampton or Townsville immediately probably means we're squandering opportunities.

As an interim measure we should be organising regional visits, selling *Green Left* and subs, and visiting contacts. For the ACT elections, NSW branches can organise a trip, and focus the nearby contacts on the election campaign. Brisbane has to plan the long trips up the Queensland coast. Hobart has to service Launceston, and Melbourne, the Victorian country towns.

But as well as keeping an eye out for regional expansion opportunities, we also have an orientation to strengthen Melbourne, with quite a large reinforcement from experienced comrades at the end of the year.

The key problem is finding meaningful, satisfying assignments for all comrades. That's especially the case in larger branches, but a generalised problem.

Marxist education

Our educational conference, 3-7 January, has the theme of '150 Years of the *Communist Manifesto*'. It will be a serious, intensive educational event, for our members and contacts primarily. We'll publicise it, with a poster shortly after the NC, and in *Green Left*, and on our web page, and leaflets.

The conference will be different from past educational conferences in that we want to encourage more active participation from comrades. Specifically, there will be reading guides for some of the classes and seminars, which will be available in the branches soon, and comrades will be expected to have done reading beforehand for the topics discussed.

In addition to the feature talks, and a wide selection of multiple choice talks, there will be two sessions on the *Communist Manifesto* in small tutorial groups that everyone will be able to attend (we've booked twenty tutorial rooms at the college), and five seminar streams which comrades should be encouraged to select in advance – Marxist economics; Uninterrupted revolution, from Marx to Lenin; Stalinism, state capitalism and Marxist theory; Internationals and internationalism, from Marx to today; and the Impact of historical events on Marx and Engels' theories.

There's also the three-week full-time school immediately after the conference for ten or so comrades. There's also the possibility of a special school for first year university comrades.

What it means to be a Marxist cadre

I want to make some points about what it means to be a cadre, today, in Australia, some things for all comrades to bear in mind, to help us exist as revolutionary cadres in these times.

1. We're *active*, not passive members. Activity is the source of our satisfaction, the way to last, and we shouldn't see it as a source of 'burnout'. We take responsibility for the party, by our activity and by deciding on its course. Participation in meaningful assignments is key.
2. We're *mobile* – footloose – revolutionaries. We're not retreating from the idea of mobility of cadres, meeting the party's needs – moving between cities, colonising new branches, moving between assignments, moving between full time for the party, into the workforce, back on full time, back to the campus arena.
3. We're *serious*, not dabblers. We're mobile, but it's also good that we have some comrades who begin to build our base in the trade unions, in particular industries. It's good also to have some comrades as specialists in different areas. We build stable areas of intervention,

and experience.

4. We're *Australian* revolutionaries. We're a very internationalist party, but we can suffer because of our emphasis: 'the grass is greener' syndrome, or trip – and then the next trip. We provide political cover, contacts, even accommodation help for comrades. But with international travel cheaper, and the interesting contacts and ports of call we can provide, we've got to be careful comrades don't see this as an *escape* from their revolutionary commitment here.

   There's also the question of whether comrades remain Australian revolutionaries, or yield to the attraction of the country of origin. A number of comrades have been feeling the need to check it out. Sometimes it's necessary, sometimes you need to get it out of your system, test it out. But mostly it will reconfirm the uniqueness of our party, the need for it, and reconfirm that the greatest contribution can be made in your own party. And let's not glorify the overseas political situation – it's *better* here. In most countries the precondition for successful political work – a Leninist party nucleus – is lacking.

5. We're dedicated socialists. Our commitment is real, not just lip service. We understand what it means to be a revolutionary. Once we accept compromises, the real norm of dedication is shattered and cynicism results. We take responsibility for our ideas and put them into practice.

How to lead, how not to

As leaders of the party and Resistance, all of us in this room have extra responsibilities on top of the above, so there are some further points we have to note: how we should lead, and how we should not.

We make full use of existing forces. The most successful leaders get the most from our existing cadres and don't give up on comrades. They don't wield a heavy whip, but politically motivate and encourage others to lead too.

Lenin's example was used by Cannon in a speech during World War II:

> We've got to grow up to the level of political people who are able to make use of members who want to belong to the party. Lenin was a great master at utilising material that wasn't 100 percent perfect and he even succeeded in making a revolution with this defective material. One of the best stories I have ever heard was the remark made by Serge Evrikoff, leader of the Left Opposition and secretary in the party under Lenin, when he was in this country. He remarked to some American comrades, 'You will never begin to understand the genius of Lenin or to appreciate him in his full stature. You know that he made a revolution, but you don't know the material he made it out of.' And every one of us should try to be a little like that and try to hold onto and utilise members of the party and kick them out only as a last resort ... You can get far more out of people by inspiring them than by nagging them and hounding them.

We don't substitute. A branch secretary, organiser, leader of a fraction or other party committee can't do it all by themselves. Firstly, it leads to exhaustion. But more importantly, it won't help train others. We have to find satisfying assignments for *every* comrade in the party. The best leaders are those who recruit, who bring on others, who find useful, satisfying roles for others, for everyone, i.e., those who teach to lead, who *expand* our cadre force.

And similarly, we can't expect solutions from the National Office or from another branch. *No* branch is big enough; the party is much too small for our tasks, our appetite. Remember, a transfer to your branch is a net *loss* to another branch.

We reject commandism. We're not a bourgeois institution, not an army, in spite of the analogies we use. We do need discipline, organisation, commitment, but we are a voluntary institution. So we'll achieve the most in the long term especially, through political motivation and comradely encouragement.

We need comradely relations, professionalism and civility within and without the party. There are no excuses for venting your anger on individual comrades. We have a special responsibility as leaders of the party to set an example of comradely behaviour.

We don't need cliquishness, but a political atmosphere. We know young people have social needs, so we should develop an attractive social milieu in Resistance. But it severely limits our ability to grow if new comrades find they're excluded from social groupings that are half personal, half political. Resistance needs an inclusive social atmosphere.

We set the example. As leaders we have to lead from the front, showing the commitment and effort that are required. For example, on *Green Left* sales; on finances; showing *real* serious commitment, not posturing.

We need a collective team spirit, but also be aware that you contribute to the team as an individual. To build the team, you have to do *your* best, contribute to the maximum. So let's have political competitiveness, not to overshadow other comrades, as happens in bourgeois institutions and society, but to help them and contribute the most that *you* can.

We're an inclusive team, encouraging all comrades to develop to the full, politically, as leaders, as cadres. We have no permanently fixed assignments. We believe in multiskilling. The Resistance leadership has to see itself also as leaders of the party, increasingly taking over leadership functions. The goal is not to kick the older layer out, but to *expand* what we can do.

International work

The Asia Pacific Solidarity Conference, 10-13 April, will be our biggest event next year. It's the big public event we really want to build, in Sydney, nationally and internationally.

Solidarity is its up-front aim. Important struggles are occurring in the region, and will increase in the future. We have to maximise the solidarity work here, and within the region, linking up the different struggles too.

We should project the conference amongst comrades as us hegemonising this area in Australia. We're heading in this direction already, with our Indonesia work, the East Timor work, our *Green Left* coverage. That is, we're gradually beating back the conservative old layer.

But the conference is also an important component of our international work, increasing our links with left forces in the region, and helping the process of socialist renewal. The conference will raise the key issues being debated on the left, internationally and in the region. Hopefully, the occasion will help important groups in the region, such as the CPI (ML) Liberation and the Philippines comrades, to take a higher profile, and not just talk about their own issues, but relate to other forces on the international left.

It will also be a party-building event, helping us recruit and integrate new DSP and Resistance members.

Links magazine will continue to be an important component of our international work. In spite of the shift to the right of some of the original participants in the project, we're reaffirming its importance. We want to make it more regular, stabilising it at three issues a year. Each issue will have a theme, a special focus, making back issues more useful for continuing sale on our bookstalls. *Links* will cater more to our own political needs, for analysis and debate that will help the education of our own cadres. It will be less academic and waffly, and reach out to the left.

The internet will be increasingly important for our work in Australia. Certainly it's now an essential tool for cheap and efficient communication between branches and the National Office. But also we can't neglect an increasingly important avenue for getting out our propaganda, for reaching people.

Is there any chance of encouraging a looser international grouping that would involve the healthier revolutionary parties, the FI, the CWI, us, others? This would entail the abandoning of cloning perspectives by those two outfits. The FI *de facto* could be heading in that direction. The CWI still sticks strongly to its narrow and inflated view of itself. We had some modest hopes with the CWI and the FI. We have political differences, but hope that the parties prosper and develop, even though their 'internationals' are an obstacle to laying the basis for real international collaboration and renewal.

We'll be attending the CWI's International Executive Committee meeting in London, and also discussing with leaders of the FI. We'll also attend a broad seminar in Paris on the 80th anniversary of the October Revolution, sponsored by the French CP, the FI and others. We'll meet with the Dutch Socialist Party, the German PDS and other left parties. I'll try to attend the Left Alternative conference in Budapest. On the way back, Doug [Lorimer] will have discussions with comrades in San Francisco.

11. A NEW PERIOD OF RECESSION AND ACTIVISM

Report to the National Committee
17-18 October 1998

Originally called an Asian financial crisis, the recession that began in Asia in 1997 soon spread through much of the world, putting paid to the triumphalism that dominated capitalist propaganda after the collapse of the Soviet Union and the Stalinist regimes in Eastern Europe. 1998 was also the year of big high school walkouts against racism, in which Resistance played an important and prominent role. And it was the year of the Patricks dispute, in which the Maritime Union of Australia and its supporters beat back an attempt to destroy the union. This report examined what this new period was likely to mean for the DSP and Resistance.

The title of this report refers to the party having entered a 'new period'. But what are its new features?

Firstly, even here in firewalled, comfortable, Lucky Country Australia, we are now in the middle of a *global economic crisis for capitalism*. It began with the dramatic Asian economic collapse last year. Now the Russian financial system faces total collapse. Latin American markets are falling. New Zealand is officially in recession. Japan's economy has been in crisis throughout the '90s and now faces enormous problems. Finally, it has now spread to the United States with a vengeance, with some very worried people in Wall Street and Washington.

It's a classic capitalist crisis of overproduction, but the unprecedented quantities of unproductive speculative capital add extra risks and instabilities to the system.

Last month's US hedge fund collapse prompted a panicky bailout. They admitted they were hours away from meltdown. According to US Federal Reserve chairman Dr Alan Greenspan, there was a 50% chance that 'the whole [US financial] system would unravel'. More is to come. International capitalism has entered a period of incredible instability and uncertainty, a roller coaster ride that's speeded up.

There's a developing loss of confidence in capitalism's stability, but also in its permanence. It's the end of the period of smug bourgeois triumphalism following the collapse of the Soviet Union. They can't stop the string of articles from Russia along the lines of 'Capitalism has failed us'.

It also exposes their myths of the 'free market', as they bail out their bad debts and bad bets with public money. They're socialising their losses, transferring even more wealth from us to them. The latest Japanese bailout promises $10,000 from every Japanese to the banks, failing financial institutions and big investors.

The Fed plays the stock market to manipulate the Dow. They did it in 1987, something only revealed years later, and there are rumours they're doing it today.

The unresolvable contradictions of capitalism are the cause of their crises. They can patch each one over – until the next one, which can be bigger, more damaging. This one could be deep, given the level of fear and panic, the amount of speculative capital sloshing around and the enormous size of the accumulated debts.

Recession doesn't automatically equal radicalisation, but each time the ruling class will be weakened. Their brainwashing becomes less effective. The consciousness of the working class can take bigger leaps. The recession will have an ideological impact on young people especially, convincing them further that the world is irrational, the system is fucked and getting more so.

The Asian economic crisis has spurred on the political crises in the region, in Indonesia, South Korea, now Malaysia. It's raised the political importance of our Asia-Pacific solidarity work to a new level.

And in all countries, the subjective factor is key, and can gain more, become stronger, as a result of a new period of class struggle opportunities in the face of the capitalist austerity drive and stepped up attacks.

Australia will not escape the global recession. The political framework is still the '90s post-collapse of the Soviet Union. Those dramatic events are still part of the framework. But it won't continue to be accompanied by the '90s economic boom! That's now ended dramatically.

Resistance high school actions

The *second* big change in this period is a change in the subjective factor here in Australia. Now, the DSP and Resistance are in a significantly new situation politically and organisationally as a result of the high school mobilisations against racism and Resistance's resulting incredible profile.

In recent years, and particularly over the last 12 months, we've made steady progress in building our bases, on campus, with our trade union work and in Indonesia solidarity. Over the last decade the left overall was weakened, although we'd grown steadily. We've improved our positions relative to our left opponents.

If at this NC plenum we were just assessing our work in these areas, the normal gains we've made, we'd enthusiastically say that we've had a great year. But that's without counting the biggest single success this year, or this decade – the fantastic Resistance national high school walkouts against racism.

The walkouts were the largest high school actions in Australia that I can remember. These actions radicalised a big new layer of young people. They mobilised 14,000 secondary students around the country on 24-28 July, and 8,000 on 28 August. Smaller numbers participated in the 30 September actions, but some branches report we made even better gains in consolidation on that day.

Resistance joined 600 new high school members. We got 1,000-plus other names on contact lists. Many of these are being consolidated into cadres. The party has had a huge increase in requests for information and inquiries about membership. We've got contacts in a dozen new towns.

But the ramifications are even bigger than this, because of the incredibly high profile of Resistance now. The media coverage – print, radio, TV – was unprecedented in our history. The clippings file in the NO is enormous, although we know it's not complete – news articles, features, letters to the editor, columns, cartoons. There's no way we'll be able to bring together all the TV coverage, although the coverage of the actions, the focus on Resistance, the interviews and features, some almost like five-minute ads for Resistance, was more than the total coverage in our history. And we'll never be able to collect all the radio coverage, talkback debates, and all the coverage that appeared in the overseas media, especially in Asia. Even 30 September, though it received little coverage here, was a front page story in the main Pakistani Urdu and English-language papers, and was also in the Hong Kong and Indonesian papers at least.

It was overwhelming. It gave a new standing and recognition to Resistance. Resistance now represents protest, youth activism, socialism, to reporters and editors, to the ruling class, to the rabid right. It was overwhelming also to millions of young people around Australia.

It was a qualitative step forward in our high school work, and it flowed on to Resistance as a whole, and the party as well. Branches like Sydney have sometimes had almost daily ITS classes. It's been a steep learning curve for many high school comrades, from fresh activists to reasonably confident political cadre in a few months. They've had to directly confront hostile political opponents and defend our politics, on numerous occasions. All layers of Resistance have been brought forward by the high school gains.

High schools are an area now where we're dominant. No organised left current can match us, even the ALP. This is an area where we can organise large numbers in our own name. We've grabbed the leadership of high school students, but have also become by far the best known socialist organisation in Australia.

Some elements of this development were unique:

- The anti-Hanson, anti-racism issue itself, which was both a moral and political question that especially related to high school students.
- Others on the left had bequeathed us the space, between the ISO's ultra-leftism trying to shut down Hanson's meetings, and the liberals' and ALPers' fear of mass action.
- The specifics of 2 July,[88] the cop attacks and subsequent explosion of publicity, and even the red-baiting helped.
- But the success was also prepared and made possible because of our correct political perspective and our previous steady work.
- We'd built a serious, national, Marxist organisation.
- We had a democratic centralist cadre force able to act quickly to take advantage of new openings.
- We had *Green Left Weekly,* a powerful tool able to intervene,

and also build cadre.
- We had a base among young people, recognising the radical role of youth.
- We'd had a record of previous successful work among high school students, going way back, but to 1995 with the wood chipping issue and around the French nuclear tests.

Changed balance of forces on left

Our Resistance high school success, and our newly expanded profile, have significantly shifted the balance of forces further in our favour. We'd been making steady gains in the '80s and '90s, and this registers it definitvely.

Others are forced to recognise this, either openly or implicitly through their sour grapes reactions that reflect their desperation.

There's certainly an effect on the bourgeoisie. They and their media and right-wing ideologues will be paying us far more attention. Sometimes we'll be able to take advantage of this through getting our views, our profile, into the mass media; sometimes they'll be more conscious about it, continue to try to exclude us.

The ruling class's state agencies are also likely to be paying us more attention. We'll come under closer scrutiny, so we have to be more conscious and careful ourselves, more professional. The far right is certainly more aware, both One Nation and National Action, with scurrilous posters in Sydney, violent attacks in Adelaide and a suspicious arson attack on our headquarters in Brisbane.

We'll see more of the reaction from the ALP, the liberal left, the bureaucracies. The Jabiluka experience was shocking,[89] but won't surprise us in the future. We could see further desperate responses from the far left, like Militant's Melbourne hijack action on 28 August.[90]

And we should be realistic about some downside effects even

among our own members. There's a let-down effect among the newer comrades once the big actions and major publicity are over. Some longer term comrades relax, start dropping their responsibilities, thinking that others are there now to take over. And some comrades might even step back because they now realise we're serious.

But overwhelmingly, the impacts have been incredibly positive.

It's had a deep impact on high school students, which we have to consolidate, and will have a continuing flow-on effect to campus that we need to foster and harvest most consciously over the next few years.

The effect on the broader milieu, the working class, will be up to us. We have to work out how to widen the breach, make it permanent, how to build on it and translate it into wider gains, and how to connect it with the DSP, *Green Left Weekly* and our other institutions.

1998 – A year to remember

1998 will probably go down in our own party history as a year to remember. Many of the projections we made for 1998 have been fulfilled.

The year began with our '150 Years of the *Communist Manifesto*' educational conference. Many comrades think it was the best educational conference we've ever had. Morale and spirit were high. We made real gains in the educational level of the party. Eighty comrades prepared and delivered talks. We had an excellent fund drive rally, with comrades pledging the largest sum ever.

Then we had the Asia Pacific Solidarity Conference. It would have been the best broad conference we've yet organised, and we've organised some very good ones. It had an excellent international impact. Pierre Rousset's report for *Inprecor* and *International Viewpoint*[91] gives a feel for this. It was excellent for our comrades, for our solidarity work and for the effect on the rest of the left.

There's been the MUA struggle,[92] the most important industrial action for more than a decade. It reinforced a very basic but dimming lesson, the importance of struggle, even though it was eventually settled for less than had already been won on the picket line. There have been other important struggles this year, and some victories, not least that by Workers First in the Victorian AMWU.[93]

Our trade union work this year has been varied and our experience is growing. Our NTEU work has been stronger; we've got a good start in the Workers First group, and we did excellent solidarity work with the MUA struggle.

Then there's been the tremendous Indonesian struggle. This inspiring mass upsurge forced the ouster of Suharto and re-emphasised the importance of our solidarity work. We need to redouble our support for the Indonesian revolution and our PRD comrades.

Our campus work has moved forward. We've got a stronger base, with more comrades, more club members, and more *Green Left Weekly* sales. And although we made no big breakthroughs in winning positions on SRCs and NUS, Resistance won every preselection battle against the rest of the left that it contested.

And of course, there's been the range of anti-racist campaigns, but in particular the magnificent Resistance high school walk-outs. Our key task is recruiting, consolidating and educating the resulting high school members and other members and contacts.

It's also been a year when we've made progress on our party-building tasks, some excellent election campaigns, good progress on our financial campaigns. We're qualitatively better positioned to respond to new developments.

Do our new gains lead us to any fundamental change in our political perspective, as a propaganda group with our main task of recruiting, building the party? No, but in this report we want to present some proposals allowing us to respond to the new period and answer the new challenges that are being tossed up to us.

Resistance section in *Green Left*

Firstly, we want to propose that Resistance builds on its already strong profile, and takes it further by having a very visible Resistance section in *Green Left Weekly*. The back page and four other pages at the back would be assigned to Resistance. They'd be Resistance's responsibility. There'd be a Resistance masthead on the back, so holding it up that way, it would appear as a Resistance newspaper.

We'll have two papers in one. The Resistance magazine will be both a special section in *Green Left Weekly* and a new publication. It will have *Green Left Weekly* page numbers, but Resistance running heads. The Resistance magazine will be a 'party' paper for Resistance, but *Green Left Weekly* will still be seen and promoted as the paper of the left, the unifying regroupment project.

It will be posted on the web as part of *Green Left Weekly*, but also posted on the Resistance web page as Resistance's publication.

Green Left Weekly will announce that the decision to allocate Resistance five pages of the paper is because of the inspiring Resistance high school actions. It's a contribution by *Green Left Weekly* to the excellent work of Resistance and the struggle against racism.

This step will address many of our needs:

- It should increase the sales participation of the new Resistance comrades. It should increase their identification with the paper. It's designed to give a qualitative boost to the confidence of high school comrades in selling the paper.

Hopefully it will also help arrest the fall in the sales rate.

- It will help make the public connection between Resistance, *Green Left Weekly* and the DSP.
- It will force the more intensive political development of Resistance comrades. Hopefully they'll read the paper more. And more comrades will have to write for the Resistance section. It will be the responsibility of Resistance branches, the organisers and executives.

It has to be oriented to the high school layer, a way to reach out to the tens of thousands whom we mobilised, the even wider layers who would be receptive. At the same time, it must be a combination paper in itself, catering to the layer of high school activists that are becoming cadres, writing for the paper, leading Resistance activities, leading the campaigns.

The Resistance section will look different, with a distinctive masthead and layout.

We can experiment with a more agitational flavour, be more irreverent than *Green Left Weekly* has been. It can contain short reports of campaigns Resistance is involved in. We can include some of the *Party Campaigner*-type reports and interesting anecdotes.

But it should also include educational material, basic articles on socialism. We could serialise *What Socialists Stand For.* We could include articles on the history of Resistance, reports and history of youth struggles internationally; certainly it would cover the current wave of French high school strikes.

There's potentially a lot of overlap with copy in the rest of the paper, of course. So it will be the ultimate responsibility of the *Green Left Weekly* editor to ensure there's no duplication or glaring gaps, and a uniformly professional publication.

We know that the paper – *Green Left Weekly*, and now the Resistance section as part of it – is essential for building the party, and integrating all our party-building and political tasks.

The role of *Green Left Weekly* sales in building and retaining cadres is especially essential in a political situation like we face in Australia today.

Australia is still the 'lucky country', compared to others. And we're in the privileged position of an imperialist power, living off the exploitation of the region, and there are still some large crumbs for the working class.

The very act of selling is a commitment of time and effort that helps steel our comrades. And the fact that it's a *public* act, a statement of opposition to the status quo, sets us apart from the capitalist consensus, helps us resist cooption.

So the recent Adelaide sales victory[94] is especially significant. It sets an important precedent, similar to the right won to leaflet on Melbourne's streets during the campaign against the Vietnam War. Adelaide branch waged a magnificent campaign, winning wide support and many friends.

Leadership – party and Resistance

A second proposal, resulting from Resistance's successes and higher profile, is to shift the weight of leadership for our tendency more towards Resistance, and at the same time increase our overall investment in our full-time apparatus.

There's a thinning older layer of comrades. We're thin already, and each casualty makes it stand out more. We will recruit from all ages, and more in the future as workers radicalise. But right now there's a very real need for the youth to take over the reins of leadership of the party even more.

However, with the heightened importance and profile and size of Resistance, we can't just graduate the Resistance leaders to lead the party. They need to make way to an extent for the even younger leaders coming on, but they're also needed to train and organise a larger Resistance than before.

So perhaps we have to make more tasks the responsibility of Resistance. Resistance comrades could become a larger proportion of the National Office and *Green Left Weekly* and the full-timers in the branches. The Resistance section in *Green Left Weekly* fits in with this.

We'll need a larger Resistance NO, expanding it to three comrades, and also plan to have Resistance leadership comrades in other NO departments. In some branches, the Resistance organiser will be the full-timer.

Resistance comrades will have to lead in campus and high school work, in our major political campaigns, in organising sales and finances, in representing the tendency, in writing and educating. So our task is to build well-rounded Resistance leaders, who can lead the party and stick it out to do so.

More Resistance comrades, *all* Resistance comrades, have to be ready to go on full time. We have to draw more younger comrades into challenging full-time assignments, assignments that are difficult, where you have to think things out politically, make hard political decisions, learn to lead.

The second aspect is the proposal to increase our full-timers overall in this period. We need the staff in the NO to be able to take advantage of the new openings, to cope with the increasing workload.

We need enough full-timers in Sydney to take full advantage of all the opportunities, all the contacts, new and old. We want to push to have full-timers in Adelaide and Hobart again.

It will be a worthwhile investment; otherwise we risk losing the gains of 1998. It's time, with the deepening global capitalist crisis and impending recession, and with our greater profile and weight on the left, to invest further in our full-time apparatus. In a way it's a gamble, but what better time to take such a gamble?

Sometimes it will be a gamble on individual comrades. So this is an appeal to more experienced comrades: *help* the new comrades to lead, to learn; encourage them to take on more responsibility.

And it's also an appeal to younger comrades to step forward. Volunteer to go on full time or transfer. Be determined to take the reins of Resistance and the party. We have an increasing number of comrades who have to become leaders, or else the process blocks up, and more drop out.

Consolidation through responsibility

Thirdly, we want to encourage a range of new party units, so that everyone has the chance to lead and learn through leading. We need to expand the positions of responsibility, and train a whole new generation of leaders. There are many ways we want to do this:

- Campus Resistance branches.
- High school Resistance branches.
- Dividing branches.
- Locality party propaganda teams, election committees, on-the-way-to branches.
- Functioning, intervention-oriented fractions.
- Geographical expansion.

Any of the developments proposed here have to be seen as flexible, not schematic. The fundamental purposes of such new structures or units are to allow new comrades to grow and learn and take responsibility, and to allow the party to grow. We have to resist the temptation to generalise any of these in a wrong way; otherwise we can make the mistake of retreating, abstaining, from the real political struggles in each city.

We've seen a big jump in the size of the weekly Resistance meetings, certainly in Sydney Central branch, and in most branches. We can't just keep increasing the size of executives, though that is happening. But to have even a chance of relating to the huge number of new Resistance members and contacts, we have to quickly have the structures where every current activist takes on responsibilities for organising, recruiting and leading others.

This problem – a good problem to have – has to be addressed in the party as well. Recent Resistance recruits have started to join the party; it's likely to be a much bigger flow in the coming year.

Sydney Central and Melbourne branches already face problems of size; comrades get lost, it's very hard to organise units that large. It's been a problem we haven't really successfully resolved over decades, and it's going to get more acute. Medium-sized branches are also starting to experience those problems of size.

The experience of Western Sydney branch has been good. The branch has settled down with a real political life and style of its own. It survived well the shift of headquarters from Penrith to Parramatta, has recruited and has contacts around it. A Resistance branch is now established, and it will be stronger next year, with its own campus base.

Our style of organising has been based on a very active use of a HQ. Could we build more units or branches in a city without multiple offices?

The very successful community actions against racism that we organised in Melbourne, Brisbane, Sydney and Adelaide this year help point us in the direction of how to expand the larger branches. The marches were easy to build. Branches will want to continue with them, in new suburbs, and try them on other issues too.

Such actions allow us to connect with the local communities, the migrant groups, more directly. In Footscray, we even got fed. And they make the local media, where much larger actions in the city get boycotted by the major dailies. It's always been easier to break into the local media, but the coverage this year was often pure gold front-page advertisements for us.

An important role for such actions could be in helping us spread responsibility in large branches, and eventually dividing branches. These local actions help us develop new party units, and give them a political focus in their area.

A key focus of such locality units will be our election work. The suburban teams proposal for elections was raised at the December 1995 NC plenum, and we tested it partially in the 1996 election campaign. It needs further testing.

But most importantly, such teams should be seen as propaganda teams: for organising *Green Left Weekly* distribution, stalls at the key shopping centres in the area, for contacting, chasing up sub renewals and organising our periphery for fundraising in the area. Now we see clearer possibilities for actions also, community rallies and marches that we initiate.

Locality/suburban teams or branches can be important for presenting comrades with sufficient challenges and excitement and responsibilities when they leave Resistance. We're clogged up in the party unless we create more challenging responsibilities.

Intervention-oriented fractions can also be important for the training and retention of comrades, for taking on leadership. However, at this time it's not a blanket solution to direct comrades into union work, where retreat still dominates, and the possibilities for extensive, rounded, exciting political work won't always be available.

Geographical expansion is another way comrades can take on responsibility. Lismore comrades still haven't recruited the party members to make a branch yet, but the Resistance branch is lively, they have a sizeable periphery and have been doing a lot of good work. In Rockhampton we have a small nucleus that's done good work too.

Geelong is the largest city where we don't have a branch, and some comrades are interested in going there next year. It's possible they could achieve more for the party overall by such a move.

The PLP [Progressive Labor Party] milieu is not unfriendly; our comrades had good experiences on polling day there. Workers First has strength there, and a comrade could get work.

Regional trips should not be restricted to the perspective of building a branch in the near future, but we get gains, widen our impact and consolidate supporters and subscribers from such trips, so let's see what branches can organise over summer.

It's important for new comrades to quickly get a sense of ownership of the party, through discussions and participation in decision making in branches, at conferences and through their own hands-on experience.

Marxist education

Fourthly, we want to make Marxist education a central priority for comrades and branches. We all have to look for ways to strengthen our education work, collectively and individually.

Party education, and comrades having a clear understanding of Marxist theory, will take on added importance as the international economic crisis deepens and recession bites in Australia. How will this affect our work?

1. There'll be greater opportunities for and receptivity to socialist propaganda, the chance for the education of a whole new layer of workers and youth.

There's less certainty about the stability of capitalism. The working class is still not convinced of the feasibility or necessity of socialism. But the door is open half way. There will be more openings for explaining, defending socialism. There'll be benefits from a more specifically socialist image.

2. Struggles and possibilities for agitation will rise. We'll have to make the most of the opportunities for actions and mobilisation as the crisis bites and the capitalist class tries to take it out on us. There will be more possibilities for leading struggles.

There are many differences between 1998 and the Great Depression 60-70 years ago, but it will be worth our while to be familiar with the historical experiences here and overseas, both the responses of the capitalist class and the lessons from working-class history.

The Communist Manifesto Conference was an excellent educational experience, but there are a lot of resources and educational materials that we still haven't made available from the conference.

With all the new Resistance members, there's a great demand for our class series, ITSs, ITMs etc. And it's great to see comrades who were themselves in a class just a short while ago, now giving classes to new comrades. Seminars and camps during the summer break will be important consolidation activities for Resistance branches.

We'll be holding a three-week full-time school on Marxist political theory immediately after the [January 1999 18th DSP National] Conference. We'll have others during the year as well.

For Easter 1999, we're proposing that branches organise city-wide or state-wide educational seminars.

The regular weekly educational activity for all comrades should be reading *Green Left Weekly*. We're in a battle of ideas with the ruling class and those peddling ruling class ideas. So we need constant historical features, educational features and articles that put socialism up front, steering clear of jargon, but reasserting our socialist language and concepts.

Comrades mostly don't focus enough on honing their Marxist theory to understand the capitalist economy, concentrating instead on compartmentalised issues. We need to redress it through education on Marxist economics, which can come from actual debates, but even more importantly, from applying Marxism to try to understand the actual, developing, capitalist economic crisis.

Continuing education and propaganda on women's liberation issues are also important, both in winning the new generation of activists, on high schools and campuses, and in consolidating and taking them further.

By also focussing on issues fresh in comrades' minds, we can consolidate recent lessons and the already entrenched lessons.

We can use the web more for our education, as increasing numbers of comrades have access. Our sites now contain quite a considerable archive of our material, documents, pamphlets and talks. There are also extensive resources elsewhere, which we should map and link to our sites.

In giving priority to Marxist education, we have to make it possible through running efficient, well-stocked bookshops, and a comprehensive program of publications.

Propaganda offensive

Fifthly, we need our own stepped-up propaganda offensive – a publications program and publicity offensive – that can build a counter to capitalist brainwashing, both the open neoliberal offensive and the more subtle undermining. We need the educational resources for our expanded periphery, for our new recruits and for our cadres.

We need to expand and make better use of our already extensive multipurpose arsenal – *Green Left Weekly*, *Links*, books and pamphlets, web pages.

We need a Resistance pamphlet on the whole high school experience this year, so that knowledge about it is spread wider, the memories retained, the lessons consolidated.

We've continued to publish a good range of books and pamphlets this year: including our hot seller, *Bludgers in Grass Castles* by Martin Taylor, now into a third edition; a new edition of *What Socialists Stand For;* our *Organisational Principles* booklet; a new edition of our abortion pamphlet; *MUA Here to Stay!* and our handbook on Marxist economics.

We want to propose an even more extensive publications program for 1999.

While we still have adequate stocks of the three-volume sets of Marx-Engels *Selected Works* and Lenin *Selected Works*, they don't meet all our needs. We need to gradually build up our own editions of key Marxist classics with our own introductions. Many of these could be grouped under a series title such as 'Library of the Marxist Classics'. Getting this off to a solid start would be the major focus of our 1999 publishing program.

We will shortly have our own 80-page edition of the *Communist Manifesto*. Other possibilities would be Lenin's *State and Revolution, Imperialism* and *'Left-Wing' Communism* and Engels' *Socialism: Utopian and Scientific*. These would all be books in the 80-120 page range with prices from $6.95 to $8.95.

We could also plan a number of Marxist readers – comprising selections from Marx, Engels, Lenin and Trotsky – designed primarily for our educational needs but also packaged to appeal to a broader audience.

Other possibilities for 1999 are:

- *Socialism and Human Survival.* Dick Nichols has almost finished updating it, and it should be printed by the January party conference.
- A booklet on the Indonesian revolution by Max Lane.
- A book on historical materialism, packaging the pamphlet series we have in a single book, once they're reworked by Doug Lorimer.
- A book on the history of the DSP and Resistance. This would include my current two talks, plus episodes from the history of Resistance, plus a chapter on the 1980s and early 1990s by Jim McIlroy, and a chronology and introduction.
- *The History and Lessons of Australian Communism,* based on

> my six *Green Left Weekly* articles on CPA history that have been printed, plus six or seven more that are only in outline form so far.
>
> * *Maoism and Stalinism in China* by Doug Lorimer, which is about two-thirds done.
> * A book by Renfrey Clarke on Russia.
> * *Capitalism and the Countryside,* based on Chris Spindler's talk.
> * *The Origins of Women's Oppression,* a booklet Pat Brewer is planning to do.

We would also need to schedule more quickly produced topical pamphlets, often based on a feature or series that would first appear in *Green Left Weekly,* or as an extensive party statement. This year we've produced the DSP statement on 'Imperialism and the Asian Crisis' and *Green Left Weekly* compilations on *The Asian Economic Crisis* and *Maritime workers: fighting for all of us.*

We should also be more conscious of producing pamphlets that register our successes our victories, or mark an important historical struggle.

All this would be a very ambitious publishing effort. It would be fantastic if we produced half the titles next year. We'd be forced to further step up our effort to improve and streamline our distribution system or it will be too great a financial burden. We need to get the branch bookshops functioning more effectively. We also need to put serious effort into attracting orders from libraries, campus courses and bookshops.

As a result of the successful Resistance high school actions and the extensive media profile we gained, it's much more realistic for us to think of ambitious ways to launch a publicity offensive.

We know it's possible to make greater use of the capitalist media than we ever have in the past. And we've got more experience with media work and more individual contacts as well. We have to follow up on this excellent base. We can be the people they turn to for comment on issues of racism, and youth.

We also have to persist in trying to get our own articles published in the bourgeois media. Certainly we should be much more persistent and professional in writing articles for campus papers. We can rewrite and cut down articles we'd be writing anyway, and keep submitting them to the media under the name of our activists who have a profile.

Any guerrilla protest actions or stunts we organise are now more likely to be picked up by the bourgeois media. We should be more creative in thinking about quick, easy, daring actions. Respond quickly to a politician coming to town. Get a small picket out to protest every particularly heinous statement or action by a big corporation or prominent millionaire. If the media turn up, great. If they don't, it's a sales opportunity anyway, and an educational and exciting event for the new comrades.

The web pages are becoming an increasingly important part of our propaganda arsenal. The high school actions and resultant publicity brought thousands of new visitors to our sites. It's settled down now at approximately 200 visitors a week to the DSP site, 200 to Resistance, 260 to ASIET, 60 to *Links*, 500 to *Green Left Weekly*, 50 to CISLAC. (The total hits per week on all pages of all our sites are probably in the tens of thousands.)

We're now getting a large number of electronic 'clip-offs' from our sites, as well as book orders. We can publicise the sites more, in all our print publicity, and over the web, and make even greater gains from them. The party email list serve, DS_NET, is growing continuously. We need to have a similar list for Resistance. The Resistance web discussion list has a number of limitations, including exclusivity and security problems.

Our publications, propaganda and publicity can't be separated from our financial campaigns, though, as we get better at it and as we grow, our publications can make us money. Our publicity successes can also make us money, as long as we consistently target our widening milieu for donations.

We've faced a financial challenge over the last 20 years. We pushed ourselves, gambled on growth, bought buildings. But it's been a continuing struggle, with deficit budgets, and survival made possible only by rising property values. We now have a more positive outlook, with balanced budgets, and are winding back the accumulated deficits.

It's just in time too. If we're heading into a global recession, we'll face increased financial pressures and increased opportunities to build the party that will need money.

Socialist leadership

Actions in our own name, once we do them, and especially once we succeed so well, seem so natural. The gains for both the anti-racist movement and ourselves from the Resistance national high school walkouts are so overwhelming.

Local community marches also helped break through the roadblocks of fake 'united front' committees, and the roadblocks in our own heads. Again, they were a confirmation of our clearer thinking on the united-front question.

The Resistance high school anti-racism actions had unique features that led to their success. We should not relinquish these campaigns in any branch. Resistance has to continue as the leader of the fight against racism, and as the leader of high school students.

A goal ahead of us is to win leadership on campus, to establish our hegemony there. It will be harder because it's more bureaucratised. So we'll use united-front tactics, and anything else, including anything that will raise Resistance's profile, and keeping an eye out for actions that we can call to expose the inaction, the misleadership, of LA, NOLS etc. We haven't found the ways yet to extend our high school gains to campus.

Another area where we should not rule out the tactic of modest actions in our own name is among young workers and unemployed. They're not organised, but thus not under the sway of the Labor bureaucracy as much as older workers. The impending recession could make this layer more open to suggestions for action. We could initiate them, especially through our suburban branches or branches in smaller cities.

Further attacks on the rights of young people to the dole or social services are likely. Unless we lead, other tendencies could jump in.

We've already had many positive experiences of actions initiated by us, on East Timor, various environmental issues, the sex diary, French [nuclear] tests, native title and many solidarity campaigns. And we should be ready to call guerrilla actions on all sorts of issues.

We can campaign on issues such as opposing the GST, with petitions and stalls, and motions in our trade unions and so on. But we shouldn't have any illusions that we're going to be able to substitute for the lack of any mass action on the issue called by the trade unions or the ALP.

A major gain of our Resistance high school actions is that they legitimised socialist political activity. It helped that we were standing up to Hanson and debating [David] Oldfield.

High school students at the rallies were extremely receptive to socialist ideas. They haven't yet been properly brainwashed by capitalist society. It's harder with other layers, just as they're also subject to more bureaucratic control.

United-front lessons

Grasping the value and reclaiming the need and possibility of initiating and organising actions in our own name does not negate our support for the united-front tactic as an essential party-building tactic. Comrades should refer to Doug Lorimer's 1995 article 'Mass Action, Alliances, and the United Front Tactic'.

What we're doing is rescuing the united-front tactic from misuse and misunderstandings that had been endemic in sections of the Trotskyist movement over the years. It's a clarification on the united front, not rejecting the real use. We had been saddled with habits and traditions that reduced our vision of the tactical options available.

Our more recent thinking helped us prepare politically for the correct steps this year. Our perspectives resolution adopted at our last conference mentioned the possibility of us initiating actions, but the reports and discussion in October last year spelled it out more clearly and explicitly, that we shouldn't rule out leading and initiating actions in our own name.

The original use of 'united front' by Lenin and Trotsky in the Communist International is a far cry from the way it's splashed around today. The united-front tactic was a proposal for joint action by the Marxist parties to the mass reformist parties, for joint action in the interests of the masses, and as a way to expose the misleadership of the reformists in the eyes of the masses, and to enable the Marxist parties to demonstrate in action the superiority of their political line and tactics.

United front approaches to the ALP are difficult today. Mostly they can afford to ignore us. So other tactics are required to show as many people as possible that the reformists are sell-outs, don't lead struggles, and that the Marxists are the best organisers, the best activists and leaders.

Obviously a key way to do this is to call actions in our own name. Sometimes this is the most appropriate organisational form; sometimes, however, it's appropriate to set up a campaign committee open to all left groups and independent activists. What is appropriate will be judged by what will enable the largest mobilisation and political advance of the masses, and also what will best build the Marxist forces.

In the case of the Resistance national high school mobilisations, the form they took was clearly correct on both counts for us. If we mean by 'united-front work' the effort to draw in the broadest range of support and allies into joint political activity or protest around specific issues, there can be no doubt that the Resistance high school walkouts were very successful. Deputy lord mayor of Sydney, Henry Tsang, the South Australian Trades and Labour Council, people from the Aboriginal community, Jabiluka Action Groups, trade unionists, student union representatives, members of the ALP, Greens, Democrats, the NDP and most left groups spoke at the rallies around the country. Thus, the fact that Resistance called the walkouts in no way restricted their political impact.

Behind the 'backlash'

Any gain by us is a threat to the bureaucrats and makes it that much more expensive for them to pull off the inevitable deals and sell-outs. We're used to fighting with the bureaucrats in these types of campaigns, to democratise the committees. But the nature and ferocity of the attack on Resistance are worse than usual.

Events like this are useful in highlighting who our friends and enemies are. We have tactical differences with the blockaders and Ploughshares activists (non-violent direct actioners), but recognise their sincerity, commitment, lack of self-interest, compared with the careerists and job-seekers in the peak bodies, the ALP and liberal currents.

Recent attacks on us in NUS by Left Alliance, NOLS, and NAL spring from the same motivations. They're totally to be expected. There will be pressure, and more as we succeed more. We need to steel and educate members, old and new, to understand and resist such pressure.

But we should also be conscious of not making enemies unnecessarily; enough are going to get thrown up by the struggle anyway. So we should reassert the principled, non-sectarian, political way of operating that we've fought for over the years.

Tiredness? Period and perspectives

This has been an exciting, excellent year, but there have been some casualties too. We're all feeling tiredness.

After the Communist Manifesto Conference, the APSC, Indonesia, MUA, high school anti-racism actions, plus all the usual campaigns and party-building tasks, it's not surprising that comrades are tired. It's partly a tiredness from jobs well done. We can easily recover from that, with a bit of a break or a change of pace with a pre-conference discussion period and a decision-making conference.

But there are some longer term trends and factors that we know we're fighting against. Many comrades have put in long stints of struggle, in fairly difficult conditions. The last fifteen years have been hard – thirteen years of the Accord, defeats in Nicaragua and Grenada, defeats in the Soviet Union, Eastern Europe, capitalist restoration in China, often hollow victories where they've happened, as in South Africa.

So even though we're wiser, better organised, have more resources and weaker competitors as a result of the struggle, it takes its toll on comrades.

And although capitalism is facing a deep economic and ideological crisis, this hasn't yet translated into a radicalisation sweeping masses in our direction. We've been recruiting, but attrition is still a problem of the period.

We know that the main cause of the attrition of younger comrades is a lack of political perspective. Comrades reach a point, at the end of university, or when they graduate from Resistance, or go off full time [for the party] after a stint, where they are faced with other life choices. These are very capable comrades, with potentially interesting careers – as far as they can be under capitalism – if they reject a revolutionary career.

We can minimise this through better Marxist education, through improving all areas of the party's work, through creating more possibilities for participation and responsibility, through consolidating worker activists with meaningful areas of trade union work.

Sometimes the attrition rate rises just at the very time we're succeeding, recruiting, growing! Possibly it's a hanging on syndrome: 'Now I can let go, someone else can take over'.

There's also the 'all or nothing' syndrome, which the period contributes to. We need to find a place in the party for leaders who step back, or who want to take a breather. Comrades can also step forward again, and no grudges are held. Activism and commitment are still crucial to building the party, but we also need to find a place for the experienced older comrades who take a step back. Don't feel guilty if you can't be a 100 percenter at the moment.

We need all those experienced comrades. We also need to re-gather some who've dropped away, and also develop a framework for recruiting as members or supporters the healthy survivors from the CPA and other parties. The role of *Green Left Weekly* is crucial here.

We shouldn't really need to repeat this, but again I find us having to dispel the weird notion that comrades with political differences with the positions adopted at our conferences can't join or remain in the party. We're not monolithic. We have the structures for discussion, PCDs, the conferences, many times in *Green Left Weekly* and normal party life. But if your view's not adopted, so what? As long as you agree with our main perspectives and are loyal to the party, there's a valued place for you.

Providing a thoroughgoing Marxist education and a satisfying political activity are the most important things for keeping comrades. But we shouldn't underestimate the importance of a healthy, comradely atmosphere in the party also. We strive to build a team leadership, try to dispel competitive attitudes and individualistic hangovers. We put politics first, but we need to build a party that works together in a comradely fashion.

International network

Our party-building perspectives are increasingly interconnected with our developing international network. There are enormous possibilities and responsibilities with our international work. There's more for us to do, more groups to relate to, more ways in which we can be helpful.

The APSC was a great success, from many points of view. It won space for us in the region, it consolidated our network, and laid the basis for closer and more frequent discussions and collaboration between Marxist-Leninist parties in the region.

On the whole, the increasing collaboration between left parties that we've been in contact with has proceeded well this year. The significant exception is the sectarian turn by the CWI/ Socialist Party of England and Wales/Militant.

Recall our assessment of the CWI at our October 1997 NC plenum:

> The CWI still sticks strongly to its narrow and
> inflated view of itself. We had some modest hopes
> [with them]. We have political differences, but hope
> that they prosper and develop, even though their

'international' is an obstacle to laying the basis for
real international collaboration and renewal.

Since then our fears have been realised. They do seem to have
dropped their opening-out approach of a few years ago. Their
politics, and the dynamic of their conception of an international,
have led them to very sectarian interventions, in Pakistan and in
Indonesia, here in Melbourne, and it looks like in Scotland too.

Developments this year allow us to draw a clear balance
sheet on our relations with the CWI. They've clearly reverted to
a sectarian factional course in their international work, which
looks as though it's been spurred on by their decline in England
and Wales, and reinforced by the major setbacks they've had in
Pakistan and Scotland.

As a result of the events in Melbourne, we've also been able to
draw a clear balance sheet on our relations with Militant here.
They'd ground to a halt before this, but the 28 August events[87]
made the political issues absolutely clear.

We've been completely open to our members and to Militant
about where we stand politically in relation to the requirements
of unity. The Militant leadership has been dishonest with us, and
probably dishonest with its membership.

Contrast the relations with the CWI and the Fourth
International today. We seem to be settling in to a comradely
relationship with the FI. We're able to use useful articles and
analysis from FI groups and *International Viewpoint;* they're
able to use our material too. We're able to have useful comradely
discussions when they visit, without any hint of factionalising,
and we're able to attend their conferences in a fraternal way also.

These developments reaffirm our understanding of what
principles for relations between parties are necessary, and what
sort of international collaboration is needed.

While processes of regroupment, alliance and recomposition

still occurring at national levels of course require flexibility and special agreements, firm organisation and democratic centralist organisation are needed for parties themselves.

For relations between parties at an international level, what's needed today is a network rather than an exclusive, rigid structure. And we need to reaffirm the principles of mutual respect and solidarity, and non-interference, non-factionalising in the affairs of other parties.

Such a network of parties from different backgrounds is developing in the Asia-Pacific region.

Links magazine will continue to provide a forum for discussion and exchange of information and views for parties all around the world. But it will be increasingly important in furthering the collaboration and common political thinking of this developing network in our region.

12. GLOBALISATION AND THE WORK OF THE DSP

Report to the National Committee
10-12 June 2000

*Beginning in 1999 with a major demonstration in Seattle, USA, an
international movement emerged opposing globalisation as represented
by organisations like the World Bank and International Monetary
Fund. At the same time, the development of international ties over the
previous decades was now bearing fruit: among other things, a large
international attendance at the DSP's Marxism 2000 conference and
plans for a major international solidarity conference in Indonesia.*

We should begin the assessment of our international work by
focussing our attention back on the Marxism 2000 conference.

We all know Marxism 2000 was a great success, more successful than any of us had hoped – 440 registrations, 53 international guests, 15 plenaries, four major sessions, 84 workshops
and seminars, $90,000 pledged to the fighting fund from the
conference rally.

In relation to building the party in Australia, the conference
was extremely successful. It shows the internationalist approach

we have leads to excellent party-building gains here. We recruited eleven new comrades, and we would have made a very favourable impression on all the other new contacts and supporters who attended. The conference was extremely useful in the education and consolidation of our cadres.

But making an overall political assessment of the conference in an international framework is not so easy. The large number of interesting international delegations overwhelmed us to an extent; there was such a lot to take in.

After the [1998] APSC, some overseas comrades commented, 'You don't fully understand what you've achieved'. Again with Marxism 2000, we move on, get subsumed in political work and don't fully appreciate what we've achieved.

Internationally, we can assess the conference at two levels. Firstly, with respect to individual parties and countries in the region. Secondly, in relation to the collective gains, the qualitative steps made in furthering the building of a collaborative non-sectarian international network of revolutionary Marxist parties.

The growth of our international work

This report reaffirms the main positive projections for our international work, confirmed by the conference and events since. But also where necessary it will answer the perspectives of a) the liquidationists and b) the sect builders.

In the last few years we've noted the enormous expansion of our international work. When we left the Fourth International fifteen years ago, we had ambitious plans, breaking out of the narrow restrictions of an organisation like the FI, but it's only in recent years that it's really mushroomed.

In 1985-90, our focus was very much on many efforts at regroupment here, blocked by lack of progress in Latin America and the Caribbean, and the developing collapse of the Soviet Union.

In the early '90s, we had to make a turn to consolidating, re-stressing party building here. We broadened out with *Green Left Weekly,* organised the Socialist Scholars Conferences, and set up European and Moscow bureaus for the paper.

That laid the basis for a further step-up in our international work, with the International Green Left Conference in 1994, the foundation of *Links,* enabling us to respond to the political developments in Indonesia, the founding of the PRD, and the split in the Philippines Communist Party.

By 1998, with the Asia Pacific Solidarity Conference, we had expanded further our interesting range of contacts with Marxist parties in the Asian region, especially India and Pakistan. In 1999 we had a further impact with our exemplary solidarity work with East Timor.

The expansion of our international work is partly relative, the result of the decline of many left currents, especially the crisis of the dominant left current, Stalinism. Thus our weight and responsibility are greater. But it also reflects some objective changes, such as the economic, social and political crisis in the Third World, Asia in particular, with the expansion of left organisations and our contacts.

We've benefited from identifying with the dynamic of growing support for constructive, non-sectarian united approaches, contrasting with continuing left crises, splits and sectarianism (though so many still persist with that approach).

We're now moving into a more *active* role internationally, from gathering information and contacts, to more often being able to have a political impact, to *help* with a solidarity campaign, to *influence* people with our views on internationalism, internationals; on permanent revolution; on the national question; on building Leninist parties broadly based on those fundamental four points outlined in our Appeal.[95]

We can be proud of our healthy achievement of gathering a

loose network of collaborating parties in the Asian region from varied backgrounds, and real implantations and each with important contributions.

(The FI in Europe refers to this as 'the Sydney process'.)

The international anti-IMF-WB-WTO movement

The whole international anti-IMF-WB-WTO movement is certainly very significant, a very real development demonstrated dramatically at Seattle [1999], and at other protests in Europe and North America at various summit meetings. We're relating to this sentiment and movement in whatever ways we can. We'll be centrally involved in any demos or action here, such as 11 September in Melbourne [2000].

But we should be conscious our analysis and approach are different from the anarchist currents – anti-capitalist, but without a strategy or an alternative – or people who see this movement replacing traditional class struggles somehow.

How can we better intervene in the whole anti-globalisation activity, even with all its rationalist or bandaid or NGO distortions? One problem is that in the Asia-Pacific region it is primarily dominated by European- and North American-funded NGOs.

Unionists Against Corporate Tyranny[96] will be a campaign designed for our intervention here, with signatures and sponsorship, leading to a conference that we want to set down for Melbourne 27 August, which can lead to some sort of organisation. It can play an educational role in the unions here, and be a structure allowing cross-union political interventions by us. But it also has the potential for future international use, allowing us to intervene in international forums where parties get excluded.

We're throwing our full support behind the 11-13 September demonstrations in Melbourne, and will do what we can to publicise them internationally. They're not causing much of a ripple yet – the World Economic Forum meeting in Melbourne is a relatively minor event.

Proposals have arisen to link up the campaigns of the G77 nations with the NGOs opposing the impact of global capitalism. This could have a useful dynamic, although I suspect some of the motivation might be from the NGO heavies to give them a political edge. The important link that needs to be developed is the connection between revolutionary *parties* North and South.

We also have to look at other tools for our interventions, such as the possibility of a solidarity-aid organisation 'that won't take any funding from governments', i.e. is independent of government, that we can contrast with Community Aid Abroad etc. and conservative organisations.

Spanish and LA networks

We haven't just been experiencing exciting developments with the developing Asian network and Marxism 2000. As Dick [Nichols] reported in his Latin American Left and Cuba report earlier today, there are remarkably similar discussions and re-compositions taking place in the Spanish-speaking world.

Dick's reports from his seven months in Europe and Latin America have been extremely useful in filling in the political picture in a number of countries. Some of these are written out available for NC comrades to read.

The contact Dick developed with Manuel Monereo (on the *Links* editorial board, on the United Left leadership, the United Left International Commission, and best of the Spanish CP currents), who is keen to collaborate with us, has led to some specific proposals.

Monereo and the FIM (Fundación de Investigaciones Marxistas – Marxist Research Foundation) are involved in building a network of Marxist theoretical journals with a practical, non-academic bent and want to include *Links* in this network. In particular, the FIM plus *America Libre* plus some other journals will be holding a seminar in Rio and want us to participate. We'd like to attend.

Monereo is working towards a 'new international' network for the Luso-Hispanic world in much the same spirit and with much the same approach as we are doing in our region. The orientation is to spell out eight to ten key points of agreement for practical anti-capitalist collaboration, and to promote the widest possible discussion among the anti-capitalist left. We'd want to engage with this.

He's also keen to get to know the left in our region, and would like to do a tour that started in Australia and included Indonesia and the Philippines. They would arrange this to include the Jakarta conference.[97] This is a valuable opening for us that we need to take seriously.

Cuba

As a result of Dick's trip and several other developments, it seems that the possibility of developing closer relations with the Cuban CP is greater than ever before. Over the last few years there's been a consolidation of the right wing in the Sao Paulo Forum [SPF]. At this Forum, the left decided to counterattack, and the Cuban CP (with a delegation of 20) played the key role.

First, they planned an ideological intervention, with their document, 'Alternative to Neo-Liberalism', which we'll run in the next issue of *Links*. Secondly, they organised to shift the axis in the working group to the left, replacing the Dominicans with the Puerto Ricans, and bringing the Partido Trabajadores [Workers Party] of Mexico onto the working group. (They began as Maoists; hold a continental cadre school each year, inviting all parties, accommodation free.) The FMLN would offer to work on the secretariat. So we're headed for sharper political clashes at the SPF in future. Cuba wants unity at all costs, but the price is no frank discussion. The Cuban CP will leave it to others to put the boot in.

The right wing of the Forum has already established links with Asian and European parties. Dick talked with the left, and the Cubans, and they want from us a written description of the APSC and the players, and they want to get a Cuban delegation to Jakarta.

The Cubans and the Argentinian CP (the leadership current, led by Patricio Echegerai) urged us to get involved in the LA left/ SPF directly.

The Colombian group 'Present for Socialism' (led by Fermin Gonzalez) is constructing an urban social and political front and is producing some draft documents for a meeting in August. They would like our comments on their four-point program:

1. Support for the Cuban Revolution;
2. A clear view of the dynamics of revolution in Latin America (not an ultra-left Trotskyist schema);
3. Socialism and democracy;
4. Internationalism.

(Compare with our appeal!)

Resistance has now got this 'Footsteps of Che' tour to Cuba jointly organised with Ocean Press.[98] The next big important event in Cuba is the November solidarity conference, where there are likely to be 4,000 people. The Cubans are looking for allies around the world. We want to maintain better contact, send all our documents and pamphlets. For the Cubans, as always, the proof of the pudding is in the actual practice. The more we achieve politically in Australia, and the more we achieve internationally, the more they will relate to us.

Role of Appeal

The 'Appeal for International Collaboration and Socialist Renewal' has been to a large extent superseded by further developments. Certainly it's no longer a projection of four parties. But it still might have some use, as long as it's not given too big a weight and a role that's fixed, especially given similar documents getting projected on the healthy Latin American left. Let's exchange discussion documents.

We printed it in the *Activist* and sent it to other parties before the conference on the basis of it being a contribution to the discussion by the DSP. That was its role at the conference.

The development of a real network has gone beyond a document like that, and we don't want it to serve as a brake on the process. The 'network of four parties' has been overtaken even before there was agreement from the other three parties with the document.

One area where I think we should consider adjusting our virtual statement is on the question of Cuba. Perhaps we should add this in? It would put us more in sync with the processes happening in Latin America.

From Latin America comes a similar push to ours, with a suggestion for four points for unity. It's similar, but has the necessary Latin American flavour, and does teach us something. At the top of the list, they had support for the Cuban Revolution. Like our affirmation of the validity of October 1917, that defines you as a revolutionary there. It's not so much a theoretical point, but how you react to Cuba does define you politically, in the sense that here's a revolution that has to be defended, revolutionary Marxists that have to be respected.

Even comrades coming from traditions not oriented to the Cuban Revolution, if they're revolutionaries, instinctively adopt a positive approach to the Cuban Revolution.

Our political perspective, thus the content of the Appeal (four or five points) seems simple and very basic. But it can encompass a lot politically: the Russian Revolution, Leninism, the Cuban Revolution. This perspective is the goal of renewing the international left on the fundamentals.

More friends

On top of the main feature of our international work, the collaboration between real, independent parties from different traditions, in recent years there's also been a secondary feature developing.

A growing feature of our international contacts is the range of small groups, from a few individuals to a couple of dozen, trying to establish Leninist groups, in difficult circumstances. They've split, or been expelled, or stranded, from anti-Leninist or liquidationist organisations.

And there's a growing list of individual collaborators, who have respect for our politics and/or our organisational achievements, and who relate to us directly. They're either not in a party, ex-SWP, ex-CWI, ex-FI, or in parties that have many limitations. These comrades have lots of political experience, and can make a big contribution, to *Links,* or writing for *Green Left.*

Scottish Socialist Party

The Scottish Socialist Party is one of the most exciting developments in the English-speaking left. They still haven't made the final break with London, although London now has an openly declared faction operating inside them. They're being courted by quite a few networks and internationals, including the FI. This is an extract from their conference resolution on international links that they adopted:

> Over and above collaborating around particular initia-
> tives socialists need to find ways to organise permanently
> on an international basis. We need to work towards an
> international alliance of socialist parties. It would be
> premature to attempt to launch such an alliance today.
> But we are ready to participate in all international
> conferences and forums which bring together socialist
> and working-class forces from different countries.
> We actively seek to establish links with those
> organisations in other countries who share our
> vision of a democratic socialist society.

We obviously want to develop the closest possible relations with these comrades.

The New Zealand Alliance, now that they're in a coalition government with Labour, are less likely to be having similar concerns as us internationally. They'll often be to the right; ours is a left project. The Dutch Socialist Party also seems to be shifting further to the right. Max [Lane] attended their NC, which he described as 'boring, parliamentary cretinism at its extreme'. They've set up a youth organisation, 'Red', with an 'anti-hunting campaign', which he described as a left-wing Rotary Club.

We should maintain our broad contacts, even with types going to the right. Their project is not our project, but we should maintain relations, avoid sectarianism, force our space, the legitimacy for a revolutionary stance. We'll put the onus on the right and centrist currents to make the sectarian moves.

More enemies

The higher profile that our party is achieving, with our confer-ences, the reputation of *Green Left*, *Links*, the developing Asian network and the clear stance we've taken on political events such as Kosova, Indonesia and East Timor, and theoretical questions like permanent revolution, has several consequences.

We get more contacts internationally, more respect, more chances for subscriptions to *Green Left* and *Links,* orders for our publications and gains for the party here.

But it also means that more sectarians will be gunning for us. Not just the ones we know, the CWI and some in the FI, but people on the internet discussion lists that we've never heard of. There are a few real weirdos out there who think the DSP is the new Great Satan.

Peoples Asia Pacific Solidarity Conference

Coming out of the Marxism 2000 Conference, a main proposal was announced, plans for the next Peoples Asia Pacific Solidarity Conference, to be held in Jakarta in June 2001.[99] Discussions to get it off the ground have been held, and some progress made. A draft letter and agenda are getting finalised; Pip [Hinman] went to Indonesia to help with the first steps, and Max [Lane] went there to help finalise it.

An email list of more than 1,500 left groups around the world of all hues will be mailed with the initial proposal, and then later with the full agenda and details. Prospects for Cuban and Latin American attendance look good. It's likely to encourage broad attendance from Europe. And from the Asian region we hope to get a huge attendance.

We project a big delegation. We'll organise exposure tours that will include the conference, and encourage comrades to plan their holidays to include it.

It will be the most important international left event for a long while. It could have a big impact on Indonesian politics, a big impact on the left in the region, and contribute to the consolidation of our Asian network.

Discussions since the conference have also clarified our own needs. In addition to the Jakarta conference, we then need another international conference here. We'll have our decision-making congress next January, a student International Solidarity Conference at Easter a few months before the Jakarta event and an educational conference in January 2002, but we want to propose that the next really big international event here be held at Easter 2002.

We'll bill it as an APSC. It won't be just a repeat of APSC in 1998; there'll be more Marxism in the workshops, and more emphasis on parties. The visiting parties themselves will be asked to run classes, not just give country reports. There'll be many more opportunities for discussions. We want to book the date now, book Glebe High School. We'll aim for 1,000 registrations, with 100 international guests. We'll get the poster and leaflets out by February 2001.

Links

Now that the regularity of *Links* has improved, and it's getting more established, with better content, more debates, more timely and relevant analyses, we're confident we can expand support for it further. We will adjust the boards before the next issue, and attempt to change them further, both to broaden out and to reflect our main collaborators and new forces in the Asian region. But it should still be broad, politically and geographically.

We have to improve the circulation and distribution, especially among DSP and Resistance members. *Links* should occupy a much more central role in the political life of comrades, in education, in theoretical discussion. Have a *Links* table at the Resistance conference. We propose to put all articles up on the web. We think this won't cut into subs. We have an impressive list of contents for the first fifteen issues, and there was a good response to emailing our long email address list.

I mentioned the idea for a *Links* supporters pledge to help finance distribution to Third World parties. We also will have to have a price increase to $8, and increase the price of overseas subs. But it will still be excellent value; what's holding our sub base back is only our own efforts at promotion. We'll get out an attractive brochure with the contents of all back issues. We need a subcommittee of comrades to make sure all the extra work gets carried out.

We'll also be going on a big push to involve other parties and members of the *Links* board in its promotion much more actively. We want to actively involve others in shaping the issues, helping in editing, soliciting articles, promoting it and getting subscriptions. *Links* can be an important stepping stone towards a more solid network.

General objectives of our international work

Can we further clarify some of the general objectives of our international work following on from the conference? I think we can be a bit clearer now by formulating some of our objectives and the objectives of our collaborative, non-sectarian network in the following ways:

1. Removing the growing space, even the germinating space, for sects and fake internationals in the Asian region. I think the network is starting to have that balance of forces and spread that contributes to this objective.
2. Providing all the half way useful or perceived functions of fake internationals:

    a) International conferences (APSC, a pattern is getting set)

b) A journal for discussion and theory (*Links;*
there's nothing really competing)

c) An international news service (*Green Left*
makes a big contribution)

d) A publishing house (we make a partial
contribution here)

e) A school for international cadres?

Of course in no way do we want even to contemplate any of the useless and *negative* roles that fake internationals give themselves.

3. Giving political and ideological leadership, fostering a revolutionary Marxist trend and parties internationally. Along the lines of the Appeal, whether sharply formulated or more general, set down in a document or promoted in various ways.

4. Leading on the key issues:

- Kosova
- The national question
- Indonesia and East Timor solidarity
- Clarity on role of UN interventions
- Permanent revolution
- Cuba

We can characterise our approach up to now as having 'a foot in all doors'. We still want to keep all these doors open, but with all these opportunities, we're going to have to be selective about what we give priority to. Fostering the Asian network is our absolute priority. And we have to solidly promote our 'process' and our perspectives, in *Links, Green Left Weekly* and other publications, and through the internet.

Our political work on the ground here in Australia and our international work are increasingly interconnected. It's always been the case for us, from Vietnam to Indonesia. But we should understand that in this period, it's even more likely that it will be international issues that help break the ideological chains in the union movement. The anti-corporate tyranny movement will be not just politically important, but increasingly organisationally important.

We're seeing the connection between the political-ideological issues we're leading on internationally and the actions that we can lead on politically here.

Crises are escalating as a result of the growing imperialist stranglehold on the world and the onslaughts of neoliberalism. The growing crises, coups and irrational violence in the Pacific region bring home to us the urgency of our international tasks: helping rebuild the left around the world, building Marxist parties in all countries that can give direction, anti-capitalist leadership to the frustration of the masses. Fiji and the Solomons are on our doorstep, but this is the state of the *world* – Iraq, Afghanistan, Ethiopia, Mozambique, the Balkans, Philippines, Sri Lanka, Colombia, the former Soviet Union, Sierra Leone, Zimbabwe, Palestine.

Big political events are happening, and can surprise us at every turn, and we and the left internationally are woefully ill equipped to respond adequately.

The masses will be expecting more of the revolutionary Marxist parties, not in decades, but in the coming years and months. Big crises are looming, and changes in the objective situation can occur very quickly. Our international work takes on extra relevance and extra urgency. What we do with this work matters, and can make a difference, sooner than we think.

13. RENEWING THE INTERNATIONAL SOCIALIST MOVEMENT

Report to the 19th Congress
January 2001[100]

*In this report John looked at the longer term impact of the collapse of
Stalinism in Eastern Europe and the discrediting of social democracy
by its repeated betrayals of working class interests. These events had
opened a process of what he called recomposition in the international
socialist movement, in which parties from different traditions that
sought to maintain a revolutionary outlook were increasingly able to
collaborate with each other. The report noted two different trends in
the anti-globalisation movement: traditional liberalism and a radical
anti-capitalism and suggested how the DSP should act in this situation.*

Revolutionary Marxists are internationalists. Our goal is the
unification of the working people and oppressed of the world
in the complete overthrow of the capitalist system and the
ushering in of a classless, socialist society. But capitalist power
is concentrated at the level of state power in national states, so
the instruments we need to overthrow that power are nationally

based revolutionary working class parties.

Building such parties to defeat our own bourgeoisie is our prime responsibility. But because we're internationalists, we're eager to help others to build revolutionary parties, to build better collaboration, to build a real network, to build parties that can make revolutions, in all the countries of the world.

From the early '80s, after breaking out of the narrow framework of the Fourth International, the Democratic Socialist Party has had a perspective of trying to renew and rebuild the communist movement. The collapse of the Soviet Union gave this perspective of renewal added impetus and urgency. Since then we've witnessed the enormous expansion of our international work.

In the early '90s, we broadened out with *Green Left Weekly*, organised the Socialist Scholars Conferences, and set up European and Moscow bureaus for the paper.

That laid the basis for a further expansion of our international work, with the International Green Left Conference in 1994, the foundation of *Links,* enabling us to respond to the political developments in Indonesia, the founding of the PRD and the split in the Philippines Communist Party.

By 1998, with the Asia Pacific Solidarity Conference, we had expanded further our interesting range of contacts with Marxist parties in the Asian region, especially India and Pakistan. They come from many traditions, and will continue to have a varied assessment of historical experiences.

In 1999 we had a further impact with our exemplary solidarity work with East Timor. The Marxism 2000 Conference last January expanded this Asian network further, linking us to the developing Marxist forces in South Korea.

The past year has added a new dimension to our international work, with the development of the growing movement against neoliberal globalisation.

Social democracy and liberalism

The objective social and political circumstances we face as revolutionary Marxists have certainly changed during the course of the 20th century, but the irreconcilable contradictions of capitalism, and the need and possibility of socialist revolution, still remain.

With the end of the long post-war boom, the bourgeoisie's neoliberal offensive over the last 25 years has beaten back the working class internationally, taking back gains won in previous struggles. The wealth gap continues to widen between rich and poor in the imperialist countries, and is widening even further between the exploited countries and the imperialist countries.

The capitalist class's neoliberal offensive has often been implemented by social democratic parties by preference. They can more effectively blunt working class resistance. In recent decades social democracy has increasingly abandoned any charade that it had fundamentally different goals and allegiances than capitalism and its parties.

But what is the *nature* of the setback for the working class? Certainly the attacks on our rights and conditions are a setback, but *not* the fact that now these parties are increasingly exposed as just another capitalist party.

The real tragedy of the 20th century for the working class has been social democracy/liberalism, a current fundamentally committed to the continued existence of capitalism. That's been the key divide, the main betrayer. The social base of this current is the labour aristocracy, living off crumbs from imperialism's table.

Sometimes parties that retain the name Communist have policies and practices that are classic social democratic, even participating in governments and ensuring the maintenance of capitalism and the implementation of the bourgeoisie's neoliberal austerity policies.

Today, we see a new layer developing with a new base, professional NGO careerists.

Also, with the collapse of the Soviet Union and Eastern Europe, the final fruits of Stalinism, the second 20th century betrayer of the workers' movement announced its departure from the scene. Certainly, the Soviet collapse had terrible consequences for workers there, experiencing drastic falls in their standards of living and life expectancy under mafia capitalism, and it has heightened the isolation of liberation movements in the Third World. But is it a setback for the working class and the prospects for revolutionary change that Stalinism no longer has the strength and the prospects for misleading the movement?

Some on the left have reacted with despair. 'It's all changed for the worse', they wail. They themselves then add to the retreat.

Some left currents, concluding it was bad times for the left, circled the wagons, drew back from any outreach initiatives they had started to dabble with.

Other currents were impelled to divide even further, to return to their 'true line orthodoxy', to set up their own new 'international'.

Many of the academic left, the latest in a long list being the magazine *New Left Review*, have given up on fundamental social change altogether.

A new movement in the imperialist countries

But for us, the exposure and discrediting of Stalinism and social democracy have a positive side. It opened the way for new parties, a new movement. We expected it. And in recent years it has been emerging, North and South.

New parties are developing with varied origins. New alliances have been built. People have been radicalising around environ-mental issues, women's struggles, national questions. Former members of the old parties and trade unions have been joining socialist parties. New links are being developed between parties with very different origins and traditions. There's a process of recomposition.

And the retreats demonstrated bad timing. The capitalist ideologues gloating about 'the end of history' have been shown to be premature and laughingly short-sighted.

When all seemed to be going imperialism's way in the Middle East, Palestine erupted with the second *intifada.*

And did they really think that the US boom of the '90s would be everlasting?

Perry Anderson's editorial for *New Left Review's* new series, declaring its peace with capitalism, would have been written at the same time as Seattle was ushering in a whole series of demonstrations opposing neoliberal globalisation, showing that there's a growing movement of anti-capitalist activists in the imperialist countries.

Mass upsurges in the Third World have been frequent, even if imperialism was coping through its standard repression and corruption. But with this new movement, the First World is now catching up. And it's worrying for the capitalists.

Seattle was the most dramatic, but it was building up before that. The wonderful experience with S11[101] here in Melbourne really brought it home.

This new internationalism in the imperialist heartland means they're in danger of losing the youth once again. Compare it with the protests against the war in Vietnam, which was focussed against a war, and extended to a radicalisation on racism, sexism, gay rights, environment etc.

This movement encompasses a general rejection of imperi-alist exploitation of the whole Third World. It's a reaction to the poverty, the exploitation, the glaring gap. Sometimes it focuses on a specific issue, a particular piece of environmental destruction, a particularly crass multinational corporation. And as yet there's no universally decided list of demands. But many general propositions would be agreed on, against imperialist institutions and capitalism itself.

Key questions in the new movement

The new movement against capitalist globalisation is very diverse. There's now enough experience to analyse the different currents and the important political issues that differentiate them. We can identify the two key trends: labour bureaucrats and radicals.

Both are 'anti-capitalist' in the sense that the liberals are still in conflict with the bourgeoisie, wanting a return to the period of concessions characteristic of the postwar long expansionary wave, before the turn to neoliberal policies by imperialism. They want a return to Keynesianism – propping capitalism up with more government spending.

In the actions we'll push for a united front. We need that broad alliance of all the forces encompassing many different political perspectives campaigning against global capitalism through some form of mass action.

But we also need to be clear on the differences, the dividing lines, the challenges, and what pushes are likely to come from the ruling class.

Doug Lorimer outlined in the international political situation report what central political demands we should be pressing in this developing movement:

- abolition of the IMF-World Bank-WTO;
- unconditional cancellation of the Third World debt; and
- preferential trade treatment for the Third World.

The position of abolishing [the three institutions] has gained momentum in the movement, even among many NGOs, especially given that the line of the institutions themselves has had to switch to one of putting on a human face, reforming themselves, humanising themselves. Unconditional cancellation of the Third World debt is also a demand that's more accepted.

Exposing the dead end of chauvinist protectionism has been harder. It's been the scourge of the Australian trade union movement.

In the Seattle and Washington [protests], this was the line of the AFL-CIO: to protect US jobs, keep China out of the WTO. Many on the left misunderstand this issue.

Socialism and the party question

But a central principled question for the movement that so far has been mostly ignored is where to go beyond capitalism, what can we replace it with? Socialism.

Sometimes this actually appears as the party question – the right to have the socialist alternative raised in the discussions, the right to have parties as part of the united front. If parties are excluded, then we just get restricted to the language of 'civil society', 'communities' etc.; you can't take the discussion or the demands out of the framework of capitalism.

This anti-party anti-socialist theme often gets picked up by naive but well-meaning anarchists who think they're extra radical, but they're actually implementing the agenda of those committed to the preservation of capitalism.

The anti-party theme has also been taken up by the NGO/civil society/community movements milieu.

It looks increasingly like the FI sees these NGO non-party international gatherings as the key regroupment. This seems the tenor of discussion at the last few IEC meetings.

Pierre Rousset, for example, saw the [1998] APSC as more impressive than Marxism 2000 because the APSC had more non-party groups, more non-left forces involved, whereas we were more excited by Marxism 2000 because of the extra serious Marxist forces attending.

But we know parties can't be bypassed. The movement feels the pressure for a healthy party where none exists. And there is no halfway structure; any half-hearted attempt is going to be weaker and reinforce people's prejudices against parties. A wiser tactic is to jump in and try.

In South Africa, the SACP had the potential to move forward, to mobilise, to build a strong party. It made an initial critique of Stalinism, but lapsed back into its old framework and chose to tag along behind the ANC government, with its neoliberal austerity, privatisation, anti-worker policies.

There are many activists and campaigns and committed socialists outside the SACP. There is also the usual range of little sects, none growing particularly at the moment. It's clear that the ANC and SACP are not providing the answer, but people are not going to jump into one of the sects. But the left activists there are holding off on any new party project, afraid it would be just another little sect. But if they don't act, one of the small sects might grow. And activists will get disillusioned.

In the USA, where there's a broad layer of activists and a multitude of campaigns, the socialist movement has been sorely lacking. Solidarity, the organisation we've had closest contact with, unfortunately is founded on an anti-Leninist principle, eschews organisation and thus squanders opportunities. With no newspaper, they're invisible at the actions, and rarely coordinate their interventions.

What sort of renewal?

What sort of socialist renewal and regroupment is possible around the world? What sort of party is needed? Can it just be on a broad anti-capitalist basis? Or do we need revolutionary Marxist parties right away?

Perhaps it depends on each country. There are varied social circumstances, and very different political situations. Movements and parties are at different stages of development, and have different political heritages. We can't be too prescriptive on this.

Some countries will need a broad, anti-capitalist regroupment, with the revolutionary Marxist forces just functioning as a current within the broader movement. Sometimes revolutionary Marxists will be able to lead the regroupment, as in the Scottish Socialist Party. Sometimes the revolutionaries will be in the minority. Sometimes there will be a variety of Marxist currents.

Certainly there's a need for a conscious anti-sectarian stance in order to succeed.

Also, it's clear that we don't need international factions, or the fake internationals with delusions of grandeur. We've experienced numerous actual negative effects of such internationals.

But the *goal*, the task, is to get to a revolutionary Marxist party, a Leninist, Bolshevik party. Without it, a revolution won't succeed. So we shouldn't make a virtue, or necessity, out of a temporary, partial step or stage.

Similarly, we shouldn't make a principle of a retreat, a lesser form of organisation that has to be accepted because of political and organisational weakness: for example, the idea of the 'pluralist left' that's emerged in some places as the description of the only acceptable parties.

Certainly, we're all for the right of tendency, the importance of discussion and debate. But unfortunately some have interpreted this to be the most important defining principle of a party, and made a principle of being anti-democratic centralism, anti-Leninist. This can lead to a slide to the right, a slide to a social democratic political position, and a retreat from the party-building project altogether.

Leninism

The FI's Pierre Rousset has characterised our position as contradictory – between our hard Leninist past, which we cling to, and our opening up approach of the present. But there's no contradiction at all. We're consciously relating to the state of flux with many parties/currents, not cutting off relations. But at the same time we have a clear line ourselves for party building, which we both push by example, with our practice in Australia, and argue for in *Links* and *GLW* and our other publications.

It's our implementation of our understanding of Lenin's practice in building the Bolshevik party. The distortion has been the Stalinist and Trotskyist practice of the last seventy-plus years.

The task in imperialist countries is to build working-class parties able to think for themselves, independent of capitalists and their institutions.

The task in the Third World is also building revolutionary parties, not sects taking direction from some mother party based in the First World. Look at the ISO in South Korea: it vanished without a trace, it had no roots in the real movement. They and the CWI and others have been trying in Indonesia. Their influence could only be disastrous.

So we stress: parties on a national basis; networks or alliances of parties internationally.

While rejecting any idea of a new structured 'international' today, the dynamic in practice is towards an international network or alliance of socialist parties. This is based on the reality of the emergence of new parties in a number of countries, and greater contact and collaboration between parties coming from different traditions. We have a de facto alliance with a number of the parties in the Asian region.

Key role of Cuba

For years the revolutionary government of Cuba has provided political inspiration to the best of the movements in the South. At Seattle they helped provide a link between the governments of the South inside [the official meetings] who rejected the WTO round and the new movements on the streets outside.

For years Cuba has been waging a lonely leadership battle at these international summits, first on the debt question and now on neoliberal globalisation. But the post-Seattle movement signalled that Cuba was no longer fighting alone on this front. At the G77 Summit of the South in Havana last April, Fidel Castro hailed Seattle as 'a revolt against neoliberalism'.

As one of the few fighting revolutionary movements with state power, Cuba will help pave the way for the other revolutionary movements in the South to link up directly with the anti-neoliberal activists in the North.

The Cubans have stepped up their role in the international left in the last few years, and this was seen clearly in their intervention in the Sao Paulo Forum meeting in February last year.

At the same time our friendly relations with the Cuban CP have improved tremendously, helped by visits of comrades to Cuba, and given a boost through our intensive discussions with the Cuban political reps who accompanied the Cuban Olympic team to Sydney in September.

Comrades would have heard of the very successful second International Cuban Solidarity Conference just held in Havana; 4,347 delegates from 118 countries gathered to express their condemnation of the US blockade. This tremendous conference would have given a boost to the solidarity campaign with Cuba, but also boosted the struggles against imperialism throughout the world.

As you know, our delegation of five comrades was given a tremendous honour. At the concluding demonstration of 12,000 people outside the US special interests section, two conference delegates from each of the five regions of the world were invited by the organisers to address the crowd, and Pat Brewer from the DSP was one of them! The three-hour rally was televised fully throughout Cuba and broadcast internationally. Fidel congratulated Pat on her speech.

Quebec City

The next global demonstration and confrontation will be in Quebec City during the April 20-22 Summit of the Americas. Having failed to restart the WTO negotiations since Seattle, the US is now stepping up its attempt to broaden NAFTA to establish the Free Trade Area of the Americas, and to expand its mandate to cover many non-trade matters. Representatives of 34 countries (Cuba excluded of course) will be there, meeting in the walled old city protected by thousands of police and military with a four-mile exclusion zone.

Opponents have already divided into two camps. An alternative Peoples Summit is being organised, with seminars, demonstrations and an attempt to shut down the summit.

The more anarchist and confrontationist-inclined forces have walked out and set up the Anti-Capitalist Convergence (CLAC), with a platform for a real shutdown. They're refusing to participate in the Peoples Summit, saying it's taking government money.

European regroupments

In Europe there are also new networks developing of anti-capitalist parties similar to the processes taking place in Latin America and Asia.

The Communist parties of Europe were already in decline before the collapse of the Soviet Union. We have analysed such parties as having had two roles, as both instruments of the Stalinist bureaucracy in Moscow, and as social democratic, often based on the trade union bureaucracy, similar to the role of the ALP here. Following the collapse, the first role disappeared, and for some the second continued, with some of the larger parties able to maintain themselves in a weakened state. The past decade has been a testing time.

Some of the smaller parties dissolved completely, as in Australia and Britain. Others made the complete transition to social democratic or liberal parties.

Some of the more hardline Stalinist parties still struggle to maintain the forms and rituals, without the content. They gathered earlier last year in a Meeting of Communist and Workers Parties in Belgrade, and later in Athens in June. The fall of Milosevic removes some of their impetus, which wasn't very dynamic anyway.

In some cases the crisis of the CPs has pushed sections to the left, or led to parties allowing different currents, or contributed to new alliances or blocs. The process still continues.

There's been a recomposition of alliances and networks, as well as a greater openness to parties coming from different political traditions. In the European Parliament there's the New European Left Forum, and the United European Left-Nordic Green Left Group. We shouldn't cut ourselves off from any of these parties, many of whom are still in flux.

Last year we saw a push to bring together the more

anti-capitalist left parties in Europe, partly initiated by the Fourth International. An initial meeting was held of some of these parties in Lisbon earlier last year, and a second gathering took place 4-5 December in Paris. It was hosted by the French LCR. We were invited to observe. The parties involved have varied origins and outlooks.

There is also talk of setting up a 'Fifth International' that has been getting raised in Europe in recent months, and it seems some, including some in the FI, see the possibility of furthering this scheme at the Porto Alegre [World Social] Forum. This envisages not just parties, but trade unions and NGOs and other organisations participating – harking back to the First International. This type of project is much more problematic and would by its nature preclude a socialist program.

It's also been noted by bourgeois organisations, and the phrase is being bandied around. The June-July issue of *Actualité*, a French employers organisation, notes the 'plural dissatisfactions' of the trade unions, and was especially worried by 'alliances of another kind which are being made in order to form an anti-capitalist front aiming to fight against globalisation'. In *Actualité*'s opinion, 'these organisers ... must be taken seriously. What is involved is nothing less than a Fifth International'.

Scottish Socialist Party

The Scottish Socialist Party is one of the most exciting developments in the English-speaking left. The SSP strengthened from an alliance of most of the left forces in Scotland (except the SWP, who are now negotiating to join). They elected Tommy Sheridan to the first Scottish parliament for 300 years. New branches are getting formed all over, even in the highlands and far-flung islands. They have about 2,500 members.

It's led by capable comrades who, as of this week, are still formally in the Committee for a Workers' International, but undermined by a small [Peter] Taaffe faction based in Dundee.

Catriona Grant, a Central Committee member who attended the CWI's International Executive Committee meeting last November, has already publicly circulated a call for 'an amicable divorce' from the CWI. The final break is likely to come soon.

They're pro-Cuban in practice; their conference in February gave a standing ovation to the Cuban ambassador, while the CWI and FI guests sat on their hands.

They're being courted by quite a few networks and internationals, including the FI, although they favour an international alliance of socialist parties, not a narrow fake 'international'.

We obviously want to develop the closest possible relations with these comrades. Perhaps we should propose a tour of Tommy Sheridan or Alan McCombes to promote their book.

A key goal is to convince them to assign a number of comrades to the *Links* editorial board, and distribute *Links* in quantity, something they're seriously considering and have already debated out with the CWI leadership in London. We can learn a lot from them about popular agitation and organising. We can also help them when they cut loose from their old international ties, by providing the extensive international news and discussion we already have access to.

The decision on whether the SWP in Scotland joins the SSP (giving up the public distribution of their paper, but having all the democratic and tendency rights that all political currents in the SSP have) will be taken at the SSP's conference this February. (We'll have comrades attending.)

In the rest of Britain, Socialist Alliances are being extended after successfully standing in the London council elections. The Socialist Alliances bring together the SWP, the SP, half a dozen other left groups mainly from the Trotskyist tradition and independent socialist activists. First steps towards left unity have been taken in Ireland too. The SWP faces a big test in these Socialist Alliances: whether they're serious about building a real opposition to Labour. But the biggest test will be posed in Scotland – whether they're just there on a raiding mission. If they're actually changing their spots in Britain, we'd expect some serious changes among some in the ISO here.

Next Australian event

Our next big international conference in Australia will be at Easter 2002 in Sydney. We'll bill it as an International Solidarity Conference. But it won't be just a repeat of APSC in 1998. There'll be more Marxist discussion leading up to the conference, and in the workshops, and more emphasis on the regroupment of parties, and connecting spheres of struggle in different regions of the world. The visiting parties themselves will be asked to run classes, not just give country reports. There'll be many more opportunities for discussions, and we hope it will be an opportunity for all the parties in the Asian network able to attend and discuss face to face.

We want to book the date now, book Glebe High School. We're aiming for 1,000 registrations, with 100 international guests. We'd like to get the poster and leaflets out soon.

14. 11 SEPTEMBER AND IMPERIALISM'S OFFENSIVE

Talk to Socialist Education Conference January 2002

This talk was delivered only a few months after the 11 September terrorist attacks on New York and Washington. In this respect, it was different from the other reports in this book. While those reports presented specific proposals for the DSP's activities in the coming period, this talk was intended to present the party leadership's views on the significance and meaning of recent events. In this talk, much of the emphasis was on the ongoing changes in relations on the international left, developments that many in the audience would not yet have had the opportunity to become very familiar with.

The 11 September [2001] terrorist attacks and the imperialist response have certainly created a new world political situation. But the main features were already in preparation and developing – the world economic recession, neoliberal attacks on the working class, imperialism's war drive and the aggressive hegemonic designs of the US ruling class.

These major developments govern very much the situation on the left, and how we all respond to September 11 and imperialism's offensive is a crucial test. We have to assess the new party-building needs and possibilities, and how our international work, and the possibilities for building the socialist movement around the world, have been affected.

This is not a war against 'terrorism', let alone Bin Laden, or al-Qaeda. It's a war on the semicolonial world and on the working class and dissidents within advanced capitalist countries. It's not just about oil. Imperialism's goal is to push world politics to the right under US hegemony, and to deliver harsh blows against all the main opponents of the US at home and abroad.

They are targeting in particular the global justice movement, the Third World, their capitalist rivals in Europe and political opponents at home. It is also aimed to help Washington achieve key US political and economic targets – economically the absolute domination of the corporations and US world leadership politically.

To help them achieve and consolidate these aims, they have launched major attacks on democratic and civil rights – in the US the PATRIOT Act; there is similar legislation in the UK, Europe and Australia. In Bolivia, shortly after 11 September, we saw the arrest of Oscar Olivera, the leader of the successful anti-water privatisation struggle. It was a portent.

They want to use 11 September to criminalise dissent and to push back all the gains made since the struggle against the Vietnam War. They want to use it to beat back the movement against neoliberal globalisation and reverse the momentum that had built up to Genoa[102] and after.

This war for US hegemony is a long-term campaign. The US ruling class had been preparing and planning for such an offensive, and were ready to go when 11 September happened. As Bush said, this will be 'a war that will go on for years'.

International left reactions to 11 September

Most of the left around the world has responded well, with general agreement on the major political questions. Not too many have succumbed to the huge imperialist propaganda barrage.

A further swag of liberal intellectuals *did* fall into line behind the ruling class, but mostly you could attribute their fall to demoralisation from events of the last few decades – skittles on the verge of toppling anyway. In the US the pressure was most intense, of course – if you didn't plant the stars and stripes in your front yard or on your car, you must be a traitor or terrorist, and various former leftists wrote accordingly, the most notable being Christopher Hitchens. There's a similar circle here. There was a most disgusting piece by Dave McKnight (ex-CPA leader, ex-Trotskyist) in Saturday's *Sydney Morning Herald,* attacking [Noam] Chomsky and [John] Pilger. In Britain, where there's a much wider liberal opposition to the war, even the tabloid *Mirror,* with a circulation in the millions, has been carrying John Pilger's trenchant articles on its front page.

But on the left, while most opposed the war and the bombing of Afghanistan, there were a number of interesting tactical differences and different ways of looking at the war.

The key differences on the left have related to the question, Are Islamic fundamentalism and imperialism equal enemies? The group that stuck out as answering 'yes' was Workers Liberty. Solidarity in the US also veered in this direction. The key test would have been, Did you feel good or bad about Washington's 'victory' in Kabul? Some groups in the US came out a bit soft on this. Malik Miah has written an indirect polemic in Solidarity's magazine *Against the Current.*

We also saw the danger of going along with any of imperialism's fake aims, such as the 'liberation of women in Afghanistan'.

Similarly with any notion that the US military is bringing 'democracy' to Afghanistan. That takes you down Hitchens' slippery path.

Another question was, Do you openly state your condemnation of the terrorist attack? Most socialists thought this was fairly basic, but the UK SWP/ISO had a unique position on this, arguing that we shouldn't publicly condemn the attack. Their reasoning was that by refraining from condemning, we would 'broaden' the antiwar movement – most of the left couldn't understand this logic, rightly arguing that the reverse would be the case, unless it was Taliban supporters you wanted to include in the antiwar coalition, and I don't think anyone advocated that.

There was also a gradation of pessimistic and optimistic reactions to the new situation.

There were differences discernible in the debates at the Sao Paulo Forum, and also in Brussels at the conference of the European Anti-Capitalist Left, but in general there was broad agreement.

Finally, we should note the very positive role of our statement, in quickly orienting our comrades and supporters in Australia, but it also helped in other countries.

Washington's war fiercely divided the New Zealand Alliance. As always, war puts wavering elements to the test, and there the majority of Alliance parliamentarians voted for war and sending troops, falling in behind Bush, including Matt Robson, a former Trotskyist who should have known better. The parallels with 1914 and the Second International are stark.

The majority of the party ranks, the conference and the National Council are against the war. Sue Bolton attended their conference on November 10-11. Immediately after it, a fierce and dirty factional struggle erupted. There was intense pressure to stamp out dissent, blackmail the ranks and staff into line behind Jim Anderton. A split seems unavoidable.

Paradoxically, this test provided a chance for the healthy militant wing to survive, and not be dissolved by parliamentarist coalitionism. In addition to the question of the war, another basic issue has come to the fore: the question of who runs the party, the members or the parliamentarians.

Building an antiwar movement

A fundamental duty for all those on the left, all those claiming to be progressive, is to actively organise against the war. The left responded quickly in Australia, with large organising meetings (200+ in Sydney) and good initial actions. The issue of the refugees and the impending election campaign served to defuse the movement a bit after a while, and the military victory in Kabul will mean smaller actions until the next stage of their offensive. A similar process seems to have occurred in the USA – initially quite large actions and coalitions. The most successful demonstrations seem to have been in Europe: 300,000 in Italy, 50,000 and 75,000 in London, 30,000 in Germany.

We can apply lessons learnt in earlier campaigns against imperialist wars, such as in Vietnam, to this struggle. The campaign is best built through mass mobilisations, with clear principled demands and a democratic and non-exclusive movement.

We can carry on some of the positive and negative lessons this time into the next stage of the campaign, since the strike on Iraq will require a huge response, and will revive the antiwar movement where it's become confused after the initial attacks.

A lesson learnt during the Vietnam War, and strongly reinforced this time, is that a 'firm stand gets the response'. That is, a principled, clear stand against imperialism results in greater participation than a supposedly 'broad', general weak demand or wish that makes concessions to Washington's offensive.

Capitalist economic crisis

But we can't look at the war and imperialism's offensive sep-arately from the economic crisis confronting imperialism. This was very clearly under way well before 11 September. The US recession is now officially recognised as beginning in March.

Fidel Castro made the point very strongly in his 2 November speech:

> … the economic crisis is not a consequence of the 11
> September attacks and the war against Afghanistan.
> Such claims could only be made out of total ignorance
> or an attempt to hide the real cause. The crisis is a
> consequence of the resounding and irreversible failure
> of an economic and political conception imposed on
> the world: neoliberalism and neoliberal globalisation.

The recession can be clearly marked by the unemployment figures (in the US, 1.2 million lost jobs) and other indices, but the immediate cause is the chronic problem of overcapacity in capitalist industry worldwide in manufacturing, in automobiles, in electronic goods and equipment.

A trillion dollars of excess capacity was destroyed as a result of the recent crisis in the IT and telecommunications industry. We [in Australia] experienced firsthand the airlines crisis with the collapse of Ansett and other airlines, but its most graphic expression is the ghostly graveyard of hundreds of mothballed planes in the Arizona desert that some of you might have seen on TV.

The extent of world steel overcapacity was reported in the 18 December *Financial Times:* the US's own estimate of total over-capacity is 200 million tonnes, out of a global capacity of 1 billion tonnes. The US is planning to impose tariffs of up to 40%, and is pressuring the Europeans to cut their capacity. The beauties of free market capitalism!

For the first time in a long while, we now have internationally coinciding recessions, in the US, Japan and Europe, as well as in much of the Third World. And with Enron, we have the biggest ever bankruptcy of a company, and with Argentina, the biggest ever bankruptcy of an economy.

The four-year crisis in Argentina finally led to catastrophic collapse. With a foreign debt of US$130 billion, 20% unemployed, 40% below the poverty line, wages and pensions cut, bank accounts frozen, pension funds seized – we see the other side of the anti-neoliberal globalisation protests. Huge demos, more than thirty dead, government and president fall – who'd want the job of running capitalism there? The new cabinet has already resigned, and the new president followed.

Argentina won't be the only victim, in spite of the capitalist media trying to reassure themselves that 'the contagion won't spread'. Economic crisis and political explosions are likely to hit other Third World countries in 2002. We'll have to be looking at Indonesia very closely.

In spite of periodic reassurances from capitalist ideologues that they'd eliminated the boom and bust cycle, and the idiotic claims after the collapse of the Soviet Union that it was now 'the end of history', that the pinnacle of life on Earth was capitalism, all the fundamental contradictions are still there. The gap between the ruling classes and the peoples of the world are increasing, the gap between the rich and poor is widening massively.

Has imperialism overreached itself?

US imperialism is militarily ultra-confident and aggressive. They feel they've got the righteous excuse to take the US working class with them. They've had their first victory, with few body bags. With a little more preparation, they'll move onto their next targets: Iraq, via Sudan, Yemen, Somalia? Will their coalition hold for their next adventures? They say: who cares, they'll go it alone.

The US ruling class is at the peak of its power, they are the only superpower. But it is a *grossly overconfident* ruling class.

And it is a ruling class totally bereft of ideas.

At the Sao Paulo Forum, one of the best and most militant contributions was made by Shafik Handel, from the FMLN in El Salvador, closing the debate on the final day. He pointed out that, when the first meeting of the Forum was held in 1990, the world situation was marked by two overwhelming factors: 1. the collapse of the Soviet Union and Eastern Europe, and 2. the victory of neoliberalism. The combination of these two factors had a two-sided effect on leftist thinking. Today, the situation is exactly the opposite. Neoliberalism has led humanity to disaster and capitalist economies to crisis. It has failed both for the people and for the capitalists.

Their system has failed. People are angry. Increasingly people are questioning the system itself.

The signs of the developing movement, only partially arrested by 11 September, were most powerfully demonstrated in Italy. In Genoa, 300,000 marched, and 300,000 the following week to protest the murder of Carlo Giuliani. Before Genoa was the powerful Italian metalworkers' strike.

But since 11 September in other countries also. In Madrid, 350,000 students took to the streets, responding to attacks on their education and conditions. In Argentina, how they played that down! 'Looting!' The president resigns and lifts off in a helicopter, with half a million angry workers at the gates!

We should be ready to go from the defensive to the offensive, linking the antiwar movement to anti-imperialist campaigns, and linking it to social campaigns and workers' struggles, as the recession bites.

Brussels demonstrations

The Brussels demonstrations during the EU meeting there in mid-December are also very encouraging signs.

The trade union march on 13 December was big, probably about 80,000, which is the cops' estimate. Even though the political thrust of it might have been limited – demanding a 'social Europe' with public services and workers' rights – and the trade union leaders didn't want to link it directly with the anti-globalisation march the next day, it was extremely important. The march itself was lively and colourful, though the noise was provided by whistles, bands, firecrackers and horns rather than many chants and slogans. There were some banners, but most of the colour was provided by huge numbers of flags identifying the particular unions, and by coloured plastic smocks printed with the union initials or slogans.

The anti-globalisation, anti-EU march for 'global peace and justice' on Friday the 14th was again a big success. About 25,000 marched (the police in Brussels apparently give accurate, or even slightly high, figures for demonstrations for some reason).

There were many sound trucks and live bands, with more chants and slogans than the day before. There were lots of banners, placards, balloons, dragons and other constructions, and organised contingents. It was similar to our demos, but with a few differences. The contingents of social movements and parties were more strictly organised, and the majority of the marchers seemed to be in specific contingents. This was assisted by the assembly process, which took place along a street, rather than at a speakers' platform like our demos, which serves to mix up the contingents.

The SWP and their European groups had a fairly sizeable contingent, but the biggest would have been the Maoist Workers Party of Belgium. Their new younger leaders don't make a big thing about Stalin now. The big banners they carried were Marx and Che. And they had smocks at both demos, printed with the Che image and the slogan 'CHEnge the World!'

The CWI had a fair-sized contingent, with a lot of youth, but I sensed they were a bit subdued, although it might have been their natural disposition. The next day they had their founding conference in Brussels of 'International Socialist Resistance'! They had their own meetings advertised for after the march as well.

The LCR contingent, together with the other FI groups, had a reasonably sized contingent, but it was very noticeable that they didn't have a large number of youth. There was a separate JCR[103] contingent marching behind the LCR, but some FI comrades complain that the JCR today suffers from a certain rigidity and conservativeness, not willing to test new manoeuvres or new movements. I got that feeling a bit from looking at them also. At the front of the march was a fairly large ATTAC (Association for the Taxation of Financial Transactions for the Aid of Citizens) contingent, and I imagine some of the FIers would have been in that as well.

There was a fairly large bloc of anarchists and similar types, although they didn't have too many banners. But in the march overall they were a very tiny element. The march took place almost without incident, and I didn't see a single cop throughout the whole very long march. But towards the end, after most of the marchers were inside the gathering place, some anarchists smashed some bank windows and attacked a disused police station. This brought the police in, with water cannon and ominous-looking armoured vans. This, of course, was all that appeared on the news that night, and might be what made the TV screens around the world. The cops blockaded the gathering place for a while, and as we left we could still see the lines of police and barricades and their vans and water cannon.

The overall impact of both actions will be very important, I think. Following 11 September, it was going to be a test: would the movement be cowed by imperialism's war drive and assault on democratic rights and dissenters? These demos were big enough to allay any fears on that score. For Brussels, they are very impressive demos. The effect should be felt not just in Europe, but in the rest of the world as well.

Another encouraging feature was the participation of youth. There were a good number of young people at the trade union march (although it was predominantly male and white). At the anti-globalisation march, youth were definitely in the majority.

The demos also showed the possibilities of youth and workers uniting. Two delegations of Belgian workers from the Thursday demonstration also joined the anti-capitalist march. They were the Sabena Belgian airline workers, who have faced 12,000 redundancies after the company went bankrupt in October. A delegation of Belgian postal workers fighting privatisation also marched. After the demonstrations, the head of the Belgian trade unions made a very significant comment on TV, saying he had no problems with the second march, he supported that as well as the trade union march. This seems a step forward from the strict separation imposed by the trade union leadership at Nice.

Brussels showed that 11 September has not been able to break the momentum built up to Genoa. But the actions from now on will necessarily have an antiwar, anti-militarism thrust to them, further contributing to the political education of the new generation of activists.

Urgent need to build parties

With imperialism on the offensive, and overreaching itself, and healthy signs that the movement still continues, the potential for the left should be promising. But we know the biggest weakness still.

The organisations, the subjective factor, are very much lacking. Marxist parties are still very weak. And some confusions exist about parties that hinder the full possibilities of taking advantage of the new situation. Some of these confusions are longstanding prejudices and misunderstandings, for example the views of Solidarity in the US.

Also, in the anti-neoliberal globalisation movement, there are still many prejudices about parties, resulting from old parties and past practices, that haven't yet been overcome. In the founding statement of the Porto Alegre World Social Forum, for example, parties are formally excluded. The right-wing parties get in as parliamentarians and so on.

The most encouraging party development is probably the PRC in Italy, where the movement seems the strongest. The party is growing, reaffirming a communist perspective, and an important draft from the [Fausto] Bertinotti leadership is being discussed for their congress. It's in the context of combating the 'Stalinist' (old parties), and a healthy 'return to the origins of the communist movement', but perhaps still retreats a bit too far on the central role of the party.

The new parties that are being formed or refounded in many countries today are developing collaboration among themselves in a new way also. They're increasingly building relations of comradely collaboration and exchanges, avoiding the narrow fake internationals that will block that collaboration and growth.

In the Asian region we've been fortunate to see the considerable independent development of new revolutionary parties, or parties being transformed through splits or other events, coming from a variety of political experiences and traditions.

There are enough examples now to recognise a trend, the emergence of a second wave of vanguards, that are completely new, or new because they're transcending their previous form.

The first wave was associated with struggles for independence and national liberation after WWI or after WWII.

SSP and ISM

The Scottish Socialist Party, the party in Europe that many are looking to and want to work with, arises from an expulsion from the CWI. The SSP plays an important role in Britain and an increasingly important role in Europe.

The main leaders of the SSP and its full-time staff are members of the International Socialist Movement platform, formerly Scottish Militant Labour, which was the CWI section. The ISM held its conference in September, and Greg Adamson represented us there.

One of the three conference workshops was a debate on 'Is Cuba Socialist?' with Tommy Sheridan arguing the case for. (The essence of the debate is really 'Is the Cuban leadership revolutionary?')

Given the respect for the SSP and ISM throughout the British and European left, their line on internationals and internationalism takes on added importance. They have developed an approach very close to ours, opposing the formation of or affiliation to narrow 'internationals', drawing on their CWI experience, and favouring loose collaboration of parties through an alliance or network.

The FI – nature of the 'mutation'

Where is the Fourth International heading? When we left the FI in 1985, we said we wanted to continue comradely collaboration with the FI and the healthy parties in it. That didn't happen at first – Ernest Mandel wrote a huge polemic against us, and there was no collaboration. In recent years, there's been increasing collaboration. They've allowed us to attend their IEC meetings and World Congresses as observers.

We've been trying to figure out their trajectory, understand the contradictory pressures they operate under, with two generally counterposed trends – the real parties, doing real work in the class struggle, and the smaller groups with the badge concept of politics, the FI as 'the only revolutionaries', the one true program, the flag concept.

For several years we've been trying to work out what they mean by the 'mutation' they were supposed to be undergoing that they talked about at the last FI World Congress.

In recent years we'd have to recognise that there have been some positive changes. Some of the FI groups, in Europe and Brazil, are doing some real, non-sectarian work. The FI was very much responsible for the Euromarches and building the anti-globalisation movement in Europe. In the last eighteen months, they were able to take the initiative for the meetings of the European Anti-Capitalist Left.

They've had many positive experiences with alliances – in the French elections, in Portugal, Denmark, Britain, Luxembourg, Switzerland. They also have undergone some negative experiences, and disasters still not overcome, such as the debacle in Spain, where they united/dissolved a strong group into a Maoist organisation and still haven't recovered, or the liquidation of the small group in Holland.

The balance recently seems to have shifted away from the smaller sectarian components of the FI. There are still those small 'sections', still hanging on to the badge as their *raison d'etre,* but their weight seems less. Socialist Action in the US has split. More groups have had to consider alliances with other forces.

And some in the FI might be increasingly able to draw the conclusions from seeing the sorry results from other Trotskyist groups claiming to be internationals. The CWI has demonstrated its sectarianism and narrowness with the expulsion of its two healthiest groups, in Pakistan and Scotland, that were able to start thinking for themselves. The IST similarly has expelled its largest group, the US ISO, that was starting to debate some questions, and the IST leadership in London has split many of the other IST groups.

We had drawn the balance sheet on the FI and narrow Internationals in the first half of the 1980s. We concluded such structures were obstacles. We needed a totally new way of relating between parties. The way forward was not going to be adding on to existing 'internationals'.

Can the FI be reformed? We said no in '85, and the evidence mounts, no. Nevertheless, with the FI in the '90s, it has mostly been possible for us to relate to the FI and the healthier parties in the FI in the way we insisted when we left – in a collaborative way between parties. We can discuss, work with where possible, observe conferences and IEC meetings and congresses (though every now and then they'll still make a proposal that we 'join', or accept 'organised observer' status).

They have tossed around a comparison, a new international more like the first, movements, or a combination of the First and Second, movements and anti-capitalist parties. But a general problem is the FI disclaimer about 'not leading the movements'. In fact in many situations they do, but in reaction to narrow Trotskyist sect behaviour, they've even worsened their traditional weaknesses on party building.

Meeting of Anti-Capitalist Left in Europe

The meeting of the European Anti-Capitalist Left was held in Brussels 12-13 December. This was the third meeting; the first was in Lisbon eighteen months ago, and the second in Paris a year ago. We've had observers at all three now. There were about thirty-five at the meeting, held in the European Parliament building courtesy of the LCR MEPs Rosaline Vacchou and Alain Krivine.

Attending were the founding group/preparatory committee of four parties: France, LCR; Portugal, Left Bloc; Scotland, SSP; Denmark, Red Green Alliance. Plus Francois Vercammen, who is from the FI in Belgium, and was running the show.

Also there were: Italy, PRC; Switzerland, Solidaire; Spain, Espacio Alternative; Spain, left faction in United Left, CP; Luxembourg, La Gauche; Holland, SP; Turkey, ODP; Britain, SWP; Britain, Socialist Alliance; Britain, SP of England and Wales.

Francois Vercammen opened the meeting, and summarised its history and its nature. He explained the purpose was not to set up an international, but to build a broad anti-capitalist alternative. The founding group/preparatory committee of four parties functioned loosely. There had been other requests to attend, but it was based on the countries of the European Union, so requests from Eastern European parties had been declined, as were tendencies in CPs.

It was useful seeing the SWP intervention in this conference. It seems that what they want and what guides their tactics is the desire to break into France, Italy and Spain. Therefore they have to deal with the LCR. Thus they try to contrast their activity, to try to show up the LCR.

They'd organised a big public meeting after the conference, and after the trade union march that afternoon. The meeting would have been a big success, at least in terms of size. The auditorium had 500 seats, and 7-800 people tried to cram in. People were sitting in all the aisles, listening in bunches outside the doors, and people were turned away.

The most interesting development in Europe is what is happening with the PRC in Italy. Obviously the mass demonstrations have given them a boost, and strengthened left-moving tendencies. Even before Genoa there was the very important metalworkers' struggle, the first time in thirty years where the whole trade union organisation was on strike. So the two things were linked, Genoa and the metalworkers' struggle. And although 11 September obviously has had a negative impact, the antiwar demonstrations in Italy have been huge.

Bertinotti has openly announced a break with Stalinism, a break with the Togliatti tradition, and they are calling for a fundamental change in the party, so as to involve the new movements and activists. They see the time of CPs as over, the time of social democracy as over. They were having an important CC meeting late in December, where major new perspectives were to be confirmed. An important document from Bertinotti has been translated into English, and some of it was printed in the latest *International Viewpoint.*

Role of Cuba today

The Cuban Revolution is an important target for imperialism's offensive. It's been top of their list for four decades. But compared with Afghanistan, Iraq, Somalia, Sudan or Yemen, Cuba presents a very different obstacle for them. The Cuban people overwhelmingly support their revolution and will defend their independence – as Fidel pointed out, 'We're just like an ant hill, people would descend on them like ants if there was an incursion'. So their initial attacks might be indirect, via Colombia and Venezuela.

So Cuba will be both a key aspect of our international solidarity, and in the coming years the focus of world attention, from both the left and right. And it will also be a key test for the left, increasingly, and in a major way. Many on the left still persist in blindly refusing to assess the Cuban Revolution, trying to pretend it doesn't exist. Our Cuba resolution can be a useful tool internationally, and there have been several requests to get it translated into Spanish.

Cuba's internationalist perspective and revolutionary credentials cannot be doubted – Che's outlook and actions, the Cuban role in Africa, Angola, their medical assistance to the Third World. After the collapse of the Soviet Union, the Cubans and the Brazilian PT initiated the Sao Paulo Forum 11 years ago, as a way to regroup left parties and counter Washington's new-found confidence. Over the years with the move to the right by the PT, and the increasing dominance in the Forum of right-wing, parliamentarist parties, the Cuban CP again initiated a push to the left, and we translated and printed in *Links* 17 the document they presented to the 2000 SPF. The November 2000 Cuba Solidarity Conference was also an important conference, and we sent a strong delegation, ending up with Pat [Brewer] being asked to speak to the rally.

The invitation from the Cuban CP to this recent Forum stressed two important roles for it: increasing solidarity action in support of struggles in Latin America and the Caribbean, and strengthening coordination internationally among left parties on other continents. It was an invitation we couldn't refuse.

Balance sheet of Sao Paulo Forum 2001

The forum provided an even more timely venue for discussing 11 September, the war and imperialism's offensive against the Third World. There was a lot of discussion about specific tasks for solidarity in the region: how to thwart Washington's attempts to subvert the Chavez government in Venezuela; how to defeat Washington's Plan Colombia;[104] how to support the Puerto Rican struggles for independence and close the Vieques naval base; how to defend Cuba and defeat the blockade; how to defeat NAFTA.

There were many general gains from the conference, as a broad forum for discussion, breaking down sectarianism between parties, discussions on the possibilities of coordinating solidarity. It stands out as a meeting place for parties, compared with the World Social Forum, where parties are specifically excluded.

The Cuban organisers seemed pleased with the success of the forum, certainly in terms of the size and breadth of the delegations. More than 500 delegates, from 82 countries, with 73 member parties and 138 invited parties, attended. This was bigger than forums held in the last few years. Certainly many of the international guests would have come only because it was being held in Cuba, and the comparison would be with the last one held there, in 1994. The forum also served as an expression of solidarity with Cuba.

The Cubans also referred to the fact that some of the – more right-wing – members were not there this time. And the fact that it was in Cuba, and the push from the Cubans from the last forum to move it to the left, plus the sifting out process of the right, would have meant a generally left dominance at this forum. And thus it resulted in a reasonably left statement (within the negotiated framework of the forum – anti-imperialist, but not specifically socialist).

But the Cubans are still within an international framework defined by:

1. Their state diplomatic needs. These are legitimate and understandable considerations given the precarious struggle for survival waged by the Cuban Revolution against imperialist blockade, subversion and assaults of all kinds. Thus the priorities given to international guest speakers, those coming from ruling regimes, even with dubious politics, such as Iraq, Libya, Syria, Zimbabwe, who all got a platform. It's also part of their considerations regarding the left in Latin

America – thus the importance they give to Mexico and Venezuela, and the delicate dual state and party relations they have to maintain.

2. Their old network of Stalinist parties, big or small, brownish or red. These still get priority over newcomers like us. They avoided having to put this to the test this time regarding Australia, not giving the call to either myself or [SPA's Peter] Symon.

3. Regarding the left in Latin America, I suppose their approach is to encourage all, not giving preference to a particular one. They'll favour a country struggle, as at this forum with Puerto Rico, to strike at Washington. And Venezuela, because of its importance for them. But for Colombia, they didn't favour the FARC, giving equal time to the ELN and seeming to rely on Fermin Gonzalez, of Present for Socialism in Colombia, for a lot of the SPF work.

What were the limitations and gaps at the forum? Obviously it has a limited and specific role, and would be structurally incapable of going beyond that. We should not expect it to do more than is structurally possible, certainly not expect it to be any sort of 'international'. [Dr. José R.] Balaguer, head of the international department of the Cuban CP, put it clearly in his opening address, how the forum had faced two errors: 1. Of becoming an 'international'. 2. Of negating the role of political parties. Nevertheless, it would still be fair to make some criticisms along the following lines.

1. Perhaps it hasn't responded enough to the anti-neoliberal globalisation movement that has spread across most of the advanced capitalist world. In most countries of Latin America and the Caribbean, of course the crisis is much more acute and the struggles are on a higher level than the struggles in the advanced capi-

talist countries, and certainly the forum discussions did relate to the new movements, but I felt more of an active, conscious bridge could have been built.

2. One of the intentions outlined in the invitation letter was to have the forum serve as more of a vehicle for coordinating action on the Latin American left. The forum itself adopted the main lengthy resolution, and other consensus resolutions, but not much in the way of specific action seemed to be planned. Perhaps this will be initiated by the working group using the authority of the resolution. On the other hand, the speaker who most clearly outlined an action perspective for the forum was Fermin Gonzalez, and he seemed to be working closely with the Cubans. In his speech he pointed out, 'If 11 September changed the world, although the crisis was already in the making, we must change this structure also. We're seeing a regression of imperialism to neo-colonialism, so we must unite and fully integrate this forum. It's a yearly discussion, but we're capable of doing more. We must unite to act, unite the social factors with the political factors, and stand up and say that the people of the world are ready for action.'

3. The Cubans were conscious at this forum of expanding the contacts and collaboration to other continents. This was a specific theme of the invitation letter. But it was still limited and concentrated on certain areas. Europe was the main continent related to, and the links with the left European parliamentarians seemed to be top of the list. While this no doubt was an important goal for the Cuban leadership in ensuring their international survival in the context of the aggressive offensive by US imperialism, the forum could perhaps

have been better used to highlight collaboration with revolutionary organisations on all continents.

4. Specifically, Asia was massively under-represented in the participation and discussion. Of course, Asian parties are poorer and find it difficult to make such an expensive trip under their own steam, but there are many interesting parties, old and new, that would have benefited from the exchange with Latin American Marxists, and which could have contributed to the breadth and enthusiasm of the forum. An aspect of this is lack of information – I had a formal meeting with Oscar Martinez Cordoves, the second in charge of the Cuban CP's International Department, after Balaguer, and he seemed genuinely unaware of many of the parties and developments I outlined to him in explaining the participation at the Easter [APISC] conference.

5. Perhaps some of the structural aspects of the conference agenda could have been improved. The preparation of a conference statement and its discussion and amendment at a plenary session are an integral part of the forum. The plenary sessions where all member parties and invited delegations can try to present their view, are another essential aspect (although in the time available not everyone got a go, and too many of the international speakers seemed formalistic and boring). But there might have been better organisation of workshops, country reports/discussions etc. (The three regional workshops were flat, apparently.) Also, the evening sessions could have been used to feature other major Cuban, and other, leaders with interesting talks, as was done apparently at the last one in Havana. This time it all fell to Fidel, with a monster five-hour closing speech, which wouldn't have been very effec-

tive after the first hour.

6. They could have organised various commissions the day before and publicised them well. The Youth Commission was not well publicised – we hadn't heard of it – and it could have been better. One commission was held for parliamentarians, but other commissions could have been on trade unions, women, indigenous struggles etc., each without a formal status or task, but helping with the preparation and discussion. As it was, the youth discussion did not get injected into the main forum much, and although there was a report, the Cuban Communist Youth, UJC, leaders didn't seem to attend much of the forum.

7. A big mistake of the forum was not to allow the setting up of stalls for books and magazines and papers from the various parties. As well as making it so much harder for individual parties to do their reach-out and networking, as in our case, it also diminished the political liveliness of the forum. So what if one party publishes a polemic against another party, in the same country or elsewhere? This is the nature of a big all-in discussion like the forum, unless you're going to restrict the discussion to diplomatic greetings and banalities.

There were a number of specific arrangements resulting from the forum. The UJC is sending one of their leaders around the world on a tour, around mid-May to mid-June. There's a conference in South Africa they'll be attending, and they can spend three days in Australia, and would like Resistance to organise events here.

We're still not sure whether a Cuban CP comrade will be able to get to APISC. Abelardo Cueto, the comrade who attended our congress a year ago, is the Cuban CP comrade responsible for South Asia and Australia, and there are CPI and CPI-M congresses in India at the end of March, but unfortunately they overlap slightly with ours, so it might not be possible for him to get to all three.

The meeting with Cordoves went well, I think. Cueto was there, and was described by Cordoves as a friend of our party, indeed 'a member', so he's probably been putting in good words for us. There were all the usual formalities, but the main point was convincing them about the importance of the Easter conference, and the importance of sending someone to it. After I had rattled off all the parties confirmed as attending from the Asian region, and giving information on the ones he might not have known about, it certainly seemed a very impressive list to me, and certainly impressed Cordoves, and he said as much. He said they will try to come, depending on availability of comrades, finances of course and other events they could combine the trip with.

Later in the conference Cueto conveyed an invitation from Balaguer for me or another party delegation to visit Cuba to be their guest for five days sometime this year before their congress in October. We will see if we can accept this invitation, trying to combine it with other international events.

But an OSPAAAL[105] speaker at the Easter conference is almost definite. Ocean Press is launching several books based on articles from OSPAAAL's magazine *Tricontinental,* and they're bringing a speaker, possibly Ulises Estrada, the editor of *Tricontinental,* out here to coincide with the Easter conference.

Porto Alegre World Social Forum

The first World Social Forum was held in Porto Alegre a year ago. It was big and diverse, and although partly dominated by NGOs, parliamentarians and social democrats, was a strong boost to the morale and fighting spirit of the global movement against neoliberalism. Dick [Nichols] and Jonathan [Strauss] represented us there, but among 15,000 people we couldn't achieve all we would have liked.

Our intervention this year will again be too limited, when the WSF will be even bigger – they're talking about 40,000, 60,000 etc. Dick will be attending again, as well as Ben Reid. There were a number of other possibilities, but none have been confirmed. We'll have a stall this time, and have scheduled a workshop. It will be an excellent opportunity to further advertise the APISC.

What to expect at WSF 2002? All the political debates circulating on the international left will again be raised, with the imperialist offensive being at the centre. The Argentinian collapse will surely impinge in a big way. The social democratic-right-wing NGO forces will again try to stamp their politics on the event, and we and others on the left will try to counter this, stressing both the party question and the state question. (Excluding parties actually also implies a political exclusion, i.e. raising the question of state power.)

The state question could be raised by the possible participation of Fidel Castro, and Hugo Chávez from Venezuela. This could help push the conference to the left. But strangely enough, this possibility is seen as a negative by some, including the FI, who claim it will take attention away from the grassroots movements. Of course, it relates to their overall position regarding Cuba, and weaknesses on the party question. In my discussion with Cordoves, I offered my 'grain of sand' in the balance, and urged that it would be great if Fidel were to attend.

Countering the Latin American and European right-wing push at Porto Alegre is made harder by that initial exclusion of parties. For the third WSF, it has been proposed that the venue be India. This would make it easier for a larger intervention by us, and a much larger participation by Asian parties and movements, and there would be more of a chance to bypass in practice the exclusion of parties.

There's clearly the need for an intervention between APISC and the Indian WSF. A network of collaboration between Marxist parties in Asia now exists and needs to develop further. The APISC will be an important opportunity to do this. In the regional sphere, we hope that we can use APISC for a call by some or all of these parties for a preparatory meeting of Asia-Pacific organisations interested in cooperating to promote a left agenda at the 2003 World Social Forum.

Certainly we can organise a meeting of left parties and left forces in the days before the Delhi WSF. It would be another important opportunity for a gathering and discussion for the growing range of left parties in the Asian region that would be a complement to the WSF, and help organise our intervention.

But we should investigate whether it's also possible to have a meeting of left forces before the end of the year. Finances will be the determinant.

There are many opportunities and challenges for the new or refounded parties. Following the collapse of the Soviet Union, the choice was succumbing to demoralisation or drawing the lessons and continuing the fight:

- responding to imperialism's new offensives, such as Iraq;
- being part of the new movement against neoliberal globalisation;
- responding to 11 September and imperialism's global offensive;
- analysing the social and political forces in their own countries, thinking things out for themselves, building a leadership team and developing a Marxist perspective for leading the struggle forward.

There's increasingly a good framework for constructive international discussion.

Links magazine has had an important role, and its unique nature can give it even greater importance in the coming years.

And we've got the framework for the increased international solidarity work that will be needed in the coming year, with CISLAC and ASAP.

APISC

The main focus of our international work in the next period will of course be the Asia Pacific International Solidarity Conference this Easter in Sydney. It also links up and connects our party-building work here. It's establishing itself as an extremely important international political event – certainly for us, for the Australian left, and important internationally.

We've had big impressive conferences with major international speakers before – the Marx Centenary Conference in 1983, the Social Rights Conference in 1984, the Socialist Scholars Conferences in 1990 and 1991, the International Green Left Conference in 1994, but it was the 1998 Asia Pacific Solidarity Conference that set a new standard, with more than 700 participants, including nearly 60 international guests. Then Marxism 2000 in some ways had an even more important international representation, of serious Marxist parties.

With the Asia Pacific International Solidarity Conference we can expect a bigger, broader and even more internationalist event. A year ago at our congress we projected a possible attendance of 1,000, with up to 100 international guest speakers. That looks to be achievable. Already the number of confirmed and likely international guests is about 77, more than attended in 1998 or 2000.

The three main themes for conference talks and discussion will be:
- war and imperialism's offensive;
- the anti-neoliberal globalisation movement;
- collaboration between left parties, nationally and

internationally.

We will put forward some resolutions, including a resolution on the world political situation, although we won't want the conference diverted into very detailed discussions on wording. We'll use the conference to relaunch ASAP, promote and build *Links* magazine and establish closer links and collaboration with left parties around the world.

The socialist goal

At the Sao Paul Forum, one of the opening speeches was given by Lula [Luiz Inácio Lula da Silva] from the Brazilian PT. He used an extensive (but false) recounting of Hemingway's story 'The Old Man and the Sea' to try to justify his increasingly right-wing and parliamentarist line – the old man constantly went to sea for the big fish, but when he finally hooked it, the sharks got it, and by the time he got back to land there was nothing left. Lula argued that we should just aim for the small fish: at least we'd get something.

In presenting the closing speech in the plenary discussion, Shafik Handel from the FMLN told us a parable of his own, about the scorpion and the frog, which was a thinly disguised counter to Lula's right-wing line. The scorpion and the frog were both on a river bank, wanting to cross. The scorpion tried to convince the frog, 'Ferry me across on your back'. The frog says no, you'll sting me. The scorpion persists, and the frog relents, reasoning that if the scorpion stings him, they'll both drown. Halfway across, the scorpion stings him, and the shocked frog asks, why? The scorpion replies – 'That is my nature'. The lesson from Shafik Handel was, don't trust the capitalists, they'll bring the whole world down. Don't help neoliberalism cross the river, no matter how 'smart' it may seem on the grounds of 'modernity'.

At this point Fidel intervened, as he is wont to do, and he has the authority to get away with it. 'Let me get it straight about the scorpion and the frog … but also remember that if the scorpion didn't have venom, we wouldn't have communism', or something like that. 'I agree with everything you have been saying', allowing him to add his weight to the anti-Lula, anti-reformist line.

The point is, we *can* land the big fish, as Cuba has done, and if we work and struggle together to fight off the sharks, we can win. We're at an interesting stage of renewing and rebuilding the socialist movement today, the movement of those willing to try for the big fish.

Our international experiences in recent years, and especially our work this year, reinforce our assessment that the healthy components for the new socialist movement will come from a range of traditions. What's central is: what response do we have to the real challenges facing the working class? Can we provide leadership, build a party in our own country and relate with solidarity and non-sectarian collaboration to the new parties developing, and the parties that are leading key struggles?

There are many tests ahead. Let's meet them confidently.

15. WHY WE GOT THIS FAR, AND HOW WE CAN GO FURTHER

Report to the National Committee
9 June 2002

In the previous chapter, John had outlined the DSP's views on how US imperialism was using the events of 11 September and what it hoped to accomplish. Following a period of growth, this report examined what changes the new context might require in the organisation's practices and what in the party's traditions and perspectives needed to be reaffirmed.

This report tries to take a long-term look at building the party, as well as addressing our current party-building tasks and perspectives.

It's in the context of a significant change in the world situation. Although imperialism's offensive against the people of the world is just as fierce, just as irrational, there have been many examples of significant fights back in recent years – the anti-neoliberal globalisation mobilisations, from Seattle to Genoa and Barcelona; the general strike in Italy; the defeat of the Venezuelan coup; the huge gatherings at Porto Alegre; even the huge outpouring in the streets in France against Le Pen. Something does seem to be turning in our direction.

It's also in the context of the party having had significant growth in the last year and a half. The total number of full members is 12% higher than it was through 2001, and 30% higher than it was through the 1990s. Our cadre base is stronger than ever before.

We have to be very clear on issues relating to the party question, because an international debate is looming in the movement in which we will be intervening. We have a record, and some respect, from what we've built here, and the network in Asia. (But we also have to be clear why we haven't had more growth, why not quicker growth.)

Our party-building perspective

We're the strongest party on the Australian left: still tiny, but with a solid group of cadres, varied political interventions, with the most respected and widely circulated newspaper, a strong youth organisation, a solid national spread and extensive and varied resources, from the buildings we operate out of to an impressive publications program.

This position in relation to others on the left is partly by default, but also by our own efforts and the political perspectives we had and stuck to: our understanding of the class nature of society, the need for a revolutionary overthrow of capitalist state power by the working class and, at the centre of it, our understanding of the need for a Leninist party to lead that revolution and the traditions and skills in building that party, our party-building perspective.

This perspective is always under challenge.

It's always under challenge from the ruling class, of course. There's a constant barrage of propaganda and ideological influences to keep us passive, meek and unquestioning and confined to the 'proper' channels of protest if we do find conditions unbearable.

And the revolutionary perspective is always under challenge by opponents of Marxism and Leninism in the workers' movement. Even currents that recognise that capitalist class rule has to be overthrown baulk at the lessons of history that point to *how* it can be done. They refuse to acknowledge that a revolutionary party built along the lines of Lenin's Bolsheviks is needed for the task.

Under challenge internationally

In the demonstrations and the debates over tactics and structures in the anti-neoliberal globalisation movement around the world, we see a resurfacing of the struggle between anarchism and Marxism, as anarchists try to impose their tactical and organisational recipes on the whole of the movement. This is probably less of an aberration than a few years ago, as more of the new generation of radicals get a deeper political and historical understanding.

But there is still an endemic anti-party, or non-party mood that gets promoted and encouraged. And even among parties and international currents that have an understanding of Leninism, the experience of the Bolshevik revolution and other successful revolutions, there's a lot of confusion and pressure to adapt to the anti-partyism, which ultimately comes from the ruling class.

Of course, the enemies of Leninist parties have been given many easy targets in past decades by the caricatures of parties passed off both by the Stalinists, and also unfortunately by so many of the varieties of Trotskyism. But we're now in a period when we should be able to shake off the horrors of Stalinism, and enter a period when genuine renewal of the socialist movement is possible. Part of that renewal will be re-establishing the strategy of building genuine Leninist parties.

We can see the impact of this anti-party sentiment at the World Social Forum in Porto Alegre, where an exclusion policy against parties openly participating was written into the founding platform.

There's a constant repackaging of the anti-Leninist perspective. [Antonio] Negri and [Michael] Hardt's *Empire* book is one of the latest, and of course it gets featured constantly in the bourgeois media. This gets echoed among the less sophisticated activists in the new movements. It's the non-party individuals who get promoted, the Naomi Kleins. And the Zapatistas – non-party – were the new heroes of the opponents of the 'centralised' Leninist party, although there isn't anything much more centralised and elitist than an army structure, which is what the Zapatistas have.

One form this assault on Leninism takes is an anti-'Zinovievist' push, claiming that those defending Leninism today are actually following in the footsteps of Zinoviev and the party tradition implemented after Lenin's death.

There are a variety of hostile anti-party, anti-Leninist, anti-Marxist trends. But there are also parties creatively working in broad alliances, in new situations, for example the new experiences with the Scottish Socialist Party. Their discussions on how they handle relations between the International Socialist Movement platform and the SSP will be useful. They're going through the experiences we would have had to cope with if, for example, in 1987 the CPA hadn't pulled out of the New Left Party process we were going through with them.

Under challenge in new movements here

The party idea, and our party as often the most effective and forceful proponent of that idea, has always had its opponents in

the movements here. Under the impact of the worldwide movement against neoliberal globalisation, the attacks on partyism
have gotten more aggressive at times. The various anarchist
currents were in the vanguard of this, of course. They had an
inflated view of themselves; often they just looked pathetic as
balaclava-clad loonies. But they do pander to a sentiment.

Our own ghost from our distant past, Bob Gould, has been
more prolific with his regular shit sheets against the DSP, handed
out at our major events (and even at other tendencies' events).
His main attack is that we aren't with him in the ALP, and that
we're trying to build a party outside it. There's a rumour of a book,
that he's writing our history for us. Comrades could suggest he
write his own history and compare his three decades or ours.

And the ISO has been re-raising distorted history regarding
Students for a Democratic Society in Australia and the US
and 'participatory democracy'. Why a 'revival' of discredited,
disproved experiences? What happened to SDS in the US and
Australia? They collapsed! They built nothing.

Sniping from sectarians and small opponents and individuals
on the left will grow as we grow. The Pilger meeting[106] brought
a lot of fear and snide remarks to the surface. There'll be many
more such excuses for others to complain that we're getting too
big, wanting to have a say beyond what they think our true place
should be. And the target will frequently be our party-building
methods, our Leninism.

How we developed our tradition

Our party-building perspective, our tradition, has two sources.

Firstly, we learnt and borrowed from the tradition of other
parties around the world, at one stage copying rather blindly.
Initially, we copied from the FI, especially from the US SWP. Then
we began to study other experiences more closely, for example

the Cubans. And we then looked beyond, to where our sources took their traditions from, and seriously studied the Russian Revolution, went on a 'back to Lenin' kick. In those early years, the examples of other parties from different traditions, in different situations and circumstances certainly, were invaluable. They were passed on by certain books, by reports of other experiences, often set down in records of factional struggles.

Secondly, as we went on we were able to add to our party-building tradition more lessons of our own that were won in practice and struggle, in real hands-on party-building experiences in our own situation. In some ways these lessons were the most important: lessons learnt in struggle are lessons well remembered.

Marxism vs anarchism and liberalism

We learnt some of the most basic lessons, the superiority of Marxism over anarchism and liberalism, in the late 1960s, when our current began.

In 1967, with the formation of Resistance, we had a struggle against anarchist tendencies who preferred to retain the original name of SCREW (Students Cultivating Revolution Everywhere). And over the next few years in the '60s, Resistance was in contention with SDS with their liberal politics and anarchist tactics.

In 1969-70 we fought for and won on the very fundamental principle of building a party, and split with Gould, who'd originally recruited us to Trotskyism. The struggle was fought out in Resistance over basic questions of having a democratic, structured organisation that could rise above the anarchic star leader system. We'd really been fighting on this issue from 1967. A major step was the final break with Gould in 1970, the Resistance national conference and setting up *Direct Action*.

The first *Direct Action* editorial registered that gain:

> To publish a paper without an organisation to build and
> be built by it is political irresponsibility. It is to play with
> politics. Only when a paper has an organisation to build,
> and that organisation has a program to guide it, does a
> little left-wing venture such as ours take on any meaning.

A further milestone came in January 1972 with the founding
conference of the Socialist Workers League. The right to have a
party was something we had to fight hard for, but a hard fight
built a strong base.

Shortly after the founding conference of the SWL, we registered a further consolidation of that party principle, and broke
with the group around Roger Barnes and Sylvia Hale, who'd been
in the old FI group. We insisted we were building a serious, committed party, and made a further stand against the inherited line
on entryism and illusions in the ALP.

What type of party?

From the beginning we recognised the importance of a revolutionary party being based on the rebelliousness of youth. Young
people radicalise quickly in response to capitalism's multitude
of injustices. They question the established order, think about
alternatives, different worlds. And they provide the energy and
activism needed for change.

We've been at the head of continuing youth campaigns and
mobilisations. In 1968 the high school politicisation and struggle against the Vietnam War mushroomed and we launched
Student Underground. We had a major high school walkout in
1972, the sex diary campaign in the early '90s, the anti-Hanson
walkouts in 1998 – all reinforcing our current's leadership role
among young people.

The party we fought for and built over the years was a party organised on the principles of democratic centralism. This was a key issue in the original fight with Gould; it resurfaced in the tussle with Roger Barnes; it's been injected into many of the other debates and disputes in the party.

From the beginning also we knew we had to be an *internationalist* party. We were born in the struggle against the war in Vietnam in the 1960s. We were in solidarity with those in struggle around the world, in Asia, Africa, Latin America and also in Europe (France, May-June '68), and with the US antiwar movement.

An internationalist outlook is absolutely essential for revolutionaries, especially in an imperialist country like Australia. We've backed this up with all our solidarity work since, on all important struggles – our solidarity with Latin America through CISLAC and, especially important, the solidarity with struggles in our region, through CAEPA, AKSI, ASIET, ASAP.

We also established that we're a *serious* party, serious about resources, finances, commitment. You'd think this is also basic for anyone claiming to be a revolutionary, but so often you see outfits made up of dilettantes, dabblers.

It was thirty years in March since we bought our first building, in St John's Road in Glebe. It's been almost twenty years since we moved into this building [in Abercrombie Street, Chippendale]. These assets were acquired by the dedication, the pledges and fund drive commitments of our members over the years.

We also demonstrated time and again that we were building an *inclusive* party. We're always on the lookout to expand, not only our ranks, but our leadership team. We're not building an exclusive club.

In 1970, we linked up with the former Flers in building the *Socialist Review* group and founding the party, even though we had to part company two years later. In 1972, we fused with the comrades from Brisbane Labor Action. These comrades split away later that year and formed the Communist League, partly under the pressure of the factional divisions in the Fourth International, but in 1976-78 we were able to force through fusions with the Communist League comrades, in advance of the divisions in the FI being resolved.

And in the 1980s, we made many other attempts to unite with others, to build broader formations, and expand our party: the Nuclear Disarmament Party, the New Left Party with the CPA, socialist unity with the SPA, efforts with the Greens, and fusions with Socialist Fight, the Rosebery [Tasmania] miners and Turkish comrades from Revolutionary Path.

We established decisively that we're an *independent* party, with its own leadership team, that thinks for itself; we're not just a branch office of an overseas parent. In 1983 we broke definitively with the US SWP, as they went off the rails, and reduced their supporters around the world to obedient caricatures of Marxist groups. And in 1985 we left the Fourth International, recognising that such internationals were in the end fetters on the development of the independent revolutionary Marxist parties that were needed in each country.

Four principles

In 1980 Jim Percy presented an NC report on 'Four Features of Our Revolutionary Party', reviewing the lessons of our first 10 years. He pointed to those central features: an inclusive party, an independent party, a party based on Leninist organisational principles and an ambitious party. Jim made a number of important reports to NCs and conferences around this time, which could usefully be reprinted for comrades today in the form of another book. Perhaps this could be a project, since we're coming up to the tenth anniversary of Jim's death in four months' time.

We did get out a book of Jim's talks from the early '90s, reports that often summarised our understanding and party-building perspectives from the first twenty years. The four reports in that book are extremely rich, and relevant for us even today, and worthwhile for all comrades to re-read.

In the early '90s, after the failures of all our best efforts to unite with others, to broaden out the party, we felt the need to re-emphasise our party-building norms, to 're-cadreise' the party – the word we invented for it. We'd abolished provisional membership, and thrown the doors open to people wanting to join directly, and you can see that reflected in the membership graph. But we had to adjust back, as the political situation wasn't developing in a healthy direction, and our opening out was actually resulting in less effectiveness for the party. We had to reassert the need for a Leninist-type party.

In 1994-95 a current in Perth wanted us to go down a different road, a looser, all-inclusive party. We had a thorough discussion leading up to and at our January 1995 congress, and the party overwhelmingly reaffirmed our perspectives.

We can be proud of our very rich party-building tradition. We benefit from the experiences of other parties in other countries, but our own history is also an invaluable asset. It's worth remembering, and worth having it recorded; otherwise we repeat mistakes and don't build on the foundations we've already laid.

How we can go further

What's changed since 1991-92, when Jim gave those last party-building reports?

Certainly there have been many changes in the objective political situation. The Soviet Union was in the process of collapsing, but we hadn't seen the full ramifications of that final defeat, for example US imperialism's stepped-up offensive as sole superpower and the drive to war. But we're now also witnessing the mass fights back around the world, the international movement against neoliberal globalisation, some victories for our side.

There've been big changes in the subjective situation we face, a very different balance of forces on the left. There's the collapse of the CPA, formerly our largest left opponent, now dead for more than ten years. We're clearly the largest and strongest Marxist current.

Our largest opponent, the ISO, seems to have continuing and severe internal problems, and their decline is visible on campus, on the streets, at their events. Ten years ago they were in much more of a position to challenge us. Even compared with the balance around S11 2000, their student base is much diminished.

Partly occupying some of the space getting vacated by the ISO, Socialist Alternative has a strong base on Melbourne University, and strong starts in a few other places, but they're still very weak.

The CPA/SPA is ageing and inactive, not very visible. Other left groups are tiny, mostly confined to one city, mostly Melbourne.

In addition to our actual size, our resources, and the activity and visibility of our cadres, another indicator of how we're faring in building our party has been some of the struggles we've led in the last five years, where we were able to have a significant impact. For example:

- 1998 anti-Hanson high school walkouts;
- 1999 East Timor solidarity demonstrations;
- 2000 S11 blockade of the WEF in Melbourne;
- 2001 M1 stock exchange blockades.[107]

Another measure of our steady progress has been the successful public conferences we've held: in the 1980s, the Socialist Scholars Conferences in 1990, 1991, and the International Green Left Conference in 1994.

But we seem to have made a qualitative advance with the Asia Pacific solidarity conferences in 1998 and this year, and also the Marxism 2000 Conference, if not in total attendances, then in the extensive international attendance and impact, and the value for our party and contacts.

We also seem to be able to get increasing media coverage. Resistance especially is well known, the place to go to interview/feature radicalising young people. And *GLW* is increasingly well known and respected in wide circles.

Our geographical spread is a further indicator of our growth, establishing branches in cities and towns in recent years where we'd never been before.

All these advances, especially our DSP membership growth, are a real vindication of our party-building methods.

How do we make further progress, both continue the steady gains, and make major leaps? Firstly, we must not jettison all the lessons about party-building and the gains that have gotten us this far.

Party building

We defend the whole party-building perspective. We know a Leninist party is necessary to make a revolution, and if we don't have a perspective for building one beforehand, it's not going to miraculously appear when a revolutionary situation arises.

We've developed an understanding of this perspective, this necessity, through debates and struggles going back to the early days of our tendency. We've won this perspective as our own.

We refine the lessons and build on the gains, and today we have a more sophisticated understanding of the party question than in our early days.

We also defend the specifics of that perspective, for example, that the organising principle for the party is democratic centralism.

Reaffirming the centralism doesn't mean tightening up. We reaffirm both aspects: we do want more discussion, but we do reassert that the party directs the work. For example, we recently lost a few comrades in Darwin who didn't understand and didn't agree with this.

But secondly, in addition to reaffirming our fundamental party-building principles and perspective, we have to resolve to continue to push on all the components of that perspective: recruiting, finances, education, sales and all the organisational tasks associated with building the party.

The most important gauge of how we've been going, the most direct measure of our success, is the simplest one: recruitment and growth. Assuming we're maintaining our standards of commitment and activity, the size of our membership indicates how our party-building project is going.

And in the last year or two, we can see clearly what we haven't seen for quite a while: actual growth, a very real upward turn in our membership graph.

Small and regional branches

We'd like to reaffirm the positive experiences of the new, small and regional branches. It's been correct to push on this; they're flourishing and can grow further and integrate new members. Comrades in such small branches have to take on big loads, but they surprise themselves continuously. They *have* to do all the tasks, assume a range of organisational and political responsibilities. In a larger branch, new comrades can get lost, be ignored.

The next possibility for a new branch might be Launceston. Certainly this is the hope of Hobart comrades, building it through the Socialist Alliance[108] election campaign coming up, and other work we've done there.

A future possibility might be Townsville, where we have one comrade and contacts. It's the next major town with a uni. Alice Springs is regularly throwing up contacts, a member there now. We know about the political ferment on refugees for example in many country towns, and the good sales rate in many of them. There are six other country towns where *GLW* is now getting distributed. We need to have a regular box ad in *GLW:* Are you interested in taking a bundle to sell in your area?

District functioning

But given the high concentration of Australia's population in a few major cities, the big hurdle for future qualitative party growth is building new suburban branches in the bigger cities. We've attempted to establish suburban branches and district structures several times in our history, and the Sydney and Melbourne districts seem to be well established now, although they still have many things to resolve. Sydney Inner West has relocated to Bankstown.

We also have to realise that we won't be able to have a HQ for every branch. We will have to make more direct use of campus facilities in some cases, e.g., Macquarie Uni, UNSW. And try to get the use of halls free, and make full use of our central district offices. Well-functioning offices have been essential for our party-building activities, but as we grow, and get many branches in a city, we can't let the old style cramp our possibilities for further growth. And even worse, we can't make a fetish of having an office and fork out hefty rents for one that's hardly used. Or put all the effort into housekeeping and duplicating all the functions of the central office, to the detriment of time put into political activity and developing a vibrant political life for the branch.

A further lesson is that we need the politics for our branches, and sometimes, as in the case of Sydney West, we have to actively create the possibilities for our own political activities, organise our own actions, not expect others to be there for us to intervene in, and not sink to the local level, not get bogged in idiotic local campaigns.

An area that we're still working through is how to do Resistance in a district setup. There will be more DSP branches where we don't have a Resistance branch. While the branch will work hard to remedy that, there's no reason in those situations that we can't recruit youth directly to the DSP, and the DSP branch will have to do things normally carried out by Resistance branches.

Other units

In addition to more small regional branches, and more sub-urban branches in district structures, we might be able to make use of other types of units to help train and integrate a larger membership. We need other institutions for their own political value – for example, a labour solidarity centre that we've talked about, or a better resourced CISLAC, or ASIET institutions or centres that we've had in the past. Such centres would help the party's outreach and political impact, but they can also help the party grow, providing more of the skeleton we need.

Having more units requires more leadership teams, and that pressure for more leaders helps train more leaders. Some of this can be provided by better functioning fractions and organising units.

The essential unit will still be our branch meetings, and here it's important we continue to push to make them interesting, political and inspiring. Have well-prepared educationals; have relevant reports where real decisions have to be made; encourage discussion that involves everyone; and cut down purely organisational reports.

We should put regular forums back on the agenda. This will vary from branch to branch, but the ideal would be to make them regular in as many branches as possible. Let's make full use of the great party offices we're accumulating.

We surpassed ourselves with the Pilger [Sydney] Town Hall

meeting: 2,100 people and hundreds turned away. But it shows what can be done. The Tariq Ali visit here also showed the possibilities; we packed out [Sydney] Newtown Neighbourhood Centre with 250 people, with rather modest publicity.

We can see the potential for this type of left meeting, if we can get well-known international guest speakers. We can do it with others, such as Howard Zinn, Edward Said or Robert Fisk. There is a milieu out there that we partly tap into with *Green Left Weekly*. If we can provide big-name left speakers, we can expand our profile, expand *GLW* circulation, build Socialist Alliance out of them. We can use the big ones to publicise well in advance a program of regular forums – local, but interesting.

Finances

To dramatise it, we've sometimes stated that finances are the key to our party-building tasks. And over the years you'd have to say that we've done well – prompting some on the left, including [the British SWP's] Alex Callinicos, to actually describe us as a 'rich' party. We certainly have faced much more encouraging budget reports, and felt less panic about our finances, in recent years. That reflects progress, our solidity and also the dire situation we've dragged ourselves out of: we paid off our big mortgages, eliminated the enormous deficits. But it mainly reflects the tremendous consciousness and commitment of our comrades in the past.

This year again there's no *huge* crisis, although we're $16,000 behind where we should be at this time. But that balance is partly due to some fortunate breaks – a very successful Pilger public meeting, for example – and ongoing political developments giving a higher [paper] sales rate.

There are specific problem areas. There is too much unevenness between branches in financial performance. Resistance finances need a lot of improvement. Cultural Dissent income is also considerably down; we are getting less than a third of what should be feasible.

But the relative success of recent years has bred a bigger problem, a consciousness problem. Our younger generation of comrades takes many things for granted. They assume our resources are a given, they just fall from the sky, are inherited. But it took commitment to get where we are, and that's only a very small step along the way.

The most significant area where this problem impacts is on pledges, the bedrock of our party finances. Our overall total of comrades' pledges, and the average level of pledges from comrades, have been declining, not merely not keeping up with inflation, but going down absolutely! At our conference, we set a goal of getting the national pledge total up from $6,300 to $7,000 per week by the end of the year. It's actually slipped back to $6,100, and this at a time when the full membership of the party has risen significantly!

The percentage of comrades not pledging has improved from 23% to 15% but that's still far too high. And a lot of these are very token pledges.

We think this should be our most important financial campaign – to reach that target for total pledges, reduce the number of comrades not pledging and increase the average pledge level for working comrades.

Another consequence of our relative financial stability is complacency about fund drive events. We don't get the maximum from these events, after having put effort into building them.

Our members provide the overwhelming bulk of our finances, even though we should be organising to get more from our supporters, by putting in more directed *GLW* ads, and reminders regarding bequests, for example.

If we call a halt to the push we've made throughout our history to finance ourselves, to get assets, apart from not going forward, it could lead to softness, a tendency to slip back in the financial consciousness and seriousness of our cadres. Comrades perhaps will take for granted that we've got these buildings, we don't have to pay rent, and thus not develop and continue that high level of consciousness and commitment that got us where we are today.

We should have those goals ahead of us to force us on, even to develop cadre, so we get *more* resources, *more* offices, some proper bookshops, and build a stronger frame on which we can grow.

We know that money makes money – that's capitalism – and that process has been increasingly helping us in recent years. We've increasingly relied on the gains from past real estate purchases, the profit from a blockbuster Pilger meeting, rather than the hard grind of comrades' commitment through pledges and fund drives – capitalist rather than proletarian sources. We want to turn that around, to have a more proletarian balance in our finances, which will result in a much stronger financial base and allow us to move forward faster.

But to do this, we need to politically inspire comrades and give them real political and tangible goals to aim for. So we want to foreshadow some specific political projects that have financial implications.

1. Purchase another building, probably in Adelaide or Darwin, where there are still possibilities for real estate bargains, or at least fairly reasonable prices.

We should also stretch ourselves to buy some items of capital equipment that in the end will save us money: for example, a PA system that can be used for our conferences and other events; we'll recoup the cost in just a few years.

2. We need more party full-timers, both branch organisers and in the National Office. We can't take up all the opportunities currently in front of us. We need more organisers to do it, not

substituting for the branch members, but helping organise them. The political situation warrants it. Our party-building indicators warrant it: the sales, finances, membership figures.

We also need to have our next expansion goals in mind: a workers' solidarity centre; real bookshops; our own party school again; and the resources to organise the next major political campaigns we have to mobilise on.

But while putting this consciousness-raising campaign up front, we can't slacken, and indeed must further improve, our existing money-making departments. For example, our bookshops must become more like Melbourne's situation of providing $300 income per week to the branch.

Sales and subscriptions

Green Left Weekly is now approaching its 500th issue, a significant milestone. By now branches should have organised ambitious events to celebrate, to raise funds, to raise our profile and to increase *GL*'s subscription base.

We've set a subscription campaign around the 500th issue. We'll start two weeks before, starting 8 July, so branches can combine it with contacting people for 500th issue special events. Our subscription base did get up to 941, but has fallen back, so ongoing follow-up of renewals has to be emphasised in each branch. We're also proposing a second subscription campaign later in the year.

We reached 4,094 sales with our January blitz. We're proposing two more sales blitzes for the year: one for the beginning of campus second semester at the beginning of August, and one for the last issue for the year.

Comrades can see from the charts that we've made some progress this year compared to 2001. There's been a small jump in sellers (not quite yet reflecting fully the jump in membership), and a small jump in hours sold. But the rate improvement has meant a considerable jump in average sales: from 1,916 to 2,441, and when you add in subs, from 2,711 to 3,353 (that doesn't include membership subs, country bundles and overseas subs and bundles, which are about another 550).

Having fewer pages has obviously created some difficulties. There are some areas that we can't cover as well as previously. But it hasn't been a major problem (some comrades still don't read the whole paper!).

We have to keep campaigning to raise the sales effort of comrades, increase the level of participation and the number of hours comrades sell for. A worrying development is that some comrades seem to think it's not cool selling our paper at movement events. Why the reluctance? We mock the ISO student non-sellers, but some of our comrades seem to have been infected by the same anti-party, anti-paper pressure.

Are there any improvements or changes in content that would be useful? Perhaps we could do with a more systematic coverage of the Asia Pacific to reflect the importance of our role in the network we're developing in the region, even if it's shorter articles. *GLW* is a combination paper. And perhaps there could be a bit more educational, analytical, even polemical material, for the education of our new members and recruitment of our periphery.

Education and integration

There's always a danger that younger comrades can fall into a far too narrow definition of what party building consists of and not give sufficient emphasis to Marxist education, to having the party and our cadres develop integral connections with the campaigns and movements, to developing a rounded political culture and long-term perspective.

We're conscious of the low level of general political knowledge amongst so many new comrades. That's a function of both the insularity and conscious miseducation of capitalist society today (in spite of the hype about globalisation) and also a function of the smaller left milieu. And often the low level of training makes many comrades unconfident or unable to intervene in campaigns and committees.

This just accentuates the absolute importance of our continuing Marxist education process for the party, at all levels.

An important part of our education experience for comrades today is our national conferences at January and Easter. We cram a lot in – this year, nine full days.

We have a good range of branch education classes and useful study guides, but unfortunately classes too often get squeezed by other priorities. Regular Marxist forums can add another element.

The recent schools for branch organisers seem to have been successful. A return to a permanent school is something to stretch us in the future. The problem is not getting the physical building – that could be organised. It's not even the finances – we could probably overcome the obstacles there. The real obstacle is the shortage of cadres, the short-term sacrifice we'd have to make.

Education shouldn't be seen as just the formal process. Informal political discussions where we pass on our traditions, history and politics are vital too. Perhaps at the moment it's work that's 'not recognised', but the time spent talking to, helping educate and integrate new comrades, new contacts, is 100% useful time.

We also need to reaffirm the importance of active versus passive education. Debates and political fights are often where the biggest advances in understanding are made. Thus, our comrades should be throwing themselves into battle, figuratively speaking, going to other forums and speaking out, using even the smallest events for practising and gaining confidence.

Thus, the importance of our comrades having projects, areas of investigation, small or large, in politics, theory or history that they pursue, becoming experts for the party, developing their skills. We need to be developing ourselves as Marxist thinkers, researchers, both for its own sake, the political gains, but also for educating ourselves.

Improvements we can make

What improvements can we make to be more effective and grow even more quickly? Are there other areas we can improve, other areas we can look at and understand why we haven't moved faster?

Getting bigger in itself, and having broader layers of educated cadres and more of a working-class base, will of course reduce some of the problems. But are there some *subjective* reasons why we haven't gone further, why we had that membership plateau, had that too high a turnover, that we can address now?

We've no strong trend within our party that questions or rejects our Leninist party-building perspective. But over the years we've lost many valuable comrades from the revolutionary movement, both newer comrades who decided after a time that the revolutionary life was not for them, and some more experienced comrades, who'd put in years of struggle, comrades who were leaders of our party.

And often the underlying factors, the political issues in dispute, were related to the party question. People on the way out found our discipline a fetter and the commitment expected an interference in what they really wanted to do with their lives, becoming the focus of their opposition. And even if it didn't culminate in an open political dispute, it would often contribute to the process of drift.

At each important struggle we were right to stand up and defend our party and our organisational principles. But we can still regret the departures of comrades who had put in hard years of service to the movement. They had experience, which is now lost to us. So we can regret, but often couldn't prevent, some former party leaders seizing an opportunity to get off the train.

But on top of that political dynamic, and overlapping of course, is a dynamic that perhaps we can address, and things that we can do to improve our functioning so that we slow down the process of drift. We don't want to burden the party with people who have been too burnt out and cynical about our project. But we continually have to find a way to make full use of all comrades, and make them feel comfortable about staying in and helping out in whatever way they can.

We do have to worry about all the people who joined our ranks and whom we didn't take further, whom we didn't integrate and encourage to play a role in the party. OK, we know there's always some sorting out process, but we have to ask ourselves honestly: have we slipped up, consciously or unconsciously, and made it easier for some comrades to fall away, when they should have been integrated? Have we, by our rudeness, selfishness, competitiveness, cliquishness, individualism, self-aggrandisement even, alienated comrades who otherwise would still be with us, making a valuable contribution?

We're still basically a propaganda organisation. But we know where we have to go, and have to be extra conscious about combating the negative influences and side effects of the actual situation we're in.

Can we say that in some respects we haven't fully broken away from all the failings of a circle spirit, the circle spirit that Lenin condemned so vehemently as he fought to build the early Bolshevik party? We criticise the 'circle spirit' in our educationals, but in many respects some of the vices of that type of existence are still with us, not just the lack of seriousness about building a democratically centralised workers' party, but all the individual-istic and elitist attitudes that ultimately are relics and pressures of the society we're fighting against.

The type of individuals we are matters. In his letter on *Man and Socialism in Cuba,* Che Guevara wrote:

> [R]evolutionary leaders must have a large dose of humanity, a large dose of a sense of justice and truth, to avoid falling into dogmatic extremes, into cold scholasticism, into isolation from the masses. They must struggle every day so that their love of living humanity is transformed into concrete deeds, into acts that will serve as an example, as a mobilising factor.

The socialist example we have to set is for reasons of *efficiency,* to build a stronger, bigger party, a more inclusive party. And in a situation where a small party such as ours is taking on so much responsibility and faces so many opportunities for political ac-tivity and growth, it's natural that the pace of work can lead to tensions. There can be an erosion of tolerance for one another.

So it's vital we do all we can to curb individualism and hierar-chical thinking, gossip and back-biting. We know we have to put politics first, but the other side of that is not to use our political power and knowledge and experience to put down other com-rades. We have to be especially conscious of public or semi-pub-lic denigration of other comrades' abilities, their writing ability, their theoretical ability, other skills.

I've heard comrades actually laugh at other people's work. I've done it myself: editing the paper thirty years ago, I said such and such a comrade 'couldn't write'. The comrade became a central leader of the party, and wrote a lot of excellent material. I regretted that remark for years afterwards. We shouldn't put people down. Rather, let's encourage, support, teach and train, consciously not depriving comrades of the political space to make a satisfying contribution to the project.

In the intensity of the revolutionary struggle, in different times and different places where the class struggle is a lot sharper than here, where political decisions and performances by comrades can be a matter of life and death, these questions probably don't have as much impact.

Here, as we've noted in the past, the less visible 'bullets of the bourgeoisie' can hit home. In capitalist countries like Australia in this period, they can have a greater impact on us. The first step in warding off such bullets is to be conscious of them, and then work out ways to prevent them doing damage in the party.

We have a right to select our members, but after that we have to build an inclusive party, a party where everybody feels at home, feels that they have a contribution to make, where all contributions are valued, where comrades aren't put down.

There will be a turnover in a revolutionary party. Revolutions are great devourers of cadre, but we try to minimise this.

Part of the process of recruiting is a selection process. Some test the party out, we test them out. Some conclude that they're not going to make life as a revolutionary their perspective. Certainly that's the case with many of the young people – the 1,000-2,000 who join Resistance each year. But the worry, the problem, is that too many of our experienced comrades, including a big layer of comrades who have played leading roles in Resistance, don't stay around, even after getting the big picture and developing a rounded Marxist outlook.

Dropouts are often the result of the defeats, the downturns, the grind of the struggle against capitalism. But those objective factors are always with us – we could face further setbacks – and are not the only cause.

It's partly our fault that some leave who shouldn't have. We need to inspire and educate the new, younger comrades. We also need to politically inspire the older layer of comrades with our long-term vision. Exhorting with organisational reports is not going to work with these comrades, and by themselves it won't work with any comrades. We need to overcome in the party any apolitical attitudes and apolitical approaches to leadership questions, or rather, alien class approaches: petty-bourgeois methods, rather than working-class, collectivist methods.

At the moment, we're overwhelmingly still recruiting students or comrades who've had some tertiary education. Our leadership is mostly made up of comrades from that background, even if today they're working in industry.

We'll change, as we grow and the working-class struggle heats up, but in the meantime we have to be careful to make the party a place where workers don't feel put down, or looked down upon. We need to encourage worker comrades in all aspects of party work.

Given that an increasing percentage of the working class, and probably a majority of the industrial working class, are migrant workers, workers from a non-English-speaking background, or from Asia or the Middle East, we have to be especially conscious of this if we're going to be able to recruit and integrate such workers.

Similarly, we have to be especially conscious about encouraging the full political participation of women in the party. Recently we've taken some steps back in this regard. Only six of the 16 Resistance organisers are currently women, compared to nine just a little while ago and, earlier, nearly all.

How to remedy this? We know that the quota system doesn't work, that it is in fact counterproductive. There's a dangerous feature of the current period compared with the '60s and '70s. There's a layer of women today whose expectations have been raised. They expect equality, to have equal opportunity, equal rights. But their experience is increasingly one of inequality, and there's a tendency to put it back on themselves.

In the '60s, as women fought to catch up, their consciousness was raised, and they got a true feeling of liberation from seeing the problem and trying to do something about it. Today, they see the problems of women's oppression and can get increasingly depressed, in the absence of any ongoing fights. The impact can lead to individual crises.

So perhaps we need to give new attention to our women's liberation work, to find ways to fight against the all-pervasive backlash.

To begin with, we can step up an ideological offensive, in the pages of *Green Left Weekly*. We need a campaigning approach in the body of the paper – there are certainly lots of things to be angry about – so that women see the paper as their campaigning paper.

Secondly, how can we revitalise our women's liberation work, to lift it above the ritualistic schedule around International Women's Day and Reclaim the Night events? We need a fresh look, not just going into another committee to organise a march, but creatively looking for fresh ways to organise aggressively against the backlash.

We also have a special responsibility in recruiting and integrating young people. We often take it for granted: throughout our history young people have been a permanent source of cadres and strength, and we continue to recruit youth. But how to improve, to get more recruits and to have more staying as revolutionaries for life?

One reason for the attrition is the small size, the small impact we still have. That's a function of the overall period.

But there are also subjective factors, things that we *can* change. There are the general points that apply to the party as a whole, but some of them apply even more so to young people.

We need to develop more of a campaigning culture, and recruit and integrate activists around this.

We won't tolerate hierarchical attitudes. That's not a youthful trait. It can be encouraged by our two-tier structure: Resistance and the party. But let's elevate the importance of Resistance; remind comrades about our early history, how Resistance *built* the party, and expect just as much energy, enthusiasm, activism from young people today.

We need more leaders. We know all members lead. But if we're to grow, incrementally and by leaps, we need the right sort of leadership. We need leaders who put politics first, who lead politically and in struggle.

We reject a star system of leadership, but are building a *team* leadership, always oriented to party-building rather than individual advancement.

There *are* problems with our nominations commissions and closed sessions. No one of us can be completely happy with how recent DSP and Resistance closed sessions have turned out. Too often they've provided an arena for reckless denigration of other comrades. And we see it continue in the branches afterwards, with self-appointed experts on 'personnel' loudly voicing their psychological assessment of other comrades.

And because we have a large NC in relation to our size still, and because, although we meet only two or three times a year, the NC meetings are interesting, very political events, comrades who can't attend do miss out. We have the *Activist*, which we use to try to make the reports quickly available to all comrades. But it is still the case that comrades who move off the NC – and there will be a continuing process of comrades coming on and going off – find it hard. It's not just there's no 'badge'; it's missing out on interesting political discussions. So there's an element of individualistic competition relating to our leadership bodies.

All of us should strive to do our best, but also examine the reasons. Healthy socialist competition can build the party, but individualist competitiveness can harm it. Use the first, but be conscious it can easily slip over into the second.

There is a layer of new comrades who aren't too confident, or at least don't openly display confidence. In such a situation it's even more important that we're conscious of rooting out any remnants of elitism, of the noisiest, most outspoken, being automatically elevated. Don't neglect the quiet achievers, the ones who mightn't look confident, but who can sometimes stay the longest and make the more lasting contributions.

Peter Boyle ended his summary of the party-building perspectives discussion at our NC last September on the following note:

> Finally, we must have respect for the party membership. It is very important that we have a strong consensus on this, a respect for our membership. It means a thorough rejection of elitism and privilege. Leninism is not elitist, despite what some bourgeois writers claim. It is the opposite. We believe in a centralised party, in unity in action; but elitism – no. It is foreign to our party tradition and you have got to hate it and look out for it in our own behaviour. Don't look down on comrades who are new, who may know a little less or are less confident. And also respect comrades who raise differences.

I'd like to thoroughly endorse those sentiments. We're building a Leninist party, defending the principles of democratic centralism, and the necessity of this form of organisation in building a party that can overthrow capitalism. So in a situation where there are challenges to our type of party – from the bourgeoisie, and from within the movement – it's all the more important that we do it properly. We can't tolerate any distortions or misuses of our organisational methods. Our methods build the best teams, the most democratic type of party, and we don't want new recruits to have any doubts about that.

AFTERWORD

The reasons for writing – and reading – a history such as this, as John Percy stressed in one of the reports included in this volume, is to seek to ensure 'that our struggles of today and tomorrow are grounded in the lessons of past struggles, both victories and defeats'.

Today, as the world is threatened by major environmental and social collapse, movements resisting capitalism's disasters are building all around the globe. From Lebanon to France, from Bolivia to Hong Kong, masses of people are rising up and taking on the ruling classes. The reports that John Percy wrote in the 1990s can still be of use for us in building such a movement in Australia. We can be sure that if he were still alive, John would not only be writing reports: he would be out there in the thick of it demonstrating, protesting for justice and against oppression, and working to build a revolutionary party. John Percy, *presente!*

ABBREVIATIONS

ACU: Association for Communist Unity
AFL-CIO: American Federation of Labor-Congress of Industrial
                Organizations
AKSI: Indonesia Solidarity Action
AMWU: Australian Manufacturing Workers Union
ANC: African National Congress
API: Asia Pacific Institute for Democratisation and
                Development
APISC: Asia Pacific International Solidarity Conference (2002)
APSC: Asia Pacific Solidarity Conference (1998)
ASAP: Action in Solidarity with Asia and the Pacific
ASIET: Action in Solidarity with Indonesia and East Timor
ATEA: Australian Telecommunications Employees
                Association
ATTAC: Association for the Taxation of Financial Transactions
                for the Aid of Citizens (France)
BISIG: Union for Socialist Ideas and Action (Philippines)
CARPA: Campaign Against Repression in the Pacific and Asia
CC: Central Committee
CI: Communist Intervention
CISLAC: Committees in Solidarity with Latin America and the
                Caribbean

CoC:	Committees of Correspondence (USA)
CPA:	Communist Party of Australia
CPA (ML):	Communist Party of Australia (Marxist-Leninist)
CPI-M:	Communist Party of India - Marxist
CPI (ML)	Liberation: Communist Party of India (Marxist-Leninist) Liberation
CPP:	Communist Party of the Philippines
CPSU:	Community and Public Sector Union
CWI:	Committee for a Workers' International
DEETYA:	Department of Employment, Education and Training and Youth Affairs
DSEL:	Democratic Socialist Electoral League
EYA:	Environmental Youth Alliance
EZLN:	Zapatista Army of National Liberation (Mexico)
FI:	Fourth International
FMLN:	Farabundo Martí National Liberation Front (El Salvador)
FSLN:	Sandinista National Liberation Front
IEC:	International Executive Committee (of FI and CWI)
IGL:	International Green Left (Conference)
ISO:	International Socialist Organisation
ISM:	International Socialist Movement
IST:	International Socialist Tendency
ITM:	Introduction to Marxism – DSP class series
ITS:	Introduction to Socialism – DSP class series
JCR:	Revolutionary Communist Youth, youth group in solidarity with LCR (France)
LA:	Left Alliance
LCR:	Revolutionary Communist League (France)
LPP:	Labour Party Pakistan
MR:	Manila-Rizal section of the CPP
MUA:	Maritime Union of Australia
NAFTA:	North American Free Trade Agreement

NAL: Non-Aligned Left
NC: National Committee for the DSP, National Council
               for Resistance
NE: National Executive
NLP: New Left Party (Australia)
NO: National Office
NOLS: National Organisation of Labor Students
NOWSA: National Organisation of Women Students of Australia
NSSP: Nava Sama Samaja Pakshaya (New Equal Society
               Party, Sri Lanka)
NUS: National Union of Students
ODP: Liberty and Solidarity Party (Turkey)
PCD: pre-conference discussion
PDS: Party of Democratic Socialism (Germany)
PLP: Progressive Labor Party
PRC: Party of Communist Refoundation (Italy)
PRD: People's Democratic Party (Indonesia)
PSU: Public Service Union
PRT: Workers' Revolutionary Party (Mexico)
PT: Workers Party (Brazil)
RACLA: Resource and Action Committee on Latin America
SACP: South African Communist Party
SP: Socialist Party (England and Wales)
SPF: Sao Paulo Forum
SLL: Socialist Labour League
SRC: Students' Representative Council
SWP: Socialist Workers Party in both Britain and the United
               States, and in Australia the name of the DSP until 1989
UJC: Young Communist League (Cuba)
WEF: World Economic Forum

NOTES

1   An organisation of followers of the Russian revolutionary Leon Trotsky, who fought against the Stalinist degeneration of the Soviet Union. The Fourth International was founded in 1938 and remained the largest of Trotskyist organisations despite later splits over subsequent political developments internationally.

2   One of the problems with this theory as espoused by Trotsky's followers was that they often disagreed as to its precise meaning. However, its basic argument was that democratic revolutions in lesser developed countries could succeed only if they quickly became socialist revolutions.

3   The bulk of John's political archive and his political poster collection now constitutes the John Percy Collection at the National Library of Australia in Canberra. A smaller part is collected at the International Institute of Social History in Amsterdam. Most of John's extensive collection of political books has become part of the Katakultur Reading Room Library in Yogyakarta.

4   AKSI: Indonesia Solidarity Action. This was the organisation through which the DSP conducted public solidarity actions. It was later expanded into ASIET in 1996 to include East Timor solidarity as well. In 2002, the latter became Action in Solidarity with Asia and the Pacific (ASAP) which was then transformed in 2007 into Asia Pacific Solidarity Network (APSN).

5   CISLAC: Committees in Solidarity with Latin America and the

Caribbean.

6   EYA: Environmental Youth Alliance, active mainly among high school students.

7   *Active Unionist:* a DSP supplement in *Green Left Weekly.*

8   *Fantastic Sex Facts:* In early 1992, the NSW Family Planning Association's planned *Fact and Fantasy File* of sexual information for young people, in the form of a school diary, was blocked by the withdrawal of federal funding, after a brief censorship campaign by the Sydney Sunday Telegraph. Resistance then published and distributed 5,000 copies of Fantastic Sex Facts, containing all the information in the *Fact and Fantasy File.*

9   DSEL: Democratic Socialist Electoral League. This was the organisation officially standing DSP electoral candidates. It was created so that election laws could not be used by government to pry into DSP membership and non-electoral activities.

10   *Student Underground:* A publication for high school students launched by Resistance in 1992, dealing with 'issues such as student rights, the environment and social justice', according to *Green Left Weekly.* Another edition was launched in 1995 focussed mainly on the anti-nuclear campaign. It had its earliest incarnation in 1968 and for some time after that during the movement against the imperialist war in Vietnam.

11   APPM dispute: Associated Pulp and Paper Mill workers in Burnie, Tasmania, resisted a company attack on union rights that was part of a plan to reduce the workforce significantly.

12   Cultural Dissent: The label used in *Green Left Weekly* for leftist music and other cultural activities.

13   After the Communist Party pulled back from using the New Left Party Charter to seek unity with the SWP, it set up an NLP consisting mainly of former members or supporters of the CPA.

14   *Broadside Weekly:* A paper produced by supporters of the New Left Party project. The paper lasted about a year before folding.

15   Rainbow Alliance: Established in 1988, this was an attempt to form

an alternative to the Labor Party. See *Against the Stream* by John Percy, Volume 2 of his History of the DSP and Resistance.

16   Marxist Workers Organisation: a Maoist-influenced group based mainly in Melbourne, which included some tramways and Telecom union officials.

17   Phil Cleary: independent candidate who won the Wills by-election in April 1992, becoming the first non-ALP member for that electorate. He was re-elected in the March 1993 general election but lost to Labor in 1996.

18   Left Alliance: Formed in 1983 by university students aligned with the CPA and promoted as a vehicle for broader left participation in student politics. Resistance participated in Left Alliance, but pulled out at the end of 1988 because of differences over orienting to the National Union of Students. Left Alliance was influential in the first half of the 1990s, especially at Sydney University, but it had largely disintegrated by 1998.

19   Gus Hall: Long-time leader of the Communist Party of the United States.

20   Association for Communist Unity: Formed in 1984 by a minority from the SPA who supported the ALP-ACTU Prices and Incomes Accord. Its founders were influential in the Building Workers Industrial Union. In 1995, the Association changed its name to Marxist Initiative.

21   Communist Party of Australia (Marxist-Leninist): Maoist party.

22   Split in CPUSA: Formation of the Committees of Correspondence for Democracy and Socialism by a dissident wing of the US Communist Party.

23   International Socialist Organisation: At the time, the main organisation in Australia that characterised the Soviet Union and all similar countries as state capitalist. Allied with the Socialist Workers Party in Britain.

24   AIDEX: Australian International Defence Exhibition, held in Canberra in November 1991 as part of the Labor government's effort to expand

Australian military exports. There were large protests against it.

25   Followers of Militant or Militant Tendency, a Trotskyist current in the British Labour Party. In the early 1990s, it abandoned the 'entryism' strategy, leading to a split by a minority.

26   Gerry Healy was the leader of the Workers Revolutionary Party in Britain, 1950-1985.

27   David North: The leader of a US group of Gerry Healy's followers who split with him.

28   Dr John Troy: Labor MLA for Fremantle 1977-80. Denied preselection in 1980 because of his support for Palestine, he became close to the Socialist Labour League and stood as an independent candidate for Fremantle in 1989 and in a by-election in 1990.

29   Andrew Watson: Vehicle Builders' Employees' Federation shop steward at the Mitsubishi factory in Adelaide.

30   Introduction to Socialism classes were designed to win DSP contacts to join the party. Introduction to Marxism classes were intended for the education of new members.

31   Fractions in the DSP and Resistance consisted of all the members involved in a particular area of political activity. A fraction would discuss and plan details of its work, and periodically report on its activities to the branch, which set the overall political direction.

32   Hawkesbury Agricultural College, in Richmond, NSW, was for many years the venue for DSP decision-making and educational conferences.

33   In a subsequent report (see Chapter 2), John Percy explained why this plan was not realised.

34   The book was *Feminism and socialism: putting the pieces together* (1992. Chippendale, NSW: New Course). A second edition was published in 1997.

35   For a time in the early 1990s, the WA Greens legally controlled who could use the name 'Green' in an election.

36   DSP members paid dues, monthly or quarterly at different periods. These were not large; they were collected by branches and sent

entirely to the National Office. The most substantial source of
finance, which was in addition to dues, was a weekly pledge by
members, who were encouraged to give according to their means.
The pledge was collected by branches. Branches then sent a portion
of their monthly income – from pledges, paper sales or any source
– to the National Office for its use; this money was called a sustainer,
and was intended to be constant over several months, not to
fluctuate with temporary ups and downs in branch income.
Additionally, the DSP conducted annual fund drives to help pay
for the production of *Green Left Weekly;* DSP members normally
promised a contribution over the course of a year, and branches
also actively sought donations from non-members and raised funds
through public dinners and other social events.

37   In the early 1990s, the DSP began collaborating with members of the
Manila-Rizal (MR) organisation of the Communist Party of the
Philippines who were breaking from the party's Maoist politics, in
particular from its rural guerrilla warfare focus, emphasising open
urban mass politics.

38   BISIG: Union for Socialist Ideas and Action.

39   Senator Janet Powell: The leader of the Australian Democrats from
July 1990 to August 1991, when she was deposed by an internal
coup. After resigning from the Democrats in 1992, she spoke publicly
about a possible regroupment of greens, independents and leftists.

40   Jim Percy died on 12 October 1992.

41   New Zealand Alliance: Formed in late 1991 from the New Labour
Party, the 'social credit' Democratic Party, the Maori Mana Motuhake
and the Greens.

42   Pegasus Networks: The first internet service provider in Australia.
It focussed mainly on progressive groups and activities. *Green
Left Weekly* articles were posted on Pegasus and could be accessed by
its subscribers in Australia and internationally.

43   CARPA: Campaign Against Repression in the Pacific and Asia. This
was established by the DSP in 1978 as a vehicle for solidarity work in

the Asia-Pacific.

44   NOWSA: National Organisation of Women Students of Australia.

45   DSP member Susan Price was on the ballot in Brisbane Central as an independent in the Queensland state election. The final official tally gave her 9.0% of the vote.

46   On 10 November 1992, there was a 24-hour stoppage of workers on Victorian state awards in opposition to anti-union legislation of the Kennett government.

47   The DSP organised Socialist Scholars Conferences in Sydney in 1990 and Melbourne in 1991.

48   The International Green Left Conference was held at the University of NSW, Sydney, 31 March–4 April 1994.

49   A reference to *Links* magazine, which was launched at the International Green Left Conference.

50   See Chapter 2.

51   A report to the October 1993 DSP National Committee meeting by Dick Nichols described *Solidarity* as intended to 'draw together … class-struggle currents and promote debate on how to strengthen the class-struggle and socialist pole in the trade unions'. The trade union work report to the January 1995 DSP 16th National Conference proposed diverting *Solidarity*'s coverage into *Green Left Weekly.*

52   Tasks and perspectives meetings in the DSP were intended to map out a branch's intended activities for several months ahead. They usually followed a National Committee meeting or national conference and dealt with implementing the decisions of that meeting.

53   Jim Percy *The Democratic Socialist Party: Traditions, Lessons and Socialist Perspectives.* 1994, Chippendale (New Course)·

54   At the September 1993 ACTU congress, members of AKSI (Indonesia Solidarity Action) and Indonesian democrats attempted unsuccessfully to have the congress vote on a resolution critical of the Suharto government's repression of trade unions and the Australian government's support for such repression. They also

unsuccessfully lobbied for the ACTU to recognise new
non-government unions.

55   The youth work report to this National Committee meeting referred
to two actions by Perth Resistance: a '200-strong youth rights
demonstration' and 'high school comrades using a petition around
the federal budget Austudy changes to raise consciousness at schools
and get students to their anti-budget action'.

56   The Challenge team in the ACT Public Sector Union, in which DSP
members participated, won seven of 12 positions in the union's
November 1993 election.

57   On 16 November 1993, Resistance and Secondary Students Against
Cuts organised a walkout of nearly 1,000 secondary students in
protest against the ACT Labor government's cuts to education
funding.

58   *Suara Aksi* (Aksi Voice): A newsletter produced by AKSI.

59   An international conference in solidarity with the struggle of East
Timor was held in Manila 31 May-4 June 1994. It was attended by
more than 500 people from the Philippines and more than 50
international participants, despite the Philippines government's
efforts to prevent foreigners attending.

60   UNCED: United Nations Conference on Environment and
Development, held in Rio de Janeiro in June 1992.

61   The nominating commission at DSP decision-making conferences
consisted of delegates from each branch, who would hear members'
proposals on membership of the National Committee and prepare a
slate for presentation to a conference plenary session; other
nominations by individual delegates could also be made.

62   This planned book appears not to have been published. Doug
Lorimer wrote most of the material explaining the DSP's changing
view of the class character of the Chinese state in the 1990s. See for
example http://www.sa.org.au/node/3941 and http://links.org.au/
node/2773

63   Dulce Maria Pereira of the Brazilian Workers Party toured Australia in

April 1994 and spoke at the International Green Left Conference.

64   Christabel Chamarette: Greens Senator from Western Australia, 1992-96.

65   Search Foundation: Set up to receive the remaining CPA assets when it voted to dissolve.

66   James P. Cannon (1890-1974): National secretary of the US Socialist Workers Party and its predecessor organisations from 1928 to 1953.

67   Telstra defence: the campaign attempting to prevent the privatisation of Telstra, carried through by the Howard government in 1997.

68   Shearers and Rural Workers Union: set up in 1994 by workers splitting from the AWU because of its conservative leadership.

69   *Dare to Struggle:* Official DSP industrial bulletin established in 1995 to 'raise the party's profile in the union movement, to explain and popularise the ideas of revolutionary trade unionists, to present our proposals for action during strikes and other disputes, as well as taking our movement campaigns into the unions' – from Doug Lorimer's report to the December 1995 National Committee meeting. The report also indicated that DSP branches and union fractions were expected to produce their own copies of *Dare to Struggle* for intervention in local campaigns.

70   When NUS was set up by ALP students in 1987, the DSP and Resistance opposed participation in it as being essentially a Labor Party front. After the election of the Howard Liberal government in 1996, much of the opposition to the government's education cutbacks began to be channelled through NUS, and the party and Resistance therefore decided to change tactics and collaborate with left forces inside NUS.

71   Demonstrations in solidarity with East Timor and against the Australian ALP government's recognition of the Indonesian annexation were held in many cities over 23-25 August 1996.

72   RACLA: Resource and Action Committee on Latin America, a group set up by CPA members and some liberal allies who split from CISLAC.

73   World Bank appeal: An international petition headed 'World Bank/
      IMF/WTO: Enough!', circulated on the 50th anniversary of the
      Bretton Woods agreement.

74   *Frontline:* Free monthly paper produced by unions aligned with the
      Pledge (left) faction of the Victorian ALP.

75   Beatrix Campbell: British writer and a former leader of the
      Communist Party of Great Britain, self-described as a 'post-Marxist'.

76   Bob Leach: Long-time lecturer in history and politics at the
      Queensland Institute of Technology and a leader of efforts to set up
      a New Labor Party modelled on the New Zealand NL Party. He died of
      a heart attack in December 1997.

77   Peter Murphy: A former leader of the CPA.

78   John Woodley: Australian Democrat senator from Queensland,
      1993-2001.

79   The Zapatista Army of National Liberation (EZLN) held an
      Intercontinental Meeting for Humanity and Against Neo-liberalism
      in the province of Chiapas, in southern Mexico, 27 July-3 August
      1996.

80   Irwin Silber, in *What Went Wrong? An Inquiry into the Theoretical
      and Historical Sources of the Socialist Crisis* (Pluto Press 1994), argued
      that the material conditions for socialism had not been created in the
      past nor in the present, in any country in the world.

81   On 27 July 1996, thugs working on behalf of Indonesian dictator
      Suharto attacked the offices of the Indonesian Democratic Party of
      Megawati Sukarnoputri. This was followed by demonstrations and
      rioting. The dictatorship sought to blame the PRD for the unrest.

82   DSP members were involved in National Challenge, a rank-and-file
      network in the CPSU. The reference here is to a campaign in the
      Department of Employment, Education and Training and Youth
      Affairs to resist attacks by the Howard government.

83   ACTU leaders called a rally outside Parliament House on 19 August
      1996, in support of the ALP's effort to amend the government's
      Workplace Relations Bill in the Senate. A large number of people in

the crowd of 25,000 tried to take their views directly to the parliamentarians inside, forcing open the building's doors and hanging banners from the building.

84   *Resist!:* A four-page publication of Resistance and the Democratic Socialist Party produced from time to time to popularise DSP positions on a particular topic. Eva To found an issue 10, dated April 1998, in John Percy's archives; it is not known if there were later issues.

85   *Intercontinental Press* (originally called *World Outlook*): Weekly (fortnightly in its last years) magazine produced by the US SWP from 1963 to 1986 on behalf of the Fourth International.

86   API: Asia Pacific Institute for Democratisation and Development. This was the official organiser of the first Asia Pacific Solidarity Conference, held at Easter 1998 in Sydney.

87   *Green Left* journalist and Friends of the Earth campaigner Jim Green exposed numerous safety issues and government misinformation being used to justify government plans to build a new nuclear reactor at Lucas Heights in Sydney.

88   A high school walkout against racism, organised by Resistance in Sydney on 2 July 1998, briefly occupied the foyer of John Howard's office and was violently attacked by police.

89   Influenced by conservative advisers from some environmental bodies who were seeking to centralise control of the campaign against the Jabiluka uranium mine and divert it into campaigning for the ALP in the upcoming federal election, officials from the Gundjeihmi Aboriginal Corporation tried to ban Resistance from even using the word Jabiluka.

90   After opposing the holding of the 28 August national rally in Melbourne, Militant members on the day forced their way onto the platform by threatening violence against the Resistance organisers.

91   *International Viewpoint:* An English-language magazine of the Fourth International.

92   This refers to the 1998 Patrick's dispute, in which the Howard

government and the Patrick Corporation attempted unsuccessfully to smash the Maritime Union of Australia.

93 The militant Workers First caucus in the Victorian Australian Manufacturing Workers Union won most of the positions it stood for in May 1998 elections.

94 After a six-month campaign by the DSP and other supporters of press freedom, Adelaide City Council abandoned an attempt to impose a $10 fee for the public distribution of *GLW* or other non-commercial papers.

95 The DSP's 'Appeal for International Collaboration and Socialist Renewal' was discussed at the June 1998 NC plenum and the January 1999 congress and circulated initially to the Indonesian PRD, the Philippines MR and the Labour Party Pakistan and later to other parties in the region. It proposed four points of adherence: (1) revolutionary Marxism; (2) a Leninist party; (3) democratic socialism; (4) comradely relations among parties based on mutual respect and non-interference.

96 Unionists Against Corporate Tyranny: This organisation was launched in July 2000 to oppose the capitalist globalisation policies of the WTO, IMF and World Bank. Its main activity was supporting the 11 September 2000 Melbourne demonstration against the World Economic Forum.

97 The Peoples Asia Pacific Solidarity Conference, held in June 2001.

98 Ocean Press in Melbourne: The main publisher in Australia of books from and about Cuba.

99 The conference was attended by Indonesians and by activists from the region and as far afield as Europe and North America. On 8 June 2001, police and right-wing militias raided and broke up the conference. Foreign attendees were arrested and many of the Indonesian participants were physically assaulted, some being seriously injured.

100 Initially, the DSP referred to 'decision-making conferences'. At this time, it changed to using the more common designation, 'congress'.

101   The 11 September 2000 demonstration in Melbourne against the World Economic Forum.

102   Some 300,000 demonstrators protested against the G8 summit held in Genoa, 18-22 July 2001. Vicious police attacks killed one demonstrator, Carlo Giuliani, and wounded 600 others.

103   JCR: Revolutionary Communist Youth, youth group in solidarity with LCR.

104   Plan Colombia was a program of increased US military intervention in Colombia and elsewhere in South and Central America, under the pretext of a 'war on drugs'.

105   OSPAAAL: *Organisation of Solidarity* with the People of Asia, Africa and Latin America.

106   On 1 March 2002, John Pilger spoke to a meeting of 2,100 people in Sydney Town Hall, organised by *Green Left Weekly*.

107   On 1 May 2001, actions against stock exchanges in eight different cities involved more than 20,000 people.

108   The Socialist Alliance was established in February 2001, on the initiative of the DSP and the ISO, as an electoral alliance. In 2005, the DSP moved to convert the alliance into a 'broad left' party, leading the ISO and other participating organisations to end their involvement.

NAME INDEX

"I hope the story will be interesting and the lessons useful
to a wider readership, not just those of us who have been
engaged at some time in this narrative, or those who are
committed activists today. I hope the history of this struggle
will inspire new young comrades to take up the banner.

– John Percy

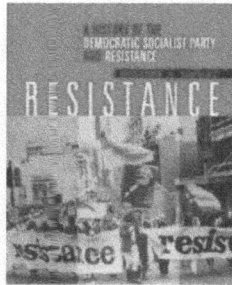

Resistance: A History of the Democratic
Socialist Party and Resistance
Volume 1: 1965-72
John Percy
Resistance Books 2005

First of a projected three volume history of the Democratic Socialist party, and
the youth organisation Resistance, which constitute the main current of the
Australian far left. This volume covers the tumultuous period from 1965 to 1972.

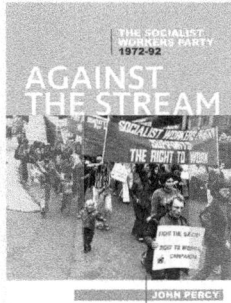

Against the Stream: A History of the Democratic Socialist Party and Resistance Volume 2: 1972-92
John Percy, edited by Allen Myers
Interventions 2017

This second volume of The History of the Democratic Socialist Party and Resistance covers the exciting and turbulent 20-year period that opened with the election of the Whitlam government in 1972. It was a time of change and struggle:

- "Kerr's coup" sacking the Labor government
- Battles between the Fraser government and unions trying to protect wages against surging inflation
- The ALP's Prices and Incomes Accord
- The Hawke government's deregistration of the militant BLF and airline pilots' union
- The rise of anti-uranium and environmental campaigns

Throughout this period, the late John Percy was a central leader of the Socialist Workers Party as it became a party based in the industrial working class, developed and modified its political understanding and grew to surpass the Communist Party as Australia's largest socialist organisation.

This is not an academic history, but an insight into the successes and mistakes of twenty years of campaigning for socialism. It will be of value to everyone struggling today.

"As well as having been a member and leader of socialist organisations since the mid 1970s, Tom has also popularised Marxist theory and developed powerful analyses of many important aspects of Australian capitalism. His influence, especially through his writings, extends well beyond his current organisation and has for many years equipped people on the left with ideas and arguments they need to combat capitalism's mystifications and lies, in struggles against its immediate consequences and for socialism."

– Rick Kuhn, recipient of the Deutscher Prize

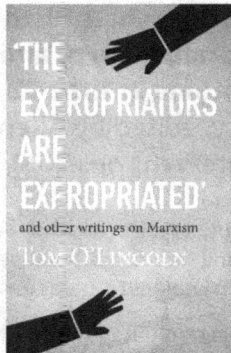

THE
EXPROPRIATORS
ARE
EXPROPRIATED'
and other writings on Marxism
Tom O'Lincoln

'The Expropriators are Expropriated' and other writings on Marxism
Tom O'Lincoln

Tom O'Lincoln has been active on the left since 1967, in Germany, the US and Australia. He is the author of *Into the Mainstream: The Decline of Australian Communism, Years of Rage: Social Conflicts in the Fraser Era, United We Stand: Class Struggle in Colonial Australia* and *The Neighbour from Hell: Two Centuries of Australian Imperialism.*

Tom is a member of Socialist Alternative.

─────── ALSO BY INTERVENTIONS ───────

"His clear and meticulous research reveals a continuity between Lenin's revolutionary organisational perspectives of the early 1900s with those advanced during the revolutionary mass upsurge of 1905 – and this in a way that can be useful for revolutionary activists of today and tomorrow. Freeman highlights the dynamic interplay of theory and practice, of Marxism and mass struggle, of intellectual activists and radicalising workers and mass insurgencies that shaped the past and are the hope of the future."

– Paul Le Blanc, author of *Lenin and the Revolutionary Party*

Lenin's Interventionist Marxism
Tom Freeman, edited by Sandra Bloodworth
Interventions 2017

Tom Freeman was a lifelong revolutionary and a member of the International Socialist Tendency for nearly 30 years. Tom Freeman's work stands as a valuable contribution to what can be considered the field of "Lenin Studies" that has been blossoming over the past decade, taking its place with the varied, important contributions of Lars Lih, Antonio Negri, Alan Shandro, Tamás Krausz, August Nimtz, and others.